ALSO BY CHRISTINE BRENNAN

The Miracle of Miami

Beyond Center Court (with Tracy Austin)

$\mathcal{I}$NSIDE EDGE

A REVEALING

JOURNEY

INTO THE

SECRET WORLD

OF FIGURE SKATING

BY

CHRISTINE BRENNAN

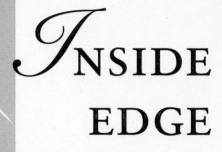

ANCHOR BOOKS
DOUBLEDAY
NEW YORK   LONDON   TORONTO
SYDNEY   AUCKLAND

AN ANCHOR BOOK

PUBLISHED BY DOUBLEDAY
a division of Bantam Doubleday Dell Publishing Group, Inc.
1540 Broadway, New York, New York 10036

ANCHOR BOOKS, DOUBLEDAY,
and the portrayal of an anchor are trademarks of Doubleday,
a division of Bantam Doubleday Dell Publishing Group, Inc.

Inside Edge was originally published in hardcover by Scribner in 1996.
The Anchor Books edition is published by arrangement with Scribner.

Set in Adobe Sabon
Designed by Jenny Dossin

Library of Congress Cataloging-in-Publication Data

Brennan, Christine.
    Inside edge : a revealing journey into the secret world of figure
    skating / by Christine Brennan.—1st Anchor paperback ed.
        p.   cm.
    Includes index.
    1. Skating. 2. Skating—Tournaments. I. Title.
    GV850.4.B74   1997
    796.91′2—dc20   96-38832
                                                              CIP

ISBN 0-385-48607-3
First Anchor Paperback Edition: February 1997

10 9 8 7 6 5 4 3 2 1

FOR MOM AND DAD

ACKNOWLEDGMENTS

I have many people to thank for their help as I researched and wrote this book. Some of them simply pointed me in the right direction. Others agreed to an interview, helped with a phone number, arranged a trip, sent a videotape. A few read the manuscript or rescued me from several months of self-imposed house arrest.

Without these people, it's safe to say, there would be no book.

First, I want to thank my editors and colleagues at the *Washington Post* for their support and guidance. The *Post* graciously gave me the leave of absence I needed to write this book; for that I thank executive editor Leonard Downie, managing editor Bob Kaiser, assistant managing editor/personnel Tom Wilkinson, and, especially, assistant managing editor/sports George Solomon, my boss and friend.

There are dozens of people at the *Post* whose encouragement is deserving of the most heartfelt thanks. They include Don Graham, Ben Bradlee, Chris Spolar, Sandy Evans, Ken Denlinger, Mike Wilbon, Tony Kornheiser, Gail Shapiro, Athelia Knight, Molli Yood, Don Beard, Andrew Salomon, Elaine Sung-Salomon, Len Shapiro, Bill Gildea, Sushant Sagar, Don White, Tony Cotton, Dave Sell, Tracee Hamilton, Jeanne McManus, Pat McLaughlin, Mark Asher, Steve Berkowitz, Mark Maske, David Nakamura, Bill Brubaker, Shirley Povich, Angus Phillips, Gabby Richards, Ben Gieser, Gene Wang, Effie Dawson, Pat O'Shea, Joel Richardson, John McDonnell, Jill Grisco, Sarah Trott, Suzanne Tobin, Wendy Carpenter, Bobbye Pratt, Mike Sandler, Saul Wisnia, Jim Brady, Colleen Dumont, Len Hochberg, Richard Justice, J. A. Adande, Frank Ahrens, David Aldridge, Bob Fachet, Steve Goff, Karl Hente, Neil Greenberger, Stephen King, Andy Beyer, Vinnie Perrone, Tom Boswell, and Jim McGee.

Outside the paper, there were dozens of loyal and supportive friends and colleagues. They include Marty Aronoff, Deborah Klein, Randy Hall, Steve Hoffman, Scott Swanke, Paul Anger, Mike Moran, Harvey Schiller, Laurie and Bob Saxton, Bob and Sandy Brennan, Marlene and Bill Kerdyk, Meredith and Barry Geisler, Sharon and Jerry Farr, Amy Rosewater, Dewey Blanton, Jim Gallo, Julie Cart, Frank Deford, Rachel Alexander, Cal Thomas, Nye Lavalle, Lydia

Owen, Kim Oberg, Mike Beckius, Bruce Schoenfeld, S. L. Price, Mark Schramm, Tom Goldman, Julie Anderson, Shelley Wolson, Kelly Whiteside, Joe Valerio, Sandy Bailey, Jane Leavy, Michele Himmelberg, Lesley Visser, Matt Amodeo, Brian Creighton, Lois Elfman, Joe Gallaher, Victoria Churchville, Wes Heppler, Nancy Jackson, Sherry Krsticevic, Leslie King, Jeff Finkle, Sandra Stevenson, Kathy Peterson, Shawn Sylvia, Robin Tunnicliff, Gerri Walbert, Ron Rapoport, John Walsh, Ron Reid, Ike Richman, Kate Boyle, the gang at Intersport, Grace Lee Nikkel, Nancy Yasharoff, Atlanta's Bob Brennan, Steve Bull, Gayle Bodin, Peter Bhatia, Sandy Macomber, Dick Schaap, and many other friends and relatives.

Several colleagues were especially helpful along the way: Sandy Davis, Mary Lou Foy, Heinz Kluetmeier, Dave Black, Dave Barry, and Mark Lund.

The world of figure skating is known to be an especially close-knit, private place. But I couldn't have felt more welcome. To thank everyone I spoke with would be to simply reiterate many of the names that are found in the book, each of whom graciously gave me time and consideration in order to write their stories. A few, however, deserve special thanks: Frank Carroll, Michael Carlisle, Kathy Casey, Tom Collins, Christopher Dean, Lisa Ervin, Carlo Fassi, Stan Feig, Catherine Foulkes, Randy Gardner, Ronna Gladstone, Shep Goldberg, Carol Heiss Jenkins, Slavka Kohout, the Kwan family, Jean Leidersdorf, Jeanne Martin, Juli McKinstry, Tamara Moskvina, Moira North, Peter Oppegard, Nick Perna, Tracey Cahill Poletis, Debbie Prachar, Michael Rosenberg, Evy and Mary Scotvold, Caroline Silby, Jerry Solomon, Gale Tanger, Debi Thomas, Jayne Torvill, Debbie Turner, Bob Weaver, Ben and Mary Louise Wright, Carole Yamaguchi, and the kind people at Sun Valley, Lake Arrowhead, and the Fairfax Ice Arena.

Others allowed me to drop into their lives for considerable periods of time. These people were invaluable to me: Audrey Weisiger, Brian Boitano, Linda Leaver, Michael Weiss and his family, Brian Wright, Tina Noyes, Peggy Fleming, Joe Inman, Janet Lynn, Bonnie McLauthlin, Mary Cook, Jenni Tew and her family, and Mike Burg.

The U.S. Figure Skating Association made my life—and research—very easy. Kristin Matta and Matt Pensinger deserve special notice for their professionalism and courtesy always. Thanks also to Claire Ferguson, Morry Stillwell, Jerry Lace, Beth Davis, Heather Linhart, and Jay Miller.

I especially want to thank the people of the Stars on Ice tour for allowing me unlimited backstage access. The skaters—notably Scott Hamilton, Rosalynn Sumners, Kristi Yamaguchi, Paul Wylie, Katarina Witt, and Kurt Browning—were extremely generous with their time.

Byron Allen and David Baden made sure the bus never pulled out without me. And a special thank you to Lynn Plage for arranging everything in her usual cheerful, top-notch way.

With television being such a big part of figure skating, several broadcast people were very helpful in this project. Thanks to Jirina Ribbens, Meg Streeter Lauck, NBC's Jennifer Arnold, ABC's Beth Schmidt and Leslee Sherrill, and CBS's Robin Brendle. Throughout the fall of 1994, one of my great pleasures was bumping into the folks from CBS, including Bob and Margaret Fishman, Verne and Nancy Lundquist, Tracy Wilson, Rob Dustin, Hamilton, Jeff Greenholtz, and David Winner. I'll never forget their support from day one.

The Professional Figure Skating Writers of America (pronounced Poof-Swa) deserve special mention. Haven't heard of this organization? You're not alone. It's a small, chummy group with this motto: "We just want to write our best and stay focused," based on the sport's most-popular quote, "I just want to skate my best and stay focused."

These are some of my very best friends in the business. Thanks to Poof-Swa alums Michael Janofsky and Steve Woodward, secretary general Philip Hersh, competition-committee chair Michelle Kaufman, Dinner Mint chair Jere Longman, Pacific Coast chair Randy Harvey, magazine-division chair Johnette Howard, European-division representatives Chris Clarey and Bill Glauber, members Mark Starr, Mark McDonald, John Powers, Linda Robertson, Julie Vader, Diane Pucin, Bonnie DeSimone, Debbie Becker, Don Markus, Bob Ford, Karen Rosen, and the rest of the reporters in the pressroom.

I must mention several dear friends who helped turn this book from idea to reality. I first thought of doing a figure-skating book in 1992, but never went any further. Then came a pivotal event: the First Annual Figure Skating Video party. In the summer of 1993, Kristin Huckshorn, Tim Larimer, Tony Reid, Tracy Kerdyk, and I got together to watch a skating highlight tape given to me by Huckshorn and Larimer. That night, we talked about the book. Their words to me: "Write it."

Chris Calhoun joined up along the way, becoming not only a superb agent, but also a great friend and confidant.

Then came the final piece of the puzzle. I talked to Lisa Drew, a dear friend and the best book editor I know. She liked the idea. Pretty soon, I was writing it, and she was editing it.

In addition to Lisa, I want to thank Marysue Rucci for always being on the other end of the phone at Scribner; Pat Eisemann, who is one of the few people in America who really understands figure skating; and Carrie Lewis, who is another.

Once this book was being written, several friends were there to help it along. A very special thanks to Kerdyk, Reid, Howard, Kaufman, Aronoff, Klein, Winner, Woodward, Martin, Cook, McLaughlin, and Weisiger for their thoughts and advice.

And then, there is my family. The Brennans have not won any national figure-skating titles, but I doubt any family had more fun on the ice than we did growing up in Ohio. My mom and dad would freeze the patio and we would skate for hours. Truth be told, I probably was the worst skater in the family. My sister Kate could actually land a single toe loop, and my brother Jim was a wonderful amateur hockey player. My sister Amy was better than me, too. My father came out and joined us, but no one could compete with the overall package presented by my mother, not because she was so good, but because she had the best skates. They were blue patent leather with gray faux fur. The judges would have loved them.

Now there is another generation of skaters in the family: Brad, Jennie, and Leslie Backoff. They're at the stage where they are learning how to pick themselves up after they fall down. They're my kind of skaters.

To all of you—and to Tom, too, of course—thanks a million. For everything.

CONTENTS

"THE BEST SPORT"

"Figure skating is the best sport."

Several years ago, a colleague came up to me in the pressroom of an NFL game and whispered those words. He didn't want anyone else to hear what he said. We had covered Super Bowls and spring training, college bowl games for the national championship, opening ceremonies at the Olympic Games. We had seen and talked to thousands of athletes.

And now, with a smile on his face, he quietly anointed figure skating as his favorite sport.

Figure skating?

I shrugged. "Let me think about it."

I don't quite remember watching Peggy Fleming win her Olympic gold medal in 1968. Later on, though, when we skated in our backyard in Ohio, she was the one we pretended to be. My Olympic recollections start with Janet Lynn, the blond pixie from Illinois. I knew she was one of the best skaters I ever would see, but she won only the bronze medal at the 1972 Games. An Austrian who was painstakingly perfect at tracing those dull compulsory school figures easily defeated her. I realized right then that something was wrong with the judging and scoring of this sport.

Then came Dorothy Hamill. I stayed home from a high school basketball game to watch her skate that night from Innsbruck, Austria, site of the 1976 Olympics. But I already knew she had won, because I had been pacing in my bedroom in Toledo, Ohio, that afternoon, anxiously waiting for live radio dispatches from the Olympics. When the reporter at the event shouted into his microphone that Hamill was spinning through the last few seconds of her program, and that it was certain she would win, I leaped for joy. As he spoke, I could hear the music in the background. For a moment, I felt as if I were there.

Watching Hamill win on TV that night was not the least bit anticlimactic. I jumped up and down all over again and even got my eight-year-old sister Amy so excited, she leaped from her chair. I'll never forget Dick Button exclaiming that flowers were "raining" onto the ice as

Hamill finished. "She has done it," Button said. "I am sure." I never had heard more delightfully certain words spoken by a sports commentator.

Four years later, during a dance marathon at Northwestern University, I watched Tai Babilonia and an injured Randy Gardner withdraw from the Lake Placid Olympics. For a few seconds, our frivolity waned. In 1984, Scott Hamilton, who grew up in northwestern Ohio at the same time I did, won the gold medal, just as everyone knew he would.

By 1988, I was attending the Olympics as a journalist. While "The Battle of the Brians" was stunning, nothing matched the sadness I felt for Debi Thomas a week later. I had been writing a story in the press center in Calgary and ran across a pedestrian bridge to sit in the stands for her performance. I'll never forget the buildup to her first crucial jumps—a triple-triple combination. I clenched my teeth as she went up for the first jump. She landed it, but came down awkwardly on the second one. My heart sank. A few moments later, she made another mistake, and the gold medal was gone. It was all there for her, and she couldn't do it. If only she could have started the music over and tried again.

The Debi Thomas–Katarina Witt battle showed me something wonderful about skating. As Thomas skated toward her first two jumps, the music built to announce that something important was about to happen. If Thomas landed those jumps, she would be on her way. But if she stumbled—and she did—she would be in big trouble.

I realized that no other sport heralds its precise moment of ultimate importance as figure skating does. No other sport can be sure exactly when that moment occurs. But in figure skating, the program is planned; reporters and TV announcers have the script. The music builds. *This is it!* In baseball, when the seventh game of the World Series is in the ninth inning, a single pitch might turn into the winning RBI—or it might be fouled off behind the plate. Figure skating does not allow for the next pitch.

Figure skating for me became not so much a sport of elaborate costumes and delightful music as it did a fascinating mixture of tantalizing qualities: impending doom, living on the edge, and the chance to witness a career made or destroyed in a split second. Its enticement is the lure of imminent disaster, the subject of every skater's nightmare—falling. It's lovely and horrifying at the same time; the only activity that makes room for both Rodgers and Hammerstein and Alfred Hitchcock.

When a skater goes up for a jump, it's a make-or-break moment unlike any other in sports. When Brian Boitano left the ice for his triple axel in the short program at the 1994 Winter Olympics, he was a gold-medal favorite. When he landed on his hands little more than a second later, his chance for a medal was gone. Full of hope when he leaped into the air, he was ruined when he landed.

I've covered the Super Bowl, and it doesn't quite compare. A quarterback can throw an incompletion near the goal line on third down with ten seconds left in the game, and he still has fourth down. The decisive moment is negotiable. And there's a whole team to share the joy or soften the blow.

Figure skaters exult or suffer alone. They are out there by themselves for four minutes or more; even hockey players take a break after two minutes. What these people do astonishes me. I've skated my whole life—on our frozen patio or in public sessions at local rinks—and when I try to skate backward, I feel as if I'm going to fall over at any moment. I might hit a good golf shot on occasion or put a tennis ball just where I want it, but I will never, ever, be able to leave the ice and spin in the air and land safely back on my skate blade.

Because they are out there all alone, there is no one for a figure skater to blame. An opponent doesn't throw a ball or send a fist at them. No one is playing defense. They could, of course, blame the judges. But skaters rarely fall back on that. Journeyman Paul Wylie won a serendipidous silver medal at the 1992 Olympics, and when we asked him if he should have won the gold medal that night—and he probably should have—he replied, "How great of a Cinderella story do you guys want?"

While figure skating has been made out to be a fantasy world of pretty dresses and caked-on makeup, it turns out to be the sport that most closely mirrors real life. Strangers—judges—make decisions about a skater based on appearance, gossip, and on what they did in the past. Skaters might not realize it until later, but, in this sport, they are getting a fine introduction to the rest of their lives.

I have two conflicting emotions when I watch figure skating. It takes my breath away. And it cracks me up. I'll never forget my friend Kristin calling me with the news that Midori Ito had actually jumped out of the rink at the 1991 world championships, and that—not to worry—she had it on tape. When we watched it, we thought the best part was the fact that one second Ito was stumbling around a TV camera, and the next, she was charging back onto the ice, never missing a beat, as if nothing had happened.

Tonya Harding's dress fell off in front of us once. Katarina Witt came out of her dress, too, but we weren't there for that one. I must say, however, that someone obtained the tabloid photos very quickly.

My friends and I along press row were challenged to come up with colorful descriptions of what we were covering. I said that Kurt Browning's fiery orange pants looked like the USA Today weather map on an extremely hot day. Jere Longman, working at the time for the Philadelphia Inquirer, topped that by describing a dance couple as dressed as "after-dinner mints." From that moment on at the Washington Post, figure skating ceased to be called figure skating. I was assigned to the "Dinner Mints."

How seriously could you take a sport with an actual place called "Kiss and Cry"? There were signs pointing the way to Kiss and Cry at the 1994 Olympics in Norway. The area where skaters and coaches sit and wait for their scores got its name because of what went on there. Skaters and coaches kissed. Then they cried.

Even at the Norway Olympics, in the midst of the saga involving Tonya Harding and Nancy Kerrigan, there was laughter. A group of us were diagramming a practice collision involving Oksana Baiul and another skater.

"Nancy was skating here," I said, putting an X in my notebook.

"Oksana was here," someone else said.

"And Abraham Zapruder was filming it all right here," said another journalist, swooping in with his pen to add another mark on the page.

If my affection for absurdity appears callous, I apologize. For all the silliness surrounding them, the Dinner Mints are the nicest people around. They're not like tennis players. They didn't grow up as pampered rich kids. They're usually in their twenties when they become famous. Although many of them have been tutored through high school and never gone to college, they do come with a strong helping of street smarts. It's unlikely that any other sport, with the exception of golf, demands its athletes spend so much time alone thinking about what they're doing and where they're headed. There are some airheads in the group, but by and large, figure skaters are people with something substantial to say. Off the ice, most of them have the sensibilities of a neighbor down the street, not a sports superstar.

Brian Boitano, for instance, told reporters at the 1994 Olympics that he would rather spend time with us than with his Olympic teammates. This is not something that an NFL player likely would have said to the writers who cover him.

Yet Boitano is a huge hero to the people who love his sport, which happens to be more people than we think. Figure skating is to women what football is to men. Women grab the television remote control and tell their spouse to either watch in silence or leave the room. Ac-

re is," Kohout told me, "a magic to skating on ice, a romantic
akin to flying. It's just a wonderful sensation to glide on the
captures people and doesn't let them go."

ot long ago, I was thinking about what my friend in the NFL
ssroom had said to me. I thought of the fiasco involving Tonya
arding, I thought of Nancy Kerrigan's stunning performance in the
idst of that mess. I tried to remember what Janet Lynn looked like. I
hought of Brian Boitano's titanic victory over Brian Orser, of Scott
Hamilton's unbridled joy on the ice, of Paul Wylie's stunning artistry.
And I thought of Dorothy Hamill and the sound of her music in the
background in the radio dispatch from Europe in 1976.

Quite a few women skated in Norway before Tonya and Nancy
and Oksana got their turn. As I sat along press row, my cellular phone
rang. It was my sister Kate, calling from Toledo. She wanted an up-
date. I told her the big names were still an hour or so away.

A woman was skating as we spoke and my sister wanted to know
who it was. I told her the name; neither of us had heard of the
woman. It didn't matter. Kate thought it was so exciting. "I can hear
the music," she exclaimed. "I almost feel like I'm there."

I told her I knew exactly what she meant.

We said good-bye and I went back to watching the skating. I
started smiling and I couldn't stop.

My friend from the NFL pressroom wasn't at those Olympics, but I
sure wish he had been. I would have rushed over right then to tell him
that he was right.

cording to various demographic stud
popular sport among U.S. women and
tional study conducted by Sports Mark
women's figure skating as the second most p
States behind NFL football. The study also
skaters were among the eight most popular
States. Gymnast Mary Lou Retton was first,
Hamill in second place, and Peggy Fleming in th.
was eighth. Who was in between? Hank Aaron wa
Jordan and Willie Mays tied for fifth, and Babe Ruth

Some point out that it must be the artistry that dra
the costumes, music, beauty and grace that are such a
world of figure skating. Is it sport? Or is it art?

The answer is that it is both. Figure skating does a grand jo
ing its athleticism under layers of disguise. Pretty costumes
the purple bruises from dozens of crash landings. Makeup cov
intense, furrowed brow. "The whole point is to make it look ef
less," said U.S. ice dancer Elizabeth Punsalan. "If we were huffing a
puffing and sweating, you'd see how athletic it was."

"No one sees me at six-thirty in the morning," Boitano said, "when
I'm wearing my workout clothes in a freezing-cold, dingy rink and
spinning so fast I can't stop my nose from running."

During the Harding-Kerrigan drama, when I was traipsing through
courthouses and FBI offices waiting to hear what one figure skater
knew about the clubbing of another figure skater on the knee, I began
to wonder what it would be like to spend a season with these athletes.
Then I realized there is no season in figure skating, at least not that
anyone really knows about. They gear up in the summer, compete
once or twice in the fall, and focus completely on the national and
world championships in the winter. Then they take a few weeks off
and begin looking forward to the next year.

This kind of schedule brings the happiest moments in life to the
lucky ones—Boitano, Hamilton, Wylie, Kristi Yamaguchi—but it con-
demns most to a life of anonymous, unceasing practice. It turns figure
skating into a sport of personalities and tours, of one-on-one battles,
of unrequited dreams. Increasingly, too, it has become a sport of
money and agents, of tiny girls and pushy parents. You wonder sometimes if anyone really knows why they're skating anymore.

That's what I asked Slavka Kohout, the woman who coached Janet Lynn.
What with the lack of control over their own fate and the renowned bud-
get-breaking expense of it all, why would someone skate?

OCTOBER

*T*HE

SEASON BEGINS

1

THE
CURTAIN
RISES IN
SUN VALLEY

The Learjet was little more than a dot in the clear night sky, the tiniest point of light over the imposing Idaho mountains, as two tired young men sat waiting in a dark van.

The lights of the tiny airstrip were off; the airport was officially closed. The air traffic controller could have been dozing; nobody would have known. It was almost two in the morning on a black, chilly October night—an unusual time, the two men agreed, for a flight to be landing in Sun Valley.

A bellman and a security guard had been dispatched by the Sun Valley Lodge for a pickup in the middle of the night at Friedman Memorial Airport in nearby Hailey. They had punched a four-digit security code to enter the airport through a locked gate, pulled up beside the runway, turned off the engine, and waited.

They knew it wouldn't be long.

Without warning, the slumbering airfield began to awaken. The white runway lights, the airport's electronic welcome mat, popped on. The two men shifted in their seats and peered into the sky. The bright light coming from the south grew larger. Within minutes, it was upon them.

At 2:02 A.M. mountain daylight time, Saturday, October 8, 1994, a cream-colored private jet with a green stripe touched down on the concrete slab wedged between the menacing peaks of the Sawtooth Range. It taxied and came to a stop a few steps from the van.

The jet's door opened and a little man in blue jeans, sneakers, and a black letter-style jacket poked his face out and flashed a wrinkled, weary grin. He breathed deeply and gulped down the cool mountain air. Six hours earlier, he had been skating in an ice show in Atlanta. Now, after a police escort to the airport there, a commercial flight from Atlanta to Salt Lake City, and a late-night rendezvous with the corporate jet that would bring him to Idaho, the most charismatic figure skater in the world had been delivered safely to his destination.

Scott Hamilton had landed in Sun Valley. The figure-skating season could officially begin.

"I can't beat Boitano in the wind and the sun at altitude."

It was 9 A.M. The sun already was beaming down on the perfect patch of ice beside the veranda at the Lodge. Hamilton had had four hours of sleep. His thirty-six-year-old body felt stiff and his mind felt stale. He was complaining—with a smile on his face. Hamilton always wore a smile. He was living a charmed life and he knew it.

"How could anyone top Boitano in these conditions?" he wondered.

When they were amateurs, Hamilton beat Brian Boitano all the time. Hamilton was the anointed one, all the way through 1984, when he won his Olympic gold medal and turned pro, leaving the ice to Boitano. Boitano quickly rose to the top, winning the next Olympic gold medal. As a professional, Boitano, thirty-one, had become better than Hamilton, who juggled a three-month skating tour with countless hours in the CBS broadcast booth. But who was better than whom was inconsequential at this stage of their careers. Figure-skating people didn't compare Hamilton and Boitano; they simply revered them both for the different things they brought to their sport.

Hamilton credits Boitano's superb jumping ability with making "the sport a sport." He said Boitano's favorite time is "in the air." Hamilton's respect for Boitano is immense. Boitano is one of the most powerful skaters ever, and the most particular. What and how he practices, how he laces up his skates, when he goes to the bathroom before he skates—it is all fastidiously regimented. Boitano's attention to detail has served him well in a sport where a man moving at twenty miles per hour must land a three-revolution jump precisely on a one-quarter-inch blade while sliding on ice.

Hamilton, on the other hand, has more sheer fun on the ice. He has the fastest feet in the sport. He skims along the ice, playing to the crowd with reckless abandon. He measures his skating with an applause meter. The crowd means everything. For instance, Hamilton does a backflip in most of his performances; Boitano never has tried one. The backflip is one of the easiest tricks in the sport and the crowd's absolute favorite move. It's skating's cheap thrill. Boitano would rather not waste the time. Hamilton lives for the roar from the crowd when he lands it.

Hamilton and Boitano have skating styles determined by their size. Boitano is massive by skating standards at five feet eleven and 170 pounds. Hamilton is five feet three and a half and 120. Hamilton skates blithely on top of the ice, while Boitano digs in. If Hamilton rents the ice, Boitano owns it. Hamilton selects light music, funny stuff. It is a show to him. Boitano is grander and majestic. For him, it is serious athleticism. In the classic figure-skating argument—Is it art? Is it sport?—these men give different correct answers.

Neither man had expected to be in Sun Valley the weekend of October 8–9, 1994. Hamilton had his show in Atlanta; Boitano thought he would spend the days at home in San Francisco, practicing for the start of a new professional season that was scheduled to begin later in the month.

But then the phone call came. The voice on the other end of the line was sounding rather nervous.

It had happened again.

Another woman figure skater.

Another knee.

Could they please get to Sun Valley?

The plan, formulated in the mind of a thirty-six-year-old North Carolina television executive named Mike Burg, had been simple. He wanted to stage a professional women's event, followed by an amateur women's event. The outdoor rink in the mountains at Sun Valley would be the site of both competitions. It was perfect, Burg thought. Sonja Henie, the most beautiful figure skater of all, had made a movie there, although, truth be told, she actually did her skating scenes in a Hollywood studio. Now, Burg would bring Henie's present-day successor, the magical Oksana Baiul, onto the Sun Valley ice to start her professional career. The sixteen-year-old Ukrainian orphan who had won the 1994 Olympic gold medal had signed a $1.5-million deal with Burg to skate in ten made-for-TV events in the next year and a half; Sun Valley would be the first.

Burg sold the idea of a series of figure-skating competitions to CBS. Television executives who had watched ratings soar at the 1994 Winter

Olympics wanted more of this sport. This was especially true at CBS, where Fox had swooped in and stole the NFL, leaving the network with just about nothing on Sunday afternoons. The Tonya Harding–Nancy Kerrigan night of skating at the Norway Olympics was the sixth-highest-rated television program of all time, behind the last *M*A*S*H*, *Dallas*'s "Who Shot J.R.?", an episode of *Roots,* and two Super Bowls. Other figure-skating events—even stale, months-old exhibitions—garnered too-good-to-be-true ratings. CBS Sports saw a chance for salvation: figure skating, figure skating, and more figure skating.

Baiul came to Sun Valley several days early to practice. Just as she finished a number, she dislocated her left kneecap and tore a piece of cartilage. While curtsying.

In football, players blow out their knees when being tackled. In basketball or baseball, knees are injured in collisions or falls or when an athlete is running or jumping. In figure skating, the knee goes during a curtsy. It's just that kind of a sport.

A knee had been the catalyst for the strangest sports competition story in U.S. history, the Tonya-Nancy saga, precipitated, of course, by the Whack Heard Round the World—the attack on Kerrigan's knee. Now, another incident with another woman's knee was threatening to postpone the start of figure skating's newest and most unpredictable season.

Burg was frantic. CBS trucks were parked beside the rink and workers were laying cable and setting up cameras at the moment Baiul went down. She had arthroscopic surgery at a nearby hospital and was back practicing within two days. But the women's pro event was scrapped; Baiul would not be ready in time. With CBS crews stopping in their tracks, Burg came up with another idea: a *men's* professional event.

He scrambled to the telephone and began dialing numbers. He called Linda Leaver, Brian Boitano's coach and manager in Los Altos, California. He was wondering if Boitano would like to compete in a professional men's event in Sun Valley in a week. Leaver said no, he wasn't yet quite ready for a competition. He was gearing up for late October. Burg called Hamilton. Hamilton said the same thing. No.

Burg had to have them. He just had to. Hamilton was the best "people" person in the sport, and Boitano was the Master of the Ice. So he changed the offer: it would be an artistic competition, much easier than a strict jumping contest. No one would be counting triple jumps. Coaches and ex-skaters who were their friends would be the judges. Burg could offer thousands of dollars up front, a $40,000 first-place prize, a nice weekend in the mountains. Boitano agreed and flew over from San Francisco the day before the event. Hamilton, who was CBS's skating analyst, knew his obligation. Although he had the commitment in Atlanta the night before, the people who ran Sun Valley would personally see to it that their corporate jet got him there.

Burg stopped and sighed. He called skating's new season "the Wild West," and he fashioned himself as Jesse James. Lawlessness prevailed. Competitions were beginning to pop up on the landscape. If you could get a network interested and sign some skaters, you had yourself an event. You made up the rules as you went along. Burg had never been a major player in running the sport. Until now. He had represented Katarina Witt from 1991 to 1993, working with the crafty former East German on endorsements and made-for-TV skating shows. That was his start. Now, with television interest high and sponsors wanting to jump on the bandwagon, Burg gladly leaped into the fray. He controlled Baiul, and he had deals with Kerrigan and Boitano, Kristi Yamaguchi, and Paul Wylie. The old guard, led by skating icon Dick Button and the sports-marketing giant International Management Group, still had its foothold in professional events and marketing and managing skaters, but Burg was coming on fast. His empire, he was convinced, would mark time from Sun Valley.

In addition to Hamilton and Boitano, Burg rounded up a third Olympic gold medalist, Ukrainian Viktor Petrenko, who already was in Sun Valley with Baiul. Wherever Baiul went, Petrenko followed. They were a team; Petrenko had encouraged his coach and mother-in-law, Galina Zmievskaia, to take in Baiul two years earlier. The whole gang had moved from the Ukraine to Simsbury, Connecticut, after the Olympics. They lived next door to one another in an apartment complex.

Burg filled out the roster for the men's event with three other skaters—Mark Mitchell, Petr Barna, and Gary Beacom, a show skater who doesn't do triple axels, but does wear sunglasses and perform headstands. Burg was putting three Hall of Famers with two Triple-A ballplayers and—in Beacom—a class clown. But what did Burg care? Figure-skating fans never complained. They were thrilled to see anyone skate on TV. CBS had an event that would get fine afternoon ratings when it ran on Thanksgiving weekend. The skaters had work and exposure. Everyone was happy.

At the former-women's-now-men's pro event, the competitors did two programs each. Unlike an amateur event, there was not a short and long program. This was show and show: one show program, followed by another. And outdoors, no less. Skaters never competed outdoors anymore, unless they were in Sun Valley. Jumping from sunlight into shade was difficult; finding the ice on the way down was tricky, like trying to hit a baseball thrown from sunshine into darkness.

For the first number, Hamilton wore purple pants and a multicolored vest to accompany his fancy footwork to the rock song "Walk This Way," blowing kisses and winking at the sun-splashed gathering of 2,300 along the hotel veranda. Boitano was all business, performing to Pavarotti's "Nessun Dorma." He did this in pain. His feet were scrunched into black skate boots that were too tight. This was a typical skater's lament. The boots were new, worn for just one week, and he was furiously trying to break them in. If he ran into a problem, he said with a smile, he would "just do what Tonya did"—prop his skate on the judges' table and plead for mercy.

For a second number, Hamilton did "In the Mood," and Boitano brought a red folding chair out on the ice with him to sit on, jump over, and fold up as "Missing You" played over the loudspeakers. Boitano thought up the number on his own, without a choreographer, after watching a ballerina use a chair as a prop during a performance he attended.

Boitano felt a bit silly bringing a chair onto the ice with him. Everyone else came up with crazy stuff, but he was reluctant to push the envelope artistically, to threaten his own high standards. He didn't want people to think him stupid out there. He laughed as he took the red chair to the ice to practice, saying, "It's my new partner; a really, really thin Katarina." The chair had a life of its own. At a skating event in Ohio, Boitano set the chair backstage, and when it was his turn to skate, he couldn't find it. He anxiously approached a group of fellow skaters sitting around a TV set watching the closed-circuit feed. "Anyone seen my red chair?" They all looked around and shook their heads. But Robin Cousins, the 1980 Olympic gold medalist, turned around on his folding chair.

"Ah, Brian?"

Boitano looked at him.

Cousins was sitting on Boitano's irreplaceable prop.

Petrenko, the 1992 Olympic gold medalist, was the artistic opposite of Boitano. They played against all the stereotypes; Boitano the Californian was an arch conservative on the ice; Petrenko, the quiet Ukrainian, loved the outrageous. In Sun Valley, he skated to a number he liked to do on the show circuit. He pinned a piece of paper with a No. 21 to his back and skated as if he were competing in a ballroom-dancing contest—without a partner. His music was "Cherry Pink and Apple Blossom White," something men like Boitano and Hamilton never would skate to. But Petrenko's world was entirely different from the Americans'. Petrenko was sitting around one day at home in Connecticut, fascinated by the offerings of cable television, when a commercial for great music of the forties and fifties came on. He called the 800 number, and in a few weeks twelve compact discs arrived. That was one of the songs.

No matter what music was playing, Petrenko was a master of flirting with the judges. He camped out at center ice and winked and smiled at them at the beginning, middle, and end of almost every program. Some of his programs featured more winks of the eye than revolutions in his jumps. Spectators on the other side got to see a lot of his back. He did that with the ballroom number, and he did it in his second effort, a rap number, of all things. A blond Ukrainian with a baseball cap on backward swiveling his hips and preening to rap music caught the audience by complete surprise.

Among the seven judges were four coaches who had women skating in a so-called amateur event the next day on this ice. One of them, judge No. 7, sitting in the shade wearing sunglasses, was Evy Scotvold.

Scotvold is the self-assured, silver-haired coach who, with his choreographer wife, Mary, led Paul Wylie and Nancy Kerrigan to Olympic silver medals. He was coaching seventeen-year-old Lisa Ervin at this event and had kept the whole weekend in complete perspective. When the men's event was over, he announced, "We're now going to have a judges' meeting—in the bar."

Scotvold gave Boitano lessons during the summer a long time ago and was a great friend and former coach of Hamilton's. Scotvold helped both of them along their way. Petrenko was another matter. Scotvold had no allegiance to him.

The Cold War is alive and well in figure skating. There are two different schools in the sport: the American school stresses jumping. The Eastern European school emphasizes ballet. U.S. skaters and coaches roll their eyes at their European counterparts, but that style goes over well with the European judges who dominate Olympic and world judging. In skating, the Iron Curtain lives a glorious afterlife. Big skating decisions, like Baiul's five judges to four Olympic victory over Kerrigan, still break down exactly along old East-West lines.

Scotvold had seen Wylie skate the performance of his life and lose to Petrenko at the 1992 Albertville Olympics. Two years later, he watched Kerrigan skate the performance of her life and lose to Baiul. The score was Team Zmievskaia 2, Team Scotvold 0. Evy Scotvold said he spent no time worrying about it, but he was not the kind of guy to take too kindly to a man on skates winking at him.

Scotvold gave Petrenko the lowest marks he received from any of the judges: 5.5 and 5.4.

Boitano won the event easily, with Hamilton second, Mitchell third, and Petrenko fourth. Hamilton gamely tried to make it close by attempting a triple lutz, the second hardest of the triple jumps, in his second number. He pushed off the ice with a vengeance, believing that the wind swirling around the rink would hold him back. It didn't. He overrotated and went crashing to the ice.

Not that it mattered. This wasn't exactly cutthroat competition; professional skating rarely got that serious. The Olympic or world championship medal was what a skater lived and died for. Professional events were fluff and everyone who was in them knew it. The skaters' pride was on the line, but, at the end of the day, no matter how they did, they still had their Olympic medals. It was rather anticlimactic: there were no make-or-break moments remaining in their careers.

As a boy, Hamilton had a mysterious intestinal malabsorption condition. It caused him to stop growing for a few years. Doctors didn't know what was wrong and eventually prescribed special diets and exercises, including skating. The condition eventually vanished, and Hamilton grew up to become the stud of the sport. Now that was an oxymoron; a five-foot-three-and-a-half-inch figure-skating hunk, the sport's macho man.

Hamilton's friends and colleagues at CBS joked that over the years, with his penchant for associating with beautiful women, Hamilton had tried—single-handedly—to alter the sissy image of the male side of figure skating. It wasn't just his girlfriends. There was the wardrobe, too. When he was competing in the 1984 Olympics, he eschewed sequins and wore plain, one-piece jumpsuits. He was trying to be as nondescript as a skater could be. The last thing Hamilton wanted to do was sparkle.

But no figure skater could completely extricate himself from the trappings of this peculiar, delightful sport.

"Are you wearing makeup?" Boitano asked Hamilton behind the curtain separating the rink from backstage.

"Do I look like I have makeup on?" Hamilton replied.

"No, but you should. You've got to wear makeup, but you never would, so you always look like a corpse."

Hamilton laughed. "Nah, nah, it's not for me."

"You should wear it, just Pan-Cake though, nothing else," Boitano said.

Jamie Isley, a female choreographer who came to Sun Valley to assist Mark Mitchell, chimed in, "I took Scott to buy his first makeup, at a mall in Florida, remember, Scott?"

Chagrined, Hamilton shrugged. "Oh, yeah. But I'm au naturel now."

Not entirely. Hamilton uses brown eye shadow religiously—to hide the bald spot on the top of his head.

The next day, Hamilton was in the CBS booth, wearing a tuxedo and talking into a microphone. On the ice were other skaters, a handful of women and girls who had received the coveted invitation to come to Sun Valley. Michelle Kwan, Nicole Bobek, Tonia Kwiatkowski, Kyoko Ina, and Lisa Ervin knew it meant that they were in America's gold-medal pipeline, which would carry the chosen few to the Winter Olympic Games in 1998 in Nagano, Japan. It has been said that an Olympic gold medal in women's figure skating can be worth $10 million to the skater who wins it, especially if that woman is an American. For organizers to think that these five women were good enough to someday be that skater, to be invited to the coming-out party on the most famous outdoor rink in the world—that was really something. None of them would have missed it. But there were drawbacks. It was too early in the Olympic cycle for anyone to know who they were. While the men's event was sold-out, organizers had to give away tickets to the competition between the five unknown women. Then again, no one would have come to see Nancy Kerrigan and Tonya Harding in 1990, either.

For the women's competition, the judges were real judges. There were no meetings in the bar. Backflips were disallowed. So were sunglasses. In a deal worked out by Burg and the U.S. Figure Skating Association, the governing body for the sport, Burg would give the organization Baiul for one of its pro-am events in the 1994–95 skating season if the USFSA sanctioned Burg's women's amateur event. Burg needed the sanctioning or he could not have held the amateur women's event. The USFSA needed the competition as well to begin to publicize its future stars. The organization was battling the professional events for sponsors and fan support. Everyone wanted TV time.

In figure skating, there are two different competitive divisions. There is the so-called amateur, or Olympic-style competition, known officially in figure skating as the "eligible" style. This is the division of Kwan, Bobek, and the other young women and men. It is the career maker or breaker. It's the kind of skating that leads fathers to drive Zamboni machines at 6 A.M. to clear the ice for their sons' and daughters' practices; that breaks up families and takes children out of school; that consumes the lives of an entire family for a decade. Although the families of eligible skaters always complain about money, those at the top of the eligible heap can now earn more than $100,000 a year from competitions and shows. That's why the term *amateur* is dated for the country's top skaters. *Olympic division* is the accurate term.

The so-called professional, or exhibition-style, competition is for those who already have an Olympic medal tucked away in a safe-deposit box, like Boitano, Hamilton, and Petrenko. Skaters in this category are called, in figure-skating jargon, *ineligible,* meaning they are not able to compete in the Olympic-style or "eligible" events, such as the annual U.S. national championships and world championships, or the quadrennial Olympic Games. This is the victory tour of skating, with judging by celebrities, ex-skaters, and coaches, occasional world-class performances, and phenomenal TV ratings. Some of these skaters are millionaires. The proper title for their skating is *professional division.*

Because professionals never had many competitive opportunities, they used to fade into oblivion in ice shows, leaving the spotlight to the new, up-and-coming stars. Now, they were sticking around—and there was a huge market for them. This development did not make the USFSA happy.

It was too early in the season to make any judgments about the next crop of American women skaters. An Olympic-division figure skater's season isn't a calendar of competitions; it's a series of practices with a couple big events thrown in. A skater's season lurches like a car with gear trouble—it lulls, it jerks, it stops, it starts up again. There's not a game a night; there's not even an event a month. It's basically practice interrupted by the national championships. A qualifying event or invitational trip can also break the monotony.

There were two teenagers to watch in Sun Valley: tiny fourteen-year-old Michelle Kwan and streetwise seventeen-year-old Nicole Bobek, who were second and third at the 1994 Nationals behind Harding, who won and later was stripped of her title for hindering the prosecution in the Kerrigan attack. Tonia Kwiatkowski, Kyoko Ina, and Lisa Ervin filled out the roster. Ina, nearly twenty-two, had been to the 1994 Olympics as a pairs skater; Kwiatkowski, a twenty-three-year-old college graduate, and Ervin made the world championship team in 1993, but had not done much since then.

With Kerrigan gone, someone would rise to the top and win her first title at the national championships in Providence, Rhode Island, in February. Kwan was the early favorite. But she was growing, and height and weight on a little girl can wreak havoc on her jumps. In less than two years, Kwan had grown seven inches and gained nineteen pounds to five feet two and ninety-six pounds. While most girls would be thrilled with that kind of natural progression, her coach, Frank Carroll, knew it could be a problem. He worried that an extra pound or two on her hips would throw off the triple jumps they had worked so hard to master at their mountain retreat east of Los Angeles. He was looking at her as a skater, not a young lady. He was paid handsomely—the top coaches in the country can make $150,000–$200,000 a year—to think that way.

Michelle Kwan was a skater in a hurry. She zipped through the ranks from novice to junior to senior (the top category) much faster than most. With the elimination of the compulsory school figures in 1991, it was easy to rush. A decade ago, a little jumping bean would have been stopped in her tracks by the school figures, the painstaking tracings of variations of figure eights that required patience and maturity and gave the sport its name. Future stars were mired in juniors for several years, stalled by those confounded compulsories. Now, there was nothing holding the little girls back—except for the judges. They still were looking for grace and style, however that was defined. Often, the older girls and women were the most poised and artistic. That played a big role in determining a winner. The subjectivity of judging, then, could place a heavy hand on a tiny girl's progress.

Kwan, however, was rising quicker than even her coach knew. There are skating tests that are required to move up from one level to the next. Carroll wasn't aware that Kwan was going to take the test to move up to seniors when he went out of town one weekend in May 1992.

Carroll was shocked, but knew there was no going back. "Okay," he told Kwan, "we're going to have to work our butts off because you are going to make a dismal showing unless you develop some maturity and presence and discipline."

Danny Kwan, Michelle's father, was not unhappy with this turn of events. His aggressive attitude toward the sport had pushed Michelle and her older sister, Karen, also a strong national skater. One day, leaving their rink in Torrance, California, he got so angry with his daughters' performances that he flung their skates into the parking lot.

"The way you skate, don't skate!" he yelled.

Karen ran over and picked up the skates.

Michelle just stared at him.

Another time, Danny Kwan overheard Michelle talking in her sleep.

"This is nothing," she was repeating over and over. "This is nothing."

Kwan recognized the words. They were what he and Carroll were saying to calm Michelle about her senior debut at the 1993 Nationals.

"I got a tear in my eye," her father said.

Danny Kwan said he began to calm down about skating, but

Michelle did not become a recreational skater. She and her sister moved to Lake Arrowhead, a two-hour drive from Los Angeles into the mountains, to train. The first year, her father drove "up the hill," as they call it, every night to sleep in his daughters' tiny cabin. For the 1994–95 year, their mother, Estella, moved into the cabin to live with both girls. They took Michelle out of school—she was an eighth-grader—and hired a tutor. The family also signed an agent—Mary Lou Retton's representative, Shep Goldberg—which sent the purists reeling. Thirteen years old and already signed up. The Kwans said they did it to keep reporters away during the Tonya-Nancy saga, when their daughter was besieged for interviews as the Olympic alternate. But a media packet on Michelle was readily available in the fall of 1994.

For all the upheaval in their lives, the Kwans were seen in skating circles as a model of how to raise a daughter in the sport. The USFSA sent out-of-control parents to talk to the Kwans. And little Michelle was a joy to be around. She was respected and treated as an equal; Hamilton walked by her at the side of the rink in Sun Valley and yelled out, "Michelle, don't still be skating when you're thirty-six, okay?" With her immense talent, her quiet, polite demeanor, and a close-knit family willing to do anything for her, there was no telling how far she could go.

If Kwan was America's most balanced little skater, Bobek was its greatest wild card.

The daughter of a single mother, Bobek traveled the country with her mother and her mother's female companion in search of figure-skating nirvana. Every coach who ever taught her—eight in all, three in 1994 alone—knew she could be something if she ever decided to work at it. She loved making up her own dazzling skating moves to music. But Bobek often loafed at practice, rarely saw the inside of a school, liked to smoke, and had been known to sneak out of her hotel room on a skating trip.

Most of the greats had coached her, including Carroll, the legendary Carlo Fassi, Colorado Springs' Kathy Casey, and Scotvold. A strict disciplinarian, Scotvold had tried to tame her for a few weeks earlier in the summer at his rink on Cape Cod. He quickly washed his hands of her—and her mother and her mother's friend, whom everyone called her "aunt."

"Every little horny dude on Cape Cod was there within four days," Scotvold said. "But she was funny and sweet. We got along really well. We kept the mother and the aunt away. She just doesn't have any discipline."

The Bobek gang left Scotvold when Nicole wanted to go to the Goodwill Games to make a few thousand dollars, while he strongly suggested she stay home and practice. She landed in the suburbs north of Detroit, at the rink of Richard Callaghan, known throughout the sport as a coach who closely monitored the lives—and training habits—of his skaters.

Slowly, Callaghan said, he started to see progress. Bobek was carrying a few extra pounds on her hips when he brought her to Sun Valley to see where she ranked with Kwan. While Kwan looked polished and sharp, Bobek was erratic and immediately announced to CBS reporter Tracy Wilson that she was competing with a fractured hip.

Word of the interview got back to Callaghan.

"A fractured hip?" Callaghan said. "She had a bad fall on Wednesday, but nothing is broken."

After the event, Wilson pulled Bobek aside for another interview. This time, Callaghan was in eavesdropping position. But Wilson then said she didn't need Bobek after all, and let her go.

"That was one of my best interviews," Bobek said with a naughty laugh and a twinkle in her eye. "I didn't say anything to get myself in trouble."

The summer of 1994, Scotvold had coached both Bobek and Ervin. They looked alike, two teenage blondes with a world of skating talent. But they couldn't have been more different. Their peers had labeled Bobek the "evil twin"; Ervin, the "good twin." They were not friends.

Bobek and Ervin both represented the United States at the 1993 world junior championships in Seoul, South Korea. At the time, Bobek was being coached by coach number six, Kathy Casey. Casey couldn't make the trip, so she sent a colleague, Lorraine Borman, who had coached Rosalynn Sumners to the Olympic silver medal in 1984. Keeping Bobek in the room they were sharing and away from impromptu parties became Borman's greatest challenge. One night, Borman recalled, Bobek pretended she was sleeping, then got up, went into the bathroom, and flushed the toilet. She then dashed across the room and tried to open the door and escape before the flushing stopped.

"Nicole!" Borman said. "I know what you're doing. Get back in bed."

A few minutes later, Bobek slipped out of bed again and began putting on her clothes. Borman flicked on the light. Bobek explained that she had gotten cold.

"No matter what you think, you are not leaving this room," Borman said.

Borman then got out of bed, sat down on the floor, propped herself against the door, and looked at Bobek.

"If I have to, I will sleep here all night," she told Bobek.

A half hour later, with Bobek finally asleep, Borman crawled back into bed.

While Bobek was attracting the usual attention, Ervin had become an innocent tourist. One day, she went hunting for bargains with other skaters in Itaewon, the bustling shopping district in Seoul. She was interested in a leather jacket. The shopkeeper told her it was $100.

Fine, Ervin said, and began to get out her wallet.

Her friends tried to stop her. You were supposed to negotiate a price in Itaewon.

"Ah, Lisa," they said, "you don't have that much money."

"Oh, yes, I do," Ervin said earnestly, forking over the $100.

The night before they left for home, Ervin was sitting in a room with most of the other members of the American team. She ordered one chocolate sundae from room service, then another. "You guys have to promise not to tell Carol," she ordered. Carol was Carol Heiss Jenkins, the 1960 Olympic gold medalist and Ervin's coach at the time. Ervin, who had had a spectacular rise to the top of her sport in the 1990s, was about to fall completely out of the picture. Difficulty with weight—and a desperate attempt to drop pounds by starving herself—would prove to be her undoing.

That same night, according to several coaches, Bobek was hanging out with a group of Estonian skaters. Soon, their minibar was empty and they had no money to pay the bill. The front desk called American team officials. "A blond American girl was the culprit," the manager told them. They knew it wasn't Ervin, so they went to find Bobek. She wasn't in her room. Borman had given up control of Bobek to her mother. And her mother had lost her.

The U.S. team was rousted and told to try to find Bobek. No one knew where she was. They called Casey in Colorado. Exasperated, Casey said she would pay the minibar bill. Just find Bobek.

Within an hour, Bobek wandered back into the hotel. Where she had been, no one knew. With Bobek, no one ever really knew.

In Sun Valley, the blond twins had latched onto new coaches. Scotvold was asked by CBS's Wilson as they ate lunch if Ervin was now his main skater.

"Oh, no," Scotvold said quickly. "We've still got Nancy and Paul."

It was soon apparent why Scotvold had been so reluctant to claim Ervin as his own. Her performance was dismal. She fell on the only triple jump she tried and could not even complete a double axel. This was a girl who in 1993 finished second in the nation to Nancy Kerri-

gan with four triple jumps. In less than two years, her weight had fluc-
tuated from 110 pounds up to 130, down to 105, back up to 130. She
was throwing away her lunch in trash cans at the rink in an effort to
keep off the pounds that would ruin her jumps. Some days, she didn't
eat a thing. The next day, she would eat everything in sight. Scotvold,
who said he did not know exactly what Ervin was doing, was weighing her a couple times a week in hopes that she would get back to
110. The pressure on Ervin to reach that weight was immense.

Ervin's father, Bill, was with her in Sun Valley. He worked for Du Pont
in Buffalo; his wife and only child lived in a two-bedroom town house
on Cape Cod, near the Scotvolds' rink. He visited once a month.

When Lisa was seven years old, Bill and his wife, Jeanne, sent her
to Cleveland to live with another family and train with Heiss. Now
Heiss was watching from afar as Ervin skated worse than she had
when she was ten. They had had their disagreements but had parted
as friends. These kinds of things happened all the time in skating.

The Sun Valley event was over by early afternoon. To no one's surprise, Kwan had won it easily. Bobek had been a sloppy second. That
also surprised no one. Kwiatkowski and Ina had come next. Ervin
was last. When Scotvold found out there was a way to catch a flight
that would get them out of Idaho that evening and to Boston the next
morning on a red-eye, he asked the Ervins if they were willing to try
for it.

"You bet. We'd love to get out of here," Bill Ervin said.

Since it really didn't matter who won in figure skating in October,
every one of the five women could smile broadly when a photographer arranged them side by side on the ice and asked them to hold still
as the sun—still high over the mountains—sparkled off their spangles
and sequins.

They would leave each other there, perhaps to meet again at the
1995 Nationals in Providence, Rhode Island, in February. Over the
next four months, one of them would nearly live up to the lofty expectations the skating world had for her.

Another would continue undeterred along a journeywoman's career path, hoping that there still was a place for a college-educated
adult in women's skating.

A third would divide her time between singles and pairs skating
and find more success in the latter.

A fourth would be arrested.

And the last girl squinting into the sun would not compete again.

2

THEY
CALL THEM
LADIES?

Tonya Harding didn't come to Sun Valley. Her invitation wasn't lost in the mail. It was never sent.

Had Mike Burg asked her to come, which he never seriously considered, Harding couldn't have done it without the permission of her probation officer. The terms of her three-year probation on the felony charge of hindering the prosecution in the Nancy Kerrigan case allowed travel only in her home state of Oregon, in Washington state, and in California, where she was making a thoroughly forgettable grade-B movie, *Breakaway*.

If Idaho had somehow been added to the list, and she had been invited and had accepted, she would have performed a one-woman show. No one in figure skating wanted to be around her. Solidarity with Kerrigan was not particularly the reason, because some in figure skating didn't want to be around her, either. It was just that figure-skating people had known Tonya Harding for years and, having known her, had had more than enough of her.

It was not because of the attack on Kerrigan. It was because of everything she did before the attack. Her fellow skaters looked at Tonya as a screwup. Harding possessed more raw jumping talent than almost any of them. More than Kerrigan, Oksana Baiul, Michelle Kwan, Nicole Bobek, Peggy Fleming, Dorothy Hamill, Kristi Yamaguchi, Sonja Henie. Harding had it all.

Contrary to what she believed, figure skating didn't do a number on her. She did a number on herself. She didn't train properly or make good strategic decisions, which ended up costing her any chance for an Olympic medal. While it is true that she came from a tough background, with a difficult mother and an inability to pay her own way through an expensive sport, Harding received more financial help than she ever let on. Even the skating officials and judges who personally couldn't stand her still appreciated her enormous talent enough to award her two national titles—one was later taken away—and two trips to the Olympics. If they wanted to punish her, why did they send her to the Olympics *twice?*

Harding first entered the national stage in 1989, finishing third at the national championships. She had the potential to become America's greatest female jumper. Coaches saw that. And the compulsory school figures were being phased out at just the right time for her. It would be a jumping contest, and the girl with the most jumps should win. Harding was that skater. You could make a case that with her talent, and with the figures being eliminated, and with two Olympic Games coming in 1992 and 1994, she could become a two-time Olympic medalist.

But she was a perplexing woman—or lady, as the figure-skating world insists on calling female skaters. In 1990, for instance, Harding was a participant at a U.S. Figure Skating Association elite training camp. Others at the camp included Yamaguchi, Bobek, and Lisa Ervin. While a couple of top coaches taught the skaters how to stroke (skate) with style and how to become more graceful, which is a requisite in the sport, Harding stood in a corner with her arms crossed, refusing to participate.

A year later, she was the national champion. In 1991, she became the first American woman to land the difficult three-and-a-half-revolution triple axel in competition. Had the judges not wanted her to win, they would have placed her second to Yamaguchi. It would have been controversial, but they could have done it. Yamaguchi came in as the favorite; she was a jumper, like Harding, but she was more graceful than Harding, and more consistent. The title could have gone to Yamaguchi, but the judges awarded it to Harding and her triple axel. Yamaguchi went home and cried.

"I was really down on myself," Yamaguchi said. "A good two weeks after U.S. Nationals, I was a mess on the ice. Almost every day, I had tears. There were comments on my program, maybe it should be changed. I just felt nothing was going to be right, I felt kind of bitter. So I told myself, 'Change this for worlds, it's a whole new start, a different attitude.'"

Harding, on the other hand, went home and stopped practicing. She took a week off, said her coach, Dody Teachman, and when she returned to the ice, she took it easy. When she fell or got angry, she stopped in the midst of her program. That was a recipe for disaster for any skater. She, Yamaguchi, and Kerrigan, the third-place U.S. finisher, went to Munich for the world championships. There, Harding again landed the triple axel, but made other mistakes, and Yamaguchi took the title away from her.

Because she seemed so tough, because she played pool, dropped out of high school, smoked cigarettes, threatened a motorist with a baseball bat, and knew her way around the engine of a car, the outside world thought Harding was feisty enough to become a strong competitor. But the wispy Yamaguchi (in reality, she was just an inch shorter than Harding, who is deceptively tiny at five feet one) put her to shame. By the 1992 Nationals, one skater had become the perfect figure-skating package: Yamaguchi. Kerrigan finished second. Overweight and out of shape, Harding was third. At the Olympics, Yamaguchi and Kerrigan were roommates and model citizens, practicing and doing everything they were supposed to do. Harding, on the other hand, came to the Olympics on her own terms. She insisted on practicing at her home rink in a shopping mall near Portland because, she said, she had more ice time there. She flew to France extremely late, just three days before the competition.

Reporters asked if she wouldn't be jet-lagged.

"I never get jet-lagged," she insisted.

In the competition, Harding's go-for-broke attitude doomed her to failure. In the short program, the two-minute-forty-second performance that is full of technical requirements, Harding insisted on trying her triple axel, which she was having trouble landing by then.

"It's my most consistent jump," Harding said.

In a way, it was. She always was missing it.

Against Teachman's wishes, Harding tried it in the short program at the 1992 Olympics—and it ruined her. Falling in the short program is devastating; the requirements must be completed. The long program tolerates mistakes. The short does not.

Crashing to the ice, Harding dropped to sixth place in the short program and instantaneously saw any chance for the gold medal slip away. All week, even before she had arrived, there had been talk of how Harding and Japan's Midori Ito had the triple axel, which meant they supposedly could bury Yamaguchi during the competition. Yamaguchi said she had practiced the triple axel, but never had much success with it, so she would have to go with what she had: five triples, up through the triple lutz, the second-hardest jump. Reporters nagged her; she stood her ground. Yamaguchi and her coach, Christy Ness, were nothing if not brilliant at competition time. They knew she didn't need a triple axel to win if she skated well. At the Olympics, with tremendous pressure on the skaters, those unbridled triple axels might end up as nothing more than loud thuds on the ice. Yamaguchi and Ness never listened to the buzz around Harding and Ito. They just kept practicing what they knew Yamaguchi could do well.

Harding thought she needed the axel—in skating lingo, it's implied that it's a triple—but she didn't need it as much as she thought. With it, she could have won the gold medal. But without it, she still could have won. Most of all, she needed to get into position to win the gold by playing it smart in the short program—worth 33 percent of the overall score—then going for broke in the long (67 percent). In the short program, she could have thrown in a smooth triple lutz, which was a breeze for her, been no worse than third, and set herself up to challenge Yamaguchi for the gold medal. The choice was strategically easy, like a golfer laying up for a simple shot into a par-five hole, as opposed to going for broke and hitting the ball into the water. But headstrong Tonya Harding never gave it a second thought. She did the triple axel in the short. She fell to the ice. She couldn't recover in the long program and finished fourth overall, out of the medals. Yamaguchi won the gold medal; Kerrigan took the bronze behind Ito's silver.

"I was trying to just go for it all," Harding said much later, looking back. "I know now it was a little too risky. If I could change it, I would."

Afterward, the exasperated Teachman admitted what many people suspected all along.

Harding was jet-lagged.

And so it went for Harding. There was always an excuse. Retakes—skating mulligans—started happening with regularity. At the 1993 Nationals in Phoenix, a strap on her dress popped off, and before her top fell completely off, she skated to the referee and received a second chance to start over. A high-level USFSA official said months later that he thought Harding unsnapped the dress on purpose after missing her first jump.

That autumn, at the 1993 Skate America in Dallas, Harding again got a retry, this time because her skate blade came loose as she was skating. While pleading her case, she propped her skate onto the referee's table. It was a scene that would be repeated before the world in Norway four months later.

Also at that competition, Harding dropped this bombshell on reporters: she had an ovarian cyst that could explode at any moment. She was skating at terrible risk to herself, but she would skate on.

As the weeks went by, there was no further word about the ovary and the cyst. Finally, at the Olympics in Norway, a reporter asked. Oh, Harding said, the problem went away. The cyst never exploded.

Earlier that fall, a special training camp was held in Norway for U.S. Olympic hopefuls. Harding was invited, but never showed up. She informed her coach, Diane Rawlinson—Harding fired Teachman after the 1992 Olympics—that she wasn't going to make the trip with a last-minute call to Rawlinson's car phone as Rawlinson headed to the airport, according to the 1994 book *Fire on Ice*. It was the ovarian cyst, Harding told her. She couldn't travel.

But, according to the book, Harding was well enough to skate an exhibition in Cleveland a week later and to go to Dallas for Skate America. Had she called and canceled ahead of time for the Norway trip, Michelle Kwan would have had the chance to go. Instead, Harding's spot remained empty. Her fan club, meanwhile, had raised more than $800 for the Norway trip and given it to her. Harding never gave it back, the club president said.

Harding didn't stay in shape. She didn't listen to her coaches. But she got away with it. No one yelled at her. No one forced her to get in line. She was unreliable and she was undertrained.

"She felt she could take a shortcut and still deliver the goods," Teachman said.

Other things troubled Teachman even more. For nine years, Barbara Flowers was Harding's choreographer. Flowers had breast cancer and became very sick in 1993. Teachman called Harding to let her know Flowers was dying and that she would love to talk to Harding. Flowers died that November.

"Barbara never heard from Tonya," Teachman said.

Harding went to the 1994 Nationals—the Olympic trials—and won the event when Kerrigan was attacked. She told ABC-TV she wished Kerrigan luck in coming back "next season." It was a curious comment, considering everyone knew Kerrigan would be back within a couple weeks.

There were dozens of curiosities involving Harding and the attack, many of which remained unanswered. No one knows exactly what Harding knew and when she knew it, but this much is true: were it not for Harding, live-in ex-husband Jeff Gillooly and his three accomplices would not have been inside the sport of figure skating and would have had no reason to attack Kerrigan. They were doing it for Tonya because she and they thought the judges were unfair to her, and, the men thought, her only salvation was to get rid of Kerrigan. But there were two spots on the Olympic team, and if Harding skated well, one of those places was hers. Kwan and Bobek weren't ready to make an Olympic team quite yet, and no one else had Harding's ability and seasoning at the international level. So the whole ridiculous plot was completely unnecessary.

Because Harding had not been found guilty of breaking any laws at the time of the Olympics, she had every right under U.S. law to skate in Norway. But the responsible thing would have been for Harding to gracefully withdraw. She admitted knowing details about the attack well before she told authorities about them. As the USFSA—and Kerrigan—worried about who was out there and what they might do a second time, Harding knew exactly who had done what and refused to tell anyone. Instead of helping out by disclosing the culprits, she hid them. When the FBI was on to her, she quickly distanced herself from Gillooly. Her lack of concern for Kerrigan was startling. The most substantial comment she made about Kerrigan from the trials to the Olympics was that she would "kick her butt" in Norway.

Journalists who for several years had enjoyed covering Harding because she was so different began to see through her act.

"You lied to us this year about your smoking and your lawyer said you weren't truthful to the FBI in all your questions," began Jere Longman of the *New York Times* at a jammed Olympic news conference in Lillehammer, Norway. "Why should we believe anything you say that you were innocent in the Nancy Kerrigan incident?"

Rawlinson chose to answer. "We're here to talk about Tonya's skating."

Harding: "I agree with my coach."

Hundreds of journalists groaned.

For Harding to have said anything more, however, would have been completely out of character. To bow out of the Games would have been difficult, too, because she had lived her life for competing. The Olympics were so important to her that she filed a $25-million lawsuit against the U.S. Olympic Committee to prevent it from kicking her off the team.

Yet, for a woman so committed to the Olympics, she came to the Games brazenly unprepared.

She left her skate guards, the plastic runners that skaters put over their precious blades, back at home in Oregon. U.S. officials quickly got her another pair. But Gale Tanger, a well-liked figure-skating judge, the U.S. figure-skating team leader in Norway, and Harding's baby-sitter during the Games, was shocked.

"How could you forget your guards?" she asked. "How did you know what you had to walk on around the Olympic rink in Norway?"

After practicing with other blades, Harding complicated matters by changing to her lucky gold skate blades the day of her competition. "I just could not understand that," Tanger said. "You don't do it that late in the day. For reasons best known to herself, dear Tonya decided to change her blades."

Tanger, a striking, blond, forty-eight-year-old former skater from Milwaukee, tried to make sure nothing else was left to chance. She had a new dress made for Harding to replace an older model that showed too much of her breasts and was universally despised (Harding had an uncanny ability to show up in the most awful dresses). Tanger also wanted to ensure that it didn't mysteriously come apart.

"We checked that dress over and over," Tanger said. "I just wanted to know that we had an industrial-size zipper up the back. I wanted to make sure that nobody was going to come popping out of that dress at the wrong time."

On the final night of competition, Tanger thought she was ready for any disaster. As she stood beside the ice, she had a variety of implements at her disposal. Inside her blazer hung needle and thread. She had a screwdriver and a screw in her right pocket, scissors in her left pocket. Skate laces were balled up in her hand. She had tape and hairpins, "just about anything that could tape a skater together and get them through their program."

She also arranged to have an ice pick nearby in case Harding's laces gnawed through her boots and another hole had to be punched. Most skaters lace their skates around hooks. Harding had eyelets put in to better hold the boot together for the wear and tear of landing and falling on triple axels. Having the eyelets meant Harding needed longer skate laces. This became clear when she broke a lace backstage before she skated. Suspicion was that Harding might have purposely snapped it. The thought crossed Tanger's mind, but she later dismissed it.

"I think it was legitimate," Tanger said. "I know Tonya well enough to look at her and to tell."

Tanger asked Harding and Rawlinson for another lace.

They didn't have another lace.

Tanger's senses were getting dull after spending a week with Harding and her hapless support team. Still, she knew that coming to the competition without an extra skate lace was particularly absurd. "It's kind of like going to your giant-slalom race with one pole," Tanger said.

They tried a regulation lace. It didn't fit. Harding's name was announced. She didn't come out. The crowd craned to look through the tunnel backstage. After all she had gone through to get to the Olympics, where in the world was Tonya? Viewers at home, watching hours later on tape back in the United States, knew what was happening due to a well-placed CBS backstage camera. But live, in the Olympic arena, it looked like the scene from the music festival in *The Sound of Music*. If someone had come running out, yelling, "She's gone!" no one would have been surprised.

Tanger and Rawlinson laced Harding up as best as they could and sent her out on the ice. There were only seconds left before she would be disqualified.

"You've got to go out," Tanger said. "Start it, declare an equipment failure. If you can't land the triple lutz, then you always have [the option of] equipment failure."

That's what Harding did. She began, missed the jump, started crying, and skated over to the referee to show that, indeed, her equipment had failed. She threw the competition schedule up for grabs but got another chance. Backstage, Tanger and the others found a longer lace. They sent Harding back out and she actually skated well enough to move up two spots from tenth to eighth.

In the do-over, she tried that triple axel once more, but true to form, she popped it in midair. She didn't turn it into a double. She did a single. A single axel! Seven-year-old girls do single axels. All that hype over the triple axel—and Harding managed just a single. She hadn't landed the triple axel in competition in nearly two and a half years.

Harding's Olympic experience came to its merciful conclusion with an awful asthma flair-up and a bucket of tears. At the same moment Kerrigan was skating the performance of her life under the bright lights on the ice, Harding was doubled over backstage, vomiting into a trash can.

Despite her failings, Harding did a big favor for women's sports. During the controversy over her involvement in the plot to attack Kerrigan, the triple axel was a topic of conversation in the strangest places: cocktail parties, office lunchrooms, poker games. In the days before the women's Olympic competition in Norway, newspaper sports sections gave Super Bowl–sized attention to figure skating. There were charts and graphs on the sport and its jumps, as performed by women. Never in the history of sports had so much attention been focused on the woman as athlete: Would Harding try the triple axel? Would she land it? Would Kerrigan land six triples?

Unlike gymnasts, to whom they often are compared, female figure skaters are not brittle, emaciated-looking children. They characteristically have been older when they become famous: adults with apartments and driver's licenses and, in some cases, minds of their own. At the 1994 Olympics, Kerrigan was twenty-four, Harding twenty-three. But the gold medalist, Oksana Baiul, was just sixteen. Things were changing because the compulsory figures were gone, and young jumpers such as Michelle Kwan and a little twelve-year-old junior skater named Tara Lipinski were catching the public's attention. But the skating world watched with a cautious eye. "No one knows what these skaters are going to be able to become until they've matured," said America's Jill Trenary, the 1990 world champion.

In gymnastics, girls historically had trouble when they began to reach adulthood. In skating, the girls with the patience to ride out the changes and adapt to their new body were the ones who won in the end. However, there was some concern in figure skating that the sport might begin accepting a world of disposable fourteen-year-olds. In this scenario, little girls would rise quickly to the top, be splashed all over television for a year or two, then disappear with the onset of hips, breasts, and thighs. This had been happening for years at the novice and junior levels of the sport, but TV cameras weren't there to record it. Now, with media interest running so high, some feared figure skating could become gymnastics on ice.

Figure skating was not gender specific, though, in some of its demands; for instance, wanting slender, lithe bodies for jumping. Brian Boitano said judges wanted him "anorexically thin." Young men were patronized as much as young women. Judges criticized what a male skater wore as often as they'd criticize a female skater. Women were not treated as second-class citizens in figure skating. It was one of the very few sports in which women have been—and continued to be—the dominant gender. Women historically have been the superstars of skating; women had the agents and the million-dollar contracts, from Henie in the 1920s and 1930s to Kerrigan, Yamaguchi, and Baiul in the present. Recently, veterans such as Boitano, Scott Hamilton, and Paul Wylie and younger men like Elvis Stojko and Philippe Candeloro attracted the attention of the teeming mobs of female fans, but who were the biggest names in skating to this day? Kerrigan and Harding.

There was an uneasiness among other female athletes and officials in accepting figure skating as a real sport, in embracing its female athletes as their sisters in the fight for equality. All the sequins, makeup, hairspray, and nose jobs bugged them. (The nose count was at least three: Peggy Fleming, Linda Fratianne, and Debi Thomas.) But what the women's movement missed when it discounted figure skaters was that women who figure-skate are on an even playing field athletically with the men. They do the same jumps. When Kerrigan tries a triple lutz, it's the same triple lutz that Wylie attempts. Ito's triple axel is better than most male skaters' triple axels. Men attempt quadruple toe loops or salchows; so does France's Surya Bonaly. The only inequalities exist in the rules: the men skate four-and-a-half minutes, the women four.

In some sports played by both genders, men and women are not equal. In college basketball, for instance, the women's basketball is smaller than the men's, to compensate for women's smaller hands. In golf, professional women play a shorter course than professional men, to compensate for the difference in power. Even in tennis, where the dimensions and equipment are the same, the game is not. Men play up to five sets; women play three. But, in skating, a jump is a jump is a jump. At one professional event, Boitano and Wylie marveled at the lift and power of a triple axel performed by Ito. Of four women pros and four men pros competing, Ito and Boitano were the only skaters to land a triple axel. Ito's jumping is legendary. At the 1989 world championships, the word was that Ito didn't just win the women's competition, she would have won the men's, too.

Women also have much more power in figure skating than in any other of America's most popular sports. There were four U.S. singles skaters at the 1994 Winter Olympics, and three of them were coached solely by a woman: Linda Leaver (Boitano), Kathy Casey (Scott Davis), and Rawlinson (Harding). Evy and Mary Scotvold split the duties for Kerrigan.

A woman, Claire Ferguson, was USFSA president through 1994, and women were some of the top judges around the world. It's indisputable: figure skating is a sport for women, run by women.

Harding unwittingly brought all this to the surface. Although the actions of her associates altered an entire Olympic Games, her presence in Norway turned figure skating into a sport for the masses. Because of the intrigue over the involvement of a skater in the attack on a rival skater, interest soared in the sport. Skaters probably should have sent her a thank-you note. And with the increased awareness came a chance to examine figure skating, an opportunity for the mainstream media to delve into something they had undercovered for decades in proportion to its popularity.

What they found surprised them.

Popular opinion says it all started with Tonya. The cutthroat, I'm-gonna-kick-your-butt attitude. The trailer-park lifestyle. The bad dresses, bad music, bad work habits.

But popular opinion is wrong. Women who smoke and drink and swear and try to trip each other have been in figure skating for decades. Long before Tonya Harding and her associates crash-landed into the sport, women gunned for other women in practice sessions. They trashed their rivals—gossiping about nose jobs and stage mothers and bank accounts—for as long as there have been rivals to trash. The sequins are a clever disguise. Whoever thought these were genteel, teetotaling ladies was sadly mistaken.

"What happened when Nancy was attacked probably happened in people's minds as skaters for years and years and years, going back to

Sonja Henie," said Tina Noyes, a member of the 1964 and 1968 U.S. Olympic teams. "So, for a skater to see that happen, it was like, 'Someone actually did it.'"

East German Gabriele Seyfert was a menacing forerunner of Katarina Witt. Both were cunning competitors the United States would have loved to have had as its own. Seyfert's mother was Jutta Mueller, Witt's legendary coach. Noyes, a Bostonian like Kerrigan, was on the ice practicing at the 1968 Grenoble Olympics when she saw Seyfert bearing down on her.

"She had blue eyes and she was a big girl, and I could see those eyes from a distance, they'd look right through you," Noyes said. "She skated by me so hard and so fast, she almost knocked me over. Then I realized it was open market. I tried to be courteous with the other skaters, the Europeans, but she was real tough. She was like, 'Get out of the way.' So I gave her the room. She wanted to play games. You had to be real careful of those European skaters because they didn't care if they hit you."

Seyfert won the silver medal while Noyes finished fourth in those Olympics. Although Noyes and Peggy Fleming were rivals on U.S. ice, Noyes took a great deal of pleasure in knowing that Fleming denied Seyfert the gold medal.

As it prepared for the 1992 Winter Olympics, the USFSA was trying to figure out who would room with whom in Albertville. Three women made the U.S. team: Yamaguchi, Kerrigan, and Harding. Yamaguchi and Kerrigan were paired up and became fast friends. Harding was left. U.S. skating officials decided to put her with pairs skater Calla Urbanski, a thirty-something waitress who was known for screaming four-letter words at partner Rocky Marval as they skated.

"We decided that Calla would kill Tonya, or Tonya would kill Calla, and we really didn't care either way," one U.S. skating official joked.

Harding and Urbanski both lived through the 1992 Olympics and then went on to further enhance their rough-hewn images. Urbanski couldn't top the Harding saga, but she did have a doozy of a battle on the ice with Cathy Turner, the feisty Olympic short-track speed skater.

Turner was headlining with Ice Capades after the 1993 national championships. For a week, Urbanski and Marval, renowned as the waitress and the truck driver in figure-skating lore, came on board as guest skaters. Immediately, there was a problem.

"For five nights, she tried to cut me off in the finale because I was the headliner and she wasn't and she couldn't stand it," Turner said. "Finally, on the fifth night, as we did our pass in the middle of the ice, she stuck out her leg to try to do it again. But I put out my leg first and tripped her as she went by. It was very funny. She had the problem. I didn't."

Urbanski understandably has a different version:

"We were guest stars for a week and she didn't like that we came out last. When we came out for our bows, we crossed. I saw her coming at me and I knew what was going to happen, and I backed away from her and she just charged at me and knocked me over. It was like Roller Derby out there. It was a little embarrassing at the end of a show. I was on all fours. I got up and continued skating and was just fuming. I wish she would have knocked me a little harder, because I would have sued her ass off."

Ladies, ladies!

If there was one person the USFSA would have wanted to patriate and deck out in red, white, and blue, it would have been East Germany's Katarina Witt. Throughout the history of her sport, there has never been a stronger competitor, a more crafty and calculating athlete, than Witt. Man or woman. She had the look of a seductress, the gait of a truck driver. She knew what she had to do to win, and she did it. She was good when she had to be good; great when she had to be better. She wore ruffles, but she stared daggers into the hearts of the women she faced. She improvised to their music in practice. She stood by the ice when they skated and dared them to blink. You could not beat her. You simply could not beat her.

Rosalynn Sumners and Debi Thomas were two of the U.S. women who tried, and failed. Figure skating is such a small world that Witt, Sumners, and Thomas always run into one another, even now. They'll be seventy and still seeing each other at competitions or dinners. Witt and Sumners skated at a few of the same professional competitions in the fall and went on to tour together in Stars on Ice from winter into early spring of 1995. Thomas no longer skated competitively. She divorced the man she eloped with after the 1988 Olympics and was in her second year of medical school at Northwestern University. But she was not far from her old sport. She gave her opinion when TV stations called. She attended skating events. She planned to visit Witt and Sumners when Stars on Ice, which she was on several years ago herself, pulled into the Midwest in the winter.

From the moment the three women met, their lives were inexorably altered. In Sarajevo in 1984, Sumners pulled back on her two last jumps, turning a triple toe loop into a double, and a double axel into a single. She lost the gold medal to Witt by one-tenth of a point on one judge's card, the same margin by which Kerrigan lost to Baiul. In

Calgary four years later, Thomas made mistake after mistake, skating so badly she wanted to leave the ice, making it easy for Witt to win.

Years later, each American still viewed the outcome not so much as Witt's victory but as her own loss. That's what losing to Katarina did to you. She won, but you thought you lost. Time didn't change that. But what growing older did do was ease the pain, if not a whole lot, at least a little bit.

In the past couple of years, Witt and Sumners had become good friends. Witt and Thomas are another story. That friendship probably will never fully blossom.

"I remember congratulating her backstage right after it happened, and I remember thinking, 'These people want me to congratulate Katarina for them, not for me,'" Thomas said of the scene in Calgary. "They wanted this whole glorified thing, and I don't work that way. I was totally dazed and she deserved to win and all, but I was just thinking, 'I can't believe I skated that shitty.' That's all I could think. It wasn't like, 'Oh, I hate you for winning.' Even now, people come up and say, 'You should have won,' and I'm like, 'Come on, what competition were you watching?'"

Thomas didn't even win the silver. Witt won the gold in 1988, Liz Manley of Canada finished second, and Thomas dropped to third to get the bronze, becoming the first black athlete to win a medal in a Winter Olympics.

"Katarina deserved it," Thomas said. "She really has always gone out and done her best, and she's been lucky enough that everybody else screwed up when she was doing that. That's what happened to me. I've always had a lot of respect for her. I've said it again and again, 'You cannot one-up this girl.'"

After Sonja Henie won three consecutive Olympic gold medals from 1928 to 1936, ten Olympic Games went by before another woman won more than one. Katarina Witt's accomplishment in the 1980s came at a time of unparalleled athletic growth for women figure skaters. Triple jumps that once could be landed only by men now were being mastered by women. The United States was particularly strong; waves of American women rolled into international competitions, each with something more than the next. Elaine Zayak, Rosalynn Sumners, Tiffany Chin, Debi Thomas, Caryn Kadavy, Jill Trenary.

Witt beat them all.

•   •   •

In Calgary, Witt had skated well in the long program, landing four triples, but she had not been exceptional. There was room for Thomas to win. She and Thomas were the "Dueling Carmens," both having chosen music from Bizet's tragic opera. This was like arriving at a party in the same dress. They both found out several months before the Games, but neither one would back down and change.

So they argued about it in the media.

Witt insinuated that Thomas could not perform artistically to the music, that jumping alone would not win the gold medal. "You can either skate to this music or you can express it," Witt said brusquely in Calgary.

Thomas hated the glamour-girl aspect of the sport and fought to remain athletic. She smirked at the idea that Witt's Carmen died at the end.

Normally, skaters who are finished watch the others on a backstage television monitor or get so nervous they can't watch at all. Witt would have none of that. In 1985, at the world championships in Tokyo, she stood beside the boards as Chin skated. Witt maintains it wasn't a psychological ploy. Others say it had to be. Whatever it was, Chin didn't beat her.

Witt also had another habit that she maintained wasn't a mind game. It's an unwritten rule in skating practices that when your music is on, you own the ice. Other skaters practice their jumps and spins and footwork around you, but the skater whose music is playing has the right-of-way. Katarina accepted this rule, but with reservations. At the 1987 world championships in Cincinnati, when Kadavy's music came on, Witt began to make up her own routine to it. "Everybody looked at me and not her," Witt said. "I didn't do it on purpose. I didn't know I would drive them crazy and make them nervous."

Witt wasn't the only one to take over a practice session. At the 1992 Olympics, Surya Bonaly rared back and landed a backflip in front of Midori Ito. Although referee Ben Wright admonished Bonaly (backflips are illegal in Olympic-division skating), the damage was done. Ito was shaken and skittish throughout the rest of the Olympics.

When Witt skated after a competitor, she was devastating. At those 1987 worlds in Cincinnati, Thomas was suffering from Achilles tendinitis in both feet and actually applied ice shavings from an ice-making machine to her ankles before she performed. She went out and skated magnificently, landing all five of her triple jumps. She brought down the house. Everyone who was there thought there was no way Witt could beat her.

With the crowd still roaring for Thomas, Witt coolly skated into position and began her program. Thomas came out to watch. Unbelievably, Witt tried five triple jumps, even though no one thought she could *do* five triple jumps. On one, she had a slightly flawed landing, but otherwise she was perfect. Witt received a 6.0 from the East German judge—surprise!—and won the title. Thomas finished second.

Alex McGowan, Thomas's coach, was in awe.

"No other skater in the world could do that," he said, shaking his head.

The 1988 Olympics were eleven months later. Thomas was pulling off her skate guards, getting ready to take the ice. Witt stood in a group near the boards, just off McGowan's shoulder. She was staring at McGowan and Thomas. As nineteen thousand spectators in the Saddledome looked down, they saw two skaters: Thomas, and Witt.

"I wanted to see it live," Witt said.

Before actually finding a seat in the second row of the arena, Witt saw something that eased her mind. Thomas and McGowan had a habit of slapping each other's palms right before Thomas left him to skate. That night, Thomas and McGowan went to hit their hands together and missed. "I knew she was too nervous," Witt said, "I knew she would not pull it off."

Thomas, however, said she was not nervous. Quite the opposite. She came in too relaxed. The last thing you want, she said, "is a relaxed Debi Thomas. I'm much better neurotic. I just kind of zombified and went out there and was waiting for my music to start, and I said to myself, 'You're not ready.'"

As Thomas's music built to a crescendo of impending doom, she took off for a triple-toe-loop/triple-toe-loop combination, a much more athletically demanding maneuver than anything Witt had tried. Thomas landed the first triple, but two-footed the second one horribly.

Her brain sent her an ominous message: "Well, so much for the program of your life."

At that moment, no more than twenty seconds into her four-minute program, Debi Thomas wanted to give up. So she did. She had trouble with two more triples and came off the ice apologizing to McGowan. She now knows that she probably made a mistake in giving up so soon. Had she quickly forgotten about the first error and skated cleanly the rest of the way, she still could have won the gold medal.

It was just that she had her mind set not simply to win the gold medal, but to win the gold medal by skating perfectly. She wanted it all. So when the perfect performance was frittered away on the first combination jump, her objective was gone, and she gave in.

How silly it sounds now that one jump would make or break a life-long desire to win the gold medal. But much of what Debi Thomas did that year to prepare for the Olympics followed that flawed logic. She even trained that way. If she missed the combination in practice, she would stop the music and start over again.

"No, no, no!" McGowan would scream out, but it didn't matter. That Saturday night in Calgary, all she could think about was stopping and starting the music over again. But, that time, she could not.

"When she didn't hug me on the podium, it was honest," Witt said of Thomas. "She was just upset. And I can relate to that. You go to the Olympics and everyone expects you to win, and then you're not just second, you're third. And then you're out of your mind, you forget anything around you. And for me, that was somehow honest. All the hugs and everything are not honest. Some are and some aren't. She was at this time honest. She showed that she's upset, so she showed her human-being side, which I respect. Maybe yes, she should have behaved better like a lot of people said, but the whole expectation which was put into her, she just didn't know how to deal with something like this. You have to respect it. While somebody failed in this one thing, why should this one be a bad person?"

Thomas found herself preoccupied with Witt again in early 1994. Witt was going back to the Olympics, having been reinstated from the professional ranks, and Thomas was being asked by countless reporters what she thought.

"Katarina's going to win," she would say. "I'm telling you. Nobody knows about the Katarina curse. They're all going to screw up and she's going to win."

Between 1988 and 1994, Thomas had had more encounters with Witt's tremendous competitiveness. They were on a tour through Italy and neither was in great shape, so they were trying only double jumps. One night near the end of the tour, Thomas tried her triple toe loop and nailed it. Witt, skating after Thomas, saw that and threw in a triple toe loop of her own.

Then, in another exhibition, Thomas performed two triples. Witt had been practicing two herself, but that night went out and did three.

"I'm telling you, you cannot one-up this girl," said Thomas.

Witt did not win a medal at the 1994 Winter Games, the first Olympics her parents were able to attend after the fall of the Berlin Wall. She wasn't even close, although her seventh-place finish did beat

Tonya Harding. By then, at twenty-eight, she didn't have the jumps of the other women: Baiul, Kerrigan, China's Chen Lu, Harding, and several others. But she did qualify for the final group of six skaters, and she did get to skate last, performing "Where Have All the Flowers Gone?" as a tribute to the people of Sarajevo, where she won her first gold medal.

"I didn't skate the perfect free program and I wasn't really in the best shape, but I walked away and thought, 'It would have been too good to be true if I would have made a perfect program.'"

Thomas of course watched on television in Chicago.

"At first, I couldn't understand why Katarina would go back after winning all there is to win, twice," Thomas said. "But, you know, you could see it in her face. She just loves skating, and she just looked so happy to be there. It was like she really didn't care if she won the thing or not."

Months later, Thomas and Witt talked about it when they ran into each other at a skating event. "I do remember thinking, you know, her parents never got to see her compete and win those gold medals," Thomas said. "And they were there, in Norway. And so she's like, 'It was the best Olympics of all the ones I've done,' and, you know, I believe her. I truly believe that. It's like there are certain things where the emotional value is more than the actual medal itself."

The United States sends its women to the Olympics with grand expectations, but only five have met them: Tenley Albright in 1956, Carol Heiss in 1960, Peggy Fleming in 1968, Dorothy Hamill in 1976, and Kristi Yamaguchi in 1992. Several others have come extremely close, but have failed: Linda Fratianne (1980), Rosalynn Sumners (1984), and Nancy Kerrigan (1994) won the silver by the narrowest of margins.

The gold medalists form one of the most exclusive unofficial clubs in sports. Two of the five—Heiss and Fleming—married men named Jenkins. Heiss married 1956 Olympic gold medalist and Ohio attorney Hayes Jenkins; Fleming married California dermatologist Greg Jenkins. The marriages lasted. Albright and Hamill also got married, but later were divorced and remarried. Yamaguchi is still single. Heiss and Fleming, with a devilish wink of their beautifully done-up eyes, hope the kid sister goes for a Jenkins.

Albright came from moneyed Boston and later became a successful surgeon; Heiss was a baker's daughter from Queens. She had a brief career in Hollywood, got married, moved to Akron, had three children, and at thirty-eight embarked on a successful coaching career.

In 1961, the year after Heiss left amateur skating, the entire U.S. delegation—eighteen skaters and sixteen officials, coaches, judges, and family members—was wiped out in a plane crash near Brussels on its way to the world championships in Prague.

Heiss received a call in the middle of the night in Los Angeles, where she was working on a movie.

"They're all gone," said the voice on the other end of the line.

It was her brother-in-law, David Jenkins, who also had retired in 1960 after winning the men's Olympic gold medal. He was crying.

"What?" Heiss was startled.

"The plane crashed, Carol. On the way to worlds."

"Oh my God," Heiss screamed. "The whole team? The skaters and the coaches and the judges? The officials? They're all gone? Maribel Vinson Owen and her two daughters? Oh my God! The Hadleys? Mr. Hadley! Oh, no! His whole family!"

In the 1994–95 USFSA press guide, which has the results of world championships dating back to 1896, there are three breaks in the chronology: 1915–21 (World War I); 1940–46 (World War II); and 1961. For that one, there is a simple explanation: "The championships were canceled due to the death of the entire American team in a plane crash at Brussels."

Out of the ashes of the tragedy came Fleming. Spurred on by Italy's masterful Carlo Fassi, one of the coaches who came to the United States to find work after the crash, Fleming won five national titles from 1964 to 1968, and the Olympic gold in 1968. After Fleming came a magical Illinois schoolgirl named Janet Lynn, who won five consecutive national titles, but managed only the bronze medal at the 1972 Olympics.

Hamill was next after Lynn and easily won the 1976 Olympic gold medal. Then came a long drought, one that Debi Thomas cynically blames on Hamill and a mythical collection of voodoo dolls. Thomas's joke goes that Hamill, realizing the commercial value of being the reigning women's U.S. Olympic gold medalist, stuck pins in a doll resembling Fratianne, a four-time national champion who narrowly lost the 1980 Olympic gold medal. Hamill, Thomas said, had a Sumners doll in 1984 and jinxed her, too. In 1988, it was a Debi Thomas doll.

But, in 1992, so the story goes, Hamill had two dolls: Kristi Yamaguchi and Midori Ito. Hamill got confused, Thomas said, and was unable to tell the Japanese-American skater from the Japanese skater. She stuck pins in the wrong doll, and Yamaguchi won.

· · · ·

With the emergence of Michelle Kwan as the heir apparent to Kerrigan, one had to wonder if Asian women have a secret formula for success. Four of the last six world champions were Asian: Ito in 1989, Yamaguchi in 1991 and 1992, and Japan's Yuka Sato in 1994. In the professional ranks, the two top female skaters in the world are Asian—Yamaguchi and Ito. Yamaguchi trained hard with Christy Ness in Edmonton during the summer of 1994 to emerge from the long shadows of Kerrigan and Harding and regain her status as America's best overall female skater. Ito, Yamaguchi's professional rival, still was booming triple axels and beating Yamaguchi on occasion.

Why do Asian women make such great skaters?

"It's our drive and it's our bodies," said Audrey King Weisiger, a former U.S. national-level skater of Chinese descent who now coaches in Fairfax, Virginia. "You get the right personality, the family pushing its kids to succeed. You get the right body type. Asians genetically don't have breasts, and we're small boned. And then there's the diet. At home, we always ate rice, vegetables, and a meat dish. We didn't eat steak and potatoes. So, obviously, we're less inclined to have a weight problem."

Tiffany Chin became the first Asian-American woman to win a U.S. national title in 1985. Her omnipresent mother was known as the Dragon Lady throughout the sport, a nickname Chin said was not deserved.

"She was tough on me because she cared," Chin said. "She was very visible and was really vocal. The Chinese are very traditional."

Chin finished fourth at the 1984 Olympics but never made it back for the 1988 Games. She was injured and she turned professional, finally heading to UCLA, where she became one of her sport's few college graduates. She returned to skating to coach children who are not nearly as good as she was—which was fine with her.

"When and if I have children, I wouldn't want my kid to be an ice-skater," she said. "No way."

Chin soured on the pressure and expectations. Often, however, the Asian family cushions the skater from those pressures better than other families can.

Frank Carroll, who coaches Kwan, was thrilled to be dealing with her family.

"Michelle comes from a very traditional Chinese family," he said. "She's very normal, kind of family oriented. A lot of things that can happen to other people are not going to happen to her. She's really nurtured by a family environment."

Asian women make great figure skaters, Chin said, because they are "easier to control."

"It's basically, 'Listen and talk when you're spoken to,' that type of thing," she said. "They're not as likely to go off with boys. We don't have the figure to attract them."

As a Japanese-American, Yamaguchi's life is filled with irony. Her mother, Carole, was born in a Japanese relocation camp in Colorado in 1945 as her father—Kristi's grandfather—fought in the U.S. Army in Europe. Yamaguchi won her Olympic gold medal in February 1992, little more than two months after the fiftieth anniversary of the attack on Pearl Harbor and in the midst of heightened concern over the U.S. trade deficit with Japan.

"She was kind of caught in a catch-22," said Carole Yamaguchi. "A U.S. car company wouldn't use her. In Japan, too, when they went over there and tried to see if there was anything for her there, they wouldn't use her because she's Japanese. They wanted that blond-hair, blue-eyed type. But that's okay. That's all right."

"It kind of surprised me," Kristi Yamaguchi said. "I'm American and I grew up like any other American. I just never thought of me being that much different than someone else."

But when Yamaguchi was underestimated—on or off the ice—she was at her best. She signed with International Management Group a month before winning the gold medal and the endorsements eventually came: contact lenses, a fabric company, in-line skates, Wendy's hamburgers. Even an ad to drink milk.

She couldn't get more all-American than that.

3

SKATING'S
TRAGIC SECRET

It's the women in skating who keep the list. A figure-skating judge outside Boston. A famous pairs skater in southern California. A skating-magazine editor in New York. A coach in Fairfax, Virginia. But each woman's list, kept either on paper or in her mind, is not complete. There always are more names to add. The list of dead men grows longer every year.

They are Olympic gold medalists. They are respected national skaters from the United States and Canada. They are coaches, choreographers, and noted professional performers. In late 1992, the *Calgary Herald* reported at least forty male skaters and coaches from the United States and Canada had died of complications related to AIDS. Some criticized the survey as sensational. Others, like former U.S. and world champion pairs skater Randy Gardner, simply nodded their heads.

"I could name close to thirty people in skating who have died from AIDS," he said. "A lot of skaters aren't admitting that we've lost skaters to AIDS. Hell, it's a disease that people are dying from."

The list begins with John Curry, the celebrated Olympic gold medalist from Great Britain, who died in April 1994 after learning he was HIV-positive more than six years earlier. Curry was, in the words of Dick Button, "the finest stylist in the classical tradition that I've ever seen." Current skaters discuss his 1976 gold medal performance as if it happened yesterday. They talk about Curry as if he were still alive, out there somewhere, skating.

As news of his illness circulated a few years ago, Curry said in an interview that almost all of his close associates from his days of skating and dancing in New York were dead because of AIDS. The names on the list from Curry's Ice Dancing company of the late 1970s include Ron Alexander and Brian Grant. A skating benefit for the Gay Men's Health Crisis in New York memorialized the names of more than one hundred others, including two more Curry skaters: Paul Toomey and Paul McGrath, who finished first in the country as a junior in 1965 and became such a respected choreographer that the U.S. Figure Skating Association's choreographer-of-the-year award is named for him.

The man who won the Olympic gold medal right before Curry—Czechoslovakia's Ondrej Nepela—died from an AIDS-related cancer in 1989.

In Canada, Rob McCall, Brian Pockar, Dennis Coi, and Shaun McGill were decorated champions for a decade. Pockar was Canadian men's champion from 1978 to 1980 and the 1982 world bronze medalist; Coi was 1978 junior world champion; McGill was 1978 Canadian novice silver medalist and later joined Curry's company in New York; and McCall, an ice dancer with current CBS announcer Tracy Wilson, won the bronze medal at the 1988 Winter Olympics in Calgary.

One by one, AIDS killed all four.

There are more: Jim Hulick, Kristi Yamaguchi's pairs coach; Patrick Dean, who taught skating in New York and was a professional ice dancer; David Fee, a skater with Ice Capades; Barry Hagan, the 1981 U.S. bronze medalist in ice dancing with Kim Krohn; Bob Lubotina, a U.S. skating judge; and Frank Nowosad, a Canadian choreographer.

Others are known to be dying of the disease, including Richard Inglesi, a respected coach in the San Francisco Bay area who was second in the United States in juniors in 1968; and William Lawe, the 1984 U.S. national junior men's champion.

Unless they are famous Olympians, like Curry or McCall, the news of these men's illness or death rarely reaches the sports section. Some prefer privacy. Other times, it's something more. The world of figure skating would rather that the link between their sport and AIDS not be made because, to so many, AIDS means homosexuality. The USFSA doesn't know what to do. No other sports organization in the country has faced such a dilemma. How do you put a spin on AIDS? How does the organization say it has lost more athletes to AIDS than any other sport in the country? Perhaps it should say that gay men are believed to outnumber straight men, especially in singles skating. And that gay males are omnipresent in the judging ranks and represent a significant segment of coaches as well.

But if the USFSA were to do that, it would risk losing valuable sponsorship at a time when the sport is exploding in the public's consciousness, and when competition with the professional side of the sport is high. It also might scare off jittery parents who could direct their sons to other sports. What's more, figure skating's old guard—the heterosexual, Ivy League men who have been around since the forties and fifties—can't stand the thought of admitting their sport is populated, even dominated, by gays.

But if the USFSA and other skating organizations continue with the status quo, they risk the horror of losing even more skaters.

The issue of AIDS does not exist only in North America, of course. Robin Cousins, the 1980 Olympic gold medalist from Great Britain, said that, around the world, his sport must be examined "absolutely, with a magnifying glass, in terms of making sure AIDS education is brought in." He said figure skating is particularly vulnerable because its athletes can be so young.

He also is concerned for the women in the sport. "What it's done is affect the male population of figure skating," Cousins said. "What I hate to see is the first female [infected], which then does bring it down to the ground with a big thump, the way that it has done in life in general."

Figure-skating-related AIDS benefits are springing up across North America—in New York, Toronto, Los Angeles, Washington, D.C. But they're almost always spurred by the unofficial action of the friends and relatives of AIDS victims.

The last time the USFSA officially addressed the issue for all its members was at the 1993 U.S. national championships in Phoenix. There, Dr. Craig McQueen, chair of the USFSA's sports-medicine committee at the time, led an AIDS awareness seminar and issued a dire warning: "If the same thing happens here like it is happening in Canada, we could lose a whole generation of skaters, performers, coaches, and choreographers."

Every man who figure-skates has heard the jokes. "You know figure skating. It's a sport of sequins and velvet and plunging necklines and earrings. Then, of course, you have the women . . ."

Every man who figure-skates knows the story line. "I have a girl-friend . . ."

They still sometimes wear sparkling costumes. They take ballet. They flutter their arms in rhythm with soft music. They are men trapped in a women's sport. They are men defending themselves against sometimes ugly stereotypes.

"I try to pull myself out of skating and say, 'If I were looking at an ice-skater, would I think an ice-skater's gay?'" Brian Boitano said. "Maybe. Maybe I would."

"It's taken me a long time to get to this point because I was so resentful of all the teasing I got when I was in grade school and junior high," said Scott Hamilton, "but when I say that some of my best friends are gay, they are."

The USFSA might not want to talk about it officially, and most gay men in figure skating prefer to remain anonymous, but there is no juicier gossip in the sport than discussing who's gay and who's straight among the male skaters.

A few coaches, sitting around an East Coast rink on a Friday afternoon, killing time between lessons, went down the list of current male skaters expected to be trying for the '98 Olympics.

A name came up: "Don't know, probably gay."

Next name: "Definitely leaning that way."

"Oh, come on," said another coach. "He has a girlfriend."

"As if that means anything," came the reply.

Another amateur skater trying for the Olympics, a handsome man who was well-known to have had a pretty girlfriend a couple years ago, now is equally well-known to be having a relationship with a male professional skater.

The women of the sport also are profoundly affected by the specter of AIDS. Mary Louise Wright, the Boston area judge, keeps in her desk on a tiny piece of paper a handwritten list of the couple dozen men she and her husband know who have died of AIDS-related complications. Tai Babilonia, Gardner's pairs partner, keeps her own list at her home in the Los Angeles suburbs. Lois Elfman, editor in chief of *International Figure Skating* magazine, was asked to help officials put together the names of the skaters who have died for AIDS benefits. Audrey Weisiger, the Virginia coach, can recite the names off the top of her head. Their recollections form the sport's only record of the dead; no official list exists.

Little girl skaters, children barely old enough to be interested in boys, know all about gay men. "Oh, he's gay," they'll say dismissively. Their parents will casually mention a male skater's homosexuality in their daughter's presence.

When a gay figure-skating judge showed off photos in his den, he pointed to a young, handsome man.

"He's dead."

He pointed to another young man.

"That's his lover," the judge said. "He's still okay."

Weisiger has stacks of scrapbooks. Interspersed with family photos and pictures from various figure-skating trips are the ones of men—her dear friends—with their arms around each other.

One photo shows two young men—both in their thirties—lying on the floor, smiling at the camera, holding on to one another.

If you're in figure skating, and you keep a scrapbook, you have these photos.

She has another picture of her best friend, choreographer Brian Wright, with another man in Wright's Indianapolis apartment.

Who's the other man?

"His former lover," she said.

Wright is HIV-positive. Most people in skating know Wright is sick. And that's how they say it: "Brian's sick," sick being the code word in figure skating for HIV. But he is still working, and one of his skaters is Weisiger's star pupil, eighteen-year-old Michael Weiss. Of the handful of top male skaters she has had in nearly twenty years of coaching, Weisiger said Weiss is her first heterosexual.

Brian Wright, thirty-five, knows that by the time Michael Weiss makes it onto an Olympic team—if he ever gets there—Wright probably will be dead. Wright, named USFSA choreographer of the year in 1994, was diagnosed as being HIV-positive in 1986. Eight years later, it has not yet become full-blown AIDS. But he is getting sicker and spending more and more time in the hospital. He is certain he will die sometime soon.

"You go through a real grieving process for your own life and a big sense of loss," he said. "You come to the tail end of that and go, 'Well, I'm still existing, I'm still surviving,' so you get this real resurgence and this sort of confident, victorious feeling about being up for the challenge.

"But there's always that question, it pops right back up: 'I wonder how long this is going to last?'"

He has had as many as five blood clots in his right leg and has been on so much medication, he began bleeding internally. Part of his intestine had to be removed. For weeks, he was stranded in the hospital or at home, attached to an IV and not allowed to travel to competitions with his skaters. Wright is six foot two, huge by skating standards, but his weight dropped to 130 pounds. As he began to get better, he was able to eat normally. He gained forty pounds in the fall of 1994.

Wright doesn't know exactly when he contracted HIV. He does know it happened through unprotected sex with a man. He isn't certain who the man was.

.   .   .

Wright was born in Seattle, the youngest of four children of a comptroller and a homemaker. When he was eight, he watched Peggy Fleming on television at the 1968 Winter Olympics. "She did those spread eagles and I thought that was really cool," he said. "I decided I wanted to learn that."

At the same time he watched Fleming win the gold medal, Wright began to understand that he wasn't like most of the other boys in his school. They were beginning to talk about girls. And Brian was thinking about boys: "I fell in love with Kato on *The Green Hornet*." Bruce Lee played the part.

In junior high, Brian faced unmerciful teasing by the other boys. "You're a figure skater," they would say. "You're a fairy!"

The singsong teasing continued. "Brian is a fairy! Brian is a fairy! Brian is a fairy!"

Wright, mustering every ounce of a thirteen-year-old's nerve, swung around to face the boys in the school hallway.

He glared into their eyes. They were still screeching, "Brian is a fairy! Brian is a fairy!"

He screamed back, *"Yes I am!"*

Wright said his participation in figure skating made it easier for him to acknowledge his homosexuality.

"You interact with so many adults in the sport of figure skating, and a lot of the adults are gay," Wright said. "The sport is tailored to you, the gay man, because you work in isolation. You live fantastically in your own mind from such an early age, and then you get this great opportunity to perform and be yourself on the ice."

That's the inner world of skating, where sport turns to art, much like ballet or dance. What figure skating reveals to outsiders is something entirely different, Wright said.

"What's going on inside skating is hidden from the outside world because the myth is still around that gay is not good. This is the sort of isolated existence that we live. The figure-skating world says, 'You can be gay and that's certainly tolerable, but let's not force it on America. Let's not push the homos down anyone's throat because we don't want to rock the boat, we want to get our TV ratings, we want to be as accepted as possible. So it's okay if you're gay; you just don't need to tell anyone.'"

In 1993, for the first time ever, figure-skating officials began answering questions about AIDS. USFSA president Claire Ferguson held a news conference at the national championships. First, she introduced the sponsor of the event, a man from L'eggs, the panty-hose company, who was supposed to field questions about his corporation's interest in the sport. But few reporters cared about what he had to say about panty hose or figure skating. In the wake of the news of Curry's illness, they wanted to talk to Ferguson about AIDS.

When a reporter asked what the organization was doing to educate its skaters about AIDS, Ferguson squirmed. The sponsor looked at her. Immediately, spokeswoman Kristin Matta moved in and excused the sponsor. They waited until he left the room before Ferguson answered.

Ferguson started curiously, listing the names of retired male skaters she could think of who were married, without being asked to do so.

But what was she to do? She was a figure-skating judge from Rhode Island, having risen through the ranks to become the volunteer president of the organization, now thrown into an issue far beyond her expertise. The USFSA was in a delicate position. It's made up predominately of volunteers like her. How could they tackle a plague like AIDS?

She also knew she wanted to say something kind, something caring: "We're a diverse group of people. I would say a close-knit group of people. As an organization and as a sport, we're certainly aware of different lifestyles, and we have accepted that."

In the wake of the news of Curry's illness and the Canadian deaths, McQueen, a Salt Lake City orthopedic surgeon, was asked to lead the 1993 discussion on AIDS. He was a logical choice. Three years earlier, he lost his brother, a forty-seven-year-old Los Angeles journalist, to the disease.

The seminar was held on the morning of the final day of competition at the Omni hotel in downtown Phoenix, just a few blocks from the hotels housing the three hundred skaters at the event. Each competitor had been informed of the meeting. Only twenty people showed up. Not one of them was a skater.

"A lot of kids think they are infallible," McQueen said. "All the USFSA's leaders are concerned. I don't know how concerned the skaters are. That's what worries me."

Others wondered if some men and boys decided not to show up out of fear for their reputations.

Like many organizations dealing with AIDS and sex education, the USFSA is in a quandary. The last thing the USFSA wants to do is call attention to itself or cause alarm among its members. On the other hand, unlike the NBA or NFL, it is dealing with children, preadolescent boys and girls, as well as teenagers and young adults. Some of these children are not in school, but are being tutored at home. And the ones who are in school aren't there regularly.

Paul Wylie never moved away from his parents, but the better he got in figure skating, the more school he missed.

"I missed the week of sex education in eighth- or ninth-grade biology because I was skating," he said. "The USFSA doesn't say that it has a responsibility to educate, but it really does. A lot of kids are being deprived of education because they're doing what they do."

Since the Phoenix seminar, the USFSA has held discussion groups on AIDS for top junior skaters. It's a start, officials say.

"We've got to talk to these young people about their futures," McQueen said in 1993. "We've got to ask them, 'Do you want to die at age thirty? Or live a normal life expectancy to eighty or ninety?'"

Weisiger, the Virginia coach, looked at it another way: "Now I know what it must feel like for the people who are at home during a war. Losing all these young men . . . You wonder, who's next? Oh my God, who's next?"

Many male skaters, straight or gay, say that the individualistic nature of their sport captivated them. They were either not good at traditional team sports or too small to participate. "There are only so many sports that a five-four guy can do on a world level," Wylie said.

Some of them were drawn to the sport because they could skate fast and jump high. Others loved the artistry, the chance to work with music, the opportunity to express themselves. Pointing their toes, dressing in sequins, wearing makeup at competitions—this, too, was part of their world. The gay men were enticed by this; the straight men tolerated it.

"When I first looked at it, I didn't view it as a sport," said Brian Wright, who skated at the national level as a teenager in the 1970s. "I saw the costumes and the performances. The national championship was a gala, a really prissy, high-fashion gala. At Nationals, no one is spitting in the dugout."

At the 1991 Nationals in Minneapolis, Wright had a brief romantic liaison with a former world-class skater who has an Olympic medal in men's singles skating. They had both been to a skaters' reception in their hotel and happened to get on the same elevator riding back to their rooms.

Their eyes met in the elevator.

"That timeless eye signal," Wright remembered with an outrageous laugh.

"Why don't you come to my room?" the ex-Olympian asked Wright, and so he did.

They were together for thirty minutes, Wright said. He never told the man he was HIV-positive, and he said it doesn't bother him that he didn't.

"It was very safe sex. I was touching him but he wasn't touching me."

They were in bed, they were kissing, and suddenly Wright was gone.

"I was drunk and I instantly knew it was so wrong," he said. "I got the hell out of that hotel room. It meant so little to both of us. What a mistake. We don't talk anymore because it's so awkward."

The other man, who did not want to be identified, did not know Wright was HIV-positive until four years after their encounter. He quietly said he wished Wright well.

The scene at Nationals is not always so serious. Once, Wright was sitting beside a male coach at a practice. The place was crawling with skating officials and coaches. Unbeknownst to the man sitting next to him, Wright turned around to look at Audrey Weisiger, who was sitting in the stands a few rows back. He pointed to the man's back and mouthed these words: "I want to sleep with him!"

Men and boys are a distinct minority in skating. At a USFSA regional qualifying competition in Ohio, in the novice division, there were eighty-one female skaters and thirteen male skaters. In juniors, there were twenty-five females and eight males. In seniors, there were twenty women—and just two men.

"Because of the percentage of male skaters to female skaters, all of your friends in the sport are female," Hamilton said. "Your whole social life is female. I think a lot of guys in skating have acquired feminine mannerisms by hanging out with the girls, whatever the guy's sexuality is. You're spending so much time around women, around females, that in some cases, some of the guys will come up with more feminine mannerisms and ways of handling themselves."

Often, the male skater's mother or coach will make him dress and look a certain way to conform to accepted figure-skating mores. One year, Weisiger sent Weiss, her young skater, to the makeup room at the U.S. national championships. He came out wearing mascara and his hair had been curled.

"In that moment, it's like the theater," Weisiger said. "I don't know why I did that. I guess it's what we've been exposed to in skating. I was just immune to it."

Hamilton, Boitano, and Wylie all say someone's sexuality is a personal matter. But they know that won't stop people from wanting to know if male skaters are gay.

"There's something intriguing to Americans about gay people,"

Boitano said. "It's like, 'Why?' 'Why are they attracted to who they are?' They think it's something weird and odd, and that's attractive to them. It's like tabloid news: 'Why are what people perceive of as negative things attractive?' They just want to know.

"They want to know, too, about famous people. They want to know because they want to say, 'See, our life isn't that bad. At least we're not addicted to drugs. Or gay. Or this. Or that.' It's something to make them feel better about themselves."

After winning the Olympic gold medal in 1988, Boitano had a difficult time understanding the public perceptions of male figure skaters.

"It was hard for me, walking into a room, and not based on how I acted or looked or dressed, I think it was hard for me to have people make that assumption right away. But the other thing that I realized is what always overshadowed that assumption was my celebrity. So I can't imagine someone going through it that doesn't have the celebrity to overshadow it. If you walk into a room and someone automatically makes that judgment, that must be what black people go through. You walk into a room and they see that you're black and it changes their opinion of you. But if they're a celebrity, it overshadows [their race] again.

"I think that no matter what their assumption, whether I'm straight or gay, my celebrity is always going to overshadow that. But also, as I get older, I don't really care anymore. I don't care. Just because you don't have a girlfriend doesn't mean that you're gay, and it's nobody's business anyway."

Hamilton gets frustrated sometimes at the image of his sport. To combat the jokes, he wore one-piece, speed-skating-style suits at the 1984 Olympics as a reaction to those men "who were way over the top, wearing these spangly outfits."

He took it upon himself to personally try to change public opinion. "I was trying to wave this banner of heterosexuality, and I asked myself, 'What am I trying to prove? What do I hope to gain out of this?' It doesn't mean anything. I am me. If people like what I can do and enjoy what I do on the ice, fine. It really became a little bit disturbing to me.

"A lot of the hard-nosed kind of redneck, ignorant people on the planet kind of look at skating and say, 'They're all that way.' Well, I could say all football players are stupid. All baseball players are greedy spoiled children and have drug problems. That's ignorant. Just because someone is wearing something, that doesn't mean that everyone is like that in the sport."

Wylie is the most artistic of the three men on the ice. Like Boitano, he wears makeup on his face. "The TV anchor guy is wearing makeup. The sports anchor guy is wearing makeup. President Clinton is wearing makeup when he goes on TV. In the lights we use, if you're not wearing makeup, you look like Casper. You look like you're not going to make it through your program."

In the late 1970s and early 1980s, Wylie wore "flashy, Vegasy" outfits, like every male skater has worn at one time or another. "We thought it had presence or something. We were definitely on the wrong track."

He is extremely conservative on the ice now, but his vests and shirts always have some sort of symbolic meaning.

"As a skater, you are sort of like a mime," he said. "You're in the middle of the ice and all you have is really the music to tell your story. It's a very frustrating place to be, so anything you can do to tell a story, you try to do it. You can use a costume to tell people what you're thinking about."

Wylie believes two weeks of lessons in the summer of 1975, when he was ten, changed his skating forever. A young man training for the 1976 Olympics was giving lessons in the rink in Denver where both he and Wylie practiced. The skater was John Curry, who had come to Colorado to train with Carlo Fassi.

For no more than an hour a day, Curry taught Wylie how to skate.

"This guy was such a perfectionist," Wylie said. "'Point your toe,' he'd say.

"I just pointed it," Wylie would reply.

"Point it harder," Curry would order.

In those two weeks, Wylie said, he discovered what skating really was about. "I kid you not, I was a different skater after those two weeks. I learned what style is. It's not like going around and flicking your hands and kind of smiling at the judges. It's about class and a deeper sense of perfection."

In his dramatic "Schindler's List" number, which he performed the entire professional competitive season and throughout the Stars on Ice tour in the winter of 1995, Wylie struck a pose that both he and his choreographer, Mary Scotvold, immediately recognized.

"That's John Curry," Scotvold said when she and Wylie first worked on it.

"Every night," Wylie said, "I think of that."

As reverential as they are to the great male skaters of the past, including Curry, men in the sport often find great humor in the lives they lead. Peter Oppegard, the 1988 Olympic bronze medalist in pairs skating, said he once wore an outfit that was the color of "buttery cream," with peach and pink trim.

"I felt like a birthday cake," he said. "I felt weak and silly."

"We joke about it all the time," said Canadian Kurt Browning, who tours with Hamilton and Wylie in Stars on Ice. "We're always goofing around: 'Oh! That was pretty!' And it's not mean at all. It's almost making fun of everyone who's ever made fun of us."

Browning, who has a serious girlfriend in Toronto, said "lots and lots of people" ask if he is gay.

"No" is his reply.

"I didn't think so," the stranger usually says back, Browning said, "but it seems that a lot of figure skaters are."

"Well," Browning adds, "we move a little different than most normal guys that get up and go to work nine to five."

While on tour, Browning receives letters from gay men. "I'd love to take you out to dinner," they write. "I don't know if you're gay, but if you are, give me a call."

Browning's buddies in the dressing room have taken to calling him "the chosen one."

The jokes carry over to outrageous costumes on other skaters. At a time when Elvis Stojko of Canada and Philippe Candeloro of France lend a masculine air to the sport, Alexei Urmanov, the flashy, lyrical 1994 Olympic gold medalist, has become a frequent target.

"You have Urmanov saying, 'I have this designer from the Ukraine ballet that designed this outfit, and we think it's really cool,' and the rest of the world thinks it's a joke. He looks like the Jack of Spades," Wylie said.

After wearing Dutch-masters–style ruffles in 1993, Urmanov showed up at competitions in 1994 as the white swan from *Swan Lake*. He wore hip-hugging white tights and a blousy white, collarless top with wide, winglike black-and-white sleeves. He covered his skates with white cloth. White skates for a man? It's practically unheard of.

"It's a real shame," NBC skating analyst and noted choreographer Sandra Bezic said of him on the air, "because in practice, wearing simple clothes, he looks so powerful. . . . I think this is not the best artistic choice for him."

Urmanov topped the swan bit with a devastating exhibition performance to *Carmen*. He wore a white cape that got stuck around his head, blinding him as he moved across the ice and forcing him to pull it off to see.

"He's got great jumps," Browning said, "and one of these days he might step on the ice like a man and have a program that everyone's going to have to take seriously. By using the term *man,* I mean a presence. Standing out there for a reason, other than just being out there doing what someone told you to do."

•   •   •   •

Where does the joking stop and the heartache begin? U.S. skater Rudy Galindo, the 1987 world junior champion, has been the object of jokes by his peers and members of the media since the late 1980s. His life, however, has been filled with a succession of tragedies.

Whether Galindo will ever be able to articulate the incredible sadness that must be locked inside of him, no one knows. He is twenty-five and goes to funerals with the regularity of a seventy-five-year-old. He has lost one coach—Jim Hulick—and his only brother to AIDS, and a second coach, Richard Inglesi, is dying of the disease.

"I think I'm just numb," he said at his rink in San Jose, California. "I just look forward to skating."

The vast sheet of indoor ice near downtown San Jose is Galindo's refuge, if not from his personal disappointments, at least from the tragedy of unceasing death. There, he practices the beautiful programs that always earn loud ovations at the national championships—but never bestow upon him what he really wants, the respect of the judges in the skating community.

Because he is gay, like his brother was, and because he wears velvet and sequins and because he is not masculine, he believes he never will win a national championship. He doesn't think the judges will give it to him, ever. And he's right. They won't. But he is not being robbed. He doesn't deserve the highest marks because he is not the country's best male skater, and he is prone to falling at the worst times. But his point of view is different. He says his balletic moves, spins, and artistry just aren't appreciated by American judges.

"When you get to Nationals, these guys skate clean, they're really butch when they skate, they're just jump-jump-jump," he said. "Our American judges like that. They want just conservative, just really macho men. I think the other guys are going to have to fall like twenty times and I have to go clean before they put me in that third spot."

Of all the people in skating, Galindo should be forgiven for his cynicism. It's not just that he is gay and everyone in the skating world knows it. It's not just the terrible impact of AIDS, or that his father died in 1993 after several strokes, or that he and his mother live in a trailer park and he has to ride a bicycle to practice and must rely on the financial support of his older sister, affectionately known as Bank of Laura.

It's all of that.

What hurts Rudy Galindo even more was that he was so close to having everything he ever wanted. Through 1990, he was the pairs partner of Kristi Yamaguchi. They were reigning national champions and could probably have won a medal at the 1992 Winter Olympics. Galindo lived at the Yamaguchi home for nearly two years, which gave him a serious jolt of stability—for once in his life. He was so in love with the life he was leading that he even temporarily changed the spelling of his name to Rudi, to match Kristi.

But there were problems. Hulick, a former national junior pairs champion who, as a coach, put Yamaguchi and Galindo together, became sick with AIDS-related cancer. He died in 1989 at the age of thirty-eight. Galindo, who was also coached by Hulick as a singles skater, did not react well to his coach's illness and death. He began throwing fits on the ice at practice. "Kristi didn't deserve that," Galindo said. "Now I look back—what a jerk."

Yamaguchi was becoming the nation's top women's skater, and it was being suggested strongly to her that she make a choice before she ran herself ragged: pick singles or pick pairs, U.S. officials were saying, but not both. A gold medal looked like a strong possibility in singles, but not in pairs. She could completely control her future if she were on her own. It was looking as if she might leave Galindo, and who could blame her?

Yamaguchi did go off on her own after the 1990 competitive season. She won the world title the next year, the Olympic gold medal in 1992.

Galindo was devastated. He drank and said he experimented with speed. He also became jealous of Yamaguchi.

"I can't lie," he said. "She walks into this rink and everyone wants an autograph and I'm just sitting there. I don't want to break down and cry, but when Kristi comes in, I get upset. I get upset with the success that she's had, while I'm still struggling. I could have paid my parents back for all the money they spent in skating if Kristi and I had made it."

Yamaguchi and Galindo talk every now and then, but they aren't particularly close. She does leave tickets for him every time the Stars on Ice tour comes to San Jose. He likes that.

For a few years, Galindo wore his black hair long, caked on layers of dark makeup, and chose extremely effeminate outfits. He thought he was ugly and wanted to hide behind an elaborate disguise. He skated well, reaching fifth place at Nationals in 1993 before dropping back to seventh the next year.

Off the ice, Galindo took care of his thirty-five-year-old brother, George, the final six months of his life. Inglesi, who became his coach after he and Yamaguchi split, also became sick with AIDS. As Inglesi got worse, Galindo eventually found new coaches.

They suggested he tone down the makeup and the costumes and cut his hair. They didn't have to suggest he tone down his lifestyle. He already knew that.

"I don't sleep around," he said. "At competitions, I'm real conservative. I'm not flamboyant, I'm not jumping around. I've got to keep that image up."

.   .   .

Keeping the image up is important to every man in skating. When Hamilton is asked about gay men in the sport, he counts heads in the Stars on Ice bus. Seven men. All straight, he said. Gay skaters tell reporters about girlfriends who do not exist. Gay judges say they cannot come out publicly with their sexual orientation because it could affect future assignments.

And then the phone call comes, and they hear that another friend of theirs from their junior skating days or the Olympics or the judging ranks is dead or dying. No one even has to say the word AIDS anymore. They know what it is.

4

THE LAST
AMATEURS

Picking a winner in figure skating is more like choosing a sorority sister than crowning a sports champion. It's a complex decision based on gossip, nationality, résumé, and popularity. Whom you know, whom you like, and who smiles at whom makes a difference. Occasionally, skating plays a role, too. Sometimes, the result is ridiculous. Often, the process is inexplicable.

The people doing the choosing are the judges. They are not paid. They volunteer thousands of hours of their time for a task that can be nearly impossible. They are given several seconds to produce scores that rank a skater with all the other skaters in a competition, even those who have not yet skated. Their jobs are complicated by the fact that they sometimes have the worst seat in the house to view the action, they cannot confer with each other on a close call like officials from other sports, and they do not get to examine an instant replay. Even worse, the scoring system they are forced to use actually is based on the premise that some judges cheat.

With all these limitations, judges have a weighty job description. With the push of a button on a touch pad, they alter the course of a skater's career. Hundreds of thousands of dollars will move into the bank account of one skater or another, based solely on their opinion.

Judges are the most misunderstood people in figure skating. When they are judging a competition, they appear isolated from the skaters and apart from the skating world—a row of nine detached people who, for all the public knows, don't even have names.

But judges actually could not be more involved in the sport. They run it. They are the ones who are the president and vice presidents of the U.S. Figure Skating Association. They are the team leaders on international trips. They watch practice sessions. They become pseudo–press agents for a skater from their country. It's practically a requirement that they sell their skaters to the judges from other nations. They develop great friendships with skaters and coaches. They monitor the elite skaters in their cities and report back to the USFSA on their progress. They sometimes meddle in the personal lives of skaters; a competitor's weight is a popular topic for a judge. They give advice on programs, music, and costumes. Skaters from Brian Boitano on down have taken judges' words to heart; Boitano and his coach ripped up his Olympic program months before the 1988 Games simply because of what the judges told them.

Judges are omnipresent and omnipotent. They rule the skating world with a furtive glance and a raised eyebrow. Nothing happens without their blessing.

The ones who do something wrong, though, can end up in Siberia. Or the Czechoslovakian equivalent.

At the European championships in 1976, the judges were doing a number on Great Britain's John Curry. After the compulsory school figures and the short program, Curry was behind Vladimir Kovalev of the Soviet Union. The judges voted down political lines: there were five judges from countries in the Soviet bloc and four from the West.

Curry's coach was Carlo Fassi. He knew he had the best skater in the competition—and he was furious. He went to the officials running the event and threatened to withdraw Curry. This was unprecedented. Skaters never stormed out of a competition.

The officials took Fassi seriously. They told him to give them a chance to correct the problem in the long program. Curry stayed in the event and Fassi kept an eye on the scores. Curry won the four Western votes—and the first-place vote of the Czechoslovakian judge. With that, he captured the European title and swept to victory in the 1976 Olympics later that winter.

Fassi never gave his power play another thought. Five years later, at another international event, a man tapped him on the shoulder.

"Do you remember me?" he asked Fassi.

Fassi said he was sorry, but he did not.

"I was the one that switched for John Curry." It was the judge from Czechoslovakia.

Fassi thanked him.

"I just wanted to tell you," the man said, "that this is the first time I've been allowed to judge since then."

•   •   •

Other times, it's an honest mistake.

One year at the U.S. national championships, veteran Morry Stillwell was assigned to judge the senior men. He was watching Christopher Bowman skate in the short program, when, all of a sudden, his pencil broke. He glanced down to reach for another pencil. When he looked up again, Bowman was performing footwork, nothing fancy or out of the ordinary.

At the end of the program, Stillwell punched in his marks, relatively good ones for Bowman, in the low 5s.

All the marks flashed up on the scoreboard. They were not good. Many were in the 4s. Stillwell was completely out of step with his colleagues.

Perplexed, he yelled down the row to a friend of his who also was judging.

"What happened?" he asked frantically.

His friend shook her head. "He ran into the wall, you dumb shit."

Judges sometimes are pawns on a coach's chessboard. "You can call them and ask them to come and watch your skater and critique them," said Frank Carroll, who used to coach Bowman and now coaches Michelle Kwan. "And they come and look and suggest that your skater maybe can point his or her toe better. And you say, 'Thank you, thank you for coming.' You give them the courtesy of offering an opinion, you thank them for an opinion, you evaluate their opinion, but you're drawing them in because you want them to be interested in your skater. You draw people who are influential into the packaging of the skater."

The result: At the 1983 world junior championships in Sarajevo, two respected world judges from the United States were nearly as instrumental as Carroll in helping Bowman win the gold medal. Joan Gruber of Wyomissing, Pennsylvania, was judging the competition; Janet Allen of Minnetonka, Minnesota, was not a judge at the event, but was the U.S. team leader, which meant she oversaw the logistics of the trip.

Gruber, Allen, and Carroll had known each other for years. They had skated at about the same time and had grown up together through the coaching and judging ranks.

"Joan was judging him," Carroll said, "sitting with other international judges in the stands, and listening, talking, promoting, analyzing what they said. She would come down and tell me, 'They don't like his sit spin, Frank, it's not low enough,' and then back up into the stands she'd go."

At another practice session, Bowman was having trouble with his compulsory figures. Before becoming a judge, Allen had been an

Olympian as a pairs skater and had coached for six years. As she and Carroll stood beside the ice and discussed the problem, Carroll had an idea: "Janet," he said, "can you go out onto the ice and help him?"

Allen trudged out in her boots and gave Bowman her advice.

"Janet's helping him with figures; Joan's up there working on what the outcome is going to be," Carroll said. "We're working together."

Sometimes, however, U.S. judges at an international event don't promote or stand by American skaters. This happens all too often, according to U.S. skaters and coaches. American judges, they say, are too honest for their own good.

"A U.S. or a Canadian judge will bend over backwards to be fair," said Kristi Yamaguchi, who won her 1992 Olympic gold medal without a U.S. judge on the nine-member panel. "The Eastern-bloc judges will go for their skater."

"They had to," said Katarina Witt, the former East German who won two Olympic gold medals. "They were told to. They had no choice."

Part of the problem for American judges and skaters is the language barrier. Many European judges speak several different languages. Many U.S. judges speak only English. How can they promote a skater if they can't talk to their fellow judges?

"If I knew thirty to forty years ago what I know now," said Gruber, the world judge, "I would have taken German. If nothing else, I certainly could eavesdrop a little better."

"The American judges," said Fassi, "are naive sometimes. But honest."

Fassi doesn't rely on judges to promote his skaters. He gets the job done himself. He speaks three languages.

Peter Oppegard won an Olympic bronze medal in pairs skating in 1988 and now coaches at Lake Arrowhead, California. Over the years, it bothered him to watch how some U.S. judges, watching an event in the audience, would react to a Russian pair.

"I often noticed when I'd look into the stands that the first ones off their feet were American judges, just applauding and applauding a Russian skater, sometimes a mediocre performance, but they couldn't see the difference.

"Americans want to be fair," he said. "Well, that's fine, be fair. But don't bend over backwards. And remember what you're there for. The judges have to understand that it's like going to the Democratic or Republican convention. Everybody's supposed to be pushing for their own."

U.S. judges sometimes abandon U.S. skaters not because they don't want them to win, but because they want to stay in line with the other judges and not get into trouble. There is an invisible pressure on the judges—invisible from public view, anyway—to avoid what's known as "national bias." If a judge ranks a skater from his or her country higher than he or she places overall, the judge can be charged with national bias and face penalties that ultimately can include suspension. The system is in place to punish judges who cheat. But it also unwittingly penalizes skaters who perform far better than expected in major international events.

Paul Wylie went into the Albertville Olympics having never won a U.S. national title and having finished no better than ninth at a world championship. A national title is the calling card a skater hands to the judges, the ultimate entrée. Wylie didn't have the résumé. He had only his skating ability. It should have been enough, but it wasn't. Figure skating isn't prepared for the supreme upset; too much history is built into the decision-making process.

As a teenager, Wylie skated pairs with Dana Graham, whose father, Hugh, ended up as president of the U.S. Figure Skating Association in the 1980s.

In 1992, Hugh Graham was one of the nine judges in the men's competition at the Olympics. When Wylie and Ukrainian Viktor Petrenko skated to a virtual draw, the judges could have gone either way. Petrenko was the 1988 Olympic bronze medalist and a three-time world championship medalist. Wylie was Wylie. He was older than the others, in his late twenties and juggling his studies at Harvard, and always asking himself why he was still doing this. He consistently made mistakes in competitions. "Nothing that a good lobotomy won't solve," said his coach, Evy Scotvold. But Wylie thought he had the perfect performances in him, somewhere, so he kept going. In Albertville, those performances happened. A pro-American crowd cheered loudly as Wylie skated better than Petrenko, who tried a slightly more difficult program but ran out of gas at the end.

Right before his eyes, Graham watched a young man he had known since childhood skate the performance of his life. Paul Wylie, his daughter's pairs partner, was out there on the ice, finally putting it all together.

But Graham gave his first-place vote to Petrenko by one-tenth of a point on a tiebreaker. Wylie lost the gold medal, 7–2. Had Graham gone for him, Petrenko still would have won, 6–3.

Wylie won the silver medal because the judges were scared to give him the gold. They didn't want to risk being out of line with the other judges, although, ironically, none would have been out of line if they all had put Wylie first. The non-American judges didn't have to worry about national bias, but they still might have had some explaining to do if they were way out of step with their peers. Wylie's performance was such a shock, the judges hadn't expected it. The safe play was to give him the silver medal and stay out of trouble.

In the short program, Graham had put Wylie second. And Wylie had finished third. Already, Graham was concerned about getting his wrist slapped for national bias.

On the night of the long program, anticipating Wylie probably wouldn't get a majority of first-place votes to win, Graham decided not to put him first. He succumbed to peer pressure.

"Paul and I had several areas of connection," Graham said. "My daughter skated with him, he went to Harvard, as I did, and he earned an athletic letter from Harvard, as I did. You're in a position where you want to put the skaters in their place correctly. You don't want the technical committee jumping on you. If I had had him in first place, I probably would have gotten national bias."

There are a range of penalties for national bias, starting with *noted*, meaning a judge is being watched by the International Skating Union's technical committee, through *advice, criticism,* and *warning,* to the stiff penalties of *demotion* and *suspension*. In 1978, the entire Soviet Union judging corps was suspended for a year for showing obvious national bias. The suspension was a kind of lifetime achievement award. While on their year-long vacation, Soviet judges realized their skaters could win without their help. They didn't cheat as badly upon their return.

Graham said he was asked by the referee overseeing the event to explain his short-program placement of Wylie in writing. That was his only punishment. Yet even though he was not reprimanded, he said he still would not have changed his vote to Wylie.

"I don't think I have any great regrets over it," he said.

Others thought he and the rest of the judges who voted for Petrenko made a mistake.

"The winner of the men's gold medal had the worst performance since 1948," John Nicks, who coached Bowman in 1992, said immediately after the competition. "Paul Wylie should have won."

"Wylie was the best," said Canada's Brian Orser.

"We have to have judges to have our sport," Wylie said, "so we pay a price there."

Graham handled the national bias charge one way; Janet Allen handled it another.

At the 1988 Olympics, Allen was judging the highly anticipated men's event, "The Battle of the Brians." Both Brian Boitano and Brian Orser skated extremely well in the short program. Allen gave her first-place vote to Boitano. Most of the other judges went for Orser, with Boitano a strong second.

At the judges' meeting the next morning, Allen was surprised to learn she was being called on the carpet for national bias by the referee. Since she had chosen Boitano, and Boitano had not won the short program, the referee wanted an explanation.

"It was," Allen said, "a pleasure to write."

The next day, Boitano won the gold medal. No one asked for an explanation of her first-place vote that night.

For decades, figure skating has tinkered with its judging and scoring system to try to provide the most understandable and fair apparatus for the most involved of judged sports. It sounds as if it should be so simple: a panel of judges (nine at the top events such as the Olympics and national championships; seven at lower-level events) is asked to rank a group of skaters based on a scoring system ranging from 0 (not skated) through 1 (bad), 2 (poor), 3 (average), 4 (good), and 5 (excellent), to 6 (perfect).

A judge gives out two marks per skater: a technical mark, followed by an artistic mark. The two scores are added (5.7 + 5.8 = 11.5), then compared to all the other scores that a judge gives a skater, and converted into a placement: first, second, third, etc. Those numbers are called ordinals. The skater who receives a majority of first-place ordinals for the short program wins that segment of the event (33 percent of the overall score); the skater who receives a majority of firsts for the long program wins that segment (67 percent).

The scoring system is the lifeblood of the sport. "If a judge says to me, 'This girl is wonderful technically but she cannot express herself like some of the other ones,' you can be sure she will get 5.8, 5.5," Fassi said. "When a judge says, 'She cannot jump but she's so beautiful,' I say to myself, '5.6, 5.9.'"

Sometimes these ranking decisions—*Do I give her a 4.8 or a 4.9 artistically?*—mean the difference between fifth and sixth place at the Cherry Blossom Invitational. But at other times, in other places, that one-tenth of a point can be much more important.

According to coach Evy Scotvold, Nancy Kerrigan lost the Olympic gold medal not in Norway on February 25, 1994, but on March 13,

1993, the night she dropped to fifth at the world championships in Prague and allowed Oksana Baiul, barely known internationally at that point, to sneak in for the gold medal. Because of Kerrigan's performance at worlds, the international judging community had little confidence in her ability to put it together in both a short and long program at the highest levels. At the same time, the judges had a reason to give Baiul the benefit of the doubt because she had been good enough to win the world title in 1993. The term, common in figure skating, is *holding up* a skater. The figure-skating establishment held up Baiul because she was the reigning world champion. They put her in second place despite a big mistake in her short program and moved her into first place in the long, even though Kerrigan did significantly more athletically and was more consistent over both nights of competition.

How does a judge measure the difference between skaters technically (athletically)? There are all sorts of ways, from footwork to the execution of a spin to the jumps. Some say the sport has become a jumping contest. It's not necessarily so, but the six jumps are the easiest way to quantify the difference between skaters. The hardest is the axel, which is the only jump that begins with a skater going forward. The skater lands backward, so there is an extra one-half revolution in the jump. A triple axel, then, is three and a half revolutions.

After the axel, in decreasing order of difficulty, are lutz, flip, loop, salchow, and toe loop, also known as, simply, toe.

The differences between these jumps depend on whether a skater has taken off on an inside or outside edge of the blade, or if they've used the toe pick to launch themselves into the air. Anyone who hasn't skated probably won't be able to catch the differences without a slow-motion replay.

Most top male skaters can do all six triple jumps, including the triple axel, and some men can do quadruple toe loops, salchows, and loops (mostly in practice). Most world-class women reach the triple lutz, although Midori Ito and Tonya Harding have landed the triple axel in competition.

The Baiul-Kerrigan decision was the most talked-about call in the history of figure skating. In the end, a few judges either missed or ignored Baiul's obvious mistakes and gave the most coveted title in the sport to the wrong person.

Kerrigan and Baiul are very different skaters. Kerrigan is athletically superior, yet distant and remote. Baiul is a dancer, enchanting, magical. When their careers are over, Kerrigan will be seen as a solid and strong skater, one of the better athletes produced in U.S. women's

skating. Baiul will be remembered as the more gifted entertainer, perhaps even a skater for the ages.

But, over two nights in February 1994, Kerrigan was better.

In the short program, both skaters were doing the same required
elements: some spins, some footwork, and four jumps—a triple-lutz/
double–toe-loop combination, a double flip, and a double axel.

Baiul skated before Kerrigan and began with the triple-lutz/double-
toe. As she landed the triple, in a far corner of the ice, she clearly two-
footed the landing. It was obvious to the unaided eye in the arena the
moment it happened. Her right foot landed, as it was supposed to, but
her left foot was not in the air. It also was touching the ice. And it
wasn't just skimming the surface. Her left toe pick was sticking into
the ice, very likely holding her up from stumbling, or even worse,
falling.

"Most people watching on TV don't understand a two-footed jump,
where the toe goes down," said Joe Inman, a U.S. judge from Alexandria,
Virginia, who is qualified to work all international events except the
Olympics and world championships. "That little toe touch makes it easy
for you to stand up. It gives you that security to keep your body upright.
A lot of times, you would fall down if you didn't put that foot down."

Kerrigan came two skaters after Baiul. She had the same combination jump in the same corner of the ice. Hers, however, was flawless.

Yet two of the nine judges on the panel put Baiul ahead of Kerrigan
in the short program. Those two judges were Wendy Utley of Great
Britain and Alfred Korytek of Ukraine.

Utley, a thirty-year judging veteran, said she could not tell if Baiul
landed the jump cleanly or not. When in doubt, a judge must go with
the skater, assume it was a good landing, and score it accordingly.

Utley had a very good reason for being uncertain. *She was seated
150 feet away.* Almost everyone in the arena—even the spectators in
the highest corners—had a better view of Baiul's jump than she did.

Utley was judge No. 1. All nine judges sit side by side at ice level
along the length of the boards. Her chair was at the far end of the row
of judges, the greatest distance from the corner where Baiul and Kerrigan landed their triple lutzes.

The judges' seats stretch 100 feet and are centered in the middle of
the 200-foot-long ice surface. So Utley was 150 feet away from the
most important spot on the ice.

"It was almost impossible to see if it was a touch down or not," she
said.

What's more, she did not have the benefit of the replays that were
flashing on reporters' TV monitors in the press section right above her
seat. Replays are not allowed to be used in judging.

"I was leaning over, trying to see it," she explained of Baiul's jump. "This is a regular occurrence when you're at the end of the row at a competition. It all happens so quickly. In an instant, you must make a decision. Was it landed? Or was it not? Having some kind of replay would be fairer, wouldn't it?"

Korytek, judge No. 4, presumably had different reasons for placing Baiul first. His son used to be her coach.

If he was concerned about national bias, it didn't show.

Kerrigan won the short program, seven judges to two. Baiul was second; Surya Bonaly of France, third.

Two nights later, in the long program, Kerrigan and Baiul skated back to back, giving the judges the best comparison possible. First came Kerrigan, who completed five clean triples. Her only error was one of omission, turning her opening triple flip into a double flip. It seemed like such a small thing, but the U.S. judge in the competition, judge No. 6, Margaret Anne Wier, said it might have been what decided the gold medal.

"If Nancy had done the triple flip, then she would have done everything," said Wier, who happens to be Hugh Graham's sister. "There couldn't have been a question. She would have had it cold. Instead, it just gave some of the judges a little question in their minds."

A judge looking to shove Kerrigan out of the picture could fall back on her past history: she always seemed to have trouble in the long program. It must be happening again.

But it wasn't. This time was different. She went right back down the ice and landed a triple-toe-loop/triple-toe-loop combination, followed by a triple loop, a triple-salchow/double-toe-loop combination, a triple lutz, and a double axel. The only triple missing was the flip, and, of course, the triple axel, which she never did in competition.

After the attack on her knee, it was assumed that Kerrigan might receive some favoritism from the Olympic judges. If there was a sympathy vote, the thinking was, she would get it. But two things happened. The world—and the judges—grew sick of the Harding-Kerrigan saga. And more important, Baiul wrested the sympathy of the judges away from Kerrigan. Exactly fifty days after the attack on Kerrigan's knee, Baiul was skating in the long program with a gashed leg and sore back suffered in a practice collision a day earlier. Before Baiul skated, she took two shots of a painkiller approved by the International Olympic Committee. Baiul, a poor orphan who won the hearts of the skating community at the 1993 worlds, now was viewed as the skater with the more heart-wrenching story.

In her long program, Baiul landed only three clean triples—lutz, loop, and salchow—none of which was in combination, which is harder because it requires the skater to muster enough energy to do a second jump immediately after the first. She two-footed two other triples she tried—flip and toe loop. At the very end of her program, in the waning seconds, knowing she needed some kind of a combination jump to match Kerrigan, she awkwardly threw in a double-axel/double-toe-loop and barely hung on to the landing. Baiul's fans pointed to that as the ultimate gutsy act, a final message to the judges, a bold move that won her the gold medal. Others saw it as a messy sequence that pointed out Baiul's inability to reach Kerrigan's athletic standards.

Baiul was delightful when she wasn't jumping, drawing in the crowd with a medley of Broadway show tunes. She easily captured the judges' attention. Kerrigan, by comparison, moved around the ice as if the judges weren't there, which is the way almost all Americans skate.

So who won? The woman doing five beautiful triples, including the triple-triple combination? The one who did all that and also completed the perfect short program, thus proving herself to be superior over two nights?

No.

"Three mistakes in the long program—no combination and she two-footed two jumps—and she won the gold medal!" Fassi exclaimed. "I'm not usually with Evy Scotvold, but this time I have to be."

"Nancy's skating was of a much higher quality than Oksana's," said Utley, who went for Kerrigan by a wide margin in the long program. "It was mature, beautiful skating. I thought she won."

"When the marks went up, I just sat there in a stupor," said Wier, who voted for Kerrigan. "I said to myself, 'How could that have happened?'"

Judging is not scientific. Judges blink and miss a skater's mistake. Or, they see what they want to see. Even if they see an error, there are no hard-and-fast rules for points to be deducted. Only guidelines.

According to the 1994 guidelines, in the short program, a two-footed jump required a .3–.4 deduction (from the original 6.0). But a touch down was only a .2 deduction. One judge might see a two-footed jump where another might see only a touch down.

Judges, obviously, can do whatever they please.

This is how the scoring works, using Baiul and Kerrigan's marks at the Olympics (see below).

Unlike other judged sports, figure skating does not throw out the high or low mark, or multiply by degree of difficulty. The two scores simply are added, ranked, and assigned an ordinal. For instance, judge No. 9, Jan Hoffman of Germany, gave Kerrigan 11.7 to Baiul's 11.4. Those numbers turned into these numbers: Kerrigan, 1; Baiul, 2.

There were no ties by any judge in the short program between these two, but had there been, they would have been broken with the technical mark. Ties in the long program are broken by the artistic mark.

A majority of the nine judges' first-place votes puts a skater into first, a majority of seconds means second, and so forth. Even in this area, it gets dicey when, if the marks are all over the place, no skater gets a majority of firsts or seconds or thirds. It has happened where someone wins first place with a majority of seconds. That didn't happen here; Kerrigan's seven first-place votes were enough to give her

THE SHORT PROGRAM

JUDGES

	Great Britain	Poland	Czech Republic	Ukraine	China	United States	Japan	Canada	Germany
Oksana Baiul									
TECHNICAL	5.7	5.8	5.4	5.7	5.7	5.6	5.7	5.6	5.5
ARTISTIC	5.9	5.8	5.7	5.9	5.9	5.8	5.9	5.9	5.9
TOTAL	11.6	11.6	11.1	11.6	11.6	11.4	11.6	11.5	11.4
ORDINAL	1	2	3	1	3	2	2	2	2
Nancy Kerrigan									
TECHNICAL	5.6	5.8	5.6	5.8	5.8	5.9	5.8	5.8	5.9
ARTISTIC	5.6	5.9	5.7	5.7	5.9	5.9	5.9	5.8	5.8
TOTAL	11.2	11.7	11.3	11.5	11.7	11.8	11.7	11.6	11.7
ORDINAL	2	1	1	2	1	1	1	1	1

first. It is a majority vote for this reason: If the Ukrainian judge wanted to place Kerrigan, say, tenth, instead of second, the overall result would have been the same. She would have had seven first-place votes, one second, and one tenth. Her majority of seven first-place votes would have been intact.

The math then was wiped out. The blackboard was erased, and the only thing that mattered once the evening was over were the ordinals: Kerrigan was first, Baiul second, Surya Bonaly third, and so forth. Because the short program is worth one-third and the long two-thirds of the overall score, the addition was made easy by multiplying the placement to reflect that one-third total. So Kerrigan was ascribed a 0.5; Baiul, 1.0; Bonaly, 1.5; China's Chen Lu was fourth for a 2.0.

Those factored placements would be added to the long-program-

THE LONG PROGRAM

JUDGES

Great Britain	Poland	Czech Republic	Ukraine	China	United States	Japan	Canada	Germany
Oksana Baiul								
TECHNICAL								
5.6	5.8	5.9	5.8	5.8	5.8	5.8	5.5	5.7
ARTISTIC								
5.8	5.9	5.9	5.9	5.9	5.8	5.8	5.9	5.9
TOTAL								
11.4	11.7	11.8	11.7	11.7	11.6	11.6	11.4	11.6
ORDINAL								
3	1	1	1	1	2	2	3	1
Nancy Kerrigan								
TECHNICAL								
5.8	5.8	5.8	5.7	5.7	5.8	5.8	5.7	5.8
ARTISTIC								
5.9	5.8	5.9	5.9	5.9	5.9	5.9	5.8	5.8
TOTAL								
11.7	11.6	11.7	11.6	11.6	11.7	11.7	11.5	11.6
ORDINAL								
1	2	2	2	2	1	1	1	2

factored placements, which were the whole number of 1 for first place, 2 for second, etc.

In the long program, much was made of the scoring of Hoffman, judge No. 9. He tied the two skaters at 11.6. The artistic mark breaks the tie, so Baiul won, 5.9 to 5.8. That's where Kerrigan's losing margin of one-tenth of a point was determined—by Hoffman's scoring. But Hoffman, who as an East German finished second by a narrow margin at the 1980 Olympics to Robin Cousins, was not the culprit in Kerrigan's loss.

His judging was exemplary, given his feelings that Baiul's artistry was every bit matched by Kerrigan's athleticism. The fact that he tied the skaters wasn't a fluke. Hoffman planned it that way. Hoffman knew the tiebreaker in the long program was the artistic mark, and he knew exactly what he was doing giving them both 11.6, but giving Baiul the higher second mark. He didn't just throw numbers up there and see what the computer would do with them. He figured out the way to say they both were great, but Baiul should win.

Of course, when he punched in his numbers, he had no idea his scores would be seen as the deciding marks. For all he knew, the final score could have been 8–1, Kerrigan.

The questionable judging in the long program was done by judge Nos. 3, 4, and 5, from the Czech Republic, Ukraine, and China. Each placed Baiul ahead of Kerrigan *technically*. All three of those judges tied them artistically. If any one of the three had judged the technical aspect of the competition differently, Kerrigan would have won the gold medal.

The final tally was five firsts for Baiul and four for Kerrigan. The 5–4 vote broke down along old East-West lines. For Baiul: Poland, Czech Republic, Ukraine, China, and Germany (Hoffman, the former East German); for Kerrigan, Great Britain, United States, Japan, Canada. Judges and other skating insiders believe it's not a matter of politics as much as it is a question of style. The East likes its skating balletic; the West prefers the athletic.

This plays into the constant argument of athleticism versus artistry. It's not simply a jumping contest. There are spins, there is footwork, there are spirals—the move with one leg up in the air, the other gliding on the ice. Baiul was better than Kerrigan at some of these maneuvers; Kerrigan beat Baiul on others.

Once the scores were determined, the numbers were wiped out and the ordinals took over. Baiul's five first-place votes gave her the long-program victory and a 1.0 as a factored placement; Kerrigan's second gave her 2.0, Chen's third, 3.0, Bonaly's fourth, 4.0.

The factored placements from the short and long were added. The lowest total won.

Baiul:	1.0 + 1.0 = 2.0
Kerrigan:	0.5 + 2.0 = 2.5
Chen:	2.0 + 3.0 = 5.0
Bonaly:	1.5 + 4.0 = 5.5

Kerrigan's loss pointed out a flaw in the ordinal system: a big lead, which Kerrigan certainly had in the short program, receives no extra weight. A tiny margin, which Baiul had in the long program, also cannot be reflected. First is first and second is second by a whisker or a mile.

This is not necessarily fair to the skaters, but it certainly ensures that the long program is meaningful. During the days of compulsory school figures, skaters like Carol Heiss and Scott Hamilton had such big leads that they barely had to skate the long program to win their Olympic gold medals. That lack of suspense would be unacceptable to television executives and their advertisers these days.

Judging the competition is only the tip of the iceberg for a judge. The practice sessions are at the root of all their decisions.

Judges judge practice at major events. It sounds shady and conspiratorial—and sometimes it is. But the judges and most skaters say it's the most essential part of a judge's job, and wouldn't have it any other way.

There are usually between twenty-five and thirty skaters in a men's or women's competition at the Olympics. Without watching practice, a judge would have trouble ranking one skater with another. This wouldn't be a problem if there were five skaters in an event, as in the professional ranks. In that case, the judge could rely on memory. But with twenty-five or thirty, the judge has to have seen the practices.

The problem for the judges is the short program, in which skaters appear in almost any order. (The long program groups the skaters based on how they did in the short.) No matter how great the first few skaters might be in the short program, the judges must "leave room" in their ranking system for skaters who come later. They might believe they see perfection in the first skater, but they can't give out a 6.0 and 6.0 because that would mean they have determined the winner after only one skater has performed. A perfect program skated at the beginning of the short-program competition would receive something like 5.8, 5.8. The same performance coming at the end of the short program would receive, perhaps, 5.9, 6.0.

"No wonder people watch this on TV and have no idea what is going on," said Inman, the U.S. judge.

A judge giving 5.8, 5.8—a very good score—is leaving room for potentially twelve other skaters to come in ahead of that skater in the short program. Among the scores beating 5.8, 5.8 (the tiebreaker in the short program is the first mark) are 5.8, 5.9; 5.8, 6.0; and 6.0, 5.7.

With all these options, the skaters prefer seeing the judges at practice.

"I'd just as soon them get a clear picture of what the skater's all about and judge it that way than just show up blind in the night and try to throw it together," Scott Hamilton said. "There's a lot more to evaluating a performance than just seeing it once. To judge the quality of choreography and the difficulty of choreography and compare it to twenty other guys, that's asking a lot."

"If they didn't see our programs, they would be clueless," Paul Wylie said.

"You have to watch practice, or else you're lost," said Bonnie McLauthlin, a former skater and coach from Denver who judges on the national level. "You have to have an idea of what skaters are in the top five, the next five, and so on. Otherwise, you'd be lost, because they come at you in no particular order in the short program. Watching practice allows you to see who's doing what. It's a necessity."

"The judges must have some inkling of what to expect so as not to do an injustice to a skater later in the order," said Mary Cook, a national judge from New York. "You can't correct your mistakes at the end. You must be right at that instant. So you have to prepare by acquainting yourself with the field."

Judges do not hide at practices. They sit in the stands near parents and reporters, often clustered with other judges. Some, like Gale Tanger, want to be seen.

"Not only do I go there as a judge, looking for a range, how far I should spread my marks, but I also go in a support role, too," Tanger said. "I've served many teams and grown up in the sport with many of the coaches and skaters as well. I encourage them to come up and ask me, 'How am I doing? Is this right?' I say, 'You're looking good, you're right on target.'"

With this emphasis on practices, the skaters treat those sessions like a competition. At Nationals, the whole week becomes one giant performance. Although unofficial dress codes have eased considerably, no one will ever show up for a practice at a competition wearing gray sweats. Every skater dresses up; most wear costumes like those they will wear in competition, although some of the men wear T-shirts and black pants, and some of the women wear leotards.

Skaters know that a superlative week at practice can win them a gold medal, provided they don't mop up the ice in the competition. Two Olympic victories that were helped by hot practice sessions were Hamilton's in 1984 and Russian pair Ekaterina Gordeeva and Sergei Grinkov's in 1994.

The reverse is also true. "If you're not on in your practices," Boitano said, "it will affect your overall score."

Mary Cook was a skater from Illinois who quit to raise two sons and go to law school. Along the way, she decided she wanted to become a figure-skating judge, so she began going to events—both large and small—to watch, study, and do something known as practice judging. Other judges graded her work. Over the years, she ended up putting in about eight thousand hours of work—the equivalent of about three years of eight-hour days—to reach her national judging appointment. She did all of this at her own expense.

Finally, she was given her first national championship assignment, judging the senior, or Olympic-level, men at the 1990 Nationals in Salt Lake City.

She was jittery before the short program. As a former skater, she had tremendous respect for the men she had watched at practice and was going to judge that day, skaters like Bowman, Wylie, Todd Eldredge, and Mark Mitchell. She was excited and she was scared. This was her big chance, she was sitting beside the ice, as close as she could be, and she did not want to blow it.

Wylie came onto the ice for his performance, and within seconds Cook knew she was seeing something special. One of the greatest artistic skaters of his day, Wylie was racing across the ice, just skimming the surface. His feet, Cook said, "were on fire."

The moment Wylie finished, Cook didn't bother to look down at the notes she had scribbled during his two-minute-forty-second performance. She simply reached for the little box with a touch pad of numbers each judge has at their place. She knew what she had to do. She punched the 5 and the 7, followed by 6 and 0.

She was giving Wylie 5.7 technically, 6.0 artistically. Then she hit the ENTER key and waited.

At their places along the row of judges, the announcer and referee saw the 6.0 pop up on their computer.

"That's Mary," they said to one another.

Knowing she was new to national judging, they waited for the other marks to come in, hoping that another 6.0 would show up so Cook wouldn't be out there with a perfect mark all alone. That's how significant a 6.0 is to the person giving it. All judges think about the marks they give, perhaps too much so. Inman, for instance, has never given a 6.0. Nothing has moved him to do it in nearly two decades of judging. Giving that first 6.0 is like losing your judging virginity.

Sure enough, another judge also came in with a 6.0 for Wylie for his artistry. When the marks went up onto the scoreboard, the audience roared. Sitting along the ice, Cook was stunned.

"I pulled at my hair, I had to steady myself. I had more skaters to judge. Finally, I just screamed. The crowd was so loud, no one could hear me. That calmed me down," Cook said.

Wylie finished second in the short program to Eldredge. Afterward, several of her peers came up to her.

"Way to go, Mary, with that 6.0," they said.

One of her judging friends, a fellow lawyer, asked her why the 6.0, why not a 5.9.

"It's like what the Supreme Court justice said about pornography," she said. "You know it when you see it."

Then came the men's long program. As she took her seat beside the ice, the thought suddenly hit her, "What if he skates like that again? I'm going to have to give another 6.0!"

Sure enough, Wylie was superb once again. Cook, sitting there watching, knew what she had to do—again. She punched in 5.8 and 6.0. And ENTER.

But as soon as she let go of the marks, she got nervous. She pressed the call button on her touch pad.

"Yes, Mary," came a voice through an intercom. It was the referee.

Cook hesitated for a moment, saying nothing. This was her opportunity to change her mind, turn the 6.0 into a 5.9, play it safe, not look ridiculous. No one ever would know except for her and the referee.

"Never mind," Cook said into the speaker. "Just leave it."

In less than thirty seconds, the public address announcer clicked on his microphone. "And now the marks for Paul Wylie . . ."

Cook closed her eyes when the second set of marks, the artistic ones, popped up. She heard another roar. She opened her eyes to see not one 6.0, but four of them.

"What a sight that was," she said.

Wylie won the long program, but because he had been third in compulsory school figures, the last year they would be part of the competition, he remained second overall.

Cook said she learned a lot about judging from that experience. "You have to have a lot of confidence and the analytical power to synthesize the product into a whole and come up with a number. I do not worry about lining up with other judges or falling in line. It's yourself you have to live with."

Every judge brings a certain expertise to the table. McLauthlin, sixty-six, is known for her technical know-how after years of coaching.

Tanger was a dance major in college, so the look and feel of a program is important to her. Inman, forty-eight, is a burly former Texas prep football player who teaches piano. He played for the U.S. Army Band for twenty-one years and also played the piano at White House teas given by Pat Nixon, Betty Ford, Rosalynn Carter, and Nancy Reagan.

Inman, naturally, is sensitive to the way a skater uses music, something another judge might not notice.

"We all have different backgrounds," Inman said, "so they're getting nine opinions, and there should be nothing wrong with those nine opinions if you can justify and give reasons why you did what you did."

"The law of averages really weighs out," Tanger said. "With our different backgrounds, we are all going to blend."

One of the oldest stories in skating is that judges don't make decisions based entirely on skating. They judge lifestyles, too. For some judges, especially the crusty veterans, this is true. Other judges said they couldn't care less about a skater's life off the ice. Two back-to-back Nationals illustrate these different viewpoints.

At the 1993 Nationals, it appeared that being a good girl was important. Only Nancy Kerrigan was a lock for one of the three spots on the world championship team. She was a returning Olympic medalist and America's best hope for a world championship medal. While her father was a welder and she was decidedly working class, figure-skating judges thought she was perfect for the sport.

"She's a lovely lady," said a world and Olympic judge from the United States who asked not to be named. "She was raised as a lady. We all notice that."

Four other women—Tonia Kwiatkowski, Lisa Ervin, Nicole Bobek, and Tonya Harding—were going for the other two spots. When the competition was done, Kwiatkowski and Ervin, both coached by Carol Heiss, performed about the same as Bobek and Harding, the sport's two bad girls. Looking at the mistakes and the difficulty of their programs, it was a toss-up. Reporters figured the judges would pick Harding and Bobek because of their talent and potential, even if they had slipped that night.

The reporters were wrong. Ervin and Kwiatkowski joined Kerrigan on the world team. Harding finished fourth; Bobek, fifth.

Bobek took the hint and slowly began to adjust her life to satisfy the judges, whom she knew were concerned about how she would represent the country if they sent her to a world championship. This was just a couple months after her escapades in Seoul.

"I do think it's a matter of what we do on the ice, but people are also looking at you to see how you are with people, how you dress, how you act," Bobek said. "It's a consistent thing that people are always looking for. When they told me, 'We don't like your earrings,' they were out. And they didn't like my rings. So they're off.

"So I'm doing everything they tell me because I want to go out there and skate the best I can and show them that I can do it. And then at the end, I can put all my earrings back in."

Harding wasn't quite as receptive. She received all sorts of advice. She rarely listened. She was going to go her own way.

At the 1994 Nationals, Mary Cook was on the panel for the senior women. She watched practices early in the morning, she watched practices late at night. She saw Harding land triple axel after triple axel in practice. She was hoping to see her complete one in competition. It didn't happen.

The night of the long program, when Harding came out to warm up, Cook took one look and shook her head. Harding was wearing the dress with the see-through middle that revealed much more of her breasts than anyone wanted to see, the one Tanger later replaced at the Olympics.

As bad as the dress was, it apparently broke no rules. The judges are supposed to deduct one-tenth or two-tenths of a point if a woman is wearing an outfit that doesn't cover her hips or posterior; if she has a bare midriff; if she is wearing a unitard; or if she is wearing a "garish or theatrical" costume not "appropriate for athletic competition." Harding wore thin, flesh-colored fabric over her chest.

In the competition, Cook ranked Harding first. So did the rest of the judges. The costume, Cook said, had nothing to do with her skating.

"Nobody deducted for the costume," Cook said. "I didn't hear any of the judges saying, 'Oh, did you take off for the costume?' No one said that or would have done that. I think I've deducted for a costume one or two times in my life, and I can't remember when it was. We were there to judge her performance on the ice that night."

Said Inman, "People think we care about these little things. We don't. We're there to judge the skating. They could about be naked and it wouldn't matter to me."

In 1993, the lifestyle of two skaters most likely decided the results. In 1994, Harding's lifestyle didn't count at all. The lesson skaters learn is that they can't be denied if they skate well. But if they don't skate well and don't toe the line, they probably won't get any favors.

Judges are not evil people. Some have been judging too long. Some are too beholden to a coach, a skating club, or a concept; i.e., that these women still should be, ahem, ladies. But even as they counted Bobek's earrings, they did make Harding national champion not once, but twice.

Judges are human beings giving opinions on the most subjective sport in the world. They don't hate little children. They don't purposely send skaters to the bathroom in tears. They don't try to give parents ulcers. They are nervous. Their hearts sink when a skater falls. They stay up late at night wondering about a decision they made.

Cook was judging a grassroots competition in Colorado in the 1980s, a rather insignificant event in the grand scheme of things. It was an invitational. It didn't decide who would go to the national championships. It wasn't anywhere near that important.

It had been a long week of judging hundreds of skaters in many different events. Cook was working from 7 A.M. until midnight almost every day. She rested between events by laying down on the cold and dirty floor in the judges' room. She was exhausted.

The next-to-last day, a woman performed a combination jump consisting of a triple salchow followed by a double toe loop. Cook was looking right at her. She is certain of that. She *was* watching.

But Cook's brain "just shut down," as if she were daydreaming in the car waiting for a traffic light to turn green.

The skater took off for her combination. All of a sudden, "everything went into slow motion," Cook said. Her mind registered "double salchow/double toe loop." She jotted that onto a sheet in front of her and lowered the skater's marks accordingly. The scores she gave were a good two-tenths to three-tenths of a point lower than the scores her fellow judges gave the skater.

Backstage, Cook asked another judge what had happened. The judge told her the woman landed a triple jump, not a double. It was not a horrible mistake; Cook's marks by themselves did not change the outcome of the competition.

But the more Cook thought about it, the more upset she became. That night in her hotel room, she lay awake, unable to sleep.

"I was thinking, 'How could I have done that?'" she said. "You tell yourself to forget it, but you can't. I couldn't forgive myself. Even for the littlest kid, it's still important, because maybe that's the only competition they'll ever be in. That's how much you really do care."

*P*REPARATION

5

LADIES
IN WAITING

The girls in the expensive, pretty dresses were leaning against a counter in the lounge of an ice rink in the Cleveland suburb of Lakewood, Ohio. They jockeyed for position, giggling nervously, pulling on their sleeves, pushing back their hair. This group of anxious junior ladies was gathered around an empty space on a cinder-block wall, waiting for the posting of the results that would tell them if everything they had done for the past six months was a success or a failure. One piece of paper reflecting the opinions of seven strangers would tell them that.

Outside the lounge, gathered in little bunches with their daughters' coaches and some neighbors and friends, the parents of the skaters were trying to keep calm. They smiled and chatted, but it was no use. Every second or so, their eyes lifted and wandered over to that room, where their little girl waited with every other parent's little girl. *Where were those results?* They returned their eyes to the people around them, but no one could remember what they were talking about. *Where in the world were those results?* It's amazing that in the history of regional figure-skating competition, no one can remember the rescue squad being called even once to treat a parent for a coronary.

Jenni Tew, a leggy, pretty eighth-grader, was at the front of the group. For her, it was touch and go. She was fourth after the short program, having fallen on her triple toe loop after a pink petal from her dress fell onto the ice and distracted her when she started to jump. Now, in the three-and-a-half-minute long program, she had fallen again on the same jump. But everyone else had made mistakes, too. She had no idea what the judges were going to do.

Unlike major competitions or senior-level events, where the scores were announced immediately over the public-address system, junior competitions did not have open judging. The seven judges (not nine like at the highest levels) made their notes and jotted down the scores, but at the end of the competition, they had a chance to reconsider who they liked and who they didn't and change their marks. Most parents and coaches believed this system—called closed judging—was fairer overall than open judging because judges could take a few moments to think about what they were doing before they announced their decisions. But it led to one of the longest waits in children's sports.

Joel and Deanie Tew were talking to Carol Heiss Jenkins and Glyn Watts, Jenni's coach and choreographer. Heiss was telling them she thought Jenni had made it. The Tews so wanted to believe her. Heiss, the 1960 Olympic gold medalist, prided herself in predicting what the judges would do. She was funny that way. She looked the part of fig-ure skating's Goody Two-shoes, with perfect blond hair and perfect makeup and perfect nails, but her personality was more like that of some babe who played the horses. She spoke with a gravelly New York accent, courtesy of Queens, she was competitive as hell, and she always was trying to outguess the judges.

Heiss started on this path long ago. In 1964, working for ABC as a commentator at the national championships, she had this to say about an unknown fifteen-year-old girl who was skating for the first time in the senior ladies division: "She has all her jumps, she has the power. All she needs now is maturity and a little more experience. You can really imagine her four years from now in the 1968 Olympics. She could probably win a gold medal for us."

Calling Peggy Fleming's future was Heiss's grandest handicapping achievement.

Based on all the other junior ladies's performances at regionals, which she had watched and ranked in her head, Heiss thought Jenni would be third. "But I could be wrong," she said. "You never know. That's the fun aspect of this sport."

For the Tews, the wait was unbearable. What that piece of paper meant to them! When that page with the results on it went up on the wall, it would be another referendum on their life. Were they doing the right thing? Was the upheaval in their lives—the move to Ohio, the sep-aration of their family, the total chaos caused by skating—worth it?

Everyone in the rink knew the Tews. They were the ones who were so well-off, the father helped finance a rink near their home in Florida, but before it was finished, his daughter had moved to Ohio to receive better training. Thirteen-year-old Jenni, her younger sister, Courtney, and her mother, Deanie, lived in a three bedroom town house in Rocky River, Ohio, close to the Winterhurst Ice Rink in Lakewood, where Heiss runs one of the top programs in the country. Joel, a successful Clearwater real estate development attorney, lived in a condominium in Clearwater and flew to Cleveland every other weekend. They were renting out their old home in Florida. The dream house they planned on a golf course remained unbuilt.

"You should hear the advice we get from the rest of our family," Deanie Tew said. "It's like, 'We support Jenni's skating, but we'll never agree with your decision to separate your family.' "

One family member pointedly told her, "I hope that gold medal is worth it."

"You find yourself not only having to make the hard decision, but then you have to defend it to everybody and justify what you're doing," Deanie Tew explained. "Our answer has become, 'Look, it's our family. It's our life.' We just want to give her the chance to see how good she can be. When she's older, we never want her to say, 'If I had had better training, I could have done something.' "

Twenty-five girls had arrived at Winterhurst earlier in the week for the Eastern Great Lakes regional junior ladies competition. Junior ladies generally range in age from twelve to sixteen and aren't quite polished enough yet to compete at the senior (highest) level. Eight junior ladies made the cut into the finals. Four of them would move on to the Midwestern sectionals in Denver in December for a chance to qualify for the U.S. national championships in Providence in February.

Everyone else would go home, cry for a couple days, and begin practicing for next year.

"Sometimes they work so hard and because something doesn't quite click that day, it's all over," Heiss said. "Three and a half minutes and it's over. A whole year. You don't know why. They don't know why. But there's no second chance. There's no coming back next week. In other sports, you can have a rematch, another golf or tennis tournament, another game next week. But not in this sport."

Two other regionals also would send four junior ladies—they call them ladies, but they're actually young girls—to Denver, making a field of twelve at Mids, as that sectional championship is commonly called. Out of those twelve, four would qualify for Nationals. There, the four girls from Mids would face four from Easterns and four from Pacific Coast (West), plus a few who received byes for special reasons, in the national junior ladies competition. In front of all the judges and coaches and families who comprise the national figure-skating community, they would start making a name for themselves.

All skaters followed this path. Kristi Yamaguchi and Nancy Kerrigan, the two most recent U.S. women's Olympic medalists, started slowly. In 1986, their first year in juniors, Yamaguchi was fourth in the country; Kerrigan, eleventh. They remained juniors in 1987: Yamaguchi finished second; Kerrigan, fourth. They moved up to seniors the next year.

Fleming had been third at Nationals in juniors in 1963, the year before she won her first U.S. senior title. Dorothy Hamill finished second in junior ladies in 1970. By 1973, she was second in the nation in seniors.

This was how a skater got famous. She came out of a regional competition like the one at Winterhurst, one of nine that are held each year in the United States. This one, for kids from Ohio, Indiana, Michigan, Kentucky, Tennessee, Alabama, and Mississippi, happened to be held in Jenni Tew's home rink.

"I'd like to go to the Olympics and I'd like to win a medal at the Olympics," Jenni said. "That's my goal. But I think about not making it all the time. I think I'd feel so let down, so disappointed. I don't know what I would feel. I think I have the ability to get there someday, but I always wonder, 'What if something goes wrong?' "

Five minutes, seven minutes went by on a chilly Saturday night in early November in Ohio. The girls still were staring at the blank wall like school kids waiting for the posting of test results. Jenni Tew was at the front of the pack.

Finally, there was rustling in the back. The kids were parting to allow the woman carrying the single page to come into their midst.

The results were taped onto the wall.

Jenni Tew's eyes moved quickly.

Where's my name? Where's my name?

Not first . . . not second . . . not third.

Oh no . . .

There it i

Fourth. Fourth!

I made it!

Jenni hugged Deana Gerbrick, a rival of hers in the rink, but the closest person at the moment. A week earlier, Deana had hogged the tape machine that the skaters use to play their music at practice. But all was forgiven now.

Deana was third. Jenni was fourth. They both were going to Denver.

The two girls inched their way out as the pack caved in and other skaters and their friends surged to the front to look.

Deana raced to her mother. Nancy Gerbrick was so nervous about this competition that, while her daughter performed, she had retreated to the lobby and paced, head down, refusing to look up.

"Third!" Deana blurted out.

"Great!" her mother said. She exhaled loudly. She looked as if she were about to faint.

Jenni had farther to go, to her parents back inside the rink, standing with Heiss and Watts. Jenni's little sister was ahead of her.

"She made it!" ten-year-old Courtney screamed out.

"Fourth," Jenni said as she rushed over.

Joel and Deanie Tew smiled disarmingly nonchalant smiles. Inside, their stomachs were churning.

"See, there was nothing to worry about," Heiss said mischievously.

She had been wrong by one place, but that didn't matter. Fourth was as good as third. Jenni Tew was going to Mids.

Heiss soon was walking out of the rink for her hour-long drive home to Akron. She was exhausted. She has been coaching since 1978 and has been through dozens of week-long regionals as a skater and a coach. This year, she shepherded seventeen skaters, male and female, through the week-long regionals. Eleven, including Jenni Tew, made it to Mids.

Heiss said she was overjoyed, but she sounded as if she needed an ambulance.

"Regionals is the worst competition," she said. "I lose weight, my fingers ache. I feel like someone's taken me into a dark alley and beaten me from head to toe."

Deanie and Joel Tew create a pleasant picture, a handsome couple in their early forties, soft-spoken, polite, and well-dressed. But as they sat in the stands during the regional competition, they felt as if they could just die. It was that bad being the parent of a figure skater.

"I would rather go outside," Deanie Tew said from the bleachers at regionals. "I used to not be able to watch, but I'm getting better now."

For several years, Deanie Tew would walk to the women's room right before her daughter skated and stand in the bathroom for the entire performance. But a problem arose. She still could hear the music. She had watched her daughter practice the program so much, she knew exactly where the jumps came in relation to the music. If she didn't hear any applause at those moments, she knew her daughter had fallen.

"I couldn't handle that," she said, "so I would stand there and continually flush the toilet until I knew it was over."

Joel Tew had a different problem.

"I die the day before. I can handle the program. I can't imagine not watching. That would kill me to not watch. But the day before is tough for me, just thinking about it."

Deanie Tew: "Sometimes, I still can't watch, so I close my eyes. When I have my eyes open, there's such a knot in my stomach when she's skating, I could just throw up at every second. I can't breathe through the entire program. I don't see how any parent can handle it. If it's a great program, then I would be sorry I missed it. But if it's not, and if I'm not watching, I come back and I'm not that upset."

Joel Tew: "It's so hard because you can't help, and because there's no second chance."

Deanie Tew: "You know how hard they work and you know how much it means to them."

For parents of young skaters, a decade of indigestion awaits. Carole Yamaguchi and Donna Boitano, the mothers of Olympic gold medalists, guarantee it. Sitting together at a professional competition, they heard the story of the mother hiding out in the bathroom flushing the toilet—and nodded.

"Oh, sure," Yamaguchi said with a smile that confirmed it happened all the time.

She had never done precisely that, hiding in the bathroom, but nerves forced her to leave her seat right before Kristi's long program at the 1991 world championships in Munich. She got halfway up the aisle and stopped.

"You haven't come all the way to Germany not to watch," she told herself.

So Carole Yamaguchi turned around, marched back down the aisle, went into her row, found her seat, and sat down.

Within minutes, her daughter won the world title.

"How awful I would have felt if I had not seen it," Yamaguchi said.

Jan Gardner, the mother of pairs skater Randy Gardner, never could watch her son compete. She hid in the bathroom until he and Tai Babilonia finished their program. She would, however, listen for applause.

Doris Fleming, Peggy's mother, wouldn't sit in the stands. She stood at the side of the rink and peeked every now and then.

Joel Tew met Carol Heiss at a U.S. Figure Skating Association governing-council meeting in Anaheim, California, in May 1990. Tew was there trying to get his local figure-skating club in Clearwater approved for USFSA membership. He and Heiss ended up on the same side of an argument about compulsory school figures; in the wake of their elimination at the top level of the sport, both favored decreasing their importance in the skating tests at the lower levels.

After the meeting, Heiss introduced herself to Tew in the lobby. The following winter, Tew called Heiss and asked for some advice. Jenni's coach in Florida, Frances Duroure, was suggesting that Jenni was good enough to warrant lessons elsewhere. The Tews wanted to send their daughter to a summer skating camp and wondered if Heiss could help them find one. They sent Heiss a videotape of Jenni's skating. After looking at the tape, Heiss had a perfect place for them—her rink.

Jenni, Courtney, and her mother went to Cleveland in the summer of 1991. When fall came and the rink in Florida still was not finished, Jenni and her mother decided to stay in Ohio, while Courtney went back home to live with her father. Jenni was tutored for the semester and mailed her homework back to her elementary school in Florida.

They moved back to Clearwater that winter, but Jenni wasn't happy and her skating got worse. So Deanie and Jenni returned to Ohio the next summer and have stayed ever since. Courtney joined them a year later.

After renting for a year and a half, the Tews decided to buy a town house in late 1993. Before they did, Joel sat Jenni down and asked her to make a decision few little girls confront.

"We need you to be real truthful," Joel told his daughter. "Do you plan to have your skating career here in Cleveland?"

Jenni said she did, and they bought the place.

"Now everybody's happy but me," Joel Tew said.

The Tews had heard all the criticisms of this lifestyle, of asking a girl to decide what she wants to do—to the exclusion of almost everything else—at such an early age. But Jenni said she absolutely adores skating and has since she was four, when she reminded her mother that the local mall would allow four-year-olds to take lessons. At five, she began competing in tiny local events. She couldn't get enough of the sport.

By the age of seven, Jenni was setting her alarm for 4:45 A.M. to practice for three hours before going to school. She woke up at that hour every school day for three years.

"Never, ever, did Jenni say, 'I just don't want to skate this morning,'" her mother said. "We realized this kid just loved it."

The Tews faced a dilemma that the parents of baseball players, football players, basketball players, even many tennis players, did not have to confront. Figure skating at the elite level is taught well at perhaps fifteen to twenty rinks in the country, and only about ten come with the reputation of churning out champions. Figure skating is not easily accessible. It is not inexpensive. It is not part of a school's curriculum, not taught in gym class or on the school grounds. If a parent has a son or daughter who plays basketball, that child can receive useful instruction in thousands of cities and towns across the United States. If a parent has a child who wants to figure-skate, if they want their child to get excellent instruction from a national-caliber skating club, they likely will have to travel to find it.

The most impressive sites and coaches are scattered across the country: Evy and Mary Scotvold on Cape Cod; Peter Burrows and Marylynn Gelderman in Monsey, New York; the University of Delaware and its various coaches; Heiss at Winterhurst; Richard Callaghan in Detroit; Kathy Casey in Colorado Springs; Lake Arrowhead and its various coaches; and John Nicks in Costa Mesa, California. They are the Ivy League of coaches; not the only good ones, but the ones with the best reputations. Judges closely watch skaters from these rinks and expect great things from them.

Jenni Tew and Carol Heiss were a perfect fit. They both were tougher than they looked. Jenni had a refreshing, girl-next-door innocence coating the drive of a head-strong young athlete. She could do a triple toe loop consistently and was furiously working on the triple loop and triple flip. The toe loop is the easiest triple jump; she knew she would need more than that to become a top skater in the country in the next couple years.

"All the time, I think, 'I've got one or two triples now. There are five other than the axel. Am I ever going to get the other ones? Am I ever going to get enough triples to make the Olympics?' " Jenni said.

Like almost all junior skaters, Jenni's triples came and went from one practice to another. Watching a junior skater was not like watching Yamaguchi or Kerrigan; triple jumps can be an adventure for a junior. The jumps are raw and sometimes perilous. A junior skater often lands a jump looking as if she were holding on for dear life. In junior competitions, the girl with the fewest mistakes usually won. Sometimes, they all fell. A certain grittiness was necessary for surviving the junior ranks, and Heiss thought the older child of a driven, successful attorney just might possess that competitive spirit.

"Jenni is stubborn, she won't give up," Heiss said. "I think Joel sees a lot of himself in Jenni. For that matter, I see a lot of myself in Jenni. All you have to do is say to Jenni, 'I bet you can't land the next jump,' and she'll land it."

At five feet four and 105 pounds, she was just the right size to skate. After shooting up six inches in eighteen months, she hadn't grown in a year. Her mother knew all the specifics. She was keeping track in a notebook.

"If she ends up to be five-nine, then she can't do it anymore," Deanie Tew said.

It was that parent trap. All skating parents at times think, plan, and worry too much. It's not that skating drives good people bad. It just drives them crazy.

Joel Tew said he couldn't help wondering how old his daughter would be in 1998—seventeen—and 2002—twenty-one—when he heard the news that the Winter Olympics were switching to alternating years with the Summer Games.

Skating parents around the country analyze everything. Attendance at a figure-skating practice can be as high as at a Little League baseball game. Parents also are known to fall into the first person when discussing their child's participation in the sport: "We" did this, they will say, not "he" or "she." And jumps mean everything—especially other kids' jumps.

"She's got [a] triple flip," a parent will say about a skater who lives a thousand miles away.

They speak in code, figure-skating code. Before their child got into the sport, they wouldn't have known a triple lutz from a flying camel. Now, they not only know their child's jumps and spins, they keep track of rival kids' successes—and failures. When a competitor falls at a critical moment, a quiet "Yes!" might just slip out under their breath.

"I was a college baseball pitcher," Joel Tew said, "I played football in high school, I've tried cases in front of juries—and I've never gotten nearly as nervous doing anything as I do watching her skate. It drives me nuts. You know, we should all take this a little less seriously."

Unlike some parents, the Tews did not take Jenni completely out of school to follow her skating dream. She was enrolled at Rocky River Middle School, where she attended class from 8:15 A.M. to 9:10 A.M. and again from 1 P.M. to 3:15 P.M. In between, she skated for three hours and ate lunch, then skated again from 5 P.M. to 6 P.M. She was tutored two nights a week. She was a straight-A student.

"I know this is a great move, coming up here," Jenni said. "And even though I miss my dad and my friends from the skating rink in Florida, I might not have ever done what I've done if I didn't come here. And I don't know what I'd do if I didn't skate. I'm not really interested in anything else. I would be so bored, I would have nothing to do except go to school all day and come home and do homework and then just sit in front of the TV the rest of the day."

What attracted so many young girls to the sport also attracted Jenni. It's a game of dress-up on the ice: the music, the costumes, the makeup, the hairstyles, the girl stuff. It's a sport that extremely feminine girls adore because they can look pretty, be popular, and spin and jump like their heroines: Yamaguchi, Kerrigan, Jill Trenary. Jenni draws designs of her costumes and sends them to a dressmaker in Colorado. She and her mother pick out her music by listening to hundreds of compact discs at home, timing selections with a stopwatch and taking their choices to be mixed at a studio. For her three-and-a-half-minute long program this year, they decided on classical Boston Pops. For her two-and-a-half-minute short program, they threw together music from *Miss Saigon* and *A League of Their Own*.

"It doesn't sound like either go together, but they're both jazzy," Jenni explained. Her father is convinced Jenni will end up a fashion designer or a choreographer.

Despite the single-minded nature of the sport, the Tews are more than satisfied with the way their daughter is growing up.

"What's a typical childhood? Watching TV—cartoons, MTV—and shopping at the mall with friends? I'll take this over that," her father said.

"What do I really remember of my childhood?" Deanie Tew asked. "Not much."

"People applaud, it makes them feel good," Joel added. "You learn a lot about the world, that it's not always fair."

Other figure-skating parents said they were so concerned about a child getting into drugs, they were willing to go to almost any length to keep them in a disciplined sport like figure skating.

Joel and Deanie Tew said the burden of their skating-imposed separation was greatest on them, not their children. "Although it separates your marriage, you are the adults," Deanie Tew said. "And it's only five or six years, until she's eighteen years old."

Until this season, the Tews' determination to see their skating dream through was severely tested. Jenni broke her right ankle twice within six months from 1992 to 1993. When she came back, she won the regionals at the novice level (a step down from juniors) in late 1993, then went to Midwesterns in Indianapolis.

In the short program, she faltered terribly, popping a single axel, a jump she has been able to do since she was seven. She was eleventh in a field of thirteen and out of the running for one of four spots to Nationals. That night, which happened to be the eve of her thirteenth birthday, Jenni and her mother held on to one another in the bed in their hotel room. When she went to sleep, Jenni pulled the blanket over her head because she didn't want to see her mother sobbing.

"I was literally brokenhearted," Deanie said. "Why did that happen to her over a simple jump that she'd done since she was seven years old? What a terrible birthday for her."

Joel Tew saw it another way. After playing prep football in rural central Florida, he played college baseball at Davidson.

"A lot of days I wonder," he said. "You don't get a second chance in skating. You don't have nine innings or four quarters. If you come to sectionals and mess up, it's your whole year."

• • •

Splitting up a family for skating is not unusual. All the top rinks attract kids who leave one or both parents behind. Constantly getting back together every other week the way the Tews do, however, is rare.

"'Oh, you're back again,' they say. 'How do you come all the time?' It's almost like they try to make me feel guilty that I'm fortunate enough to be able to come back. And I guess I understand it because they're in a situation where maybe they can't," Joel Tew said.

"Everything is questioned," Deanie Tew said. "Everybody minds your business. We bought a dog a few months ago, and I went into the rink the afternoon after I bought it and virtually everybody knew I had bought a dog. I said, 'You people have nothing better to do than sit around talking about dogs?' "

When they first arrived in 1991, the Tews were popular. But the moment Jenni won something—the novice regionals in 1993—things changed.

"It was like walking into a whole different rink," Deanie Tew said. "It was a totally different atmosphere, the gossiping, the stories behind our back. People are always there to say they're sorry when you do badly, but they're never there to say 'Congratulations.' They resent somebody having enough money to be able to afford the sport and to be able to move and take as many lessons as you want, and pretty much do what you want to do, and they resent any success that you have.

"Jenni's first coach in Florida told me that if you want to be popular in the rink, then you have to have no money and not have a talented child," she continued. "Then everybody will love you. But if you have the money to participate in this sport, and God forbid then also have a successful child, they're going to hate you for walking in the door."

"That's probably the most unfortunate part of it, because that takes away from some of the joy," Joel Tew said. "I think you just get hardened and you get calloused, but you just get to the point where you say, 'Well, I really don't care.' We've tried to be nice to everyone, we've tried to be friends with a lot of people. It's just very hard."

"In defense of Nancy Kerrigan, when I hear the comments that are made about her, about how she's abrupt or this or that, I can almost see how that happens," Deanie Tew said. "I can see how you get so hardened that you just don't want to take anything from anybody, and you don't really care what anybody thinks anymore because you had to not care in order to survive."

It's just not worth it to Nancy Gerbrick. Deana's mother would not have minded leaving the sport immediately—and her daughter has been one of the successful ones, making it to Nationals twice and qualifying for Mids this season.

"I would never do this again," Nancy Gerbrick said. "If I had another daughter, knowing what I know now, I wouldn't do it. It's a miserable sport. The people are so cutthroat."

The stories are told throughout the sport: skate blades maliciously scratched and damaged; dresses ripped or cut; skates stolen from the locker room. At every first lesson in every rink in the country, new skaters learn one thing: never let your skate bag out of your sight. Jenni Tew knows this. So does Deana Gerbrick.

Deana was once coached by Heiss, then left for Casey in Colorado, and now was back at Winterhurst, where she was coached not by Heiss but by Sherry Marvin, another respected Cleveland coach. Nancy Gerbrick said she didn't feel at ease inside the rink, that there was tension between Heiss's skaters and the others.

Her own daughter, however, had caused some trouble a week earlier when she kept playing her music in the tape machine. Finally, Marvin walked over and took her skater's tape out so Jenni could have her turn.

"It's just like you see in any of the boys' sports," Marvin said. "They may be wearing rhinestones and they look pretty out there, but it's as tough as anything the boys are doing."

The Tews know the odds are that their daughter will not make it to an Olympics, or even onto a world championship team. There were five hundred skaters at Eastern Great Lakes, and it was very possible none would make an Olympic team. Once every four years, three women and three men (sometimes two, as in 1994), plus pairs and dance teams, represent the United States at the Winter Olympics. Other sports give kids more to hope for. During those four years, on thirty National Football League teams, as many as one hundred and fifty different men might get an opportunity to play quarterback in the NFL, figuring starters and reserves, injuries, and mop-up duty.

The best thing going for the Tews is that money is not a factor. They have enough to spend whatever they need for as long as Jenni skates.

Joel told Deanie that they never should add up the checks they write. Dresses by themselves can cost a fortune: Jenni's short-program outfit was $950; her long-program dress cost $700. If they did add everything, the cost of Jenni's skating, the town house, and all the traveling would be about $50,000 a year, Joel Tew said. They figure they will pay that kind of money for about ten years.

"If I went into this for an investment, that's the most stupid investment I've ever made," Joel Tew said. "I might as well go to Las Vegas and put five hundred thousand dollars down on one number. The odds would be better on that than on this. We don't have any visions of her being the one. I think you'd be setting yourself up for a big disappointment. If we were in it for the money, we'd be spending half a million dollars chasing a rainbow."

They say they do it for other reasons.

"When she does a great program, it's just the greatest feeling in the world," said Deanie Tew.

"I love the thrill of the competition, whether she wins or loses, I just like seeing her out there," said Joel Tew.

But there are strings attached. There is an investment now, one that Jenni herself feels. Could she quit tomorrow if she really wanted to?

"There's no way," she said. "I love it and I've dedicated too much of my life to it to stop now. I mean just to totally stop, I would waste all the work I've put into it and all the money and the dresses and everything. There would be no way."

"It would be heartbreaking because we get so much pleasure out of watching her accomplish what she has done," Deanie Tew said. "But it's always been her decision, and we've always told her that. There's no way you can make her do it."

"We would have to reorganize our life," Joel Tew said. "Our whole life is centered around the skating activities. Of course, ten years ago it wasn't. There was a life before skating and there would be a life after skating. It's the in-between part that's tough."

6

ICE
WARS

At noon on Wednesday, November 9, Nancy Kerrigan, Kristi Yamaguchi, Brian Boitano, and Paul Wylie dashed onto the ice at the darkened, empty Nassau Coliseum on Long Island. This was the Dream Team of American figure skating, the four most decorated U.S. skaters of the past six years. Friends and colleagues for more than a decade, they were practicing for that evening's live, made-for-TV competition on CBS, known as "Ice Wars."

As they sped around the ice, stopping to chat with their coaches and talking with one another, they couldn't help feeling like the luckiest people on earth. Here they were, together for the first time on the same ice since the 1988 U.S. national championships, when money was first trickling into the amateur side of the sport. Back then, they could make a few thousand dollars a year skating in ice shows. Now they all were millionaires. Between them, they had two Olympic gold medals, two silvers, and one bronze. They all knew skaters who had put in just as many hours and paid just as much money and had come up empty-handed. But not them. They were the lucky ones.

By 12:45 P.M., the happy scene was shattered. Kerrigan was leaning against the boards, calling for Stan Feig, who, with Mike Burg, was producing the event. She was furious. *Entertainment Tonight*'s camera crew was filming her and she didn't like it. Unless the crew stopped, Kerrigan was ready to quit and walk out immediately. If she left, CBS, Feig, and Burg would be without their biggest draw just seven hours before their live, prime-time event.

Quickly, Feig met with CBS's public relations officials, who reluctantly agreed to tell the *ET* crew that they could film and interview just the other three U.S. skaters. Do not film Nancy, they said. Kerrigan was so important to them, they would give in to her wishes, even if it meant losing coveted publicity for their event on *ET*'s show that night.

Entertainment Tonight was interested in Kerrigan because she was in the news. Two days earlier, the show repeated what the *National Enquirer* was reporting, in bold headlines: "Nancy Kerrigan Shares Love Nest With Married Man." The married man was her agent of two-and-a-half-years, Jerry Solomon, although Solomon said the relationship started six months after he separated from his wife. This was not good news for Kerrigan. The tabloid that once had given the world a play-by-play of Tonya Harding's life had moved on to hers.

"Ice Wars" was devised for Nancy Kerrigan, built around her, and totally subservient to her. The brainchild of Burg and Feig, a San Francisco–based event promoter, it was originally supposed to be a reprise of the Olympic battle between Kerrigan and Oksana Baiul. But Kerrigan didn't want to go through that again. So Burg and Feig made it a team concept: the USA vs. the World, i.e., Baiul, Katarina Witt, Viktor Petrenko, and Kurt Browning.

But that didn't completely satisfy Kerrigan. She didn't want to be judged individually, so Burg and Feig acquiesed again and agreed to combine the scores of the two men and two women on each side. Kerrigan's score would become part of a Kerrigan-Yamaguchi team score.

Kerrigan received $300,000, more than any other competitor, as an appearance fee. Everyone else either got money up front, prize money, or both. Every member of the winning team was guaranteed at least $100,000.

The event was as legitimate as a professional, made-for-TV skating competition could be. It wasn't sanctioned by the U.S. Figure Skating Association, so coaches like Richard Callaghan and Carlo Fassi were the judges. But it wasn't a joke; some of the competitors were trying programs that were technically quite difficult. "Ice Wars" covered two nights and two arenas—first Nassau Coliseum on Wednesday, followed by Providence's Civic Center on Saturday—and used spotlights the second night, which cheapened it considerably, making it look like just another ice show. In fact, a public relations man slipped several times and called it exactly that: "the show."

Yamaguchi and Boitano, friends for a decade from the Bay Area, used to laugh at competitions that used spotlights. "Now here we are doing them," Boitano said. "When you're in a competitive atmosphere, you want it to be competitive. It didn't make sense to use spotlights."

Perhaps they did it so Kerrigan and Baiul, the two headliners, could hide in the dark. Burg boasted that the event was like the Ryder Cup in golf, but it was more like a skins game, a skins game in which Jack Nicklaus and Arnold Palmer couldn't make a putt.

Given everything she asked for, the red-carpet, kid-glove treatment, Kerrigan was an embarrassment, and Baiul, still wobbly on her injured knee, was, too. Both were far below their Olympic standards. Kerrigan turned in two terrible performances, managing only one triple jump and one double axel in both programs combined. She couldn't remember the last time she had been so bad. The junior ladies at the regional in suburban Cleveland did more than she did. Watching and biting their nails, Yamaguchi and Boitano, who had turned in their usual top-notch performances, could not believe that Kerrigan was jumping so poorly. Team USA ended up winning, but Kerrigan, like Baiul, knew she had utterly failed to keep up her end of the bargain.

Poor Nancy Kerrigan. She never wanted any of this. She never wanted this kind of pressure. She didn't get into skating to make this much money or have to do so many TV interviews. She never thought about the money until other people started thinking about it. She was a Boston tomboy with short hair and a couple of brothers who played hockey. Her welder father and blind mother were barely making ends meet. She liked to skate and she liked to jump. Lucky for her, they got rid of the compulsory school figures just as she was ascending to seniors, so jumping was in vogue. Then, Mary Scotvold, one of her coaches, suggested she grow her hair long. Scotvold made Kerrigan elegant. Her hair went up into a bun. They put her in beautiful Vera Wang dresses. They bonded her teeth. They gave her a spiral—the beautiful move with one leg up in the air and a hand over her heart—and the media gave her a nickname, the Irish Katarina.

But they could never give her heart. She always choked in major competitions. Then she got whacked on the knee and she suddenly really, really cared. Funny, wasn't it? Tonya Harding and her thugs finally provided the one missing piece of the Nancy Kerrigan puzzle. They gave Kerrigan heart. They gave her the desire to fight.

But they also made her famous, and for that she despises them. Because she won the bronze medal at the 1992 Winter Olympics and because she had that all-American look, Kerrigan already had made what many would consider to be a fortune before she was clubbed on the knee on January 6, 1994. She signed half a dozen endorsement deals after the 1992 Olympics with companies like Campbell's Soups,

Seiko, Reebok, and Northwest Airlines—and Solomon already was working on a $2-million deal with Disney heading into 1994. This all happened before she was attacked. Kerrigan was extremely marketable because she was the only women's Olympic figure-skating medalist from 1992 returning for 1994, because she was pretty, and because she was America's best hope for a gold medal in figure skating.

Kerrigan had enough money to live on for a long, long time. It's obvious, then, that while many thought the Tonya-Nancy saga was the best thing to happen to her, Kerrigan strongly disagrees:

"Are you kidding? I never would have wanted the attack to happen. I know I don't have to worry the way my parents did when you get the phone bill and you're like, 'Oh, no, how do I pay it?' but I still don't understand all of this. I still do the same thing I always did. I go to Marshall's like everybody I know. I'm just like this kid from Stoneham, just like anybody else."

Left to her own devices, Kerrigan, twenty-five, probably would be married with a couple kids. She would skate in ice shows because she likes to perform, but she never would allow herself to be judged again. She would live near her parents so she could go over in the morning and do her mother's makeup and hair and read the newspaper to her.

It's a pleasant—if unfulfilled—scenario.

"That sounds nice," Kerrigan said.

"Nancy is a very familial person," Wylie said, "fiercely loyal to her parents. No matter what they say goes. I always said that you could never talk to her before noon or after she talked to her mother. But I love Nancy for the fact that she's a small-town girl who takes care of her mother."

That, however, is not the life Nancy Kerrigan has. Not even close. There are the professional competitions, the Disney TV specials, and the springtime tour of the United States that pays her $1 million for seventy-six performances in one hundred days. There are the appearances and the dreaded news conferences. Stoneham is a dot on the horizon many months of the year.

Kerrigan is not in control of her life. It's as if she fell into a river, was picked up in a swift current, and carried far, far from where she ever thought she'd be. The attack did it; it stole her anonymity. She enjoyed going to hockey games and speed-skating events at the 1992 Olympics, befriending Dan Jansen and Bonnie Blair, being just another American Olympian. Prior to the attack in Detroit at the 1994 national championships, she rode the skaters' shuttle bus to late-night practices, jumping in with all the teenagers. Solomon was shocked to find this out, telling her that someone like Ivan Lendl, the tennis pro he used to represent, would never do such a thing. Lendl would have a limo, a taxi, something special.

But Kerrigan liked being one of the gang. Her friends say she has been happiest around other skaters, just mixing in. She was always the one to bring the "Good luck" greeting card to the rink when another skater was heading off to a competition. She hated being singled out and grew nervous when cameras approached. At the height of the Tonya-Nancy saga at the Olympics, she and her parents told reporters they should stop talking to them and go interview other, more deserving athletes. It wasn't contrived. They really meant that.

But Kerrigan's image was another matter entirely. That look on the ice—that was a big seller. Solomon would have been crazy not to see it. All you had to do was look at that beauty on skates, so mature and exquisite and tall and untouchable. *She must be five feet ten!* No one would ever have to know that behind the camera, backstage, she was slight and meek at five feet four, uncertain and insecure, a deer caught in the headlights. And when an outsider threateningly entered that world—a camera crew, a reporter—she immediately covered up the only way she knew, with the unpolished feistiness she had learned growing up in blue-collar Boston.

A tug-of-war was going on inside Kerrigan. She knew she was the tomboy from Stoneham. But everyone said she could be so much more. Kerrigan went along. Who was she to put her foot down? She didn't know. How could she know? She was just a skater who happened to get lucky, lucky to have been born in 1969 and be the right age for two Olympic Games in two years in the 1990s, lucky to be a jumper when jumping was everything, lucky to have two of the finest coaches in the sport in the husband and wife team of Evy and Mary Scotvold, who also found sponsors to pay for all her skating expenses as she reached the top. She was just in the right place at the right time. Who could blame her for that?

In the summer of 1992, Paul Wylie, Kerrigan's best friend in skating for many years, shared a house with her on Cape Cod. They trained down the road at the Tony Kent Arena. They talked a lot, fought over the TV set (Wylie wanted to watch the Democratic convention, Kerrigan wanted *Beverly Hills, 90210*), and compared dreams.

"What do you want to do?" Wylie recalled asking Kerrigan over breakfast one morning.

"I don't want to skate forever," Kerrigan said. "I don't want to tour. I just want to do two or three more years and then I'm done."

Wylie shook his head and kept his thoughts to himself: *Then what are you doing this for? If you don't really want to go into it, why do this?*

Over the past few years, Wylie thinks he found his answer:

"It was much more for the status than for the money, needing seven or eight or ten or twelve endorsement contracts to say, 'Look, I am great. I *am* great. Look how great I am.' When you talk to Nancy, she will tell you what she's doing. It's just part of her. She needs to tell everyone what she's doing so that they affirm her. Then you have to affirm her, then she's okay. It's like, 'I affirm you, Nancy. You are great. I don't think you're not great.' But I think there's something in there that says, 'I'm not great.' "

It was the same way with her teeth. The previous summer, she had had her teeth fixed. The very next day, she saw Wylie and started crying.

"She kept saying, 'I don't understand why I had to do this,' " Wylie remembered. "It's the struggle between the small-town Stoneham, Massachusetts, girl who just wanted to have a family and the world-class skater.

"Money has never really been a factor to Nancy," Wylie said. "Her quote is, 'How much can you really spend?' "

On the ice, in competitions, Kerrigan never was quite tough enough. In 1991, after a steady rise through the novice, junior, and senior ranks, Kerrigan finished third at the national championships and headed to the world championships in Munich. With both Kristi Yamaguchi and Tonya Harding ranked ahead of her, with no expectations, Kerrigan made some mistakes but finished third behind her U.S. teammates.

The next year, at the Olympic trials, she finished second to Yamaguchi as Harding fell to third. Kerrigan went to Albertville as a bit player. Yamaguchi, her roommate and friend, was locked in the battle with Japan's Midori Ito for the gold medal. There was so little interest in Kerrigan that the USFSA's Kristin Matta nudged several reporters and asked if they would please ask Kerrigan a few questions so she wouldn't feel left out.

With next to no one paying attention to her, Kerrigan won the bronze medal. Yamaguchi turned professional, leaving Kerrigan alone at the top of U.S. skating. In 1993, Kerrigan won her first and only national title, skating well in the short program, as always, but making mistakes on several jumps in the long. As always, U.S. judges and other skating officials started to wonder if Kerrigan had the inner drive to ever put it together in both a short and long program. They looked at her on the ice, so powerful, with an elegant, beautiful line, the classic American-style skater, but they still wondered. What made Kerrigan tick? Did she feel what she was skating? Or was she just out there, going through the motions she had been taught, just moving her blades across the ice?

Still, there was no one else good enough to beat her. U.S. women's skating in 1993, and probably in 1994, would live and die with Nancy Kerrigan.

She went to the 1993 worlds in Prague, where she took the lead in the short program, her forte because it required technical skill and jumping ability. But in the long program, she fell apart.

"She went out and flopped around like a dying walrus," Evy Scotvold said. She dropped from first to fifth, a crushing performance not only for Kerrigan personally, but also for the U.S. team as a whole. She needed to be in the top three to help qualify three American women for the 1994 Olympic Games. When she didn't win a medal, the United States lost an Olympic spot.

"I want to die," Kerrigan blurted out in Kiss and Cry, the area where skaters sit beside their coach and watch their marks come up. Kerrigan was shocked by how poorly she had skated.

Evy Scotvold said the problem had been her training schedule: "She was gone every week. She took a trip out of town every week to make an appearance or do something. . . . [Kerrigan and Solomon] treated the worlds in 1993 like she was going to a coronation."

In reply, Solomon said, "Everything was scheduled with [Scotvold's] knowledge and consent."

But her friends wondered.

"Had it not been for a way-too-hectic '93, she would have easily won worlds," Wylie said. "She just didn't train enough. She was here and there, doing one thing or the other."

After Prague, the Scotvolds, Kerrigan, and Solomon decided they weren't going to let that happen again.

"It cost her and she saw it right away and Jerry saw it right away," Scotvold said. "And so, she went to work. She fought very hard all year. She trained like no woman I've ever seen train."

Kerrigan and Evy Scotvold are two stubborn people. They once got into an argument and Scotvold threw her out of the rink as all sorts of equipment rained onto the ice, courtesy of Scotvold.

Banished from her lessons, Kerrigan called Scotvold a few days later.

"The public skating's getting a little old now," she said. "I'd like to come back and train on the ice."

Scotvold allowed her back, but still refused to teach her. His wife, Mary, was her only coach until Evy cooled down.

"Nancy can be a real bitch," Scotvold said. "Oh, absolutely. She's no saint. She can be really fun and a terrific kid. She can be rude and snippy, and when she's done it to me, I've thrown her out of the rink and not taught her for weeks on end. She can give me some lip, be disrespectful, she can do that."

"Evy does a lot of negative reinforcement kind of teaching, but that's what he learned from his dad, a pro hockey player," Kerrigan said. "He'll say, 'Pretty good for a girl.' Or, 'You can't do that.'

"'Yes, I can,' I'll say. 'Watch this.' "

Kerrigan said that sometimes this coaching philosophy worked. Other times, it drove her crazy.

"You're right, I can't," Kerrigan would tell herself. "It snowballs in my head. I stink. I can't do this."

Kerrigan and Scotvold sat down again. She asked him to not be so negative. They got along much better heading into the 1994 Olympics.

After the 1993 worlds, a Boston radio station teased Kerrigan unmercifully about her dreadful performance. "I knew the guy at the station," Wylie said. "I told him, 'Don't joke around with skaters about falling. Falling is traumatic. Falling means losing in a lot of ways.' "

Kerrigan's mistrust of the media was born. Her one-word answers, her scrunched nose, her furrowed brow: reporters who wanted to pick on her had a field day. Some began to dislike her; with Kerrigan, the feeling was mutual.

The ice became the only safe place. Every morning, as they started practice by skating around the rink together, Kerrigan had some kind of story to tell Wylie. "Usually about someone she was dating," he said.

"There's a lot to like about Nancy," Wylie said. "She's very fun to be with, very laughy and kind of giggly, a fun person when she feels comfortable."

Kerrigan headed into the 1994 Olympic trials in the best shape of her life, doing triple run-throughs of her programs in practice. Prague was her motivation, she and Scotvold said at a news conference at Nationals—the trials—in Detroit on January 5.

Kerrigan was hit on the right knee after an afternoon practice the next day. Once the shock wore off and the swelling went down, Kerrigan almost immediately honed in with that same determination. Although she couldn't compete in Detroit, it was a foregone conclusion she would be placed on the Olympic team, and she and her coaches returned to the goal that they had had the day before: winning the gold medal.

From January 6 through the end of the Olympic competition on February 25, Kerrigan and Solomon and the Scotvolds conducted themselves with dignity in the maelstrom of an unprecedented athletic chaos. Every button they pushed was the right one. They were classy and kind, indignant when it was required, masterful throughout. It was as though no matter how bizarre the story got, they were standing on top of the whole mess, looking down on it, in control of it all.

The day after the attack, Kerrigan came to the media interview room, sat down, and calmly answered questions. Never one to feel at home in front of reporters, Kerrigan was outwardly measured—and, inside, fighting mad. It was a notable performance, considering the only other story of its kind was the stabbing of Monica Seles. While a knife in the back and a whack on the knee are two entirely different traumas, the way the Kerrigan camp handled this—putting Nancy back out in public the next day—was in direct contrast to what had become of Seles, who had been in isolation for eight months at that time.

They brought Kerrigan back again a day later when she had been voted onto the Olympic team. As she sat down at a table on a small platform in front of reporters, she pumped her fist and whooped out loud, as if she were in Arsenio Hall's audience. Those in the media who had been around the sport for a handful of years had never seen Kerrigan act this way. *Nancy Kerrigan was showing emotion. She actually seemed to care.*

A week later, her first official practice session was scheduled for a Monday morning at her hometown rink. A dozen reporters from around the country were invited. Kerrigan scooped them all. Getting antsy, she sneaked out of her family's home well past midnight Saturday night to practice on her own.

At her parents' house, where she was staying, the mail overflowed. The phone rang with good wishes. Seles called Kerrigan at home after the attack to wish her good luck at the Olympics. Kerrigan knew how Seles felt. This was not easy. Kerrigan was jumpy. She went to Los Angeles for a photo shoot not long after the attack and noticed the balcony doors in her hotel room were open.

"I was freaked out," she said. "I got so nervous. I looked out and saw that anyone could easily go from balcony to balcony in that hotel."

It turned out the maid had left the doors open.

As the controversy grew over Tonya Harding's alleged involvement in the plot to injure Kerrigan, she and Solomon didn't waver. Kerrigan became the perfect sportswoman. She held a news conference in her front yard as snow fell on her hair. She never said a bad word about Harding, even as Harding was proclaiming from Portland, Oregon, that she would "kick her butt" at the Olympics. Back inside her parents' home, she read details of the attackers' twisted ideas to her mother at the breakfast table, and they laughed out loud. If they weren't planning to cut her Achilles tendon, they were going to tie her up with duct tape. Kerrigan said she loved mysteries and barely could wait to see how this one ended.

Her newfound toughness continued in Norway. Kerrigan was at first furious that Harding was being allowed to come to the Games, that she would room in the same Olympic village dormitory and share the same practice sessions. But Kerrigan soon turned her anger into psychological warfare with Harding.

The day of their first practice session together, Kerrigan purposely put on her white lace dress, the one she wore the day of the attack, the one seen over and over again in the "Why me?" videotape, as an attempt to psyche out Harding.

"She wanted to make a statement: 'I'm here, I'm in the same outfit,' " Evy Scotvold said. "Nancy likes to tease a little. She wants to have fun."

When U.S. reporters ended up with a copy of a London tabloid showing topless photos of Harding, someone made sure Kerrigan saw the article.

When Harding's practices continued to be awful, when she would fall and stop skating and pout and leave early, a reporter said to Solomon, "Even her worst enemy wouldn't wish this on her."

Solomon smiled mischievously. "I wouldn't be so sure about that."

As ready as any athlete had been for an Olympic competition, Kerrigan skated perfectly in the short program and was in first place. Harding was tenth. Kerrigan had unequivocally slam-dunked Harding. She was history. Now it was just Kerrigan and Baiul, first and second, for the gold medal.

When Kerrigan finished skating in the long program on February 25, she and the Scotvolds thought she had won. Solomon, jammed into an aisle in the press section, asked reporters what they thought. Kerrigan had been in the lead after the short program and had performed five triples in a masterful long program. It looked good, they told him, but her technical marks were a bit low. Still, they were good enough to win, unless Baiul was perfect.

When Baiul came out and two-footed the landing of her second triple jump, a reporter leaned over to Solomon.

"That's it. Nancy's got the gold."

When the marks came up on the television monitors in press row, with the placements, and Solomon counted five 1s for Baiul, he was shocked.

So was Evy Scotvold.

"We were sure she had won the gold," Scotvold said. "We were absolutely positive. When we saw the scores, we were just heartbroken, so deflated, just couldn't believe it."

Backstage, Kerrigan was stunned. She had skated the performance of her life and she had lost. It wasn't fair, she said to herself. It just wasn't fair. All she went through—and now this?

"Chin up," Scotvold said to Kerrigan. "Come on, you were great, the judges sucked."

At that moment, though, Kerrigan couldn't hide her feelings. And right then, her emotions began to unravel.

"The media said, 'Oh my God, she is too good to be true—and she was for that eight-week period,' " Solomon said. "I look back on it and she literally went into a zone where most people don't ever go, and mentally she just dealt with everything. And right after that, I think she let down, naturally, which is to be expected, and nobody gave her an hour to breathe and—boom—they were right on top of her. There was a need, for whatever reason, to tear her down. And so they did."

But Solomon and Kerrigan helped them do it.

The problems began for Kerrigan in the arena when she commented about Baiul's makeup during a nearly half-hour delay before the medal ceremony. But that wasn't their first mistake. On television back in the United States, twelve minutes after she skated, came the first blunder. It was Kerrigan's Disney World commercial.

All but forgotten in the ensuing chaos, that commercial represented much of what Americans do not like about the selling of athletes. It was well choreographed, too much so. Unlike the Super Bowl commercials in which the star player screamed out that he was going to Disney World as he walked off the field, Kerrigan's commercial was filmed three weeks earlier in her rink in Stoneham.

She couldn't have filmed a commercial after she skated in Norway; Olympic rules prevented it. But by doing the Disney commercial the way she did, Kerrigan could not capture the charm of the Disney Super Bowl commercials. Those spots emphasized the randomness of fame; when the game began four hours earlier, the star of the commercial had little idea he would be the one in the TV lights. The commercial also appeared a day or two later, not the night of the game.

Kerrigan's commercial aired close to the finish of her competition. Agents who represent Olympians get anxious as the Games come to a close. They believe they better get whatever they can quickly, because an Olympian's shelflife is usually not very long. That's why Kerrigan was on the air skating with Mickey Mouse even before CBS had signed off for the eleven-o'clock news on the East Coast.

Back in the arena, it was easy to sympathize with Kerrigan's discomfort after the competition. She thought she had won, as did many skating experts, and she did not. In her mind, she was robbed.

Meanwhile, many members of the media had little idea of what kind of person Kerrigan was. The stereotyping going on by all the Johnny-come-latelies to figure skating—that is to say, all but about two dozen members of the press corps—was wrong. They looked at the hair, the dresses, the teeth, and they thought they knew Kerrigan. Kerrigan was supposed to be the beautiful lady; Harding, the tough broad.

Kerrigan was pretty, yes, but she was no sweetheart.

After the Olympic long program, Kerrigan; Chen Lu, the bronze medalist from China; and Mary Scotvold stood beside Kiss and Cry. There was a delay; they had no idea why. They didn't know that the Ukrainian anthem could not be found. All they knew was that Oksana Baiul was not with them. Kerrigan finally asked, and someone erroneously told her Baiul was touching up her makeup.

Wanting to get on with the medal ceremony, Kerrigan made a snide remark that Baiul need not worry about putting on makeup because she would only cry again anyway. It was not the worst thing ever said backstage at a skating event. It most likely wasn't the worst thing said *that night*. Kerrigan didn't swear, she didn't gesture obscenely, she didn't spit on a spectator, all of which had happened within months at professional sporting events in America. She said something she should not have said, or at least not within range of a camera and microphone near Kiss and Cry, where all skaters and coaches know they can be both seen and heard.

Kerrigan's luck with television, as she was going to learn, was awful. A camera and microphone nearby picked up what she said. It wasn't CBS's equipment; it was the world feed, available to all international rights-holders.

When the clip came to CBS's attention, Rick Gentile, the executive producer, had an easy decision to make: "It happened. We didn't eavesdrop. It wasn't even our camera. We didn't think it made her look bad. At the time, it was part of the story and we put it in."

Gentile said if Kerrigan had spoken in a private area, where only a CBS camera or microphone picked it up, he would not have used it. But this was different.

"I have no second thoughts at all," he said.

CBS's decision, as maddening as it was to Kerrigan, was journalistically correct. Had the network not used the sound bite, certainly someone else around the world would have. Eventually, it would have been picked up and shown in the United States. And TV critics would have been all over Gentile, asking him why he had not included it in the Olympic telecast.

The growing outrage over the comment took everyone in Kerrigan's camp by surprise. Other skaters who were told of the comment didn't give it a second thought. Many laughed at it. They heard things like that every day in the rink.

Like almost everyone else still in Norway, Solomon said he had no idea how the comment was playing back home. Only in the United States was this an issue, only because it had aired on CBS.

The magnitude of the controversy showed that Kerrigan, like quite a few respected Olympic athletes—and many female athletes—was being held to a much higher standard than an average professional athlete. Harding, ironically, was given more leeway by Americans because there were no expectations of her. But Kerrigan had been made out to be something better. She was America's ice princess. When she showed a nasty human side, Americans were surprised.

Jealousy? Anger? Nancy, you, too?

"You see these girls who are wearing these great-looking outfits and they're for the most part good-looking girls and they're skating to great music and it can be a little sexy, and I think the general public forgets that it's a sport," Solomon said. "And so, when you have a really intense competitor who doesn't like losing, it's incongruous with this sport, it does not fit. I think it's somewhat sexist. If Elvis Stojko, who has a macho image, loses by one-tenth of a point in his next competition and he kicks the sideboards, the people within the pristine sport might not like that, but for the most part people would say, 'Okay, he's venting.' But the female can't get away with that."

Because of the contrasts made between Kerrigan and Harding, Americans had put Kerrigan on a ridiculously high pedestal. She benefited greatly from the image of the fallen figure skater, so graceful and innocent. But when she came crashing off her pedestal so suddenly, Americans began to see that their heroine, unscripted, was not exactly what they thought she was.

"Some people didn't like the fact that Nancy was being set up as the media hero and sweetheart, because they felt that was not what she was," Wylie said. "And indeed, she was kind of miscast in a way. But then, somebody who goes out there after six or seven weeks and has the guts to pull it off and skate like she did is not going to be weak."

There also was the matter of whom she was gossiping about. It was tiny Oksana Baiul, the fragile Ukrainian orphan. Americans immediately fell in love with Baiul; how dare Kerrigan say something bad about *her*?

Kerrigan's timing and luck were just horrid. She could have picked on anyone else and gotten away with it. Anyone but the magical Baiul.

Kerrigan didn't get one benefit of the doubt. So much was made of her comment about Baiul that no one remembers her charming efforts to locate her parents after the long program, searching the stands with her eyes as she came off the ice. When U.S. hockey goaltender Jim Craig searched the stands for his father at the 1980 Olympics, it became the stuff of legend. But, with Kerrigan, no one noticed.

There is a false notion that all American athletes travel to the Olympics and travel home together, just as in the old days when the team went to European Olympic Games on an ocean liner. Fans watching at home are under the illusion that all the athletes go to the opening ceremonies and they all go to the closing ceremonies, en masse. The fact is that many top athletes miss either ceremony—or both.

Nancy Kerrigan did not go to the closing ceremonies in Norway because she was on her way home to the United States on the Concorde. Brian Boitano didn't go to the closing ceremonies either. He was sitting at home in San Francisco. Dozens of athletes and coaches at the Winter and Summer Games, especially high-paid American stars in basketball, track and field, and figure skating, do not attend the ceremonies. They come and they go from the Olympics, either for the convenience of their schedules or because they simply don't want to be mobbed by autograph seekers.

In Norway, Kerrigan did not attend either the opening or closing ceremonies, in part because of security concerns. She was in Norway for the opening ceremonies but watched them on TV; at the closing ceremonies, she was told there would be a security risk, according to Evy Scotvold and Solomon. Solomon also wanted her to get back to the States, fly directly to Orlando, and appear in a Disney World parade that was scheduled for Monday, he said, the day after the closing ceremonies.

But when Solomon stepped off the Concorde in New York on Sunday and called his Disney contacts, he was told they wanted the parade to be that day.

"I get off the plane and I'm exhausted, and the Disney people are pretty good promoters and they're not going to make a huge mistake, so I put faith in them," Solomon said.

So Kerrigan and her family flew to Orlando, got on a float, and found themselves in the midst of a parade at Disney World as part of her big commercial deal with the company.

If she had sat in a hotel room on Sunday or gone home to Boston or even been in her Olympic dorm room in Norway, no one would have missed her at the closing ceremonies, or if they had, there would have been an easy excuse. But when Kerrigan popped up that same day at another event on another continent, it was a public relations nightmare.

Worse yet, Kerrigan opened her mouth again. Obviously unprepared for the changing rules in her life, for the pitfalls of saying offhand remarks near those omnipresent open microphones, Kerrigan stood next to Mickey Mouse and uttered the immortal words, "This is the corniest thing I have ever done."

Her family and friends said she was complaining to her mother, telling her she did not want to wear her Olympic silver medal in public. She later said the same thing. But, by then, it didn't matter. Another sound bite, another disaster.

Months later, Solomon said, "I think, retrospectively, if we had moved [the parade] a day [to Monday], it would have been better. She would have been a little more rested."

Another week later, Kerrigan hosted *Saturday Night Live.* The show is a challenge for seasoned actors; for Kerrigan, it was a cuecard nightmare. Her friends were embarrassed for her.

"After seven weeks of pressure, she needed to go to an island, be deprogrammed, debriefed," Wylie said. "What happened was she wasn't allowed to come down off of that, she wasn't allowed to normalize after that, she wasn't allowed to feel good about herself, or anybody else. In fact, she was under more and more pressure. *Saturday Night Live,* Disney, missing closing ceremonies, all of a sudden, her image had spun out of control because CBS had used a bad quote. Then she's on *Saturday Night Live,* and she's destined to not have the kind of presence that even most people struggle with. That's terribly, terribly, terribly difficult.

"At that point, I have to say Jerry Solomon should know these things or should take care of his client more for the long-term as opposed to feeling they have to [do these things]. They say 'have to' way too much. She's too big a star to 'have to,' at that point," Wylie said.

"On all of these things, it's very easy in hindsight to say I should have done this or that," Solomon said. "A group of us, about fifteen people, including Nancy's family, were undergoing an absolutely grueling eight-week period of time. It wasn't easy."

Kerrigan was in desperate need of a spin doctor. In the forty-year-old Solomon, however, she had an agent who was about to become her boyfriend. "We were spending tons of time together, and over time, that just sort of evolved," Solomon said.

They started dating in the spring of 1994, he said. "Everybody was speculating that this was all going on at the Olympics, and I think that was an unfair thing. With what she was going through, and the role that an agent can and oftentimes does play, we were together all the time, and that got fabricated into this big romance, which was not happening. . . . I probably spent as much time with Ivan Lendl at various times as I did with Nancy, and yet people weren't running around saying that we were having some kind of thing going on."

Kerrigan's shattered image would have been whole had she won the gold medal. She would have been happy, the U.S. anthem would have been readily available (no waiting, no remarks about makeup), and she would have been on top of the world. That one-tenth of a point made all the difference. She is obsessed by it. The skaters taped a rock-and-roll skating special in the fall, a silly event in which MTV personality Downtown Julie Brown was a judge and actually danced on the judges' table. It was shown to historic Fox ratings on a Tuesday night in January. A camera caught Kerrigan stalking off. She was furious. She had lost to Baiul by one-tenth of a point. Again.

"She feels like it has happened several times to her, where she was the best skater and not won," Solomon said.

"I don't want to put myself in the hands of the judges again," she told Solomon.

A profound bitterness prevents Kerrigan from being happy—really happy—around skating. Family and friends still talk about how she was robbed of the gold medal, how she was decimated in the media, how it all wasn't fair.

"Nobody around her was able to tone it down," Wylie said. "Everybody was merely fueling it."

Kerrigan began to deal with her frustrations in unusual ways. At an after-dinner party honoring Winter Olympic athletes at the Washington Hilton in April 1994, she walked up to Neal Pilson, who had been in charge of CBS Sports during the Olympics, and blurted out, "With all I've done for your network, I can't believe you aired the comment from Kiss and Cry. That was a cheap shot."

As Kerrigan walked away, she turned to someone she barely knew. "Do you think it was okay I did that? I think I'm going to do more of that. From now on, I'm going to tell people what I think."

Her insecurity can be overwhelming. When Kerrigan is with other skaters at professional events, they are amazed that one positive comment can turn her head and make her feel extremely good about herself. At a professional event, she was repeatedly practicing a triple jump and was close to landing it when someone mentioned how well she was jumping.

"Yeah," Kerrigan responded with a surprised look. "You're right!"

But mention Tonya Harding, and the uncertainty vanishes. It's like the bell ringing for Pavlov's dogs. The thought of Tonya Harding becoming a counterculture martyr quietly enrages Kerrigan.

"I can't believe that I'll always be linked to her: Tonya and Nancy, Tonya and Nancy," Kerrigan said. "I read where people list the problems in sports, the strikes, O. J. Simpson, Tonya and Nancy. How do I get mentioned like that? I was the one who was hurt. I understand people saying, 'There's no way her knee was as bad as she said.' But my knee was blown up like a balloon. I was real close to having my kneecap shattered."

"Nancy's greatest disappointment in the Olympics will not be that she didn't win, but this link with Tonya, forever," Solomon said.

If she could get beyond Tonya, the entire fiasco, and the narrow loss to Baiul, if the media and the memories would allow such a thing, Kerrigan could have such a different outlook.

"Never in sports has there been as much focus for four minutes on anything as there was for Nancy Kerrigan," said Harvey Schiller, who was executive director of the U.S. Olympic Committee in 1994. "She couldn't run away. She couldn't hide. Several billion people watched her. Think about the application of technology. Give Jesse Owens all his due, one of the greatest athletes who ever lived. He did not have a camera in his face. Every muscle on her face, every emotion, every grin, every movement, was watched by every possible angle by the whole world. The press was prepared to write that she fell. The press was prepared to write that she didn't take the ice. And that kid got out there and did it."

"We all know what she did," said Gale Tanger, the U.S. skating judge who was team leader at the Norway Olympics. "What an honor to this country to overcome what she did. I'll never forget that, and nobody will ever forget that. Victory is not necessarily a gold medal."

7

TEENAGED
GIRLS;
BIG-TIME
AGENTS

Frank Carroll was giving Heather Linhart an animated lecture as they walked together from the Hyatt Hotel to the silver-tiled, igloo-shaped Civic Arena in Pittsburgh one bright fall morning. Carroll normally was refined and quiet, a proper fifty-six-year-old bachelor who is revered by younger coaches and former pupils. Occasionally as a coach, he got angry with his skaters. But Linhart wasn't one of his students. She worked in the public relations department of the U.S. Figure Skating Association. Carroll was not at all pleased with the association at that moment, and she was its closest representative, so she heard all about it.

His reservation in the Hyatt, the skaters' hotel, had been lost and he had had to spend the night at another hotel. Then, he said, he had not been told about the press conference for his star pupil, Michelle Kwan, a press conference they were walking to at that moment. Particularly galling was the fact that he said he never received a practice schedule for this event, known as Skate America, one of the very few eligible events on the calendar and one to which only the top few Americans in the Olympic division were invited.

The schedule went to Kwan's agent, Shep Goldberg. On the flight from California, Carroll told Danny Kwan he didn't have a schedule. Kwan pulled it out and handed it to Carroll.

"Where did you get that?" Carroll asked.

"From Shep."

"What do you mean Shep got the practice schedule?" Carroll screamed. "Remember me? How dare the USFSA ship out to the agent a practice schedule when it's my kid."

Agents! They were swarming around figure skating these days like moths to a lightbulb, making the sport look dangerously like women's tennis. In previous decades, men like Michael Rosenberg in Palm Springs, California, or Dick Button, or International Management Group, took Olympians like Dorothy Hamill and Janet Lynn and Tai Babilonia and Randy Gardner and helped them set up fabulous professional careers. Now a whole new group of agents—a tennis agent like Jerry Solomon, a promoter like Mike Burg, an ex–public relations man like Goldberg—were getting in on the ground floor. Solomon had signed Nancy Kerrigan when she was twenty-two. Kwan's signing at thirteen was the real eye-opener. Some in skating wondered why she still wasn't an anonymous junior, somewhere down on the farm, slowly working her way up. But she had the triple jumps, and few skaters with the requisite jumps waited anymore. The Kwans were in a hurry, and so was the sport's Shirley Temple, twelve-year-old Tara Lipinski. That's who Burg was going after.

These developments sent shock waves through the staid skating community.

"Why do you have to have an agent if you're staying an eligible [Olympic-division] skater?" asked Carole Yamaguchi, whose daughter Kristi was twenty when she chose IMG to represent her right before winning the gold at the 1992 Olympics. "Usually, an agent tries to find work for you, or a tour, and you don't need to do that [as an Olympic-division skater]."

Carole Yamaguchi was told it was done to fend off media queries.

"You can go unlisted," she replied innocently. "We did go unlisted once, after the Munich worlds."

Like Carole Yamaguchi, whose family struggled mightily to pay for Kristi's skating, Carroll tried hard to take skating's new world order in stride. But the sport he loved so dearly was turning into one mad dash for cash. For years, families went into debt to pay for a child in skating. Now, most still had trouble financially, but, for the lucky few, there was a way out. They could make money from the USFSA Memorial Fund (in honor of the 1961 plane-crash victims), they could make $5,000–$10,000 from Burg for a televised exhibition, and they could make prize money at competitions: up to a $25,000 first-place prize at two annual pro-am events. These paydays couldn't keep pace with the prizes and appearance fees at the professional events, but they took care of a sizable portion of the annual bills of a young skater.

Olympic-division skaters made most of their money on the Camp-

bell's Soups Tour of World Figure Skating Champions each spring.
This was a grand celebration held in a different city every night from
April to July. The tour would put on seventy-six shows in 1995;
Olympic-division skaters who made the minimum of $2,000 per show
took in more than $150,000 in three months. The top two women
and men skaters from the previous Nationals usually were invited,
plus the top U.S. pair and dance team. Other up-and-coming skaters
made special appearances when the tour came to their hometown.

The USFSA itself had more money than ever, thanks in part to the
Tonya-Nancy saga. It had just signed a $25-million deal with ABC to tele-
vise its events through 1999. Sponsorship was on the rise: $2.5 million
in 1994 rose to an upcoming $6.8 million in 1995. Money was flooding
into the organization, and some of it was going to find its way to the athletes. They certainly deserved it. No one was complaining about that. But
when it came to the tiny teenagers, girls who had not yet reached puberty,
there were concerns about giving them too much too soon.

Carroll liked the mild-mannered Goldberg; as agents went, he really was one of the kindest. When seven TV trucks pulled up outside
the rink during the Harding fiasco, Carroll knew they had to do something. So they signed Goldberg. But protecting Kwan from the blast-
furnace media was like sleep-walking to an agent; what agents really
love to do is make deals. Michelle was the USFSA's brightest hope for
the future, and that meant she needed to be out there, doing interviews, tours, and various competitions—all of which took her away
from practice at the rink with Carroll, from her tutoring, and from
the stability she found at Lake Arrowhead. But it did pay a lot of skating bills.

Because Kwan was the heir apparent to the national title, the USFSA
would promote her to the hilt. It would be her picture used on promos
of the Nationals during the upcoming Super Bowl. She was available on
media conference calls. For the first time ever, the USFSA was competing with well-known Olympic heroes in the pro ranks. They used to run
off with Ice Capades or Ice Follies and never be heard from again. Now,
they were on TV every week. The USFSA needed a personality to
latch onto. Kwan would carry the flag for the USFSA as it did battle
with the professional side of skating for all-important TV ratings. A
fourteen-year-old would lead them.

Skate America, the first eligible, Olympic-division competition after
Sun Valley, brought together the various factions of the new skating
world. There were the Olympic-division skaters—the kids, as the
agents called them—Kwan, Nicole Bobek, and the veteran French

jumper Surya Bonaly. The men came too: Todd Eldredge, Aren Nielsen, and Philippe Candeloro, the ponytailed French heartthrob.

Wherever the skaters went, the agents were sure to follow. This was a sport with athletes ripe for the picking. The action at the Hyatt's darkened lobby bar, called Pietro's, was more significant than what took place on the ice. Who was with whom spoke volumes about the sport.

One night, Nielsen, an artistic twenty-six-year-old who has never finished better than third at Nationals, was being wined and dined by Steve Disson, a Washington, D.C., sports marketing man who helps companies find events to sponsor. Nielsen ate in the same place the next day with two thirty-something agents, Jeanne Martin and Steve Woodward. It was looking like a game of musical chairs.

Martin is a tall blonde out of South Bend, Indiana, who is viewed by the skaters more as a big sister than as an agent. Martin is not into high-profile clients. Debi Thomas is her biggest name. She likes older skaters and the no-names whom she can befriend. Martin is into causes. Woodward became her sidekick a couple months earlier after working as *USA Today*'s Olympics reporter for nearly a decade. He enjoyed watching the figure-skating scene so much that he joined it.

They wanted Nielsen, and he decided he wanted them. Martin and Woodward had nabbed themselves another client. They would try to schedule him for shows and exhibitions. He would not be high maintenance. He might be no maintenance. There wasn't much of an audience for an older skater with no titles. But it would be a challenge, and Martin loved challenges.

At a back table in the bar, Goldberg and Danny Kwan got together to talk, plan, and get a little nervous about the competition. Michelle still was a bit off-kilter with her new weight, and some triple jumps—especially the triple loop—were not coming as easily as before. Goldberg, Carroll, and Danny Kwan tried to console themselves with what would become their motto of the year: "She's got ten more years," Danny Kwan said. "That's seventy to eighty competitions. If it doesn't happen this year, then it will happen the next year, or the next. We've got time."

Danny Kwan is a brooding, forty-six-year-old chain-smoker from Canton, China, worried about making ends meet with two daughters in skating. Having money coming in—into six figures counting the world skating tour—meant a lot to him. He knows Michelle could be one of those who is here today, gone tomorrow. He worries for her, but he also knows there is money to be made, and you might as well go for it now, because a new little kid might come around in a year or two to take it all away.

Katarina Witt, Rosalynn Sumners, and Brian Boitano at dinner in San Francisco in January 1995. (*Courtesy of Rosalynn Sumners*)

Scott Hamilton stretches backstage before a 1995 Stars on Ice show. (*Courtesy of Heinz Kluetmeier*)

Peggy Fleming visits Michelle Kwan and former coach Carlo Fassi at Lake Arrowhead for a television special in December 1994. (*Author's collection*)

Coach Audrey Weisiger and choreographer Brian Wright in Indianapolis in 1994. (*Courtesy of Audrey Weisiger*)

Rudy Galindo competes in 1992. (*Copyright Dave Black, 1992*)

At qualifying competitions such as the Eastern sectionals in Fitchburg, Massachusetts, the judges hold up their scores. Joe Inman (middle) displays a 5 in his right hand and holds another 5 on the table with his left. Taffy Holliday holds a 4.9 on far left. (*Copyright Rhonda Wiles, 1995*)

A judge's notes: some of the sheets Bonnie McLauthlin used during the men's long program at the 1995 Nationals. (*Courtesy of Bonnie McLauthlin*)

Tara Lipinski competes at the 1995 Nationals in Providence, Rhode Island. (*Copyright Paul Harvath, 1995*)

Jenni Tew practices for Nationals at the Winterhurst Ice Rink in Lakewood, Ohio. (*Copyright Roadell Hickman,* The Plain Dealer, *1995*)

Sydne Vogel skates at the 1995 Nationals. (*Copyright Paul Harvath, 1995*)

A young Brian Boitano practices a jump. (*Courtesy of Linda Leaver*)

Linda Leaver and Brian Boitano talk at practice in 1986. (*Courtesy of Linda Leaver*)

The U.S. women—Peggy Fleming, Christine Haigler, and Tina Noyes— at the outdoor practice rink at the 1964 Winter Olympics in Innsbruck, Austria. (*Courtesy of Tina Noyes*)

Tina Noyes presents Peggy Fleming with a bouquet of roses at the 1993 party celebrating the twenty-fifth anniversary of Fleming's 1968 Olympic gold medal. (*Courtesy of Tina Noyes*)

Janet Lynn almost always had a smile on her face as she skated. (*Courtesy of Janet Lynn*)

Janet Lynn at home, summer of 1995. (*Photo by Nic Salomon*)

Christopher Bowman—Bowman the Showman—at the 1992 Nationals, on his way to a second Olympic Games. (*Copyright Dave Black, 1992*)

Michelle Kwan and coach Frank Carroll meet the press at the 1995 world championships in England. (*Author's collection*)

Kristi Yamaguchi, Kurt Browning, Paul Wylie, Scott Hamilton, and Katarina Witt off the ice in New York City in March 1995. (*Courtesy of Heinz Kluetmeier*)

Michael Weiss and coach Audrey Weisiger at practice, June 1995. (*Copyright Mary Lou Foy, 1995*)

Nicole Bobek makes a rare trip to school, April 1995. (*Author's collection*)

Lisa and Jeanne Ervin at Lisa's high school graduation on Cape Cod, June 1995. (*Courtesy of the Ervin family*)

Coach/choreographer Mary Scotvold and agent Jerry Solomon join Nancy Kerrigan at a press conference after she was attacked in January 1994. (*Copyright Dave Black, 1994*)

Tonya Harding's singing debut in Portland on Labor Day weekend 1995 drew boos and flying soda bottles. (*Copyright Brent Wojahn,* The Oregonian, *1995*)

Dorothy Hamill, professional figure skater Andrew Naylor, and Tonya Harding at the rink in the Clackamas Town Center mall outside Portland, Oregon. Hamill bought the rink that Harding made famous. (*Photo by Elaine Stamm*)

Katarina Witt and Coach Jutta Mueller, together again, backstage at a Stars on Ice performance in 1995. (*Courtesy of Heinz Kluetmeier*)

Kristi Yamaguchi and Scott Hamilton sign autographs after a show. (*Author's collection*)

Paul Wylie, Rosalynn Sumners, and Kristi Yamaguchi talk backstage in New York. (*Courtesy of Heinz Kluetmeier*)

Katarina Witt has a laugh at practice. (*Courtesy of Heinz Kluetmeier*)

Paul Wylie (far left), Ekaterina Gordeeva and Sergei Grinkov (middle), and Scott Hamilton (right) are among those at the back of the Stars on Ice bus. (*Courtesy of Heinz Kluetmeier*)

Kwan, a systems analyst for Pacific Bell, lives alone in a tract neighborhood behind a Chinese restaurant his parents own. His son is in college, and the rest of the family is up at Lake Arrowhead for skating. A couple years ago, before they moved, Kwan stopped Michelle's lessons for several months because he had no money to pay the coach. But Lake Arrowhead picks up the tab for Michelle's ice time and coaching because she represents the rink and, with her success, brings it fame.

Danny Kwan had asked Michelle several times if she wanted to keep skating at this level. When she answered yes, then he laid down the law: "If you want something, then you really have to pay the price for it. If she wanted to go to a party, to go shopping, I'll tell her, 'You can't. You can't. If you want it that much, you can't afford it.'"

But was she missing something, like playing high school sports, or joining Junior Achievement, or doing anything else but skating? Danny Kwan said he didn't think so, but he wasn't sure. Who could know anymore? Kwan believed parents needed help, and signing an agent was not an awful thing to do. There were so many choices now: train, compete, do a photo shoot. Calling in an outsider who knew the ropes made sense to him.

But having an agent around also made things more tense. An agent's job is to push. But, in women's figure skating, the prize traditionally goes to those who wait. The body changes and then—only then—will it be determined if a skater goes to the Olympics. Pushing works in gymnastics, where puberty usually signals the end of the road, although new minimum age requirements might begin to change that. Patience, however, is what figure skating rewards.

Little girls always have done well in skating—Sonja Henie was fifteen when she won the first of her three Olympic gold medals; Carol Heiss was thirteen when she came in second in seniors at the 1953 Nationals—but they weren't shoved into the spotlight to make money and movies until later in their careers, after the pressure of the Olympics had abated. For one, they weren't on TV. Another reason: back then, amateur rules ensured that no one would earn anything.

Christy Ness, Kristi Yamaguchi's coach, said Yamaguchi would not have won the Olympic gold medal if she had had an agent in, say, 1989 or 1990. It would have been too much of a distraction. Ness herself set aside time every night to handle phone calls for Yamaguchi. Coaches always used to fill that role for skaters—and sometimes had fights with the skater when they turned pro and money started rolling in. Carlo Fassi and Dorothy Hamill, for instance, became embroiled in a nasty legal battle after she signed with Ice Capades following the 1976 Olympics. Fassi claimed she owed him $14,000 for skating lessons and $84,000 for helping arrange her professional contract. Hamill and her parents countersued for defamation. They settled out of court. Now, percentages for coaches are written into the contracts skaters sign with agents.

Goldberg and Burg were new to the sport. Goldberg was relatively certain Kwan would win the national title in Providence in February, but he was hoping she would come in second for a year or so at the world championships. He didn't want her to win everything the first year. They were building, he said, to the 1998 Olympics. He was an agent with a plan.

Burg, on the other hand, was building to next week. He had a dozen ideas a day. He already was representing U.S. gymnast Dominique Dawes, and had his eyes on another gymnast, thirteen-year-old Dominique Moceanu. He thought the little girls of figure skating were just as cute. Burg could sell cute. He hadn't signed Tara Lipinski, but he had paid her more than $5,000 to skate an exhibition at "Ice Wars" and was getting chummy with her parents, who lived apart—one in Maryland, near the University of Delaware rink, the other in Texas—for her skating. He looked at Dawes, Moceanu, and Lipinski as the same kind of client. In reality, they were entirely different. Dawes was at the top of her sport; Moceanu was headed there. Lipinski wasn't there yet, might take five years to get there—or might never make it.

"You're going for a kid who's still a junior?" USFSA officials asked Burg.

"She has a big-time future," he replied.

Officials shook their heads. It would take some time to get used to this.

Cautionary tales, and there are hundreds of them in skating, sounded silly to Burg. He didn't care about the past. If teenaged girls failed at the rate of a half dozen a year, he just had to assume he would pick the one who wouldn't.

"Tara's got all the triple jumps," Burg bragged, although she really did not, but it was a good story.

She sounds just like Jill Sawyer, someone replied.

"Who?"

Sawyer was better than Lipinski. A contemporary of Brian Boitano's and Rosalynn Sumners's from the Pacific Northwest, Sawyer had a beautiful triple lutz—which Tara and most junior skaters didn't have yet—and won both the national and world junior titles by fifteen.

"She was a blond bombshell with a triple lutz before a triple lutz had even been heard of for a woman," Sumners said.

Carlo Fassi called and offered the moon, so Sawyer left her coach, Kathy Casey, and moved to Colorado. But Sawyer was injured in a traffic accident and couldn't train and eventually watched an entire generation of skaters pass her by.

Now thirty-one and teaching skating in Beaverton, Oregon, Sawyer wistfully describes how Fassi referred to her in the mid-1980s: "There's the girl who should have won the last two Olympic gold medals."

The girl who could win the next two Olympic gold medals was practicing in the most beautiful indoor rink in the country, the Ice Castle International Training Center at Lake Arrowhead. One wall is mirrored to allow skaters to see themselves, as if they are in a dance studio. Floor-to-ceiling picture windows look out on the tall pines and the melting snow in the mountains east of Los Angeles. Michelle Kwan was working with Frank Carroll, both of them on skates, on a perfect sheet of white ice with no boards surrounding it. The mothers sat and watched in a corner in soft chairs, looking very much like the mothers at the country club pool. That's what the facility looks like, a silent, still pool. Of ice.

"Breathe!" Carroll was yelling out to Kwan as she churned through her long program. "Remember to breathe now. Don't hold it in."

This was Michelle Kwan's life, this little enclave of nothing but skating. Even the clapboard cabins where the skaters stay remind them of what they are there for: Michelle, her older sister, Karen, and her mother, Estella, live in Debi Thomas' Tee Pee. Other cabins are called Sonja Henie's Hideaway, Torvill and Dean's Den, and Brian Boitano's Bungalow. Since Michelle sneaked out and took her senior test, she has lived the charmed life of a skater on the move. She was sixth in 1993, her first year as a senior. She moved up to second in 1994 behind Tonya Harding, but was bumped off the Olympic team when Nancy Kerrigan was placed on it. She went to Norway anyway as a spectator. The minute Harding got kicked out of the USFSA and Kerrigan retired to the world of shows and pro competitions, Kwan bobbed to the surface as America's top female skating hope heading into 1998.

"She's a remarkable performer for her age, as far as the face and the look and the little innuendos in between," Carroll said. "She's continually learning. This is the first year, for instance, that she looks the judges in the eye."

It's a perfect fit, Carroll and Kwan. Carroll is the Mr. Rogers of figure skating, such a trustworthy guy. He misses nothing. He teaches his skaters how to smile as they perform. He doesn't just chat up the judges; he *grew up* with the judges. They in turn expect great things from his skaters, and he almost always delivers. He coached Linda Fratianne to two world championships and the 1980 Olympic silver medal. He endured the talented but erratic Christopher Bowman through the 1980s. He delights in the daily wonder of little Michelle, and deep down, he asks himself, Is this the one? Will she be the Olympic gold medalist?

She is his perfect student: intelligent, driven, capable, eager, and willing. She is a plain little girl who skates without earrings and wears little makeup. She giggles about boys, but she doesn't date them. For a coach, it doesn't get much better than that.

Carroll is always trying to think of ways to make Kwan better. He already has come up with two things for 1995–96: a triple axel and a triple-triple combination jump. She was doing five of the six triple jumps in 1994; all but the axel. She practiced the triple axel, but wouldn't go all-out on it until the spring, after the 1995 Nationals and worlds, when she could devote all her attention to it. For now, Carroll wants her sticking with the double axel, which floats effortlessly through the air. As for the triple-triple combination, he would let her try it when she has finished going through her programs for the day.

In practice, just for fun, she tried the combination a dozen times, always landing the first jump, the triple flip, but never quite getting the second, the triple toe loop. Her ankles looked as if they would snap on that second landing, then she fell over with a thud. By the time she was done, she looked like a child making angels in the snow; that was how thick the ice shavings were caked on her black tights and skating dress.

Of more concern right now was a problem she was having with another jump, the triple loop. This was a jump she had supposedly mastered, but now was not landing consistently. It's a jump that takes off on an edge, without the help of a toe pick. It requires an especially strong right thigh muscle, and Kwan didn't have the natural spring in that thigh to always pull it off.

"I'm scared the blade will flip out under me," she said. "When I go into it, I'll be like, 'Ahhhh,' and I'll open up in the air and pop it into a single or something."

"If something falls apart in the program, it's that damn triple loop," Carroll said. "But I'll never take it out. It's there. It's going to be there and she knows it's there."

Carroll never gives in with a kid who can take it. Bobek, whom he coached in 1989, was a cutup, a talented, vivacious cutup. She would stop when she missed something in a program. She didn't last long with Carroll—or anyone. How different Bobek and Kwan are. When Kwan falls during one of her programs in practice, he demands she keep on going, and she always does.

"If you miss something or trip on something unexpectedly, that may be the only time in your life you get the opportunity to practice how you recover at that instant in the program," Carroll said. "If you let that opportunity go by, then you have not practiced that possibility of something happening."

Skating is all about being prepared, Carroll says. He demands that a skater land a jump 80 percent of the time before he puts it in the program for a competition. "You try to make the body like a machine, so when the nerves take over and you're under pressure, that same technique holds you in good stead all the way through. I like to know what's going to happen when I put a skater out there."

At Skate America, when Carroll took Kwan's hands and sent her onto the ice, he told her, "Okay, darling, you go through this program every day and you land everything. Today, you're going to go onto the ice and do the same thing you do every day of your life. You know you can do it. I know you can do it. And you're going to do it."

Michelle Kwan is a woman-child who says she is doing exactly what she wants to do, and no one seems a bit concerned that there's anything wrong with it. "It's all been so fun," she said. "If I want it enough, then I'll still be around. Like in *Forrest Gump*, you know how he starts running. It's up to you if you want to keep on going or not. And he just keeps on running.

"Sometimes you say, 'No, I don't want to run anymore.' It could be the same thing in skating. But not until 1998, at least. I came this far already, why not go a little more?"

So Kwan lives a life far different from the average fourteen-year-old's. She balances algebraic equations while watching TV in the Lake Arrowhead recreation room in the morning; takes three forty-five-minute skating lessons sprinkled throughout the day; and has three hours of tutoring in the afternoon. Her social life is interacting with the other skaters, some of whom have come in from Europe to work with the Lake Arrowhead coaches, who now include Fassi. She is gone quite a bit; twice she has had to fly to San Francisco to get her skate boots fitted. Her dresses cost more than $1,000, Carroll said. This is a serious commitment, and she knows it.

"I probably would be disappointed if I didn't go to the Olympics, but I would not see it as a failure. You know it could have been one horrible day. And I also would have another two Olympic years," she said.

She will be seventeen for the 1998 Olympics, twenty-one in 2002, and twenty-five in 2006.

Older, more detached skating people are concerned for Kwan, mostly because they like her so much. Bobek, her top rival, doesn't inspire such heartfelt worry. If she could get her act together and train properly, she could become the Olympic champion. She has all the ingredients. But until she becomes disciplined, she is just a pretty free-spirit with talent. Kwan, however, is a wonderfully polite and driven child whom they hate to see ruined by the pressure cooker of skating.

"A lot of the enjoyment, the fun, the adventure, the goofing around is lost because now it's life's purpose at fourteen," said Scott Hamilton. "That's kind of a drag."

"I get scared of people who get things so quickly," said Carol Heiss. "I get a little bit afraid of the ones who get everything so fast."

But if it's possible to turn this drive toward an Olympic medal into child's play, Kwan does it. Something as serious as watching her weight becomes a game. She can have chocolate only once a week, she said, so she has to improvise.

She walks over to the blender in the cafeteria at Lake Arrowhead and pours in sugar-free cocoa mix, nonfat milk, ice cubes, and a banana. That, for a fourteen-year-old world-class skater, is a chocolate shake.

Prior to the women's competition in Pittsburgh, Bobek sat with her mother, Jana, and Joyce Barron in Pietro's. It was lunchtime. Nicole ordered a Philly cheese-steak sandwich with the works. Extra cheese, peppers, mushrooms.

Michelle Kwan, seated with her father and her agent, went for the chicken stir-fry.

The two American hopefuls skated like they ate. Bobek fell and looked lethargic, Kwan was smooth and easy on the eye. Although she popped that troublesome triple loop into a single, she finished second to Bonaly, the veteran of the group, four judges to three (there were only seven, not nine, in Skate America).

Bonaly made $10,000; Kwan quietly accepted her second-place check of $7,500 and went into the USFSA's interview room. Prior to her arrival, Goldberg tapped the microphone to see if it was working. The USFSA media-relations people already knew it was. Agents!

The USFSA sometimes felt like a traffic cop at the Indy 500 in this season of renegade professional events, but where it still could assert its control, it did. Before the competition, Goldberg placed a stack of Kwan biographies on a table in the middle of the pressroom. These bios were separate from the ones the USFSA puts out on the skaters. A couple moments after Goldberg put the bios down, Kristin Matta picked them up. Reporters, she said, would use the USFSA's bios at USFSA events.

Bobek actually came in last among the five skaters, going oh for five on her triple jumps. She shrugged her shoulders and said she still had a bad hip. She was worse than she had been in Sun Valley.

That performance led to an argument with her mother under the stands as coach Richard Callaghan stood by and watched. Nicole had been invited to skate in the exhibition the next day, which is seen as a reward for a skater. Jana Bobek saw nothing on the ice to warrant that honor and wanted her daughter to rest her hip. But Nicole said she wanted to do it—and she eventually won.

That night, she did not go to bed early to prepare for her final performance. She was out past 2 A.M., parading through the Hyatt lobby with a pack of cigarettes in her hand and a handsome blond gentleman by her side. By that time, Kwan had been asleep for hours.

Twelve hours later, in the exhibition, Kwan nailed two triples and a double axel as little girls screamed, "We love you, Michelle!" Bobek was a shimmering white chiffon spectacle caught between eight spotlights in the middle of a darkened arena. Twenty seconds into her performance, she went up for a triple toe loop, the easiest triple jump. She came down with a crash. That was the last attempt at a triple jump for Bobek. It was becoming embarrassing for her to try one.

While the Olympic division was undergoing its most bizarre year, strange things were happening in the professional events, which were being held throughout the fall, taped by the networks and shown later. The rules were different every week, confusing the skaters and coaches. Skaters did the same programs again and again; one of the participants, Canadian Josee Chouinard, performed "Moon River" five times in competitions that were to be shown in little more than a month on CBS.

Some events were run by Burg; some by Dick Button. The competition wasn't limited to the skaters; Button and Burg were going at it, too. There was big money on the line promoting these events. Convincing television audiences that their competitions were the ones to watch became an obsession.

Button devised a catchy idea in November: he brought together three recent men's and women's Olympic gold medalists for an event he called "The Gold Championship," shown live on a Saturday night from Edmonton. Katarina Witt, Kristi Yamaguchi, and Oksana Baiul would compete for a $200,000 first-place prize, as would Scott Hamilton, Brian Boitano, and Viktor Petrenko. Second place was

$160,000; third, $140,000. So everyone was guaranteed money. In its introduction, NBC called the competition "a once in a lifetime opportunity to see these gold medalists go head-to-head . . . never, ever, have we seen them compete on the same ice and on the same night."

Except that we had. Hamilton, Boitano, and Petrenko had met in Sun Valley a month earlier in the Burg event that had not yet been shown on CBS. Hamilton and Boitano even repeated numbers in Edmonton they did in Sun Valley. Boitano, Petrenko, Witt, Yamaguchi, and Baiul all were at "Ice Wars" one week earlier. That, too, was run by Burg and shown live on CBS.

Button had another event on NBC: the fifteenth annual World Professional Figure Skating Championships from Landover, Maryland. "The real championship," NBC called that one. The network also labeled this a season "of contrived rivalries and pretenders." The Landover event was a fine show, featuring an all-star cast and triple axels from Brian Boitano and Midori Ito, but the technical level overall in the men's event was below that of a national championship run by the USFSA. Two of the four professional men didn't try triple axels; the Olympic-division male skaters couldn't get away with that.

For years, Button stood alone in the competitive professional world running a couple events a year. Burg crash-landed onto the scene this year. His events were on CBS mostly, as well as Fox and cable. It was a jarring turn of events for the sixty-five-year-old Button, America's first Olympic gold medalist in figure skating and the sport's leading amateur and professional innovator. He performed the first double axel—in 1948—and the first triple, the loop, in 1952.

Button had always had the run of the sport. After winning Olympic gold medals in 1948 and 1952, he turned his sport into an extremely lucrative business venture for himself. He managed athletes and went into television and became, as he calls it, "a narrator." One might commentate on other sports, Button said, but one narrated figure skating.

Button personified figure skating to millions of Americans. He took the nation by the hand and led it into the sport. A jump wasn't good unless Button said it was. He anointed stars with a sentence. He shed a private tear for an injured Randy Gardner and his partner, Tai Babilonia, as they withdrew from the 1980 Olympics, and fans cried with him. Viewers put their faith in him. They had to, because no other sport had such an important figure. He was Arnold Palmer and Howard Cosell rolled into one, the innovative star of the sport and its leading media voice.

But Button was not entirely beloved. He was a Harvard man who was smarter than almost everyone else, and he knew it. His Landover event, an essential stop for any professional skater, was not everyone's favorite competition. Some skaters dreaded the event because it went on until midnight and was known as figure skating's longest night.

Appearance fees were paid out to the big names—fees much higher than the announced first-place prize money of $40,000. But one IMG client feared he/she was being lowballed by Button because the skater was represented by IMG while Trans World International, an IMG company, held the international TV rights for the event.

These kind of questions had come up before. Dorothy Hamill sued IMG, her former agent, in 1991, saying the company had taken $75,000 from her account, destroyed videotaped performances, and displayed conflicts of interest as her representative, the owner of some sports events, and the producer of the events' television coverage.

According to *Forbes,* Hamill said she was paid 30 percent less than her standard $100,000 fee for the World Professional Figure Skating Championships because, she claimed, the event was 50 percent owned by TWI.

IMG disagreed with Hamill's claims, saying it revived Hamill's marketability after her popularity waned. Hamill and IMG settled for an undisclosed sum in 1994.

As Button promoted and cashed in on professional events, he also kept his job "narrating" Olympic-division events for ABC. Thus he became the sport's leader in one more category: messy entanglements. Claire Ferguson, the USFSA president, charged into ABC's headquarters at Skate America one morning, steaming. She had had it with Button.

"He continues to use the word *amateur* for our events," she said. "That's wrong. And he's putting on events of his own that compete with us."

Chicago White Sox co-owner Eddie Einhorn, who negotiates the TV-rights deals for the USFSA and the International Skating Union, the worldwide federation for figure skating, followed Ferguson's lead and laid into Button in a speech a few months later.

"We have a real problem when an announcer is the promoter of competing events," he said.

ABC Sports president Dennis Swanson shot back in the press, "We are satisfied Dick has been fair and objective in his commentary on ABC Sports. He does not work for ABC on events he produces. We wonder why this has suddenly become an issue with a USFSA agent."

The answer was that Button had not been a threat all those years. But now the USFSA was being challenged on all sides, and Button's events were a major competitor. It was time, the USFSA thought, to expose Button's conflicts.

•   •   •

The most perplexing of all the professional performers in the autumn of 1994 was Oksana Baiul, who had won one Olympic gold medal, and because she was turning seventeen in November, was in a position to try for two more. By 2002, she would be twenty-four, the age Kerrigan was in Norway. Burg was so enthralled with her that he built the whole season around her. And then she injured her knee and wasn't the same the rest of the year.

Baiul did not take time off to fully recover from the injury. She couldn't, not with the made-for-TV events that were counting on her. "If we didn't have the Wild, Wild West," said CBS producer David Winner, "she might have taken two months off and been fine."

The money was important to her. Here was an orphan from the Ukraine given an opportunity to earn $1.5 million by skating in ten events over the next year and a half. She could not give that up, and who could blame her?

So she skated—and lost. She won only one out of five events, the Fox rock-and-roll special. Otherwise, with her knee wrapped, she fell or stumbled or simply failed to try the difficult jumps. She and her coach, Galina Zmievskaia, seemed confused about how to approach competitions. When the judges were looking for athleticism, she gave them artistry. When they wanted artistry, she was trying difficult triple jumps.

For a world so willing to embrace her as the next Sonja Henie—she even had Henie's agent, the William Morris Agency—it was disheartening.

"She seemed like she would be a big star," said Carlo Fassi. "Everybody was enthused about this girl. Now we realize after the professional championships, she's not that good. She's good, but not that good."

Baiul's body was changing. She was five feet two and ninety-seven pounds at the Olympics. By the end of 1994, she had grown two inches and gained four pounds.

But even with the slips and mistakes, Baiul drew raves as a show skater. Forget the jumps. The magic of Baiul's feet and hands washed over the audience. "You seduce with the fingers," Zmievskaia told her. "Your body's worth twenty kopecks, but your fingers are worth gold."

After the 1994 Olympics, the International Skating Union allowed skaters to leave the Olympic division and turn professional, then reinstate as an Olympic-division skater by April 1, 1995. This was perfect for Baiul. She could rake in the money and also ease up on competitions, avoiding the heavy lifting of the Olympic division in 1995 with the less-taxing exhibition-style events.

Conventional wisdom said the charming Baiul would enjoy the year and then return to the ISU fold to gear up for the 1998 Olympics.

But now, with the injury and her body changing, people began to wonder. Did Baiul really want to try to match triple jumps with the likes of Bonaly and Kwan? Or was it time, at the ripe old age of seventeen, to settle into the professional world and enjoy the good life?

Before the American skating world ever heard of Michelle Kwan or Oksana Baiul, a thunderbolt out of Ohio struck the sport. If anyone was headed to the Olympics, it was going to be Lisa Ervin.

She had made one of the great sacrifices for skating. When she was seven, her mother and father packed her up and sent her to Cleveland, five hours away from their home in Charleston, West Virginia, to live with a family they did not know.

For three years, Lisa saw her parents only every other weekend. Her parents' house was silent. They had no other children.

"When Lisa wanted to leave," Jeanne Ervin said, "this was so serious, we talked about it. I knew it was an opportunity for Lisa to get out and get more coaching. But in my heart I knew she was just seven years old. How does a mother part with a seven-year-old?"

Lisa was taking lessons on a small rink in Charleston and doing quite well. The coach there suggested that if she was going to get much better, she would need to move to another rink. West Virginia wasn't the place for Lisa Ervin. She should move to Ohio and train with Carol Heiss.

Bill Ervin was stuck in West Virginia working for Du Pont. Jeanne Ervin was a nurse. She said she tried to find a job in Cleveland, but could not. Heiss asked her to come. "I couldn't just leave," Jeanne Ervin said. But Lisa wanted to go. So, unlike the Tews, the parents stayed together and the child left.

"She was with a good family, that wasn't a problem," Jeanne Ervin said. "But the problem was that when something would come up that she needed us for, we were five hours away. Sometimes that five hours might as well have been five million."

Jeanne Ervin had tried to prepare Lisa to be self-sufficient. She was moving into the house of a family with four children. Jeanne Ervin knew the mother wouldn't have much time to devote to her child. So she gave her instructions, details that few mothers have to tell secondgraders.

"I felt really guilty at bedtime," Jeanne Ervin said. "At nighttime I sometimes had tears in my eyes thinking I had been so tough on my own kid. I would make her do things that I thought she was going to have to do with another family. I would make her look around her room, hang everything up on a hanger. I would make her say, 'What do you have to do tonight? What are the things you're supposed to do before you go to bed?' I was very stern with her. 'Remember, brush your teeth. Lay out your clothes for the next day.' "

Meanwhile, on the ice in Lakewood, Ohio, they were busy making a champion. With her white blond hair pulled back, Lisa Ervin was being created in the image of Carol Heiss. It was perfect: the beautiful blond coach and the little blond pupil. Strangers used to ask them if they were mother and daughter.

"This girl took my breath away," Heiss said. "She listened, she worked hard, she had the body, she had the natural ability. She was just a natural at that time. She worked very hard, but she had a gift for all of it."

When Lisa was ten, her father was transferred to Delaware and her mother came to Cleveland to join her. Jeanne began a career as a case manager for an insurance company. It was the perfect job for a skating mother. She could live anywhere.

By age twelve, Lisa Ervin had four triples. Heiss was so proud. That year, 1990, Ervin won the national novice ladies title. In 1991, she won the national junior ladies title. In 1992, three months before her fifteenth birthday, Ervin again went to the national championships, which also were the 1992 Winter Olympic trials. She entered the senior ladies competition for the first time. When a junior moved up to seniors, she usually got lost in the shuffle for several years. Ervin became a senior lady and finished fourth. Fourth! The order at Nationals was Kristi Yamaguchi, Nancy Kerrigan, Tonya Harding, and Lisa Ervin. The first three were going to the Olympics, where they would finish first, third, and fourth, respectively. Lisa Ervin was right behind them.

In 1993, Lisa Ervin did even better. She went to Nationals and finished second, behind only Nancy Kerrigan.

"It was too much too soon," Heiss said. "We knew that. When she was second, as wonderful as it was—oh, no, no, no, no. Harding didn't skate well. I said to Jeanne Ervin, 'It's a little bit of a gift. It's not a gift because you earned it, but you got there because nobody else really did their job.' "

Lisa went to the world championships in Prague. There, she fell on her combination jump in the short program and finished thirteenth. The event was a debacle for the U.S. women: Kerrigan was fifth, and Tonia Kwiatkowski, Ervin's teammate at Winterhurst, failed to make the cut out of the qualifying round.

"We kept reading stories that that was the worst U.S. team in a number of years at worlds," Ervin said. "And another Olympic year was coming up. Everything was so tense."

Ervin turned sixteen in April 1993. Her body was changing. At five feet two and a half, her ideal weight was 110 to 115. She was gaining weight, not a lot of it, but enough to throw off her jumps. She lost her triple flip. Other jumps were not coming easily anymore.

Her weight became a topic at the rink. Heiss began to weigh Ervin once a week—at Ervin's suggestion, Heiss said. For two or three days at a time, Ervin said she would eat nothing. Then she would binge for a day—and then not eat for a couple more days.

"I would starve myself and then binge," Ervin said. "Starve, binge, starve, binge. Your system goes up and down, up and down. I can definitely say I had an eating disorder. I was never bulimic. I never forced myself to throw up. That wasn't my thing. I just wouldn't eat. It was awful."

Her mother sent her off every day with a lunch, either a sandwich or salad. "She didn't know," Ervin said. "I was either at the rink or in school all day. At lunch with my friends, I would eat a piece of lettuce, say I was really not that hungry, then go and dump it out into a wastebasket."

Away from the rink, she stopped shopping for clothes. "I thought that I was horrible and that I wasn't any good because I was five pounds overweight."

Heiss knew something was wrong. When Ervin couldn't do her triple jumps, she compensated by spending an hour on the exercise bike, Heiss said. "She trained hard and was very intense, very goal-oriented. To satisfy that sense of accomplishment when she couldn't hit the triples, she pushed herself in other ways."

Ervin dropped to seventh at the 1994 Nationals in Detroit, where the Olympic team was selected. She called it a "disaster." Her meteoric rise was over.

The long relationship between Heiss and Ervin was coming undone, too. The Ervins called Evy and Mary Scotvold in Massachusetts. The Scotvolds were hot, having taken Paul Wylie and Nancy Kerrigan to Olympic silver medals. At first, the Scotvolds were reluctant to take Lisa because of Ervin's ten-year relationship with Heiss. But when Ervin said she was leaving Heiss no matter where she ended up, the Scotvolds told her they would coach her, and Ervin and her mother moved into a two-bedroom town house on Cape Cod in April 1994.

Lisa enrolled in the local high school, just as she had in Cleveland, and began to start her life anew.

DECEMBER

*N*OSTALGIA

8

BRIAN
AND
LINDA

Please, God. Please, God. Please, God. Please, God. Please, God.
PleaseGod-PleaseGod-PLEASEGOD!'

Brian Boitano couldn't believe it. Never before had his mind let go like this. Always, he was in such control, thinking of the right things during a program, technical things: balance, footwork, timing. And now this. His mind was wandering at the worst possible time, a couple seconds before the second triple axel with little more than a minute left in the long program at the 1988 Olympic Games. This was "The Battle of the Brians." This wasn't supposed to be happening *here*.

Boitano threw himself into the air. How many times had he done this jump in practice? Five thousand, ten thousand? Oh, if ever there were a time he needed to land it. *PLEASEGOD-PLEASEGOD!'* The mind was gone. His body would rely on memory. All those years of instruction: *TAKE YOUR TIME! SIT ON THE EDGE! KICK THE KNEE THROUGH!*

Gone. Forgotten in an instant. He wasn't hearing that now. No, only the shrieks inside his head: *PLEASEGOD-PLEASEGOD . . .*

At the other end of the rink, standing alone as she had nearly every day for sixteen years as she watched a little boy turn into a young man before her eyes, Linda Leaver couldn't hear the noise inside Boitano's brain.

She simply watched him go up, just as she taught him.

And she watched him come down, just as she taught him.

In her silence, in the quiet calm that enveloped her, Leaver had no idea the volume was reaching a crescendo within Boitano's head. *PLEASEGODPLEASEGODPLEASEGOD . . . YESSSSSSSS!*

· · ·

Linda Leaver met Brian Boitano in 1971, when she was twenty-eight and he was eight. When she first saw him skate, she didn't know his name. He was one of the little kids in her half-hour Saturday morning classes at the Sunnyvale Ice Palace, in the Bay Area south of San Francisco. By the age of eight, some children around the country were being groomed as elite figure skaters. Not Brian Boitano. This is how Leaver described her less-than-prestigious students: "They signed up, they were in the class. Whoever you had, you taught them."

Leaver was teaching Level 5, which included forward crossovers (the maneuver of putting one skate across the other to go around corners and gain speed), a two-foot spin, and most important, how to stop. One Saturday morning, Leaver noticed a cute little boy in the class who already could do crossovers and spin and stop. In fact, the boy was spinning so fast that he fell over.

Leaver skated over to him.

"Don't try to spin so fast," she said. "Just slow down and stand up and you can pass to the next level."

The boy listened, then began spinning again. Faster. Faster. Boom! He fell over again.

"Come on, just a little slower," Leaver told him. "I know you can do this."

Finally, the boy slowed down just enough to keep from falling over, and Leaver passed him to Level 6, which she also taught.

As she handed him a ribbon for his achievement, she asked him his name.

"Brian," he said through a huge grin. "Brian Boitano."

Lew and Donna Boitano knew nothing about figure skating. This wasn't bad. Quite the contrary. With no aspirations came no pressure. Brian was the youngest of four children, coming seven years after their third child. His father, a banker, had hoped Brian would play baseball, just as he had, all the way to the semipro San Jose Bees. But Brian didn't like baseball. Years later, he would say why: "It wasn't individual enough."

As a boy, Boitano liked to jump and spin on roller skates. When he ran into Leaver, all he and his parents knew was that he enjoyed skating. They didn't know about competitions, about real lessons, about the expense of costumes and skates. So Leaver offered some advice.

"You should really join the club here and get him in the show at the rink," she said. The membership cost $50 a year, for which a child received a two-hour skating session every Monday night, a half-hour lesson with one of the pros, and the opportunity to participate in the rink's ice show. The Boitanos signed up. Brian became a Muppet in his first ice show.

In March 1972, Brian Boitano took his first private lesson from Linda Leaver. He learned four single-revolution jumps in the first half hour they spent together. But his style was unorthodox. As he leaped into the air, he looked at Leaver.

"Don't look at me," she said, smiling.

"But I want to see if you like it."

Leaver raced home that night, walked in the door of her house and blurted to her husband that she had just found the "best little skater" she had ever seen.

"One day, he'll be the world champion."

David Leaver laughed. "Linda, you always think your skaters are good."

"Yes," she said, "but this one is different."

Linda Leaver grew up skating in Tacoma, Washington. She was good enough to make it to the national championships as a novice and a junior and had to coach herself for four years when her coach contracted hepatitis. All the while, her family couldn't figure out her fascination with the sport.

"I had no one who really wanted me to skate other than me," she said. "My parents didn't really want me to skate. They put up with it. They wanted me to go to school and be part of the family, and they thought this whole thing was ridiculous. They finally gave up when they saw that I loved it."

Leaver didn't wait long to become a full-time coach. At twenty, she began teaching skating as she attended the University of Washington, where she received a degree in philosophy. One of her pupils in Seattle was Diane Schatz, whose married name was Rawlinson. By 1994, Diane Rawlinson would be the coach of Tonya Harding. Linda Leaver had to admit it: in the family tree of coaches, she was Harding's grandmother.

Married at twenty-three, Leaver began to follow her husband around the country, from Washington, D.C., to Pittsburgh to the Bay Area. When they moved to California, she drove by the rink in Sunnyvale in denim shorts and a T-shirt, with a puppy in her arms, hoping to set up an appointment with the rink owner. No appointment was necessary. She met the owner, he shrugged and said he was a little short on staff, and hired her on the spot.

When Boitano was twelve, his kneecap cracked due to the punishment of jumping. He could not skate for six months.

At the same time, David Leaver received a tantalizing job offer in Atlanta. As he and his wife discussed moving, Linda Leaver asked her husband to turn down the job. Her reason was surprising.

"Just give me five years with this boy, that's all I ask," Linda said. "It wouldn't be right to ask a child to move. I know Brian can be world champion. Just let me have the chance."

After a month of discussion and tears, Linda Leaver convinced David Leaver to accept a less desirable job in Palo Alto so she could stay in northern California and coach Boitano.

"Why did I get David to give up a job for a kid who wasn't even skating at the time?" she asked years later. "If we had left, Brian would have stayed behind and I would have moved and that would have been that."

Leaver might have dreamed she had a future world and Olympic champion on the ice beside her, but she saw none of the trappings of greatness. The Boitanos didn't realize that their son needed $500 costumes; they thought the shirts and pants they were buying at the store for $50 were just fine. They didn't know he needed a second pair of skate boots; or that most up-and-coming skaters took several hours of lessons a day, not a couple hours a week; or that a housewife coach wasn't supposed to win in the elite world of figure skating; or that you were supposed to drag your kid out of school and send him to some mountaintop retreat to learn from a coach with a foreign accent and a chest full of medals.

They just didn't know.

"And thank God for it," Brian Boitano says now.

So Leaver began steering the Boitanos through the sport.

"I'm getting there," she told Kathy Casey, a coaching friend from the Pacific Northwest. "I'm in a world where the people just don't know. I'm in a public-session, roller-rink-next-door kind of situation, and I'm making it work."

Leaver herself took promotional photos of Brian and her other skaters to send out to competitions and local businesses. She was inventive on the ice as well. Every week, she devised contests for the kids, suggesting they try new things. One day, Brian stuck his left arm into the air as he performed the lutz jump. That looked interesting, Leaver said to herself. Years later, that little move would become the "Tano" triple, Boitano's trademark triple lutz with the grand flourish of an arm thrust high into the air.

When Leaver ran those tiny competitions, she didn't want Boitano to win every week, so she would pick out the moves her less-talented skaters did best and make the weekly contest out of that particular skill. As a result, even the worst skater could say, years later, that he or she once beat Brian Boitano.

When Brian returned from his injury, he had six weeks to train for the intermediate men's competition at the regionals. He won it. He went on to the Pacific Coast sectionals and won that. There was no national competition for intermediate skaters, but had there been, he probably would have won that, too.

Leaver's five-year plan, as promised to her husband, officially began the next year. Boitano finished third in the national novice competition in 1977. He won national juniors the next year. He then moved up to seniors, the Olympic-level competition. He was eighth in 1979. The next year, he was fifth in the country, just two spots from making the 1980 Olympic team. In 1981, he did all the triple jumps but the triple axel and moved up to fourth. He also graduated from high school that year—Peterson High, class of '81, right on time, although hardly anyone there knew him. His friends were at the rink, mostly girls, always skaters. He didn't like school, but it wasn't because, like other boy figure skaters, he was being teased unmercifully.

"When I went out the door early, they would say, 'Good luck at your competition.' I didn't know that it was supposed to be a sissy thing to do."

He went to his junior prom, but he didn't fit in. Skaters, he said to himself, act so much older than other kids.

"Skaters grow up instantly. At thirteen, I was already a man," he said. "I had to deal with juggling a schedule, going to school, competing and being judged, everything. I grew up way before anybody else in certain ways."

Boitano's steady rise delighted Leaver. She was an anomaly in coaching, the coach with one great student. Women were scattered throughout the coaching ranks in the United States, but a woman had never coached a male Olympic champion. Boitano, people realized, was good enough to someday win a gold medal. Others gossiped about her. How was she pulling this off? When would Boitano leave her for the great gold-medal machine of Carlo Fassi or the esteemed Frank Carroll or the respected John Nicks, all great coaches, all located, as she was, in the West? Somebody, anybody, with a résumé that didn't read: college graduate; wife and mother with one daughter and another to come; national titles as a skater—zero; Olympic and world champions—zero. This was becoming humorous among those who knew what skating was all about: *When would the Boitanos come to their senses and find a real coach?*

Fassi called once and talked to Brian. He chatted with Brian for a few minutes, asked what his plans were, and hung up. Fassi never specifically mentioned coaching him, but Boitano thought it had to have been a recruiting call.

Knowing that the Boitanos could leave her at any moment, Leaver pushed herself harder than she pushed Brian. She spent hours in the Boitanos' kitchen, describing what competitions Boitano should attend, and sometimes sheepishly explaining that they would need to spend thousands of dollars to send her, too, and put them both up in a hotel for a week. She took Boitano to training camps run by some of the great names in coaching. She wasn't afraid of what other coaches might do to him. She sought the advice.

Each summer from 1984 to 1987, she sent him to a different expert for several weeks. First, he went to France to work with coach Didier Gailhaguet to learn how the Europeans taught compulsory figures, which would become vitally important later in his career. Europeans stressed tracing, while Americans paid more attention to turns and the size of the circle being traced. Figures still were an integral part of major competitions, and the nine-person judging panels at the Olympics and world championships often included six Europeans. Learn their ways, Leaver told Boitano, and you can beat them at their own game.

The next two years, Leaver sent Boitano to Nicks in southern California, then to Evy and Mary Scotvold, who were in Boston before moving to Cape Cod. Finally, in order to make him more presentable artistically, she sent him to famed choreographer Sandra Bezic in Toronto.

"The idea was for him to take what he could from any great mind," Leaver said, "and assimilate the part of it that was going to work for him."

The 1982 Nationals were a pivotal event for Boitano and Leaver. They were held in downtown Indianapolis in a snowstorm. There, Boitano, still a teenager, became the first American man to land a triple axel in competition. He received a rousing standing ovation from the audience. And yet, he did not finish in the top three and qualify for the world championships. Three skaters who at the time had bigger names and better résumés—Scott Hamilton, David Santee, and Robert Wagenhoffer—were sent to Copenhagen to represent the United States. Boitano stayed home.

It was the first and last time Linda Leaver cried over a skating decision.

"I wasn't crying because he didn't make the world team, I was crying because I was totally duped by the system," she said. "I truly believed in the system, that the best skaters were rewarded. It was like I found out someone who was a good friend had been lying to me. It took me six months to recover, but I vowed to never, ever, feel that way again."

In those days, Boitano was spending much of his time with Rosalynn Sumners, whose rise to the 1984 Winter Olympics began in Indianapolis with the first of her three national titles. The night Boitano finished fourth, there was a party for all the competitors. Neither Sumners nor Boitano went. They walked together hand in hand through the snow in downtown Indianapolis, both of them blinking back tears as they tried to figure out the decisions that came out of this crazy sport of theirs.

That was the last time Boitano failed to make a world or Olympic team. As the understudy to Hamilton, he was second in the nation the next two years, finishing seventh and sixth at the world championships, and fifth at the Sarajevo Olympics. Because there was a strong American ahead of him, he knew he would not win until that man, Hamilton, retired. In figure skating, Boitano knew you took a number and waited your turn.

This was why: In the days of compulsory figures, to make sure Hamilton won, the U.S. judge couldn't push for Boitano, too. He or she was selling one man—Hamilton. The U.S. judge would tell the judge from, say, Great Britain that he or she would "look out for" the British skater if the British judge would in turn "look out for" Hamilton, the Olympic favorite. Boitano was expendable. In the wheeling and dealing, he would fall like a rock to sixth or seventh place.

The night the men's competition ended in Sarajevo, a disgusted Boitano had had enough of this. He told Leaver that he was fed up with the way he was being judged, and with what the judges were telling him. One U.S. judge had seen him eating some crackers at the 1984 Nationals. "You better put those down," he warned. "You need to lose weight."

Boitano was five feet eleven and weighed 162 pounds.

"I don't think I have the heart to do this anymore," Boitano told Leaver that night at the Olympics.

"Then you should quit."

"I need to think about it," Boitano said. "I don't want to get anorexically thin like they want me to get."

Boitano was big for figure skating. "And there I was competing against these little tiny boys. The judges always used to tell me, 'You're fat, you're fat, you have to lose weight.' "

Boitano did not quit, of course, and did lose a few pounds before the 1985 Nationals in Kansas City, the first of four consecutive titles that he won.

He weighed 154 pounds when he innocently went for a hamburger with his sister after the competition in Kansas City.

A judge came by and couldn't help herself from minding Boitano's business.

"You really shouldn't be eating that," she said. "You need to lose more weight, another ten pounds."

"You know what?" Boitano shot back. "My doctor said I couldn't go under two percent body fat. It's too dangerous for me."

Boitano said much later that he had made up the figure of 2 percent, but he wasn't far off. The judge was held at bay.

Judges nagged Boitano his entire career. Once, a judge told Leaver that Boitano didn't land his jumps on the "booms" in his music. The fact that he was landing triple jumps to the other boys' doubles didn't matter to that judge. She wanted jumps on the "booms." Leaver nodded politely and thanked her for her thoughts, but she didn't change a thing in Boitano's program. This, she learned, was the way to play the game. Just nod and smile.

Another time, when Boitano was at the novice level, Leaver ended up having a drink with about a dozen judges and a handful of coaches in a cramped hotel room at the Pacific Coast sectionals. This was her time to learn; the judges' gossip about music and programs and costumes was invaluable to her. But this particular evening, it got to be too much. She soon was barraged with all kinds of criticisms and negative comments.

A judge piped up, "Why doesn't Brian skate like [a current men's skater]?"

Someone else chimed in, "Why don't you try something new?"

Others jumped in with their thoughts. The ideas snowballed. Leaver had heard enough.

"Listen," she said, standing up from the bed where she had been sitting, "he has more talent and creativity in his little finger than so-and-so will ever have in his whole career. Don't you try to put him in your mold! Don't ruin him! Let him grow and develop at his own rate."

"I learned that you have to be able to take the stuff they throw at you," Boitano said. "You want to say, 'You know what? Nuts to you.' But you don't."

It wasn't entirely smooth sailing for Boitano to the 1988 Olympic Games. He had an injured heel bone in 1986 that made jumping excruciatingly painful at the Nationals and worlds. Leaver gave him a choice: "All you have to do is answer this: What is greater, the pain in your foot or watching your title go to somebody else?"

All week at Nassau Coliseum on Long Island, Boitano skipped practices. As he warmed up for the short program, it was time to find out if he was ready.

"Do a triple lutz now," Leaver said, "or don't do the competition."

She wanted to see the jump right then, and if it hurt him too much, he would withdraw from the competition on the spot.

He landed the jump in practice and in competition and kept his national title.

The heel flared up heading into the worlds in Geneva several weeks later. Before they left California, Leaver made the triple axel the do-or-die jump. He had not done a triple axel in weeks.

"We're not getting on the plane if I don't see it here," Leaver said. "We're not going all the way to Switzerland if you can't do it now."

He landed it, went to the worlds, and swept to his first world title, overtaking Canada's Brian Orser at the world championships for the first time. Just three years earlier, Orser had been third at the worlds and Boitano had been seventh. "How am I going to catch him?" Boitano had asked himself then. "He's so far ahead of me."

It would be Boitano and Orser, Orser and Boitano, all the way to Calgary in 1988.

Leaver's decision to send Boitano to Bezic in 1987—the last of his four summertime trips—became the crucial final piece of the Olympic puzzle.

Leaver was a technical teacher, "a mathematical type," she called herself. Boitano was her soul mate. He was a jumper, a windup toy. He didn't want to point his toes or do anything dramatic. He wanted to jump and he wanted to go fast; Leaver even had trouble slowing him down for the ninety-second "slow part" that comes in the middle of every skater's long program.

They were painstakingly particular about the finer points of jumping. Some children learn a jump overnight; many lose the jump just as quickly. But Boitano took so long to learn jumps—six months to get the double axel, for instance—that he couldn't possibly ever forget any of the mental or muscular preparation required to do them.

Leaver said Boitano "inched his way around jumps. After a thousand reps, he knew what he did to land it."

No one ever worked harder than Boitano. But he was unpolished on the ice. Bezic took care of that. She made Boitano more expressive, more brooding. At the end of the long program they were working on for the 1988 Olympics—a militaristic advance across the ice, to Carmine Coppola's score from *Napoleon*—she wanted him "marching through the streets of Paris."

"Be real cocky," she told him, "be really sure of yourself.' "

To Leaver, it made sense to give Bezic total control of Boitano's artistic life. But to many figure-skating coaches, that would have been unthinkable. Some of them are control freaks who would shudder at the thought of giving up even a shred of their power.

"Everything Sandra does is better than I can do," Leaver explained. "She's a genius. On choreography, I just stand out of the way. I think some coaches get confused. They think they're the ones that are skating. They're jumping up and down at the boards, their arms out, whatever. The greatest compliment that a coach can have is that their athlete can do it without them."

The Olympic competition in Calgary came in three parts: the compulsory figures (worth 30 percent); the short program (20 percent); and the long program (50 percent). Boitano did better than Orser in the figures; Orser was a thumbnail better than Boitano in the short program. So, on the night of February 20, 1988, the two of them met to decide the title in what was billed as "The Battle of the Brians." Never in men's figure skating had there been a more anticipated showdown on live television.

Boitano drew the first skating position in the last group, a perfect spot for him. He lived for just such a moment: to put his performance out there and let someone try to beat it. Orser, on the other hand, was such a nervous wreck that no one was sure what skating position was best for him. He had hired a psychologist, a masseuse, and a nutritionist, among others, to see him through his fears. He was the guy who hid in the bathroom when his competitors skated, turning on the shower to drown out the cheers and the scores.

What few knew then was that Boitano, too, had a psychologist of sorts, a woman who helped him spiritualize and visualize his performances. The outside world was only beginning to learn that skaters received psychological help. If there was laughter about it in 1988, it was thoroughly accepted by the mid-1990s, when many top skaters saw shrinks.

Both Boitano and Orser knew their lives would be forever altered by four and a half minutes of skating. If ever there were a time to get help, it was then. There was too much pressure to go it alone.

As Boitano took the ice, he was thinking only of skating well, not winning. He could contol the former; the latter was the opinion of the judges. He wanted the performance of his life, and if that brought the gold medal, so be it. He and Leaver had talked about how Peggy Fleming, Dorothy Hamill, and Scott Hamilton, to name some recent

American stars, had not skated the best performances of their careers at the Olympic Games.

"If you talk to them today," Leaver told Boitano, "inside their hearts, they wish they had skated better. So when you say, 'Congratulations,' there's a little thing in their heart that says, 'I really wasn't that good.' "

Leaver sent him off to skate his long program the way she always did, in silence, their eyes meeting with a quick, certain glance.

Bezic was there, too. "Show them your heart," she said to Boitano.

And off he went. One triple jump followed the other, a perfect Tano triple lutz, a superb triple axel. There were eight in all, including the second-to-last one, a second triple axel. There also were five different dramatic sections and changes in music, including a spread eagle that majestically meandered across the ice for nearly fifteen seconds.

Nearing the end, Boitano passed by the red hockey circle at center ice, which was a landmark he looked for to make sure he was on the right path for the final triple axel. He began to hear strange noises in his head. *Please God, please God.* They were getting faster and louder until he could barely stand it. As he launched himself into the air, he hoped that all those years of training would come through for him. Muscle memory, they call it. Only when that tiny blade swooped down, reached for the ice, found it, and held him upright did he know he was okay.

YESSSSS.

When he finished the program, Boitano tossed his head back, looked to the rafters, and nodded as if he were staring into heaven and saying thanks. In the background, barely recognizable standing beside a group of Olympic volunteers in white cowboy hats, Leaver applauded. Tears were rolling down her cheeks.

"I did it!" Boitano said breathlessly to Leaver when she met him as he stepped off the ice. His marks were superb, 5.9s and 5.8s mostly. Still, there was plenty of room for Orser, who came two skaters afterward. Leaver would watch Orser on a TV monitor. Boitano, like Orser before him, would not—could not—watch.

Boitano trudged to the dressing room, changed clothes, and collected his things. He walked to the bathroom, went into a stall, sat on a toilet seat, and put on his earphones as Orser got going with his program in the arena. Boitano looked at his watch. He waited about five minutes—the length of Orser's program plus time for the scores to be read—listening to mellow music on his tape player.

While Boitano sat in the stall, Orser skated nearly flawlessly to a classical, quasi-militaristic piece called "The Bolt." He was not as strong athletically as Boitano. His U.S. rival landed two triple axels; Orser did one. Boitano nailed a triple-triple combination; Orser did a triple-double. Boitano managed two triple flips; Orser did just one and stepped out of the landing on that one.

But Orser was the reigning world champion, so his marks were very good. World-champion-gets-held-up-by-the-judges good. He was behind Boitano technically, with a majority of 5.8s. But the artistic marks were better, just barely, than Boitano's. They came over the public address in the Saddledome: "5.9, 5.9, 5.8, 5.8, 5.9, 5.8, 5.9, 5.9, and . . ."

In the bathroom, Boitano pulled off his earphones.

". . . 6.0."

Boitano's heart sank.

"I lost. I lost. He got 6.0s."

He sat on the toilet seat for another minute.

"I lost."

Boitano stood up, walked to the bathroom mirror, and looked at himself.

"I skated great," he said to the mirror. "Okay, I lost. I'll stay in it for four more years. I can do that."

Boitano walked back to the dressing room, still alone. He sat down hard. Moments later, he heard a noise. His head turned with a jolt. The door swung open, and in walked Christopher Bowman, Boitano's youthful, bizarre Olympic teammate.

Bowman swaggered in, winking at Boitano. Bowman's mouth was hanging open, vaguely smiling. His hand was in the air, with his index finger extended. He was wagging one finger. No. 1.

Boitano solemnly shook his head.

"If this is a practical joke, I'm going to kill you."

"No, no," Bowman said, suddenly serious. "You won. You really won."

Bowman reached down and hugged Boitano.

"This can't be true," Boitano said. "I heard a 6.0."

"That's the only one he got."

"You're kidding."

Leaver, who was keeping track of the marks on a backstage television, knew Bowman was in the dressing room, telling Boitano that he was first. But Viktor Petrenko of the Soviet Union was skating, and if he impressed even one judge enough to place him first and knock Boitano down to second, that could have handed the gold medal to Orser. Nothing was certain until Petrenko was finished.

Leaver sent the U.S. team physician, Dr. Howard Silby, into the men's dressing room to tell Boitano it wasn't yet official.

"Hold on," Silby said.

Bowman, never known as a stabilizing influence, suddenly grew calm. Boitano began pacing.

Silby left to listen to Petrenko's marks.

He was back a minute later.

He opened the door. Boitano's eyes shot lasers into his.

"Yes!" Silby shouted. "You won!"

Boitano popped out of the dressing room moments later and bumped into Hamill and Bruce Jenner, who became the first people to congratulate him. He took a look at the TV monitor:

Boitano.

Orser.

Petrenko.

Boitano won the judges from the United States, Denmark, Soviet Union, Switzerland, and Japan, each by one-tenth of a point. Orser won West Germany, East Germany, Canada, and Czechoslovakia, again by one-tenth each. The Danish and Swiss judges tied the two skaters, but Boitano's technical mark—which was the tiebreaker in the long program in 1988—beat Orser's.

Boitano dashed back to the dressing room to put his skating outfit back on for the awards ceremony. As he was changing, the door swung open. Orser walked in, slowly placing one skate in front of the other. He looked like an old man. His mouth was open, his eyes were glazed, he had flowers hanging limply in his arms. He walked past Boitano, went to the bathroom where Boitano had been sitting as Orser skated, and laid down on the floor by the showers.

Boitano went in to make sure Orser was all right.

"What can I say?" Boitano asked.

"Nothing."

Boitano triumphantly leaped from the Olympics into a delightfully lucrative professional career, full of money and TV appearances and fame and everything but the one thing Boitano always loved most: competition. Prior to 1994, no professional skater ever was allowed back into the Olympics. But Boitano fought hard with the International Skating Union, and in 1994, he returned. So did Katarina Witt and Torvill and Dean, among others.

There was a risk involved in the comeback. Boitano knew it. If he didn't win, wouldn't he be remembered not for the 1988 gold medal, but for failing in 1994?

At the age of thirty, with a bad knee and little support from his competitors, Boitano took off eight months from touring and skating professionally to train with Leaver every day for another Olympics, the Games in Norway. In that short amount of time, he gave up at least $1 million in earnings.

After five years of touring and skating in professional events, raking in grand sums for a single night's work, Boitano was going back to the Olympic division.

It did not go as he and Leaver expected.

Boitano didn't win in Hamar, Norway. He didn't come close to a medal. He finished sixth after a devastating stumble in the short program. Skating first, he lifted off the ice to begin his triple-axel/double-toe combination, fell out of the triple axel, and clumsily felt for the ice with both hands. Boitano had performed about seventy short programs in his career. This was the first time he ever had made a big mistake. Leaver couldn't believe it. When he took off, the jump had looked perfect to her. She usually could tell something was wrong as he set up a jump or lifted off the ice. But this time, he looked absolutely perfect.

Within minutes, Boitano trudged to the practice rink adjacent to the main arena, the rink where hundreds of reporters had gathered earlier that day to watch the first practice session of Tonya Harding and Nancy Kerrigan. He sat in the stands by himself and stared blankly at a short-track speed-skating practice.

He felt horrible. It was the same feeling as hearing that 6.0 for Orser six years earlier. But that had been meaningless. This was real. "I can't believe it's happening to me," he said. "I know I'm dropping, dropping, dropping as other skaters skate. I'm thirty years old and I'm experiencing the same junk I did when I was fifteen."

He tried to tell himself that it had all happened for a reason, although that reason escaped him at that particular moment. He told himself he wasn't going to lean on excuses. A tendon in his right knee was loose and dangling, causing pain nearly every time he jumped. He should have taken the entire 1994 season off. But there were no Olympic Games in 1995.

He also had faced resentment in his comeback. Some of his American competitors had complained about his return. Boitano had had his chance, they whimpered. We want ours. He felt like an intruder at times on the U.S. Olympic team.

It was easy to feel sorry for himself, Boitano realized. After sitting in the practice rink for an hour, he picked himself up and went to a news conference and put on a good show. He talked about perspective, about realizing just how great 1988 had been. But it wasn't sincere. "That was me saying what I eventually hoped I would feel," Boitano said, "not what I felt then."

Sitting beside him, Leaver shrugged and smiled softly. There was nothing for her to say.

Boitano skated well in the long program, pulling himself up from eighth to sixth. He got out of town three days later and was home in San Francisco before Tonya and Nancy skated. When he left his house, he pulled a baseball cap down low over his eyes. He was embarrassed to be recognized. This was not how it was supposed to have been.

Boitano thought his reputation—even his career—might have been harmed by the 1994 Olympics. But they were not. In fact, all the attention and publicity was a good thing. Boitano's career, it turned out, was about to take off again.

He returned to the professional ranks in the fall and embarked on an incredible run of competitions, most of which he won. Hundreds of thousands of dollars came his way. He had the luxury of turning down $50,000 appearance fees because someone else would pay him $100,000. Or more. Promoters offered that kind of money because they knew they were getting the best-prepared athlete in the sport.

Indiana's Bobby Knight often talked about coaching against the game, not an opponent. A golfer might talk of trying to defeat the course, not another golfer. And so it was with Boitano. He often said he would rather try difficult jumps and fall than take the easy way out. It was Boitano against the ice. The ice usually lost.

Boitano bought a five-story home in San Francisco with a basketball court in the basement, putting a fictitious name on the title so his adoring fans wouldn't be able to find him—at least not without the kind of effort he had grown to expect of them. As he gutted the place, he stood in what would be his new kitchen. Looking out through the picture windows, he saw the sparkling blue San Francisco Bay, Alcatraz Island, and the Golden Gate Bridge. He couldn't deny that life was good.

Forty miles to the south in Los Altos, Leaver and her family were having their house rebuilt, too. She was showing up at the rink when Boitano asked her to, which was not every day anymore. Still, they spoke constantly on the phone, as often as five times a day. Leaver had become Boitano's business manager as well as his coach. They both had the distinct feeling they would be together for a long, long time.

9

PEGGY
AND TINA

The difference between first and second place in figure skating can be measured in many ways. At the moment the decision is made, it is a whim, a personal feeling, a fraction of a point one way or the other. Years later, it solidifies into something much bigger. It has become life itself.

Tina Noyes, a forty-five-year-old senior majoring in business at Boston College, still lives in the white Cape Cod–style house where she grew up. Her parents bought the house with its picket fence in middle-class Arlington, Massachusetts, four years before she was born. They're both dead now. Tina was their only child. She has never married. Her neighbors are what remains of a family for her, and she knows they won't be around too much longer. Most of them are in their nineties.

When Noyes looks out the window over her kitchen sink, she sees her small backyard, the hibiscus tree planted in memory of her father, and the neighbors' barbecue.

"My little world," she said. "My *Leave It to Beaver* neighborhood."

Peggy Fleming, a forty-six-year-old multimillionaire wife and mother, lives in a secluded, ranch-style house up a winding road on a lush green hillside of Los Gatos, California, an extremely well-to-do neighborhood overlooking San Jose. She and her dermatologist husband, Greg Jenkins, bought the house seventeen years ago, and it is there that they are raising their two sons, eighteen-year-old Andy and six-year-old Todd.

Their block is lined with interesting and rich people, among them Al Hakim, a central figure in the Iran-contra scandal. Another neighbor fled the country in the middle of the night rather than deal with authorities the next morning.

If it's a clear day when Fleming looks out the window over her kitchen sink, in the distance, sixty miles away, she can see the Golden Gate Bridge.

Tina Noyes sighed and forced herself to think once again of her skating career.

"I have to remember what one of my coaches once said to me, that someday people will ask, 'When did you skate?' And the coach told me, 'You might say you were on two Olympic teams, but that might not trigger anything. But if you say to them, 'Well, I was second to Peggy Fleming for four years,' they would say, 'Oh, wow, you were?' ' "

Somebody had to finish second to Peggy Fleming. Somebody had to live with the knowledge that but for the opinion of a couple judges back in the middle 1960s, she and Fleming might have flip-flopped, and the most glorious career in figure skating could well have been hers. Tina Noyes was a fine skater, quite good; a jumper, not an artist — although she tried, she really tried. Whatever it took, she tried. She knew the judges loved Fleming's look, the rich dark hair pulled back. So Noyes let her short, curly red hair grow long. The judges liked Fleming's ethereal style. Noyes could see that. So she began taking ballet. Compulsory school figures ruled the day back then, accounting for 60 percent of the overall score, so Noyes did everything she could to become good at them. But Fleming was superb at figures. Try as she might, Noyes was not going to beat Fleming in the compulsories.

As Tina Noyes looks back on it now, since someone had to be the runner-up to Fleming, it might as well have been her.

"It would probably be like having a sister who married well and you didn't," Noyes said in a staccato Boston accent. "If you were going to compare your life to hers forever, I think you'd be in deep trouble."

There were five judges in the women's competition at the 1964 Nationals in Cleveland. Three gave first place to Fleming. One gave first place to Noyes. The other gave first to veteran Barbara Roles, the 1960 Olympic bronze medalist who came back to skate after the plane crash in 1961. Roles finished fifth overall as Christine Haigler, a skater from the prestigious Broadmoor Ice Arena in Colorado Springs, jumped into third.

The five judges' votes at the 1964 Nationals:

Peggy Fleming:	1	3	3	1	1
Tina Noyes:	2	1	6	4	2
Christine Haigler:	3	2	2	2	3

Fleming, Noyes, and Haigler were the immediate future of U.S. skating. They were moving faster through the ranks than American girls ever had, simply because the women who had been above them had been killed in the crash.

The year before, in 1963, Noyes won the junior national title and Fleming finished third. One judge had placed Fleming fifth, another sixth. (Haigler already was in seniors.)

But, that next year, as they were choosing an Olympic team that was certain to win no medals, the judges changed everything—for good. Those five people weren't simply making a decision for one competition; they were pouring the cement that would become America's modern skating foundation.

Fleming and Noyes had very different styles. Fleming was graceful and doelike; Noyes was hardy and energetic. Before Noyes began her program at the Cleveland Nationals, she rolled up her long turquoise sleeves. Even ABC's Dick Button commented on that; this girl, he said, must really mean business. Imagine, in this refined ladies' sport—a girl rolling up her sleeves! Were they skating now, Fleming would be most like Oksana Baiul; Noyes, Michelle Kwan.

"Jumping was my forte. I was just a little bit early—like maybe by twenty years," Noyes said.

Had two of those judges changed their minds in 1964—not that they should have, but if they had—Noyes would have beaten Fleming. Noyes would have been the U.S. champ heading into the Olympics in Innsbruck, Austria, not Fleming, which, in those years, would have meant she likely would have received more of a push with the judges at the Olympics. (None of the Americans did very well in Innsbruck: Fleming was sixth, Haigler was seventh, and Noyes was eighth.) National order almost always was honored on the international stage back then. Had Noyes won the national title, she would have had the judges' attention as the next potential U.S. star. Going into 1965, Noyes would have had top billing. Everything Fleming had would have been Noyes's, and vice versa.

But Fleming, of course, beat Noyes. Fleming went in as the national champion; Noyes as the runner-up. Everything was set from that moment on.

"She had the grace and the beauty, I had the jumps," Noyes said. "She had such an elegance on the ice. That was the look the judges really wanted at that time. I was a little kid in 1964, just fourteen to fifteen years old. And I was tenacious, a real competitor. I knew that my only chance was if she didn't land any of her jumps. She had four in her program, and if she missed all four, then they might have given it to me. That's a teenaged competitor talking. You didn't root for that to happen, but those were the facts. She had to miss all her jumps for anyone to beat her, because she was so pretty on the ice.

"Anyway," Noyes concluded, "she never missed more than one."

Skating magazine, the official publication of the U.S. Figure Skating Association, covered the 1964 Winter Olympics. Noyes, it reported, "is a vigorous jumper with plenty of personality. She did not quite manage three turns in the air on her triple salchow, but it was a bold attempt, and the program was pleasantly lively."

Fleming, the magazine said, "came to grief once on her double lutz, but otherwise jumped well and skated with a pleasing flow of movement. She is a thoughtful skater who has considerable capacity for development."

Fleming and Noyes were closest in 1964. From then on, it was all Fleming: first-place votes across the board. As long as Fleming was skating, Noyes never had another U.S. judge's first-place vote.

"It could have gone either way," Fleming said. "Anything can happen in competition, and I knew that and I think that's where my insecurity always came. 'Well, gosh, something could happen.' I was lucky that nothing weird did happen. I got the job done and I skated well."

Fleming finished third in the world in 1965; Noyes dropped to tenth. Button wrote about the event that year in the USFSA magazine. "In the free skating event, comment should be made of Tina Noyes, who skated with extraordinary electricity," he reported.

As for Fleming: "Here is a skater who has a unique combination of athletic ability, technical control, great style, and immense musicality."

At the 1968 Olympics in Grenoble, France, Fleming won the gold medal and Noyes finished fourth. Noyes tried a triple toe loop and almost landed it. Fleming tried her trademark spread eagle–double axel–spread eagle, but managed only a single axel. She two-footed the landing on her double lutz and hung on because of the huge lead she had built in the compulsory school figures. "I messed up my biggest jumps," she said.

Fleming, who was always so nervous before a competition that she could not eat, was the two-time world champion coming into the Olympics. She had built such a big lead in the compulsory school figures that a shaky performance—and that's what it was—could not rob her of the gold medal. Her best effort had come a month earlier, at the 1968 Nationals. It's that performance, not her Olympic program, that is seen almost in its entirety on an ABC highlight film.

"I didn't skate my best at the Olympics," Fleming said. "Everyone would love to have that, to win the Olympics and have the performance of your life. Like Brian Boitano. I mean, wow, what a wonderful memory. But I don't have that."

With the Winter Olympics televised live and in color for the first time, it didn't matter. Within months, Fleming signed a five-year, $500,000 deal with Ice Follies. Another contract ensured one TV special, which then led to four more. She made commercials for products including Ocean Spray, One-A-Day vitamins, Avon, and L'eggs panty hose. A soap commercial required her to shower in a TV studio. "I wore a bathing suit, but it was a strange feeling. You knew people were whispering to each other about you," she said. By 1981, she was working beside Button at ABC.

Fleming became America's favorite skater in 1968, and even though Dorothy Hamill came along and stole that title in 1976, Fleming still had the edge on Hamill in many other ways. A squeaky-clean image. The one marriage. An impeccable business record that did not include well-publicized lawsuits with her agent and coach, as Hamill's did.

Fleming was approachable, a woman who gave out her home phone number and then answered it herself. Hamill, on the other hand, was difficult to find. Telephone messages went unreturned for months. When an assistant was located, it was suggested that the best way to communicate with Hamill would be by fax.

Fleming, understandably, became the celebrity many companies wanted as their spokeswoman. About the only controversial thing she ever did was call Joe Namath "a mess" when asked about role models back in 1969.

Namath, who hosted a television show back then, invited Fleming to be on it. He treated the incident this way:

"Say, Peggy, what are you doing tonight?"

Noyes stayed amateur the year following the Olympics. After training in Boston and New York her whole life, she moved with her mother to Colorado Springs to train with Carlo Fassi for the 1969 season. (Fleming had moved there herself in 1965 as she prepared for the Olympics.) Noyes went hoping Fassi could work his magic for her last try at a national title.

But it didn't happen. At the national championships, the judges

placed her not first . . . not second . . . but third, behind the next bud-
ding American superstar, Janet Lynn, and another youngster, Julie
Lynn Holmes.

"The message was very clear," Noyes said.

At the age of twenty, Noyes turned pro. She joined the Western
company of Ice Capades and made $25,000 a year, a paltry sum com-
pared to Fleming's deal.

"Put into nineties terms, Peggy would have had more money than
the queen of England, and she deserved it," Noyes said.

After three years, Noyes's Ice Capades contract ran out. Her
mother died and she returned home to live with her father, a sales rep
for Mobil Oil. She turned down an offer from Holiday on Ice and
latched onto a Boston-based agent. She endorsed a line of skating
equipment, wrote an instructional book, and took a job teaching skating at the Hayden Recreation Center in Lexington, Massachusetts.

When Noyes was thirty-three, her father died, leaving her alone.
Not knowing what to do, she kept on teaching skating.

This went on for nearly another decade. One day in 1992, almost
twenty years into her coaching career, Noyes stopped in her tracks on
her way into the rink.

"I've been stuck on hold for twenty years now," she said to herself.

Noyes was forty-three. It was summertime, the slow season in figure skating. She was making fund-raising speeches in and around
Boston on behalf of the U.S. Olympic Committee. She wanted to become a better writer. She decided to go to college.

She took a writing course that summer at Boston College and enjoyed it enough to keep going. She didn't tell anyone at the rink, but
she soon enrolled for a full complement of evening courses. She was
getting up at 4:45 A.M. to teach skating. She was eating dinner while
stopped at red lights in her car. She was studying until midnight.

Finally, as a college junior in January 1994, she quit her job in skating and became a full-time student. She paid for her classes—$32,000
for the three years it took her to get through—with money her late father had set aside for a rainy day.

"It's raining," Noyes proclaimed.

One class she was thinking of taking was called "Career, Marriage,
and the Family."

"Gee, that's interesting," she told her adviser. "I have none of the
above."

An invitation arrived at Noyes's home in January 1993. Greg Jenkins was throwing a twenty-fifth anniversary party in honor of his

wife's 1968 Olympic gold medal. Noyes immediately decided she wouldn't go. It would cost her $1,000 to fly to San Francisco and spend a couple nights in a hotel, she would miss some of her college classes, and she also would have to cancel some of her skating lessons. It just wasn't worth it.

The next day, she reconsidered. Over the years, she had bumped into Fleming at various skating events. The more she got to know Fleming, the more she liked her. And, after all, the 1968 Olympics had been her Olympics, too.

Tina Noyes ended up in California.

There was a skating party at a rink in Cupertino, then a dinner for 250 in a nearby community center. Jenkins asked Noyes if she would skate, perhaps put on some kind of exhibition at the rink.

"No, thanks," Noyes told Jenkins, "it's her party."

A couple of the men—former national champions John Misha Petkevich and Tim Wood—skated, and then, Fleming came onto the ice.

She announced to the guests she was going to re-create her 1968 Olympic program. In the days before the party, Fleming had studied the videotape of the performance and practiced it at the rink to try to remember all the footwork and moves.

"This is where I've landed my double lutz," Fleming said, pointing to the ice, standing still and smiling, "and now I'm going to do my slow part."

And so she did. The music—Tchaikovsky's Symphony No. 6, *Pathétique*—played in the background. It's music that will always be a part of her life. At home, her husband hums it to get her attention.

In a black skating dress and tights, Fleming began moving across the ice. She performed all the steps and arm movements that she had done in Grenoble, France, twenty-five winters earlier.

Her guests, including Noyes, stood and watched. They couldn't help but notice that Fleming was in better shape now than she was in 1968, and prettier, too. She had had her nose fixed when she turned thirty, and her husband occasionally gave her professional tips to "look and feel better," she said. His business card, after all, read "Diseases and Surgery of the Skin." (He didn't do the nose, though.)

Noyes, in her skates, hanging along the boards with the other guests, shook her head and smiled.

"Look at who she has become, this larger-than-life character," she said. "And thus she will always be."

When Fleming finished, beautifully as always, Noyes was the first to skate over to her. Wearing a brown cashmere coat draped over a lime green warm-up, Noyes handed Fleming a bouquet of long-stemmed red roses, given by David and Phyllis Kennedy, longtime fans and friends of Fleming and Noyes's from New York. Fleming hugged Noyes and kissed her on the cheek.

At the community center, after cocktails, Noyes saw that seating was unassigned, so she picked a table where some friends of hers had gathered and sat down.

Fleming was seated at another table. When she saw Noyes sit down, she got up, walked over to her, and tapped her on the shoulder.

"I want you to sit with me," she said.

And so they dined together, with only Jenkins between them, telling stories all night with Petkevich and Wood and some of the other old skating buddies.

While Noyes was in town, Fleming picked her up at her hotel and drove her back to the house on the hill. Noyes was struck by the view over the valley all the way to San Francisco.

"It was really something," Noyes said. "Just what Peggy deserved."

Noyes would hate Peggy Fleming if she didn't like her so much. Fleming doesn't act like a national icon. She is more like an old, sweet college friend.

"Along the way, even after I won the Olympics, I was never really totally impressed with myself," Fleming said. "I was real impressed when I made the cover of *Life* magazine. That kind of registered; that was really cool. I guess I really did something important. Winning the Olympics was an incredible feeling of accomplishment and relief that will stay with me the rest of my life. But I don't go around thinking about it all the time."

Peggy Fleming desperately tries to lead a relatively normal life. During the week, she makes lunches for her family and drives Todd to kindergarten in her Range Rover. She works out two hours a day, she answers her mail, and she schedules TV work and personal appearances, often related to women's health issues. When the weekend comes, her pace slows—if she is in town. On one rainy Saturday, she worked out with a personal trainer for an hour in the morning; came home to play with Todd, who was setting up a toy train on the living room floor; ran errands with assistant and long-time friend Jean Leidersdorf in the afternoon; and packed for a four-day trip to New York to voice-over videotape from a recent skating competition she had covered for ABC.

"It's tough to be a friend to someone like me," she said. "I make plans and then I have to cancel out when my work comes up."

Husband Greg was out of town himself; he had flown to the Caribbean for a few days after attending to his late father's estate. He wanted Fleming to go, but her ABC duties prevented that.

"He wanted to go someplace warm. I told him, 'Honey, our pool's open. Put on that wet suit and jump in,' " Fleming said with a mischievous grin. "He'll come home the day I come home. It's good for him to get away."

Peggy Fleming's house is full of pictures. Her two sons grow up from wall to wall in the bedrooms and the hallways. All the photos that are not hung are in scrapbooks, which are strategically placed in a cabinet by the garage door. Fleming wants to be able to grab them and run if a forest fire threatens their home.

The pictures on the walls aren't just of people. Fleming wanders into her guest bathroom: "When you're on an African safari, and you see an animal and you want to take a picture, by the time you're ready to take the picture, the animal has turned and . . ."

There, on the wall, are the rear ends of a zebra, a giraffe and an impala.

The laundry room is also something to behold.

"I painted it myself," Fleming said, giggling, opening the door to reveal a pattern of black and white cow spots. "I don't know why I did it. I just did it."

This is the Peggy Fleming that no one outside the house on the mountaintop knows.

"I come across differently on television, don't I?" she said.

Who thinks of Peggy Fleming sitting in her den barefooted, giggling about how editorial cartoonists portrayed her sport during the Tonya-Nancy saga? If she's not the teenager from California in the chartreuse dress with the hair piled high, she's that fetching fixture in an evening gown on the skating telecasts. She says the nicest things. She feels so sorry when a skater falls. She never gets herself in trouble, even in private.

"Our sport is very revealing to what the character of the skater is all about," is what she will say. "It just takes all kinds. There's no cookie-cutter form for skaters. It would make a dull world if they all were the same. This kind of spiced it up a little more. Some people would not have been able to handle things as well as Nancy Kerrigan did, and Tonya Harding did deserve to go to the Olympics, because she had not been found guilty of anything. The media circus was the most unfortunate thing."

That's about as controversial as Fleming will get.

Beautiful and reluctant at the same time, she is credited with starting America's love affair with its female skaters. Her journey was not easy. Her father was a newspaper printer who moved his family of four daughters from San Jose to Colorado Springs—and Fassi—for Peggy's skating, then drove the Zamboni at the Broadmoor rink. He died in 1966. Her mother, Doris, sewed Peggy's dresses and made sure no coach or slick businessman took advantage of her daughter.

Every night at nine, Fassi and Fleming would finish on the ice at the Broadmoor. Fassi would drive home, then wait for the phone in the kitchen to ring.

"I put down a blanket on my kitchen table, and a pillow, and I waited," he said. "Mrs. Fleming called me and kept me forty minutes on the phone to discuss the practice that day. What happened, why she missed this jump. I don't know how I did it, for two to three years, every night I got a call to discuss everything that was going great."

"Maybe she called a little too much," Fleming said with a chuckle, "but she didn't do elite sports herself and she was making sure she was doing the right things by me."

After Peggy won the gold medal, her mother said she wasn't going to turn pro. She would get married to that nice medical student and have a family and . . . whoa! Fleming did turn pro. She did have the career. And it wasn't that hard. All she had to do was be herself.

"I have a very nice life," Fleming said. "I don't get bothered a whole lot. I get asked to do different things, but I learn to say no. I feel that my private life is important to keep private because of my husband and my children. I want them to grow up in an environment that is not a big fishbowl of people looking at everything we do. I don't want them to become self-conscious that they can't be themselves because everybody knows who Mom is and we have to act a certain way."

Fleming brought no family members with her when, a week before Christmas, she visited Michelle Kwan at Lake Arrowhead to tape a television special. Fleming laced up her skates and glided around with Kwan for the cameras.

Would she jump? someone asked.

"Ohhhh, noooo," she said. "I don't jump anymore. At my age, you can really tear muscles."

She had just been to Columbus, Ohio, for a skating appearance at the local zoo. She had had no time to practice her number, and she hadn't skated in front of a crowd in more than a year.

Leidersdorf had come to Ohio with her. When they got to the rink, Fleming had time only to get dressed and step onto the ice to do her number.

"Skate around a little, Peggy," Leidersdorf said anxiously. "Skate around to get warmed up."

But there was no time for that. The music started. And, on cue, the forty-six-year-old wife and mother "went into the Peggy Fleming mode," Leidersdorf said.

"Thank God," Fleming said. "You know, the music, a little bit of costume, a little bit of support hose, it makes a big difference. That muscle memory, or that whole feeling, comes back when you absolutely have to have it. I grabbed every ounce of concentration that I could possibly muster to be able to do that. I didn't want to let those people down."

Tina Noyes rarely skates anymore. She doesn't have time with her classes and studies. But when she gets extremely worn out at school, she will put on a Walkman and pop into a public session at a nearby rink and zip around for thirty minutes. She doesn't jump anymore either.

Her life is not entirely school and studying. She has numerous social contacts in Boston, some through the U.S. Olympic Committee, and often finds herself at black-tie affairs or dinner parties.

"Life as a single woman is ever changing, unpredictable, and exciting," she said. "I feel something and someone is waiting around the corner. I'm not single by choice. I always say I've been close to marriage, but I've never bought the dress."

Fleming and Noyes usually run into one another at the national championships every few years, or even at the Olympics. Noyes always pays her own way to these events; Fleming is there for ABC, or some corporation. Noyes sits in an upper section; Fleming settles in rinkside in the ABC booth. Sometime during each trip, Tina will work her way close to the booth, hang over the railing, and yell to Peggy. Peggy always turns around and waves back.

"I wish I knew Tina better," Fleming said. "When we were skating, I was working on my own stuff. I'd look out the corner of my eye at what my competitors were doing, but that was about it. I would only see her at high-stress times in competition when we all were scared to death. But now when I see Tina, we pick up where we left off. It's just too bad that at the time, the competitive edge has to be so cold."

"Peggy and I never could have been best friends with the way we were competitors," Noyes said. "There was an archrivalry and it was one I'll cherish forever. You say, 'Thank God you had an opportunity to really have something to strive to be better than.' That, for me, was Peggy. I never was, but at least I had the opportunity to strive for it."

10

"GO OUT
AND
TELL
A STORY"

The videotape was grainy. Sometimes, there was no sound, just the image of a little blond pixie moving across the ice blithely on her skates. The tape belonged to Joe Inman, the skating judge, and to him it was priceless. It was a special night indeed when he could invite Brian Boitano, in town for a skating performance, to come over and watch it.

Boitano sat transfixed in front of Inman's television set. These performances were nearly twenty-five years old, and other than a snippet here or there, he had never seen them. By the time he had come of age in the sport, this girl was gone.

"Look at that," Boitano marveled at one of her jumps. "Look at that spring off the ice. And she lands like a pillow, so smooth."

Boitano shook his head. "There's so much stuff here . . ."

The pixie turned one-footed edgings into artwork before Boitano's eyes.

"Go back," Boitano said to Inman. "Can you rewind it a few seconds? There!"

Boitano smiled at a particularly intricate piece of footwork. "I want to steal that move."

In twenty minutes, the tape had wound its way to blackness. Boitano finally turned his eyes back to the room.

"I never had a skater I idolized when I was growing up," he said. "Now I realize I should have idolized Janet Lynn."

•   •   •   •

Accompanied by one of her five sons, a plain, heavyset, forty-one-year-old woman was waiting in a booth at a suburban Detroit restaurant. Waiting for the kind of person she almost always avoided. Waiting for a reporter, of all things.

The U.S. Figure Skating Association said it could not find Janet Lynn. No telephone number, no address. A box of fan mail sat for years in the USFSA office in Colorado Springs, collecting dust and the occasional letter. Only a woman with the world's most comprehensive figure-skating Rolodex knew how to reach her, and she warned of serious consequences if Lynn ever learned who had given out her number.

Sure enough, when the phone call was placed, Lynn immediately wanted to know how she had been found.

A couple days later, Lynn ended up in the booth at Mountain Jack's in Auburn Hills, which shares a highway exit with the sports arena of the Detroit Pistons. She brought Nic, one of her fifteen-year-old twins, for companionship and encouragement. But if it was true that she really didn't want to come, it also became true that she didn't want to leave. More than four hours after she began talking, she finally finished.

Then again, a Midwestern housewife who once signed a three-year, $1.45-million professional sports contract—the largest in history for a woman at that time—had a lot of explaining to do.

"It's very flattering that people care, but I've always downplayed what I did in the past because of our children," Lynn said softly. "I don't want them to grow up to be the children of the Olympic whatever. Those things are past anyway, and I've gone on to a different life. When we've moved to a new place, I never tell anybody what I did. They just kind of eventually find out because of something that happens, like when a Japanese camera crew shows up at our house."

Janet and Nic turned to look at each other. They giggled like siblings. This hiding business wasn't as serious as it initially sounded.

The Japanese have come calling because Janet Lynn was the most precious figure skater ever. She never won an Olympic gold medal, but if the rules in 1972 were as they are today, she would have. If most Americans don't know that, the Japanese will remind them, for it was in their country, at the 1972 Games in Sapporo, that Lynn fell to the ice on a flying sit spin and, amazingly, sat there and smiled. The next day, mobs of fans pushed to be close to her. "I was like a rock star," she said.

In the United States, Lynn won five consecutive national championships from 1969 to 1973. Had she been better at the dreaded compulsory school figures that dominated the sport then, she could have been every bit the household name that Peggy Fleming, who came im-

mediately before her, and Dorothy Hamill, who came right after, still
are today.

Except that, unlike Fleming and Hamill, Lynn was content to fade
away. It wasn't an entirely easy decision, especially when exercise-
induced asthma snatched away the last year of her pro career and
later gave her a reason to try a comeback in her late twenties. But
Lynn, unlike so many of the other stars of her sport, allowed herself to
be plucked away from skating and taken to another place, and she
lives there still.

Where that is, exactly, she won't say. She would prefer that details of
her family life remain untold, not because anything is wrong, but because she wants it that way. Her husband's government work keeps
them on the move, from Colorado to Minnesota to a well-to-do suburb
north of Detroit. Her children range in age from nine months to seventeen years old. She would prefer not to recite their names for the public.

A much warmer glow develops when she talks about her skating.
What do you think would happen if you tried to skate now? she was
asked.

"Ummmm." The skater most beloved by her peers couldn't come
up with an answer, so she laughed nervously.

Nic chimed in, "She skated once on a school trip in Minnesota."

The teachers and other parents knew her as Mrs. Janet Salomon.
When they saw her on the ice, twirling and spinning, they were quite
surpised to see that Mrs. Salomon really knew how to skate.

Nic set the record straight. "My mom is Janet Lynn."

"*Your mother's Janet Lynn?*" one of the teachers replied incredu-
lously.

Janet Lynn shrugged at this story: "That was two babies and about
forty pounds ago, though."

As a skater, Janet Lynn was sweet and vulnerable. She was a child
who never grew up. She reached only five feet one and a half inches.
Her short blond hair fell softly onto her forehead and often blew in
wisps as she glided across the ice. During practice sessions at the
Wagon Wheel Ice Palace, a resort built of logs and railroad ties in the
cornfields of northern Illinois, she would skate over to her coach and
lay her head on the coach's shoulder. "She nudged up to me like a kit-
ten," said Slavka Kohout, the woman who coached Lynn from 1959
to 1973. At competitions, Lynn would put her head on the railing and
rest between compulsory school figures, then charge off when it was
her turn again. And she always smiled. Father's orders.

"No matter what you do, smile," Lynn said her father told her.

"And I always did. He didn't care how I skated, he just wanted me to smile when I was out there."

Kohout, the daughter of a Chicago businessman who was herself a fine skater, always sent Lynn out to skate by taking hold of both her hands, staring into her eyes, and telling her, "Go out and tell a story."

"I wanted her to take her attention off the technical aspect so that she wouldn't get so tied up," Kohout said. "I knew that a fall didn't make a bit of difference if the performance was interesting. Some of these skaters go out mindlessly and just go through the motions. I knew she had good imagination, so that I always wanted her to be thinking of something and projecting something and looking into people's faces. And so I would say it: 'Just tell them a story. Listen to your music. Hear it again for the first time. Tell a story to it.' "

Lynn's skating was charming and delightful, unlike anything we see in one skater today. If Boitano's attention to detail could be mixed with Oksana Baiul's magic, Michelle Kwan's youthful exuberance, and Nancy Kerrigan's athleticism, that would come close. Lynn wasn't doing all the triples those skaters now do—no woman was—but were she skating today, with the coaching and technical advances of the nineties, she probably would be able to do most of them.

Were she skating today . . .

With no compulsory figures, with her jumping and skating ability and with her middle-American wholesomeness, Janet Lynn would be one of the most famous athletes on the planet.

The outside world has a strong and misguided sense that only in the 1990s has figure skating begun to demand that its stars be tiny pre-teens who alter the lives of their families to further their ice-skating careers. The truth is, this has been going on for years.

When Janet Lynn was in first grade in the Chicago suburbs, she took off Wednesdays from school to skate. On Tuesday afternoon, either her mother or father would drive her one hundred miles up the Illinois Tollway to the Wagon Wheel in Rockton, Illinois, so she could skate that night and all day Wednesday. They then would drive back to their home in Evergreen Park Wednesday night. After two more days of school, Janet, her parents, her two older brothers, and her younger sister would make the trip again Friday night, returning late Sunday.

Lynn spent one school year like that. Then she moved in with a family in Beloit, Wisconsin, four miles from the Wagon Wheel, for the next school year. She was seven years old. Within a few months, however, she was homesick, so her parents worked out another arrangement. Janet's grandfather moved to Rockton to take care of her the rest of that year, and by the next summer, the whole family moved to Rockford, fifteen miles from the rink. Janet's father sold his half of the pharmacy he co-owned in Chicago and got a job managing a drugstore in Rockford. They bought a house and settled into new schools. All of this was done for Janet's skating.

Also that year, Kohout suggested to Janet's parents that she have a skating stage name. At the time, Janet Lynn was Janet Lynn Nowicki. Drop the "Nowicki," Kohout thought, because it was hard to pronounce and spell, difficult to understand over the public address system, and potentially damaging to Janet in those Cold War days if judges from the Eastern bloc didn't like Janet's Polish heritage. Janet's parents went along, even though some Polish-American groups weren't so pleased later on.

A lot was happening to a little girl at a young age. But rather than feeling pushed or pressured by this, Lynn thrived.

"I was a normal kid doing something that I loved to do," Lynn said. "I know now that the reason that I loved to do it is because I was so shy that I hated to talk to people, and I found out that I could express myself in skating without talking to anybody.

"So my skating stemmed out of what I felt in my heart. I was not a natural for a lot of the technical things, but the heart that I had in skating was a gift that God gave me, and it was just a natural for me to share that with people."

The vulnerability in Janet Lynn, at age seven or forty-one, was complemented by the kindness of Kohout, now a sixty-two-year-old who recently returned to coaching in Connecticut. When the Nowickis first appeared at the Wagon Wheel and asked Kohout to coach their daughter, she had a question for them: "You mean you'll let me?"

After a fifteen-minute lesson, Lynn knew she had found her last skating teacher.

"I'd never been so captivated in my life," she wrote in her 1973 autobiography, *Peace + Love*. (The *and* in the title is represented by a cross.)

The pairing was perfect for both. Lynn was loyal and unquestioning; Kohout, innovative and unthreatening. "She was very good at imitating whatever she saw," Kohout said. "I'd show her things and she could do them. Janet always innately loved skating, the pleasure of gliding on ice. It was evident always."

Kohout taught Janet to jump both clockwise and counterclockwise, something that no skaters do now. Her footwork was intricate. Her timing was impeccable. Nothing was rushed in her programs, nothing forced. Sometimes, she would stop and wait before the next musical note pushed her on her way.

"Slavka was a genius," Lynn said. "I remember her going to have music cut, and she would take sometimes a note, one note from one album, and use it to have other music connect together. One note to have it all flow together and make it work."

Their partnership flourished. In 1966, Lynn won the national junior championship, and in 1968, not yet fifteen and in the ninth grade, she took the third spot on the U.S. Olympic team, after Fleming and Tina Noyes. She finished ninth, all but forgotten during Fleming's coronation.

But she was developing an important ally in her climb to the top of her sport: Dick Button of ABC Sports. At the 1968 Nationals in Philadelphia, the Olympic trials, Button was in his element. Lynn said it's funny to watch the replay:

"Little Janet Lynn . . . only needs to move up one place to make the Olympic team . . . she's moving gracefully, powerfully. . . . Isn't she fantastic? . . . A beautiful jump!"

Lynn wasn't entirely fantastic. She fell twice, on a triple salchow and a double lutz.

After the second fall, Button changed his tune: "Oh! I don't know what's happening to her tonight!"

But Button was smitten. Within five years, he would be Lynn's agent and he would be Kohout's husband. He and Kohout had two children, but were divorced in 1984.

In the 1960s, just as it is now, skating was terribly expensive. After Lynn won the junior national title in 1966, her mother told Kohout that Janet was going to have to quit taking lessons. The Nowickis had run out of money.

Kohout went to the owner of the Wagon Wheel and explained the problem. From that moment on, the Nowickis never paid for ice time or another lesson for their daughter.

The assumption was that Kohout knew that Janet Lynn was going to be something special, and the rink didn't want to lose her. But Kohout said that wasn't entirely true. "You never know you have anything," she said. "It's circumstances and it's luck and how you develop and the lack of injuries. But we never knew what would happen."

When Fleming turned professional, she left American ice to Lynn. Lynn always won the national championships, but went to the worlds and performed so badly on the compulsory school figures that she finished out of the medals in 1969, 1970, and 1971. Another American, Julie Lynn Holmes, ended up ahead of Lynn each of those years. It was a sign of Lynn's charisma; she often failed at the biggest moment of each year, and yet she left the arena with the crowd on its feet, chanting her name.

Then came the 1972 Olympic Games. *Newsweek* put her on the cover, but foretold of her potential problems: Lynn, the magazine said, is "a virtual cinch to enchant the Sapporo audiences with her dazzling free skating—and almost equally certain to fall short of the points accumulated by Austria's Beatrix Schuba in the dull compulsory competition."

Lynn had tried everything to get better at compulsory figures, but she just couldn't muster the steadiness to retrace her figures six times without major errors. She was a free skater. To her, the compulsory school figures weren't skating; they were drudgery. Yet they then accounted for 50 percent of the total score in 1972. And Schuba, a massive woman who clanked around the ice in the free skating (long program), may have been the greatest compulsory figure skater ever.

Lynn was fourth after the figures. Schuba was first. She had all but locked up the gold medal before the free skating began. Everyone knew Schuba was exceptionally weak in the long program, but it didn't matter. Her lead over Lynn was as wide as the ocean.

Lynn said she was lucky to be fourth: "In one of my loops, I did a little fish. I got up to the top of it and it's supposed to be a certain shape, and I got nervous and stuck and so this fish thing came out. And that was a really huge no-no."

More than two decades later, in the retelling, she could laugh. Back then, Lynn raced to her room in the Olympic village and sobbed for hours.

"I was so embarrassed. I realized that I had just ruined everything that I had lived for my whole life."

Lynn had become a born-again Christian several years earlier, and she spent much of the night praying. When she got on the ice for the long program two days later, she performed as if she had not a concern in the world. Except for the fall on the flying sit spin—which she turned into one of the crowning achievements of her career with that smile—she was perfect. She received no score lower than a 5.8, most of the marks were 5.9s, and she even received one 6.0 for artistic impression from the Swedish judge.

The *London Observer* described it this way: "There is a movement in her program . . . when she suddenly moves backwards so that her blond hair flies forward and her arms are outstretched and she is indeed a young girl in love with the world. She would say she is thanking God for so much happiness. Those who watch her can make of it what they will, knowing only that it is supremely beautiful."

Lynn won the long program but, because of the school figures, managed just the bronze medal behind Schuba and Karen Magnussen of Canada.

The next year, officials of the International Skating Union realized the public had no idea how their sport arrived at its results. Why was it that in the only part of the competition the world watched on television—the long program—Janet Lynn was first, but she finished third overall?

So skating officials added a short program. And because a short program was added, Janet Lynn stayed amateur for one more year. Figures would count for just 40 percent of the overall score; the short program would be 20 percent; the long program, 40 percent. Schuba had retired; Lynn finally had her chance.

She won the last of her five national titles in 1973, beating Hamill, and went to the worlds in Bratislava, Czechoslovakia. She traced the best figures in her life and was second, behind Magnussen. The next day was the short program. Oddly, Lynn was nervous. This was supposed to be her event. Its existence was based on her Olympic experience the year before. But, as she later wrote in her autobiography, something didn't feel right. The requirement to do certain jumps bothered her. She had never *had* to do a jump before; she did them because she felt like doing them. Now, every skater was required to do a double-double combination—hers was a double axel/double loop—as well as another double jump—hers was a second double axel. Being told what jumps to do made her uneasy.

Within forty seconds near the end of her short program, the unthinkable happened. Lynn fell on one double axel. Then, she fell on the other.

Kohout stood by, dumbfounded.

"The double axel was the most stable jump she ever did," she said. "She had double axel when she was ten years old. If I really wanted to show her off, I'd stand in the middle of the rink and have her do double axels across the ice. She had one of those beautiful ones that goes up and floats and then checks out. . . . And she fell on it, and then she fell on it again."

Lynn and Kohout, both heartbroken, didn't discuss the short program disaster for twenty-one years. In 1994, when Lynn was inducted into the U.S. Figure Skating Hall of Fame at the Nationals in Detroit, Kohout thought it was time to bring it up.

They were sitting beside each other at the ceremony.

"By the way," Kohout asked out of the blue, "what happened on the double axels at the worlds in '73?"

"Oh, my legs got so cold," Lynn replied. "There were windows open way up high in the arena, and I got so cold."

"I was just wondering," Kohout said.

Twelfth in the short program, Lynn again pulled herself together in the long program, received two 6.0s, kissed Button on the cheek as he interviewed her, and won the silver medal behind Magnussen. It was another grand leap to the medal podium, but it also illustrated her only true weakness: her inability to cope with the rigid discipline of the school figures, and, for forty seconds on the Bratislava ice, the unforgiving requirements of the short program. But when the music came on and she could skate with total freedom, she was the best there ever was.

"No one who ever skated displayed more simple joy, more love for the sport," Button said on television. Her skating, he said, "was just one smooth-flowing thread of silk."

That summer, at the age of twenty, Lynn signed the $1.45-million deal with the Ice Follies, becoming the highest-paid female athlete in the world, making more than Fleming or even tennis star Billie Jean King.

When International Management Group, which worked with Button to represent Lynn, invited her to discuss investments, she had a confession to make: she did not know how to write a check. Her life had been absorbed in training. When it was suggested by the people who ran Ice Follies that she go to a nice store and buy herself some clothes, she returned with a few relatively inexpensive outfits that she and her mother liked. Ice Follies officials took one look at the clothes and suggested she go back and spend more money.

Lynn was not a master of life off the ice. Within two years, unable to control her exercise-induced asthma after a bout with pneumonia, she quit professional skating with a year still left on that huge contract.

Lynn married Salomon, the brother of a skating friend of hers, and they started a family. Money was never a problem; she had invested most of her skating earnings, and her husband had a fine career. But in 1980, living in Colorado and itching to try to skate once more, Lynn returned to professional competitions and shows for three years. She skated with John Curry's company; she went to Button's professional competition in Landover, Maryland.

But with three young sons at the time, she and her husband decided that she should return home. "It was the best decision that I've ever made, to be home with my children, to strengthen our marriage, to be at home instead of out gallivanting."

And that is where she remains to this day, at home. But it's a constant struggle. Her religion tells her to be a good mother and wife, so she says this: "I'm much more comfortable having people know me for what I am instead of what I used to do." Lynn said she is happy being anonymous, the mother of five boys, the loyal wife working in the kitchen.

To that end, she vigorously defends motherhood. But in her words, a wistful uncertainty lingers.

"I miss so much that vehicle of expression," she said. "When you have been in the arena and your peers have been the best in the world in something, it's real hard to pull back from that and realize that, well, I'm cleaning toilets now. There are these days that I think, 'Why am I doing this?' And then I have to go through all the reasons in my mind, because I know there are logical and certain reasons why I'm doing what I'm doing, but you don't get much support from anywhere, basically."

Some of the people who knew her as a skater worry and wonder about her today. They are intensely interested in what has happened to her. They talk about how she looked the last time they saw her, seven months pregnant with her fifth son at the Hall of Fame induction. *How could little Janet get so big? And that family—five boys!* Everyone wants to know where she is living and if she is happy.

Lynn and Kohout rarely talk. Like many coaches and pupils, they went their separate ways. Their meeting in Detroit was a reunion; at the induction ceremony Lynn read an uplifting poem she had written in honor of Kohout. But, when they spoke alone later, Kohout found Lynn quite maudlin.

"She was so sad in Detroit whenever her skating came up," Kohout said. "It's almost a little sad that she hasn't followed a little of her own star."

"Sometimes I am sad," Lynn said, "because I am not out skating or doing something that brings immediate gratification. But I am more content than I have ever been when I fight through that desire to have glory for myself and realize that what I'm doing at home with my family will have wonderful long-term benefits."

Boitano stopped her the last time he saw her, at the 1994 Nationals in Detroit. He always talks about hearing music, even elevator music, and immediately picturing himself doing a routine on ice.

"Janet," he wanted to know, "when you hear music, do you still picture yourself skating to it?"

"Yes," she replied. "Always."

JANUARY

ALMOST
THERE

11

SKATING
IS A
SLIPPERY
SPORT

The Eastern sectional championships were a mere formality for Michael Weiss. No one doubted that he would qualify for Nationals. He was too good not to. No one, that is, but Audrey Weisiger, the coach who knew better—but couldn't help herself. Years ago, she got nervous as a skater, and now she got nervous as a coach. Brian Wright, Weiss's choreographer and Weisiger's best friend, told Weisiger to calm down, Weiss "could land on his ear and still make it," he said, and he was right. Four good senior men skaters had come to Easterns to take the four spots that were available at Nationals. Weiss, the youngest of them all, would earn one of those places. This was a certainty.

The competition was held in Fitchburg, Massachusetts, a small, drab town that was in desperate need of new-fallen snow. In early January, with nothing to hide under, the central part of Massachusetts was especially bleak. At the horizon, the gray sky blurred with the gray landscape. Duly uninspired, Weiss spent his time inside, either flopped on the bed in his motel room, watching the NFL play-offs, or on the ice at the Wallace Civic Center, skating far worse than he should have.

Weiss arrived on Thursday, January 5, 1995, feeling decidedly uncertain about his skating. This had been a strange season for him. Only eighteen, he was in just his second year at the senior level. There could be another ten to go. No one expected him to beat former national champion Todd Eldredge or current national champion Scott Davis this year. Or even for a couple years. And yet, there was this sense of urgency about him. If he was as good as people said, why was he having the kind of year he was having? He had barely competed, because skaters at his level got invited to only one or two international events prior to Nationals. And, when he did compete, he had been awful.

At Nations Cup in Germany in late November, a fairly prestigious invitational, he found himself surrounded—by triple axels. Everyone was as good as he was. Or better. Weiss used to go to international competitions as a junior, be one of the best skaters there, and come in first or second. Now, he was on the ice with Canada's Elvis Stojko, the reigning world champion, among others, and triple axels were bursting all around him. He couldn't help but watch.

"He's just at that age where he's starting to think and understand what's at stake," Weisiger said.

Weiss fell three times over two days and even stumbled on the easiest jump he does, the triple toe loop. For him, the triple toe loop is "like breathing," Weisiger said. Weiss finished tenth of twelve skaters. Weisiger was thrilled he didn't end up last.

They flew home to Dulles Airport, where their families met them. Weiss grabbed Weisiger, his coach since childhood, and hugged her good-bye.

"I had a great time," he said. "Don't worry. Everything will be okay."

Weiss and Weisiger had been together for a decade. Weisiger's husband, Henry, owns the Fairfax Ice Arena, located a couple miles outside the Beltway in Virginia, where she teaches skating. Weisiger, forty, was good enough as a girl to beat Dorothy Hamill a couple times in novice and junior competition. She was fourteen when she left home to train in Colorado. She got homesick, her skating suffered, and she quit. She hated feeling inadequate if she wasn't skating well, which was exactly how the top coaches at the best rinks made you feel, she said. From that moment on, she vowed that if she ever taught skating, she would never make her students feel as if their self-worth were based on "a tiny piece of metal."

She also told herself she would try not to get too wrapped up in the career of one of her skaters.

"Skating," she told herself, "is a slippery sport."

There was too much that could go wrong. There was so much more to life than figure skating.

Then, along came Michael Weiss.

Weiss is either the next great American male figure skater or a young man of great potential who will never make it because he doesn't know what he wants from the sport. This season, his lack of intensity was driving Weisiger crazy. He was too good to keep making these mistakes. *Wiping up the ice* was the term Weisiger used. *The human Zamboni* was another of her favorites.

When Michael made mistakes, Weisiger began to doubt everything. She had coached Michael since he was a little boy, yet she began to wonder why he skated at all. He had a good temperament for the sport; he remained calm most of the time, except when he flung his baseball cap after falling on a triple axel in practice. But she always had this nagging thought: One day he would up and quit.

She feared he would leave figure skating because he is not gay. Weiss has several straight male friends in the sport, but the gay men he consistently interacted with made him uncomfortable. A few years ago, he almost did leave because he felt so out of place, Weisiger said.

"I have to face the fact that the sport might not hold his interest because he's straight," she said.

Greg and Margie Weiss cringed at the thought that people might think Michael is gay because he figure-skates. Margie Weiss has taken great pains to say that her son is "all boy." She was not unusual as a parent in this regard. Joel Tew, Jenni's father, makes it clear that when strangers find out he has a child who is a figure skater, it's a daughter, not a son.

But it was so natural for Michael to become a figure skater. While most fathers played catch with their sons in the backyard, Greg Weiss had his boy on a trampoline. "Michael spent a lot of time upside down," Margie said.

Greg and Margie both were accomplished gymnasts when they were younger. Greg, who competed at Penn State, made the 1960 and 1964 U.S. Olympic teams. When they had children—first two girls, then Michael—they trained them to become athletes in their sprawling gymnastics school at their home on six acres in Maryland. Their oldest daughter, Genna, was a diver. She won a world junior title—then quit when her wrists hurt so badly she had to be helped out of the pool after every dive. Their second daughter, Geremi, chose figure skating. She finished second in junior ladies at the 1990 Nationals. She quit before the 1991 Nationals. She loved the skating, but she didn't like the traveling, or the competing. Both women went on to graduate from college and get jobs involved in sports-related fields.

Michael at first tagged along to the rink because Geremi was taking lessons from Weisiger. Then he began skating himself. As he grew, he realized he could play many sports, including hockey and volleyball. But he liked figure skating because it was so different.

"I like achieving things I didn't think I could do at the beginning," he said.

He also mischievously enjoyed disproving the stereotype that male figure skaters are wimps. In junior high, for a physical education requirement, he had to run a mile. He had never done that before. The other kids were watching. He did it in six minutes. When members of a rival hockey team found out he was a figure skater, too, they began teasing him. He asked them to get out a radar gun and have a race. He reached twenty-two miles per hour. They didn't.

But Weiss didn't skate solely to change the sport's image. He did it because he loved it.

"Everything happens so fast in skating," he said. "You don't have time to be up in the air and say, 'Oh man, this is cool.' You're up there less than half a second. The enjoyment comes in the landing more than in the air. You glide out and it feels great. You know not many people can do it, and you just did it well."

It has been a steady rise for Weiss, from the national junior men's title in 1993 to the gold medal at the world junior championships in 1994. At junior worlds, held on the ice of the legendary Broadmoor in Colorado Springs, every judge put him first. He was the United States' first world junior men's champion since Todd Eldredge in 1988.

He finished eighth in the senior men's division at the 1994 Nationals in Detroit, which wasn't bad for a first try at seniors. Even better, he caught the eye of Brian Boitano and Linda Leaver, who were back because Boitano had reinstated to try again for the Olympics. At practice, Boitano found himself watching Weiss on the ice, even though he didn't know who the kid was.

"He reminds me of someone," Boitano said.

Who?

"Me."

Leaver began to keep up with Weiss. She asked about his coach. She was told it was Weisiger. Years earlier, when Leaver and her husband were in Washington, D.C., she taught lessons at a tiny rink in Falls Church, Virginia, and occasionally skated on her own in a long-gone rink in downtown Washington. On the same ice, circling around her, taking lessons from another coach, was a teenage Audrey King Weisiger.

Now, Audrey was married with a ten-year-old daughter, spending almost all of her time coaching one skater, Michael. She found solace in Leaver's story: the housewife/mother/coach who took the boy skater to the Olympic gold medal. If it worked for Leaver, she hoped it could work for her, too.

"I'm like a mad scientist with this grand experiment," Weisiger said. "With any experiment, it's putting the right ingredients in at the right time. I'm trying the best I can to do this right, to not rush headlong into this, to realize that's where mistakes are made. But I guess I'm totally aware that, at any time, things can all go kabluey."

Plagiarism being the sincerest form of flattery in figure skating, Weisiger decided to take little pieces of Boitano's success and incorporate them into Weiss's skating. They are both big by skating standards, Boitano at five eleven and 170 pounds, Weiss, five feet eight and 160 pounds. Boitano was reared on compulsory school figures. So was Weiss, who won the national novice figures title in 1990 and was second in senior men's figures in 1991. Like the old-time skaters, Weiss was disciplined. In skating terms, it's called edge and line. He skates with a deep edge and has a nice line.

Were figures still a part of the overall competition, were things the way they were ten years ago, Weiss would have a huge advantage over most of his competitors. His compulsory marks would beat those of almost everyone else, so he, like those skaters of the past, would have had an advantage going into the short program. Unlike most skaters, Weiss misses the time spent alone on the ice, carving those designs. Those patch sessions—so named because they were performed on a small patch of ice—were expensive and time-consuming, but they also were the sport's backbone. In baseball, when a player misses a bunt, an announcer laments the passing of the sport's obsession with its fundamentals. And so it is with figure skating. The jumping is eye-catching, and the sport is judged more openly, but what happened to the intricate footwork? The stylish edge? The classic line?

Weisiger wanted Weiss to play to that heritage. For his short program a year earlier, thinking of Boitano, Weisiger put Weiss in a navy blue military-style outfit, similar to Boitano's 1988 Olympic costume.

"I'm thinking to myself, okay, Boitano was the 1988 Olympic champion, and here comes little pinheaded Michael, the youngest senior man at seventeen, why not show a little bit of the comparison?"

It would be a miracle if Weiss did what Boitano did. The timing, the luck, the performance of a lifetime at the exact right moment: this didn't happen often. Michael's parents knew that, and yet they pushed on, having altered their lives completely for their son's skating.

After the girls left their sports, the Weisses threw their collective energy behind Michael. They sold their gymnastics school and home to move into a four-bedroom, red-brick town house in Fairfax, Virginia, two minutes from the rink. They did this to save money for their son's figure skating.

Greg teaches management at Prince George's Community College where Michael, who graduated from high school a year early, takes free classes. A small, extremely muscular man who still enters bodybuilding competitions, Greg, fifty-three, created quite a stir in the staid U.S. Figure Skating Association almost a decade ago by posing in *Playgirl*. He was standing by a pool wearing swim trunks—standard swimmer's briefs. Telephones were jingling in figure-skating homes from Washington to Colorado Springs. Margie Weiss, forty-five, saw the magazine being passed around at a competition in which Geremi, then barely a teenager, was competing. Weisiger heard about it and was truly concerned. The blue-haired ladies of the sport were beside themselves: *Do we want to see this much of the father of two promising skaters? In* Playgirl?

The Weisses thought the ruckus was humorous. Greg and Margie saw nothing wrong with the photo. Working out is their passion. They are part owners of the local Gold's gym down the street from the rink. The entire family works there. Genna keeps the books; Geremi gives lessons; Michael stocks soft drinks. Greg and Margie give off-ice trampoline and weight-lifting lessons to skaters at the rink to scrape together extra money. Anywhere there's a group wanting their services, they will go. One weekend they drove all night, slept in the car, gave off-ice training lessons at a rink in North Carolina, made $2,000, hopped back in the car, and drove through the next night to be back home to teach and coach the following morning.

Money is always an issue for them. There might be millions at the end of the rainbow, but there's next to nothing at the beginning. As recently as 1988, Michael wore Geremi's old white skates, painted black. Hand-me-downs are everywhere in the Weiss family—even in the town house parking lot. Michael drives a beat-up, fifteen-year-old black Porsche that his father gave him.

Late last year, hoping to get in on some of the profit-taking in figure skating, Weiss signed with Jerry Solomon and ProServ, the sports marketing and management firm that represented Nancy Kerrigan. But because Weiss was basically unknown, companies and promoters were not beating down Solomon's door. So Margie Weiss took charge and arranged skating exhibitions involving her son to dredge up support from townspeople and local businesses. She was a soliciting machine, intensely digging up money for her son's training. She and Greg figured they would spend $49,100 on Michael's skating in 1995. To offset their costs, they had money coming in from several sources. They received a gift of $2,500 for ice time at the rink, and USFSA and U.S. Olympic Committee training grants could reach as high as $10,000–15,000.

However, another $2,500 being donated annually by an anonymous benefactor dried up when Weiss signed with ProServ. The benefactor doesn't like agents.

How does a family spend nearly $50,000 on skating?

This was the Weisses' 1995 budget:

Trips (expenses for Weiss and Weisiger):

Nationals:	$3,500
Internationals:	3,000
Special training:	2,500
Choreography:	5,000
Costumes:	1,000
(His competition costumes are sponsored. It would be another $2,000 if they were not.)	
Skates, two pair:	2,000
Music/studio costs:	600
Off-ice training:	3,000
Medicine/doctors:	1,500
Coaching:	15,000
Ice time:	12,000

Weisiger helped the Weisses by not requiring them to pay for lessons lost back home when she went on the road with Michael, a standard fee for most top coaches. The Weisses do pay for Weisiger's travel, room, and board on the road, which also is the norm.

The Weisses have trouble making ends meet, but Weisiger doesn't worry about when they will pay her. To her, they're extended family. She spends hours at the town house, stopping in for lunch or to watch skating videotapes with Michael. The Weisses have known Weisiger for so long that a five-by-seven black-and-white photo of her is prominently displayed among the family pictures.

The Weisses pinch pennies everywhere. Getting Michael and Audrey to Fitchburg was a perfect example. Margie Weiss found a good airfare for Michael and Weisiger—$178 per person. But that involved flying from Washington National to La Guardia, changing planes, and flying a propeller to Worcester, Massachusetts. They rented a tiny white Geo for $100 for the week, got a $39 room rate at a place called the Inn on the Hill, and jammed six people into two rooms—four skaters and two coaches, including Weiss and Weisiger. The women and girls were in one room; Weiss and another boy were in the other.

Sitting in the overcrowded motel room, chaperoning a bunch of skaters, Weisiger tried to maintain her sense of humor. She could have been sitting in her beautiful home with five acres of land and a pool in the Washington, D.C., suburbs. But this was more fun. She was taking a kid through skating, from the age of eight to whenever. It was an adventure, a low-budget joyride. Once, she had driven a van with no air-conditioning in the dead of summer from Washington, D.C., to Colorado, to get Michael and Geremi to a competition. It was just part of the job, what a skating coach did.

If Brian Boitano and Nancy Kerrigan and Kristi Yamaguchi were in the majors, this was Class A ball, but without the team footing the bill for travel, lodging, and food. At this level, skating was one long, bumpy bus ride. The only consolation was that no one jumped to the majors as a rookie. Absolutely no one.

Weiss arrived in Fitchburg for the competition wearing a goatee and an earring. The hoop earring was no big deal; lots of male skaters wore earrings, including France's Philippe Candeloro, U.S. ice dancer Gorsha Sur, and Canadian pairs skater Lloyd Eisler. But goatees? Successful male figure skaters didn't grow beards or mustaches until they were safely ensconced in professional shows—or in the broadcast booth.

At the first practice, Weiss landed a quadruple toe loop, a jump no American man has ever successfully landed in competition. But that wasn't what attracted the attention of the judges.

"What's this?"

Taffy Holliday, a former national novice champion and a judge from Greenwich, Connecticut, had wandered up to Weisiger at the boards and was gesturing with her fingers around her lips.

"Did you see his quad?" Weisiger replied, ignoring her question.

"Yes, I did," Holliday replied. "But what's with the goatee?"

Joe Inman, the Alexandria, Virginia, judge who monitored Weiss at home and reported back to the USFSA on his progress, teased him later:

"Hey, what's this?"

Weisiger was standing beside Weiss.

"Joe!" Weisiger was annoyed. "Come on."

"No, no, it's fine," Inman said. "You'd be mad if I didn't mention it, right?"

Weiss and Weisiger weren't so sure.

"He'll probably shave it off now," Weisiger said later, "but I'm not going to tell him he has to do it. That's his call. If he was in the NFL, do you think they would care about a stupid goatee? No. Only in figure skating."

"Give me a break," Weiss said. "Look at Andre Agassi."

Weisiger and Weiss weren't imagining things. Boitano appeared at "Ice Wars" in November with a goatee. "When I was an amateur, I never would have done this," he said. "Who knows what the judges would have done."

Perhaps nothing. But it wasn't worth taking the risk.

The short program Weiss was going to perform in Fitchburg was created by Brian Wright, the choreographer with HIV. Nearly a year earlier, Wright told Weisiger that he had an interesting piece of music for Weiss. It was a tango, "Deus Xango," a bit jarring and unconventional, but something Wright had performed in a dance theater in Seattle.

This is what Wright did for a living. He met with Weiss for several days in the spring, installing a new program the way a plumber puts in a new sink, pipes and all. "The maintenance man," he called himself. Before the meeting, he selected the music with the coach's help and mapped out in his mind the moves the skater would make to the music. For this, Weiss's parents paid Wright $2,000 for the two-minute-forty-second short program; Weisiger did Weiss's four-minute-thirty-second long program, as she had done for his entire career.

"I come in, set the feet, set the arms, go home, let the skater go with that for a while, then come in for the periodic follow-ups," Wright said. "After we go through it, I leave and the program goes to the student and the coach, and because they don't know it in and out, the student makes it his own and kind of gives birth to it. I'm sort of like the nurse, or something, when I return, pulling them along in their own direction."

To come up with ideas for how Weiss would skate the tango, Wright walked outside his downtown Indianapolis apartment during a rainstorm—without an umbrella. He wanted to get soaked to remind himself of how he felt when he had been kissed in the rain.

He also wandered into auditions for dinner theaters and other local productions, not to get a part, but just to see what the actors were doing. Anything for an idea.

For Michael Weiss, there would be no sissy stuff. Weisiger and Wright put him in a masculine costume for the short program: black pants, a Spanish-style vest, white shirt. It was manly by skating standards, a little dicey, Weiss thought, for normal everyday life. It wasn't something he would wear to, say, the mall.

"I don't know why I should wear stuff like that when I compete," Weiss said. "I don't wear it any other time. A lot of things, I'll just say, 'I'm not wearing that. No way.' I practice in shorts or sweats, a tank top, and a baseball cap. My friends ask me why I don't wear that when I skate in a competition. I don't know why I don't. I should."

Weiss also questioned the skating community's devotion to music. He left those choices to Weisiger and Wright, but he often wondered why it was such a production to pick music.

"If you skate well, you can skate to 'Pinocchio,' 'Peter Pan,' whatever you want to skate to," Weiss said. "If you're a girl and you do triple lutzes, you can skate to whatever you want to. If you're a guy doing two triple axels and triple axel–triple toe, you could skate to 'It's a Small World' and still win."

Wright knew what he was dealing with in Weiss. He wanted Weiss to look and skate like a man. Wright stood on the ice in Fairfax in the fall and showed Weiss what he wanted him to do: sudden, jerking arm movements, executed precisely to the beat of the music. There would be no rounded edges, no soft lines. Just rough, aggressive moves.

"Being gay doesn't mean that it immediately includes an effeminate quality," Wright said. "I like being a man and I like acting the gender roles. My style's always been very masculine. I'm not lightly going through life."

It had been quite an experience for Weiss to work with Wright. Never before had he spent so much time with a gay man. He surprised himself by accepting Wright so easily.

"I just think of Brian as a girl—and he does, too," Weiss said. "I understand and accept Brian really easily. I guess it's because he's just funny. He makes fun of gay people and he's gay. Maybe that's why I can hang out with him."

An hour before the men's competition began Friday night at seven, Weisiger heard the sound of a razor in the adjoining motel room. When he went onto the ice, Weiss posed in front of the judges, looked straight at Holliday, and pointed toward his face. *Hey, look! No goatee! And the earring's gone, too.*

Weiss's performance in the short program went downhill from there. He was shaky, falling on one of the four required jumps, the triple lutz. His scores ranged from 4.8 to 5.3 technically. He did get 5.5s and 5.6s artistically from the judges, who had to hold up the numbers on cards because there was no scoreboard in the rink. By the time everyone had skated, Weiss had landed in fourth place. He could fall no further.

The other three top skaters were the ones ahead of him. Shepherd Clark, twenty-three, who always wore elaborate costumes, was third after a tenuous performance of his own. Michael Chack, also twenty-three, was second, which was a gift, because he had made three mistakes, including slips on two jumps. Chack had been third at Nationals in 1993, a remarkable achievement for him. At qualifying events like Easterns, he could live off that for another year or so.

An upset of sorts had occurred, though. Jason Sylvia, who, like Weiss, had toned down for the judges by taking out the two earrings he wore in his left lobe, was first. Two years older than Weiss at twenty, but less well-known and less accomplished, Sylvia was coached by Evy Scotvold on Cape Cod.

Scotvold had been singing his praises all week, saying what a fine jumper he was, one of the best in the country. And Scotvold, who was starting over this season in the Olympic division after all those Paul Wylie–Nancy Kerrigan years, was right. Sylvia, one of two blacks in the competition, was superb, a slender, lithe leaping machine. Seven judges had him first, to one for Chack and one for Weiss. Ed Cossitt, a judge from New York, was enamored of Weiss's skating—and also remembered how Weiss had put together a program in four days for an AIDS skating benefit Cossitt had put on last fall. Cossitt despised the jumping contests that were becoming so prevalent in skating. He was a traditionalist. "In a four-and-a-half-minute program, you spend twenty-one seconds in the air," Cossitt said. "What about the other four minutes?"

Edge and line still mattered to some. Weiss received Cossitt's vote.

The top four skaters in Fitchburg all knew each other quite well. Two years earlier, some of them—and others—had gone to a training camp for top male skaters in Colorado Springs. During one of the sessions, the discussion leader asked them to go around the room, give their names, and tell something about themselves.

One of the skaters said his name and told the group that he made jewelry.

Several of the other boys couldn't suppress giggles.

They came to Weiss.

"My name is Michael Weiss, and I do *not* make jewelry."

On Saturday night, the senior men skated the long program. Each of the top four qualified. Sylvia skated without a mistake, but was given second place to wobbly winner Michael Chack. Take a number, Jason, the judges were saying. Chack's been in line much longer.

The several hundred spectators sitting in the stands began to boo. The rink had the look and sound of a high school hockey game.

"What are you watching?" one man screamed toward the judges.

It was rare that skating families and friends—who comprised almost all of the several hundred fans in the audience—would lose their temper at judges. Skating people were supposed to become immune to disagreeable decisions.

But the judges had a point. While Sylvia's jumps were superb, his technique in between was nothing like Chack's, or Weiss's. Weiss finished third after stumbling on his triple axel. He never tried the quad toe. It had been a practice jump that week, nothing more.

Clark was lucky there was no competition for fourth place. He landed only one solid triple. Sylvia, by comparison, completed seven. It was the first time Weiss ever had lost to Sylvia; the first time Weiss ever had beaten Clark. They usually competed twice a year.

Weiss skated his long program to Mozart, which wasn't his choice. The music was Weisiger's call, selected by her last spring. Like all skaters, he would use this program all year, from the fall through Nationals to the world championships, if he was lucky enough to get that far.

"I wanted to expose him to some cul-cha," Weisiger said with a laugh. "I'd rather see him in as many different kinds of programs as I can conjure up and decide which one is best when it's really critical, in, say, '97 and '98, heading into the Olympics. This was not going to be the year of his life, so why not try something new?"

Weisiger's decisions about music for Weiss's programs usually came in the car, when she listened to tapes as she was driving. "The minute I hear music, I see skating," she said.

It also can be said that the minute she sees skating, she forgets she's driving. Weisiger has had seven fender-bender car accidents in the past fifteen years, all of which, she said, were caused when she got too involved in listening to music in the car. No one has been injured, but her insurance once was canceled for a few weeks.

An hour after the competition, a videotape of the event was playing on television at one end of the rink. Weiss stood with Sylvia and a few other skaters several feet from Weisiger, watching.

On the tape, Weiss moved into some footwork.

Weisiger looked away from the TV set and toward Weiss.

"You forgot your head," Weisiger said to him sternly. At that moment in his program, he was supposed to look back over his right shoulder, but he did not do that.

Weiss looked at her and placed his index finger to his lips.

"Shhhh," Weiss said.

There were too many people around. They would talk about it later.

Brian Wright wasn't at Easterns, so Weisiger called him every night. After the final, Weisiger was upset. What in the world was wrong with Weiss? she asked herself. With his talent and those programs, he should have won the competition, or at least have been second to Chack.

"Maybe I'm making mistakes with him," she said over the phone.

"You're too paranoid to make mistakes," Wright said.

They flew home the next day, Weiss and Weisiger. Their goal had been realized: make Nationals. It wasn't exactly as they had planned, but third was as good as first, at least in this competition.

Weisiger spent most of the day telling herself that she would do whatever was necessary to make Weiss better. If it was time for him to leave her, she would step aside and help find another coach.

This wasn't the first time she wondered. When she'd brought it up to Margie Weiss several months earlier, Weiss had said nonsense, Michael was staying put.

"Audrey," Margie Weiss said, "it's not you. If he doesn't go as far as perhaps he should, it will be because of him. If he never makes it to the Olympics, it's not that big a deal."

Weisiger checked again with Greg Weiss after Fitchburg.

"He's not going anywhere," he said.

That made Weisiger feel better. One day, she approached Michael with a different question. What would he do, she asked, if she somehow couldn't coach him for a long time? Whom would he seek out for lessons?

"Oh, I don't know," Weiss said. He thought for a moment. "We're too used to each other. I guess I'd probably go do something else, play volleyball or whatever, and wait for you to come back."

In the official program at Easterns, there was a picture of Lisa Ervin among the entries for the senior ladies. That was strange, because one person who definitely wasn't competing in Fitchburg was Lisa Ervin.

A month earlier, Ervin, her parents, and her coaches, Evy and Mary

Scotvold, decided that she would not compete in any of the qualifying events leading to Nationals. Her season had ended when it started. Sun Valley had been her one and only competition of the year.

Her eating disorder had continued. On the days she wasn't eating, she had trouble at practice and felt extremely—and understandably—lethargic.

At the urging of Evy and Mary Scotvold, Ervin began working with a Harvard nutritionist on a strict plan to regulate her diet. Every day, she and her mother wrote in a diary about what she ate and how she felt, including her sleeping habits.

"I know I have a problem," Ervin said. "Some people are lucky with their weight, some people aren't. I ended up not being the lucky person."

In some ways, she was unlucky. On the other hand, she actually went to high school and had a 3.9 GPA, she was one of ten seniors out of a class of 220 to be named to the high honor roll, she had friends who knew nothing about skating, her graduation was coming up in five months, and she was waiting to hear from several colleges to which she had applied.

Around the country, this was qualifying time for Nationals. But some skaters didn't have to go through a regional or sectional. Stars like Michelle Kwan and Nicole Bobek were given byes by the USFSA because they appeared in international competitions in the fall. Even some little kids received a free pass to Providence.

Because she had been to the world junior championships, where she finished fourth, tiny Tara Lipinski was given a bye into Nationals. She did not have to attend Easterns. But that didn't mean she took any time off. Tara Lipinski could not rest.

Lipinski, the twelve-year-old, four-foot-five media darling and favorite for the gold medal in the junior division at Nationals, was obsessed with skating and, accordingly, spent the holidays flying between Delaware and Houston.

She and her mother moved north in the summer of 1993 to train at the University of Delaware, one of the country's finest skating centers. Her father stayed behind in Houston. Mother and daughter flew home to Texas to be with him for Christmas.

"I made her come home for Christmas Eve and Christmas Day," said Pat Lipinski, Tara's mother. "She was supposed to stay that week, until New Year's, but she flew out, came to Delaware for five days to train, and then flew back to Houston New Year's Eve.

"I told her, 'Well, that's what you want to do, fine, that's your Christmas gift. The extra flight, that's the money for your gift.'"

Tara and her mother flew back North again a few days later to begin the push to Nationals.

"Is this child driven, or what?" Pat Lipinski asked. "And all I want to do is just spend time together, a mother-and-daughter kind of thing. That would be nice."

The Midwesterns were held in Denver a few weeks before the Easterns. In the short program, Jenni Tew fell on her triple toe loop. But instead of plummeting to eleventh, as she had the year before with a mistake in the short program at Mids, she was sixth.

One judge had placed Jenni first, even with the fall, because most of the others had made errors, too. That judge was Beth Graham of Denver, the former wife of Hugh Graham, who placed Paul Wylie second at the Olympics.

The judges didn't know what to do with Jenni. One placed her second. Another had her third. Three placed her sixth. One even had her eighth.

When the judges got to talking in the back room before their marks were revealed to the public (at the junior level, other than at Nationals, it was closed judging), Beth Graham heard some teasing about her vote for Jenni, according to Deanie Tew:

"Did the Tews promise to build you a rink?"

Sitting in sixth place, Jenni had to leap two places in order to make one of the four spots to Nationals. She had one full day between the short and long. Her parents were glum, Joel Tew especially. Another year, he thought to himself. Another year, she comes close, but she doesn't make it to Nationals. On a day-to-day basis at Winterhurst, the thought wasn't so immediate. But in Denver, at Mids, where all anyone did was discuss when they would fly to Providence and what the practice schedules were and who would be the ones to beat, it was tough. Another year, Joel thought, and Jenni's not going to make it.

In the long program, Jenni fell on that triple toe again, but otherwise skated well. Everyone else stumbled on something or other. It was rather messy. When it was over, no one knew what the judges would do. The Tews knew Graham liked their daughter's skating, and they knew there had been some discussion of their daughter in the judges' room. That was all for the good, they thought.

But Carol Heiss, the master handicapper, wasn't venturing any guesses.

"The judges will send whoever they want to send," Heiss told the Tews. "With all those mistakes, it's just a matter of who they liked."

Jenni was waiting for the results with her parents. That was always the hardest part. The waiting. At the other end of a long hallway, the results would be posted. She was planning to go down to see them, but first, her mother turned to her. She had something to say.

"Even if you don't make it, it was a very successful year," Deanie said, looking deeply into her daughter's eyes. "You achieved your goal of making Mids as a junior lady. I'm afraid you may end up fifth, which will be the hardest thing to take, but you should be proud of yourself. You had a great year."

At that moment, Deanie looked past Jenni and down the hallway. She saw a friend from Winterhurst, 1992 junior men's national champion Ryan Hunka, rushing toward them. Hunka, who also took lessons from Heiss, missed the season due to injuries, but flew to Denver to watch Jenni skate. Now, he was running and Deanie could see that he was holding up some fingers on his hand.

Three?

Three!

It was three fingers.

Jenni had her back to Ryan. She was searching her mother's face.

"Honey, you made it!" Deanie blurted out.

In the beat of a heart, Jenni burst into tears.

The judges had placed her second in the free skating, third overall. Beth Graham had put her fourth, but another judge, Mark Hayes of Dallas, had placed her first. Maybe he was going to get the rink now.

Deanie Tew glanced over at her husband, who stared blankly into space.

"Congratulations, Dad," she said, walking over to hug him.

This was the moment he had been waiting for.

"Everything he had given up, which is literally his whole family moving away from him, I felt it all came together for him right then," she said. "We could at least say it had been worth it. All those critics who have said, 'I wouldn't let my family go off. I don't see how you do it.' He can go back and say, 'This is why I'm doing it. She's now achieved something that very few figure skaters have achieved. She's going to the national championships.'"

By the time Jenni Tew was finished crying, her makeup had washed off in rivers down her cheeks. She told her mother she had to redo it.

"Why?" Deanie asked.

"Mom, we're going to have pictures. I want to look good."

Deanie immediately thought of Nancy Kerrigan's comment about waiting for Oksana Baiul to put on her makeup. She laughed. At the Olympics or at Mids, the issues were the same. Judges, close calls, tears, and makeup.

•   •   •

When Carol Heiss got back to Cleveland, one mental picture from Denver stuck with her. It was Joel and Deanie Tew, hugging each other in the hallway.

"Parents make such tough decisions for skating," Heiss said. "We don't get into that. It's their decision. But then to see the happiness on the other end, it brought tears to my eyes."

A few weeks later, at the rink in Lakewood, Ohio, Jenni Tew, who had turned fourteen in early December, was having a jumping contest with her buddy Ryan Hunka. All the Tews were there. The weight of the world was off their shoulders.

"She's going down," Hunka yelled to Joel Tew, standing in the bleachers beside the ice.

"Oh, yeah!" Joel Tew was smiling. "You're just afraid that a girl will beat you."

After they both tried several jumps, Jenni landed a triple loop. Ryan fell on his triple flip.

"Ha!" Jenni exclaimed.

Jenni also was working on a triple flip. She kept trying. Awkwardly, she kept missing. With each fall, she looked as if she would twist her ankle. Or worse. Joel Tew stood by the boards and watched like a father standing by the batting cage helping a son figure out a baseball swing.

"Come on," he prodded her. "You can do it."

Jenni pulled herself up and stood there, hands on hips. Getting this third triple—assuming she could land the toe loop and loop that she already had on good days—was not going to be easy. Triples came and went. Sometimes, they never came back.

Deana Gerbrick also showed up at practice that day, all dressed up with nowhere to go. She had failed to qualify for Nationals, finishing eighth at Midwesterns. Her season was over.

She wore a blue-and-pink skating dress and swooped around the ice, one time cutting Jenni Tew off as Jenni practiced her long program. Jenni had the right-of-way, but had to stop in her tracks to avoid running into Deana. After the program was done, Jenni glared at Deana, then turned away without saying a word.

A wide range of emotions was on display at Winterhurst. Deanie Tew was living in a dream world. At home a few days earlier, she had caught herself smiling: "She's going to Nationals! She's going to Nationals!

"I can't believe it's true, we're going to Nationals. I get to see her in that arena, sitting in Kiss and Cry, having her scores come up on the scoreboard. It will be the first time she's ever had open judging. But we don't want to get greedy. And we don't want Jen to ever be the kind of child who stops appreciating each step, from where she's been to where she's going."

New Year's Eve came a few days later. Joel and Deanie spent the evening with their daughters in their Ohio town house. They didn't have a party to attend. This didn't bother them; their families were in Florida, and they had no strong adult friendships in Ohio. Their life up North was built entirely around Jenni's skating.

Joel and Deanie Tew went to bed before midnight. At 11 A.M. on New Year's Day, they were back at the rink, with Courtney by their side and Jenni on the ice.

12

THE
GREAT
WASTED
TALENT

Word spread quickly around the crowded rink.

"He's here! Bowman's here!"

"How does he look?"

"He's a mess."

Ann Greenthal, a judge who had been watching Christopher Bowman skate since he was eight, came up to him in the rink at Fitch-burg.

"My bunny," she said to him, reaching out to hug the nation's greatest waste of figure-skating talent, once wrapped inside black velvet, now bundled into a bulky green hunting jacket.

"I thought about you today," Greenthal said. "It's too bad you couldn't stay in shape just to do this year. All the money that you could have made . . ."

"That's what everyone keeps telling me," Bowman said. "Money, money, money. But why can't they tell me, like, Cindy Crawford will come and get down on her hands and knees for me. That's much more appealing than the money, you know?"

Greenthal shrugged. "Are you happy?"

"Of course I'm happy," he said. "I let a few people know that I had talent, didn't I? I tried to get it across. I mean, a million dollars is not going to get that across, is it?"

Greenthal stared at him. "All right. Well, you take care of yourself, okay?"

"You can count on it," Bowman said, winking.

You could count on a lot of things with Christopher Bowman. Two Olympic gold medals for starters, one in 1992, the other in 1994. That was supposed to happen. It didn't. Since 1992, he had been retired from skating, had left his native California, and was coaching in the Boston area. Coaching. That was the job description, at any rate. His top pupil, a Jill Trenary–look-alike junior skater named Amy D'Entremont, got sick of waiting at the rink for a coach who sometimes didn't show up, so she finally gave up and went to train with Kathy Casey in Colorado.

Bowman wasn't surprised to lose her.

"Can you believe," he shouted to a group of reporters a year earlier, when D'Entremont was still with him, "that somebody is actually being coached by *me?*"

The one thing you could always count on with Christopher Bowman was that you could never count on Christopher Bowman.

"I can't have a conversation with him because if you can't believe one word one human being says, what's the point of talking to him?" said Frank Carroll, who coached Bowman for eighteen years. "You can't have a conversation because it's all bullshit. You might as well say, 'Hi, Christopher. Nice tie. Good-bye.'"

The sad thing is, Christopher Bowman never had a more loyal friend than Frank Carroll.

Bowman entered Fitchburg's ice rink Friday night to watch his girlfriend skate at the Eastern sectionals. He careened through the lobby. His eyes wandered; who knows what they were seeing. He said hello; to whom, he didn't know. His breath reeked of alcohol. Talking over his shoulder, walking one way, chatting another, not looking where he was headed, he barged into the midst of the men's draw for the long program the next night. Men like Michael Chack and Shepherd Clark, skaters with half the talent and twice the desire, were picking numbers out of a box in the lobby to find out in what order they would skate. And there was Bowman, unwittingly slamming into their world just long enough to excuse himself and exit, the center of attention, as always.

He didn't look that bad, all things considered. Put it this way: he had looked worse. Skaters remarked that they were surprised he looked so, well, normal. He actually had shaved within the past twenty-four hours. The last time some of them had seen him, he had a Mohawk. The time before that, he had hair long enough to pull back into a ponytail. Now, his hair was short, he had a slight paunch over his belt, and he wore an earring, a tiny silver foot in his left lobe.

"It's because I'm always getting stepped on," he said. "Ben Wright gave it to me.

"Naw, just kidding."

Everyone laughed. Ben Wright—proper Bostonian, skating historian, international referee—would be the last man to shop for an earring for Christopher Bowman.

It was a good line. Bowman even smiled at it. He always was a very funny guy.

This wasn't as humorous: Det. Scott Heagney of the Franklin (Massachusetts) Police Department wrote up a report of what he was doing a little after 8 P.M. on Monday, April 11, 1994. It went like this:

"I was patrolling Depot Street, a public way in the town of Franklin, in an unmarked vehicle, when I observed a 1987 red Harley-Davidson motorcycle bearing Massachusetts registration WX-4131. I observed that the license plate on the motorcycle was expired. The registration expired 12/1993. I then stopped the vehicle.

"The operator of the vehicle was identified as Christopher N. Bowman. Bowman did not have any identification with him.

"I then ran a license and missing/wanted check on Bowman along with confirming that the registration was expired. Officers Lapierre and Lawrence arrived as backup.

"The dispatcher informed me that Bowman's license was suspended and that there was an outstanding arrest warrant from the Holden State Police barracks. The registration was confirmed as being expired. I then placed Bowman under arrest without incident. While searching Bowman before placing him into the rear of the marked unit, I discovered two (2) clear plastic Baggies containing a white powdery substance inside his right front watch pocket. I recognized this substance to be cocaine.

"Bowman was subsequently transported to the station for booking.

"The evidence that was seized from Bowman was tagged and placed in the narcotics depository."

The outstanding arrest warrant was for traffic and drug violations in California and Massachusetts, Bowman said. It was no surprise to Bowman that he had been caught. Again. By his own estimates, he had been arrested twenty-seven times. "Stupid stuff," he said. "Stealing people's credit cards, scams on banks, ripping off ATM machines."

In April 1994, Bowman was charged with illegal possession of a Class B substance—cocaine—as well as operating his motorcycle without a license and without registration. He received six months' probation on the license charge and was ordered to pay a $500 fine for cocaine possession.

The Eastern sectionals came nine months after his arrest. Bowman admitted in Fitchburg that he had hitched a ride with his girlfriend's parents because he was "having a difficult time" trying to get a driver's license.

"My name," Bowman said, "is like a rash all over the computer. I have no driver's license in California and none here. Everything carries over. You're out with your girlfriend, you're having dinner or whatever, and you get pulled over by the state police and she doesn't understand why they're tearing the seats out of your car, you know what I'm saying?"

In his prime, Bowman was the darling of U.S. men's skating. He was handsome, he was charming, and best of all in the minds of skating officials, he liked girls. From 1987 to 1992, he won two national titles, qualified for every world championship, and made the 1988 and 1992 U.S. Olympic teams.

During those same years, he had a "$950-a-day cocaine habit," he said.

U.S. skating officials said they knew he was in trouble. His coach also knew and tried to get help for him. Judges and officials asked other skaters to come forward and give them evidence of Bowman's drug use, but no one ever did. So Bowman kept skating and winning medals. Fans and officials kept applauding and laughing at his antics. And he kept digging himself deeper into the entertainer's netherworld of spotlights and headlines, mug shots and handcuffs.

"I was heavily into cocaine use for over ten years," he said. "I did everything. I mean, I was a human garbage pail. You name it and I would try it because to me, I was invincible. I could literally do anything. I was like, I'm an Olympic athlete, you know, take me to Disneyland, take me to the world. That's the dangerous thing about believing your own press. It can be disastrous."

Bowman always was at home onstage. He was a skater and a child actor, and he was good at both. He appeared in two hundred television commercials, he said, and had a part in *Little House on the Prairie* for one season. He played Benjamin, a blind boy.

Off-camera, life wasn't so sweet. At the age of ten, he said he smoked his first joint. When he was sixteen, he got into cocaine. At twenty, before the 1988 Olympics, he checked into the Betty Ford Clinic for a two-month stay. His coach at the time, Frank Carroll, said they tried to keep this a secret from everyone, including the USFSA, although it wasn't easy hiding a top skater for two months.

"We knew what was going on," said USFSA president Claire Ferguson. "We knew, but what could we do? We never had any record of any arrest. I think everyone tried their utmost, but when there's a dependency problem, it's much bigger than the Association."

"I was a young person with really nothing to lose," Bowman said. "And I was used to taking chances because the bigger the chance, the bigger the risk, the bigger the payoff. Unfortunately, the bigger risk you take with drugs doesn't exactly pan out that way."

When he came out of Betty Ford, he went right back to skating— and to drugs, he said. However, he said he always stopped before a national or world championship or the Olympic Games. Drug tests were being conducted at those competitions. The USFSA did not, however, conduct random tests between events.

"When it came time for the event, maybe two weeks prior, I was always very paranoid that I was going to test positive and disgrace my country," Bowman said. "That was the most important thing. My life was already a disgrace, as far back as I can remember. Where I grew up, how my life existed, was a disgrace. But my skating was not. That's how it was separated. The skating was something that gave me a sense of importance and pride, and I regarded it as such."

Yet he almost ruined everything before the 1992 Olympics in Albertville.

At the 1992 Nationals in Orlando, where the U.S. team was selected for the Winter Games, reporters vigorously pursued a rumor that Bowman had been mugged in a drug deal gone bad in Toronto the previous fall. Bowman had moved to Canada to train with coach and former Olympian Toller Cranston after an emotional split from Carroll.

At the time, both Bowman and the USFSA denied any drug connection to the mugging. But Bowman said that was, of course, a lie.

"Yes, absolutely," Bowman said. "As a matter of fact, I was dealing drugs in Toronto at the time to make money, to cover expenses. Crack, heroin, you name it, everything. That was a deal that went bad, people were pursuing me."

He said he was thrown down a stairwell and suffered a broken nose and two fractures near his right eye.

To pay for the drugs, Bowman said he used money he made from skating, including $71,000 he made in the spring of 1989 from the world skating tour. One night on the tour, he was out late and had no idea where his hotel room was, so he slept in the luggage hold of the tour's customized bus. The next morning, when other skaters came to store their luggage, they were extremely surprised to find Bowman lying among the Samsonites.

The USFSA was so delighted to have a handsome, masculine male star that it overlooked many of Bowman's transgressions.

"The USFSA liked Christopher's macho image," Carroll said. "If there was a cute girl around the corner and Christopher made eye contact, he was going to try to pick her up and take her in the back room. . . . I think a lot of people thought it was very charismatic and kind of cute when he pulled all those antics. It didn't matter what he did, all the crap he really did, it was all whitewashed because, 'Oh, he's such a ladies' man. Isn't that great? He can do anything and get away with it.' And he did."

Frank Carroll and Christopher Bowman had one of figure skating's most extreme love-hate relationships. Bowman was four when he went to Carroll to learn to skate. And Carroll took him to the Olympics. That was a grand achievement, the two of them together, like father and son, Bowman said. But Carroll also watched a young man self-destruct in front of his eyes. That was terrible.

The problems were minor at first. When Bowman was in his early teens, he was getting pudgy and not eating right. His mother asked Carroll if he could help.

After practice, he sat Bowman down for half an hour, explaining the importance of eating properly. Bowman appeared to be listening and thanked Carroll profusely for the little chat.

The very next day, Bowman's mother marched into the Pickwick rink in Burbank, California, where Carroll was teaching at the time, and produced four boxes of doughnuts.

"Here!" Carroll recalled that she said to him. "This is what your student did while I was in the shower."

Christopher had taken some cash from his mother's purse, gone around the corner, and bought four boxes of doughnuts, three plain and one powdered sugar. He took the doughnuts to his room and was eating them when his mother walked in.

Carroll was furious. "Christopher," he said, "you sit down here. You are going to eat every one of these doughnuts before you get on the ice. And you're not moving from here until every one is gone."

At 8:30 A.M., Bowman started eating. At 10:30, Carroll heard him coughing. Finally, at 11:15, Bowman was finished.

"Great!" Carroll said. "Put your skates on."

Bowman laced up his skates. The two of them went onto the ice.

"Now," Carroll said, "we're going to spin for a while."

Carroll made Bowman spin and spin and spin until he dashed off the ice and vomited into a trash can.

•   •   •

What a beautiful, robust skater Bowman once was. He jumped with the power of Atlas and landed with all the force of a feather. He was big and broad-shouldered at five feet ten and 155 pounds. He sparkled in $7,000 outfits made by Hollywood designer Bob Mackie. He knew where every television camera was as he skated. Winking and posing was a part of every routine. Nothing was forced or learned; everything looked so natural. Born and raised in Hollywood, Bowman had two nicknames as an adult: Bowman the Showman, and Hans Brinker from Hell. Take your pick.

Bowman faced the 1988 Olympic trials not long after getting out of Betty Ford. He and Carroll were arguing often; one of their fights was over whether a particular jump combination was to be included in the long program at the trials. Carroll told him to take it out. He didn't want to. Carroll told him if he didn't do as he was told, he would quit on the spot.

"Okay, okay," Bowman said. He left out the jump, but he wanted to make Carroll pay. So he refused to smile throughout the program. He skated four and a half minutes with a scowl on his face. It was so noticeable that the judges went to Carroll to ask him what was going on.

Bowman made the team and roomed with Paul Wylie in Calgary, where they played supporting roles in the men's event to teammate and gold medalist Brian Boitano. Bowman certainly looked at the Olympics as a chance to skate, but first and foremost, he saw the Games as one grand, international dating game.

"I was drinking, not doing any drugs, but drinking and partying," Bowman said. "I was winding up at various women's houses and trying to figure out how to get back to the Olympic village before anyone missed me."

Bowman terrorized Wylie by coming back to their room around dawn several times. The night after the men's short program, Bowman came in the door at 5 A.M., turned on the lights, got up onto Wylie's bed, and began dancing and shouting, "Good morning, Vietnam!"

"He was drunk out of his mind, I guess," Wylie said. "And then he tried to convince me he had scoliosis. I said, 'No, you have halitosis, not scoliosis.' He was very funny and incredibly charming, but it was a nightmare."

Wylie finally moved into another room.

Bowman finished seventh at those Olympics; Wylie, tenth. Everyone assumed that of the two of them, Bowman was the future Olympic medalist. The next year, Bowman won the national title and finished second at the world championships. In 1990, he withdrew from the national championships due to a bad back, but was placed on the world team anyway and finished third.

His performance at the worlds pushed Carroll over the edge. After missing his first jump, Bowman discarded the rest of his program, which they had worked on for nearly a year, and improvised for four minutes. He was jumping and spinning and having a ball on the ice. Carroll couldn't believe it. He crossed his arms and tilted his head as he stood by the boards, trying to maintain his well-practiced composure. Inside, he was seething. Bowman was doing things Carroll had never seen before—and in the most important competition of the year.

When Bowman came off the ice, gasping for breath, Carroll shook his head and escorted him to Kiss and Cry. As they sat waiting for the scores, Carroll turned to Bowman.

"I've never seen that program," he said dryly. "What program was that?"

Bowman later said he had changed his program to add more jumps to try to beat Canada's Kurt Browning, the reigning world champion.

"It's not like I'm some moron who forgot his program," he said.

Everyone knew what Bowman had done, including the judges, who had watched him practice an entirely different program all week.

"Christopher," Carroll said, "these judges don't have any respect for you anymore. They think you're a tremendously talented boy, but they also think you're a flake. They're sick to death of you."

That was the end for Bowman and Carroll; Bowman soon left and went to Canada to train under the artistic and dramatic eye of Cranston, the 1976 Olympic bronze medalist. But when Bowman arrived at the 1991 Nationals in Minneapolis, he sobbed through an entire precompetition news conference as he discussed leaving Carroll.

"He meant everything to me," Bowman said. "He was my life, my umbilical cord. He loved me like a son, but sometimes, you just have to let your kid go."

Carroll washed his hands of Bowman. "I love him. He loves me. But it's screwed up."

When he showed up in Minneapolis without Carroll, Bowman looked different. "The cheeseburger had to be turned into filet mignon," Cranston grandly proclaimed. "He needed to be into himself. He needed to be serious, and his costumes will reflect this. You won't see any sequins or rhinestones. The color taken most seriously is black. Christopher will be dipped in black."

"Dipped in black" went all the way to the top of his head. He dyed his hair to match his outfits: shoe-polish black.

Bowman finished second that year to Todd Eldredge, who won his second consecutive national title. In the long program, Bowman was draped in a black velvet suit with plunging neckline and a white silk collar. When he came onto the ice, a couple dozen reporters, clustered in one section of the stands at the downtown Target Center, struggled to find words to describe the outfit.

Julie Vader, covering the event for *The National,* a new sports daily, spoke up.

"It's a shawl collar."

"How do you know?" someone asked.

"I have a dress exactly like it."

In 1992, the Olympic year, Bowman was with another new coach, John Nicks, the renowned pairs specialist. Change was a constant for Bowman. In a year's time, his hair had gone from jet-black to white blond to orange to its natural dark brown.

Rumors about the Toronto mugging swirled around him that week, forcing USFSA president Franklin Nelson to announce that Bowman had passed every drug test he had ever taken. Nicks was also testing Bowman, but said he would not divulge the results. Bowman said later that he never failed one of Nicks's tests, but only because he was able to flush out his system with herbs and other masking devices.

Nationals was not the place for Bowman to come clean about his problems. That would have ruined his chance at the Olympics, where, for a while anyway, some thought he could win a medal, even the gold. So Bowman feverishly and aggressively lied. He called the media attention on the Toronto story "not really appropriate." If it bothered him, it never showed on the ice, where he pointed at and mugged for a TV camera during his performance, then grabbed ABC reporter Julie Moran in Kiss and Cry in a mock embrace.

Nicks's expectations were so low that he couldn't help being pleased.

"I thought having Christopher follow coaching instructions for two minutes and thirty seconds was the most remarkable achievement in my thirty-one years of coaching," Nicks said.

Bowman won the national title—his second and last—and went to Albertville as a medal contender. His roommate at that Olympics was Rocky Marval, the New Jersey truck driver and pairs skater.

The first night they spent in Albertville, Bowman was bouncing off the walls as Marval pulled down the covers and got into bed.

"Where are we going?" Bowman asked Marval. "What are we going to do now?"

"I don't know about you, but I'm going to sleep," Marval said.

Marval's pairs partner, Calla Urbanski, the tough-talking waitress, heard the story later and added her opinion.

"If Christopher gets out of line, Rocky will just bop him."

On the ice, Bowman stumbled on his combination jump in the short program and dropped to seventh. He leaned on his knee when he finished, shaking his head and smiling. For him, the show never stopped.

"Ouch!" he said when his marks came up. Too far down to win a medal, he skated extremely well in the long program, but ended up fourth. He had been a little too cute all week: posing for the cameras, as usual; stopping during practice to ask reporters questions and proclaiming the outrageous at any news conference he could get himself into.

"I've worked very hard to be completely different from the average skater," he said.

When he and Herschel Walker, the NFL running back turned bobsledder, bumped into each other in the Olympic village, Walker said he didn't know who Bowman was.

Bowman understood.

"There's no reason why any hardworking, dedicated, serious athlete should ever know who I am."

As he departed the arena in Albertville, Bowman exclaimed, "I came, I saw, they kicked my butt."

Three years later, Bowman didn't regret his silliness. "I was just being myself. People are attracted to people they know. They knew me. I wasn't hiding anything. With me, they knew what they were getting."

That year, 1992, was the end for Bowman. He joined Ice Capades, made some money to buy more drugs, gained some weight, got into more trouble. Bowman said he and a girlfriend slept in the street for several nights in Los Angeles after moving out of a seedy motel.

"It was just awful," he said. "We had no shoes and no money."

He knew his body couldn't keep up with what he was doing to it. He had to stop skating. He moved to Massachusetts and started coaching.

"I always knew that I could go back to my miserable life after the glory," he said. "When I was out on the ice and when I was away from the ice, I was like two completely different people. Because I was such a perfectionist, a performer, I could go out there, put on a costume, like a suit of armor, literally like a mask, and become somebody else."

What a role model Bowman had become. The skating world never got all that it wanted from him, but it got about what it deserved. No Olympic medals, two world championship medals (neither one gold), two national titles, a hundred laughs, a thousand headaches.

"I can't stress to the kids enough," he said. "You want to screw up your life forever, what I did was the way to do it."

13

ON
THE
ROAD
AGAIN

The flowers. The flowers! Every night on the tour, there are flowers. Wrapped, crushed, falling apart, wilted. It's a tradition in skating. Fans bring flowers and throw them onto the ice or give them to an usher, who personally delivers them to a stagehand, who takes them backstage and piles them on top of each other.

On Friday the thirteenth of January at the Oakland Coliseum, the flowers were stacked high on a crate during intermission. There were bouquets for Kristi Yamaguchi, Paul Wylie, Scott Hamilton, Katarina Witt, and Kurt Browning. Every one of them came with a card. "Please call me." That's what the cards said. There was a name, a phone number, sometimes a personal message.

The skaters pluck the cards and try to make sure each one gets an answer from their publicist. An autographed picture perhaps, or a note. Phone calls are out of the question. The flowers are given to the local stage crew or taken to a hospital.

Two pink carnations were lying there, addressed to Nancy Kerrigan. Kerrigan is not on this tour. Three letters for Oksana Baiul arrived at the Coliseum that day. She's not here either.

Fans hear a skating tour is in town and just assume that every skater is a part of it. Isn't that the way it always was? After the Olympics, didn't the top stars join the tour, crisscross the country for a couple years in gaudy costumes and feathered headdresses, earn a fine living, and then exit stage right, never to be seen again?

It's not like that anymore. Top skaters don't have to join the circus. They don't have to go on tour at all. And if they do, they don't have to wear a silly costume. Nowadays, they get to play themselves.

Millions and millions and millions of dollars in skating talent checked into the Fairmont Hotel atop San Francisco's Nob Hill for a three-day run of the arenas in northern California. First Oakland's, then Sacramento's, followed by a Sunday matinee in San Jose's. These would be the seventh, eighth, and ninth performances of a forty-eight-city tour called, appropriately enough, Stars on Ice.

From late December through the end of March, fourteen of the world's best-known figure skaters lead the lives of well-groomed rock stars. Their view of most cities is limited to the airport, their customized tour bus, the hotel, and the arena loading dock. They perform to capacity crowds most nights; more than half a million people saw the show in 1994–95. They cash huge paychecks, up to $10–12,000 per show for the biggest names, a minimum of $2,000 a night for the skaters without the grand résumés. They do the same thing every night—same music, same lighting, same costumes—over and over, from Portland, Oregon, to Portland, Maine. They do it because they love the skating, mostly like each other, and what else would they be doing anyway?

This tour, sponsored by Discover card, run by International Management Group, and populated with its clients, mostly, is not the only tour out there. Tom Collins, a former skater in Holiday on Ice and concert promoter from Minneapolis, owns the biggest tour of all, the Campbell's Soups Tour of World Figure Skating Champions. It travels the country every April to July. But Collins, the beloved godfather of the sport, puts a different kind of product on the ice. His is a series of stars—Brian Boitano, Baiul, Kerrigan, and the current Olympic-division skaters—doing one number each, with a few performing an encore. There's an opening and a closing with the entire cast, but the skaters are out there to show off their individual talents. Collins jams in every skater the fans would want to see and plays to 1 million people in seventy-six cities. He takes in $35 million in gate receipts in one year. For four months' work, Boitano, Baiul, and Kerrigan make $1 million each. It's their biggest windfall of the year; skaters, unlike some other athletes, make the bulk of their money touring, not in endorsements or commercials.

Other shows exist. Kerrigan has a Christmas show; Jayne Torvill and Christopher Dean play a few cities in the United States, then work Great Britain for months. Ice Capades, owned at the time by Dorothy Hamill and her husband, Ken Forsythe, ran two financially troubled tours until one was abruptly canceled in January. The other tour continued until its scheduled conclusion in March. At the same time, news leaked that Hamill and Forsythe had sold Ice Capades to religious broadcaster Pat Robertson's International Family Entertainment Inc. Hamill herself announced her retirement December 18 at the end of a performance of "Cinderella . . . Frozen in Time."

Stars on Ice began when Scott Hamilton was fired by Ice Capades in 1986. That was a time when, if you were a woman—Hamill, for instance—you laced up the skates and dressed as Cinderella and made hundreds of thousands of dollars. If you were a man, well, skating didn't need men, Hamilton was told. Do something else. Commentate. Coach.

Hamilton and his agent, IMG's Bob Kain, sat in a condominium during the week of the Lipton tennis tournament in 1986 and decided that Scott Hamilton was not yet ready to give up skating. They decided to start their own tour that autumn, professional figure skating's version of a movable all-star game. Unlike Collins's established tour of Olympic and world champions, this would be entirely for professionals. They would call it Scott Hamilton's America Tour. They would send it to five university towns in New England. They would pray they knew what they were doing.

The opening night at the University of Maine, in the midst of the finale, one of the thick wires attached to the spotlights broke and started spewing sparks from the top of the tiny arena. The spectators thought it was part of the closing number until the skaters stopped performing and ambulances began arriving. Eleven people went to the hospital with minor burns.

"If that had been New York City, we would have had one hundred and fifty lawsuits," said Kain, who in addition to his work in figure skating, managed Chris Evert's tennis career.

The tour now plays Madison Square Garden in New York, the Rosemont Horizon in Chicago, Miami Arena, the Palace of Auburn Hills. It runs on a $15-million annual budget. It's so big, it has its own official charity, the Make-A-Wish Foundation. Hamilton's name was dashed and Stars on Ice was chosen, Kain said, because of egos and longevity. But it's still Hamilton's show. He's the only one who wears a microphone and talks to the audience during the show. He performs the final solo number. If he's hitting his jumps and smiling, the entire show is uplifted. He drives Stars on Ice. It's just that the tour has a name that will last long after Hamilton retires—if he ever does.

The tour is a vast receptacle for IMG clients. All but one pair and one dance team are represented in some way by IMG. The massive sports management firm does the same thing for its golf and tennis clients. It represents them, then on occasion creates a forum from which they can work. It can create a conflict, certainly, but for the skaters, the conflict that exists when your agent becomes your boss isn't as bad as the conflict that occurs when the bills came due and the checking account was empty.

IMG had assembled a well-decorated group for its ninth season, the 1994–95 tour. The skaters possessed six Olympic gold medals between them: Witt's and pairs skaters Ekaterina Gordeeva and Sergei Grinkov's two, Hamilton's and Yamaguchi's one. They had won nineteen world championships. However, the last title any of the singles skaters or Americans won was Yamaguchi's world title in 1992, which came a month after her Olympic gold medal. Gordeeva and Grinkov won an Olympic gold medal in 1994, but they are not Americans or singles skaters or true headliners. Of the top four skaters—Wylie, Witt, Hamilton, and Yamaguchi—only one, Yamaguchi, wouldn't be at least thirty by the end of the year.

But if the skaters were getting a little old, the tour got a boost from the explosion of skating on television in the fall. Names that might have been forgotten in other years were omnipresent on weekend TV. Yamaguchi won almost everything in sight, prime time and otherwise. Wylie and Witt were marquee names at every made-for-TV event. And Hamilton, as often as not, was holding a microphone, if not competing himself. Even better for the tour, the programs they performed often were ones they were preparing for Stars on Ice.

It's a deep, regal, mysterious voice on tape over the public address system that introduces the skaters in the darkened arena. It's all names, achievements, and triangles of light shining on the ice from the spotlights above. The announcements illustrate what every skater knows: a title—an Olympic or world championship medal—is your passport in skating. Without at least one, you can go nowhere.

The voice dramatically lists the titles and the names. They come in order of importance, least to most, including:

Three-time United States champion, world champion, Olympic silver medalist, Miss Rosalynn Sumners.

Two pairs and Browning and Wylie come next.

Six-time European champion, four-time world champion, two-time Olympic gold medalist, Miss Katarina Witt.

Four-time United States champion, four-time world champion, Olympic gold medalist, Mr. Scott Hamilton.

United States champion, two-time world champion, Olympic gold medalist, Miss Kristi Yamaguchi.

•   •   •   •

Every night, these people work. If they fall or pop a triple jump into a double, it kills them. They come off the ice swearing. The show is filled with beautiful music and lighting and footwork and even some humorous lines from Hamilton, but it's the jumps they care most about.

Yamaguchi does five triple jumps every night, as well as six double axels. Hamilton does six triple jumps and a handful of double axels. Witt does a couple triples a night. Sumners stops at the double axel. "I'm the oldest woman, I don't do triples, and I'm glad to still be working."

Sumners, thirty-one, and Witt, twenty-nine, are great pals backstage. You would think they had grown up as friends. You can't say that, but you can say this: they did grow up together.

After the 1983 world championships in Helsinki, which Sumners won, the top skaters toured Europe. Each took with them a big box of chocolates they had received as a gift.

Witt, whose willpower with sweets is not one of her strengths, devoured the chocolates in a week. Sumners didn't touch hers. She saved her candy to take home as a present.

Word soon came that Witt was going to be receiving a visit on the tour from her coach, the stern Jutta Mueller. Frau Mueller knew about the box of chocolates. She also knew about Witt's sweet tooth. She told Witt she wanted to see that box of chocolates, and she wanted to see it full.

Witt sent out a plea for help around the skaters' hotel: Did anyone still have their chocolates? Sumners said she did. Witt begged. Sumners delivered. A full box of candy was sitting in Witt's room when Frau Mueller came knocking.

To thank her, Witt bought Sumners some cookies. The next year, all pleasantries aside, Witt swept into the Olympics and took away the one thing Sumners had been working for her whole life, an Olympic gold medal.

Past midnight, on the two-hour ride in their customized tour bus from Sacramento to San Francisco, Witt sat on the floor of the bus, Sumners on a sofa above her.

"I wish we'd gotten to know each other much earlier," Witt said, holding a cup of Kahlúa to soothe a scratchy throat. "In 1984, do you remember? We would be at the gym and you would do your workout in one corner, and I would do my workout in the other corner and we wouldn't look at each other. We were so competitive. Now, we're not competitive anymore."

"There are some skaters who can't be like that," Sumners replied. "Never once have I ever looked at you and said, 'I wish I had what you had.' Never once. And when you won your second gold medal, it lifted a lot of disappointment from my life. It just cemented the fact of who I lost to. It showed me it wasn't a fluky kind of loss. At this stage of our lives, I'd rather have the friendship than the gold medal."

It wasn't always that way. At the 1984 Olympics in Sarajevo, Witt skated next to last, Sumners last. Witt skated cleanly except for one slight stumble and received good marks, but the judges had left room for Sumners to win. If she won five of the nine judges, the gold medal would be hers. It was sitting there, waiting for her to take it.

As Sumners churned toward the finish of her four-minute program, it looked as if she would win. She had landed three double axels, a triple salchow, and a triple toe loop. She had two jumps left, one more triple toe and one more double axel. If she landed those, she surely would become the gold medalist. Just two jumps to go. Her mind got a little ahead of her body. She didn't mean to, but she got cautious. Her brain buckled under the pressure of being so close to winning. Sumners doubled the triple toe. She singled the double axel. The Italian judge gave her a 6.0 for artistic impression. But Witt won, five judges to four. It was so close that had either the West German or Canadian judges given Sumners a 5.9 instead of a 5.8 for technical merit, Sumners would have won the gold, not Witt.

That last double axel decided it. Sumners is sure of that. Had she done it, she would have won. The double axel. Sumners performs beautiful double axels in the show every day, two each night. Even eleven years later, they're automatic.

When they put the silver medal around her neck, Sumners was about to embark on a journey through athletic purgatory that only an American woman who loses the gold medal will ever know.

She believed she had let down her parents, who had divorced three years earlier and had spent a fortune back then—about $25,000 a year—to get her to the brink of an Olympic gold medal. She and her mother couldn't even discuss her Olympic performance for a full year. It was as if it never happened. She joined Disney's World on Ice, signed for $250,000 a year—and became almost instantly miserable. There she was, the Olympic silver medalist, now relegated to being Donald Duck's fiftieth birthday present. She popped out of a music box and skated through the whipped cream left on the ice from the previous number, which was, appropriately enough, the making of Donald's birthday cake.

She did eleven shows a week. She quickly abandoned her triple jumps; there was no time to practice them. Her weight shot up from 102 pounds at the Olympics to 125, heavy for a five-foot-two athlete. "I was depressed, I was fat, I was homesick."

Sumners always battled to keep her weight down. She loved pizza and cookies and she didn't want to give them up. Before the Olympics, trying to lose a few pounds, she resorted to taking a laxative one night before she went to bed. "I woke up with such a stomachache that I had to tell my mother what I did," she said.

Sumners said she "used to pray for anorexia" on the Disney tour. "All the other skaters ate carrot sticks with mustard for dinner. They all looked so tall and thin, like they belonged in a magazine. And there I was, so much shorter than they were. That was hard."

Disney demanded to weigh the skaters every week, and Sumners had no choice but to comply. If a woman was three pounds over or under her weight, she would be fined $10. Sumners began bringing $10 bills to the weigh-in. "I thought their rules were stupid. It was like kindergarten."

But she said no matter how intense the pressure, she never became anorexic or bulimic.

"I said, 'Screw it,' and I'd eat a pizza."

She lasted two years on tour before she quit. She moved home to Seattle, she bought a house and a horse, she found a boyfriend and a psychologist.

"She'll never work again," friends told her mother.

Then came Stars on Ice, a three-month assignment that has lasted nine years. Even without a grand portfolio, she is treated as an equal, skating one solo and appearing often with other members of the cast. At some point, some youngster will kick her into retirement. But until then, she happily fills the role of the mature, sophisticated skater. (It also doesn't hurt that she happens to be dating Kain, the tour's executive producer.)

"I knew sooner or later, I'd be in my thirties," she said. "I knew sooner or later, I'd be a confident, grown-up woman. I kept pushing and pushing and pushing through it, until I didn't have to live up to anyone's expectations anymore."

Katarina Witt was in the midst of her strangest season when she checked into the Fairmont. She went to her sixth-floor room and called Boitano, who lived a couple miles away, to plan dinner in the city, just the two of them. They used to tour together with their own show. They miss those times now.

Boitano said he might not come to the Oakland performance because it bothered him that Stars on Ice had hired the brain trust of their old show and had the look and feel of the Boitano-Witt tour.

Witt agreed with Boitano, but she knew they could do nothing about it now. She insisted he come to Oakland.

"If anything," she said, "at least you should see me."

Witt knew she was the draw for a lot of men—those she knew, those she didn't know. After she beat Sumners at the Olympics, she received thirty-five thousand love letters.

"They come to the show," she said with a sly grin, "and they fall in love."

Then again, perhaps they come because they heard what happened in Paris a few years ago. An elastic strap gave way and Witt fell out of her dress as she skated.

"I caught it at the last moment, but like halfway down," she said. "Of course, they had it on TV and so they had a still picture that ran in the newspapers. Everyone made it out that I tried to seduce the judges with it. That's really ridiculous."

Ever the trouper, Witt pulled up the dress and kept on skating. "The rest of the number, I didn't move my arms."

But in 1994–95, figure skating wasn't the same for Katarina Witt. She couldn't win anymore. At the height of the professional season, in the fall, she was terrified to jump. While training in Lake Placid, New York, for the tour, she stuck the toe pick of her skate into the ice and launched herself into the air for a triple toe loop. When she landed, abruptly and with a tremendous thud, her boot had nothing on the bottom of it; her blade had come off and was still wedged into the ice. She was lucky she didn't break her neck.

She got the boot fixed, but she still couldn't get over the feeling of landing full force onto the ice in what amounted to a street shoe. She wondered when it might happen again. "I'm scared," she said, "of this stupid triple jump." It was like diving into a swimming pool and worrying that someone might drain the water before you reached it.

Witt was still having an extremely lucrative season. She was skating competitively virtually every week, making the money she, as an East German, could never earn after her two Olympic triumphs. This was payback time, and she was awash in cash. But Witt was not eighteen, as she was in Sarajevo, nor twenty-two, as she was in Calgary. Many women were better than her: Yamaguchi, Baiul, Kerrigan, Midori Ito, as well as the top Olympic-division skaters. The story going around was that Witt no longer had the jumps to win even the U.S. junior ladies competition. It had come to this: Katarina, athletically, was a junior lady.

"A junior lady," the storytellers quickly added, "with breasts."

But Witt did not stop trying. Not quite what she once was, she changed into something else. If she was no longer unbeatable, she would create her own competitive event: the-voluptuous-woman-in-the-flowing-dress-who-will-mesmerize-you-with-her-artistry-and-make-a-statement-on-world-affairs-at-the-same-time category.

Katarina definitely would win that.

After the Stars on Ice preview show in Lake Placid in November, Witt and Sumners flew six hours together in a private plane to get to Nashville for a professional event run by Mike Burg called the American Skating Invitational. They had to throw two programs on the ice apiece and make it look good. They were competing against Baiul and Japan's Yuka Sato, the reigning world champion, among others. This wasn't a matter of winning; they weren't going to do that. It was a matter of surviving with their reputations intact.

Witt chose her Olympic long program "Where Have All the Flowers Gone?" as her first number and planned a triple toe loop and a double axel, back-to-back. Stretching backstage, Sumners knew Witt was as tired as she was from the trip. She also knew Witt was anxious about the triple jump because of the incident in practice several weeks earlier.

As Witt was about to start, Sumners found a spot near the ice that was not too distracting and watched.

The triple toe loop and double axel came quickly. Despite her fears, Witt easily landed the triple toe. She nailed the double axel. She sped around the ice and, to her surprise, caught a glimpse of Sumners in the shadows.

For a split second, their eyes met.

Sumners clenched her teeth and pumped her fist. "Yes!" she shouted to Witt.

All those years watching competitors stumble on the ice, Witt thought. And now Sumners, one of the ones who had made a crucial mistake a decade ago, was out there cheering for her.

When she was an East German, she was so mysterious to American audiences. She was the enemy, produced by the East German machine, supported by those Eastern-bloc judges. When some American skaters went to East Germany on a tour years ago, she said they seemed surprised.

"Well, did you think our grass was gray?" she asked them. "It's green, too. And we have trees."

Now Witt splits her time between Germany and her forty-second-floor apartment on the Upper West Side of New York City.

"I've fallen in love with New York City," she said. "You can get everything done in fifteen minutes. It would take me two hours to do the same thing in Berlin."

The world had opened to her since the unification of Germany. "People see me as so Americanized," she said. "They say, 'Oh, you remember this and that,' and I say, 'No.' My calendar starts in 1990 in the States. Even Cole Porter music. I got introduced to it in 1991, when we used the music in our show, Brian [Boitano] and I. Before then, I never knew about it."

At a skating exhibition of Olympic gold medalists in Boston in 1993, she was introduced to the talents of someone else. That night was the first time Katarina Witt saw Peggy Fleming skate.

Witt's signature performance in Stars on Ice is "Schindler's List." It also is Wylie's big moment.

The cast goes to choreographer Sandra Bezic, the show's director and coproducer, in the summer with their ideas for the coming show. Hamilton always calls ahead to reserve a piece of music, just in case someone else is thinking about using it. Wylie and Witt weren't so careful. They both went to Bezic at about the same time with "Schindler's List." Bezic decided to keep them happy by allowing both performances, one after the other, each with a different interpretation.

Wylie skates in gray and black with "Never Again" written in Hebrew on his vest. Spotlights create barbed wire on the ice. When he appears on the ice to begin his performance, women in the audience squeal. It happens every night.

"They're missing the point," Wylie said.

Wylie's "Schindler's List" attracts the largest group of his peers in the small space between the tunnel and the stands, where the other skaters can see the ice. Yamaguchi, Sumners, Browning, and a couple of the Russians all came out and stood in the darkness one night. Wylie becomes so emotionally drained doing it, he always feels he needs more than the fifteen-minute intermission to get back onto the ice.

After Wylie, Witt comes out in red for her "Schindler's List" performance. She is representing the little girl in the red coat, the only moment of color in the black-and-white film. This is vintage Witt, circa 1995, wanting to do more than just skate, wanting a chance to remember the children of the Holocaust in a performance in the show.

•   •   •

On the same day the tour played Sacramento, NBC aired a taped hour-long Stars on Ice special and engaged in an accepted and cunning bit of deception on the viewing audience.

Early in the TV show, Browning came on the ice, skating one of his two individual show numbers, Joe Satriani's "All Alone." Forty-two seconds into the performance, he landed a triple axel.

"Wow," exclaimed Sandra Bezic, who, in addition to directing and choreographing Stars on Ice also analyzes skating for NBC. "The triple axel . . . three and a half revolutions, making it the most difficult triple."

Bezic's call of Browning's jump was worthy of an Academy Award. So, too, was the jump itself. What Bezic knew—and what viewers did not—was that her comment, taped later and placed into the telecast, described Browning's *fifth* try at a triple axel in that program that night.

NBC's cameras were at Baltimore Arena December 29 to tape the show. Browning had had trouble with the triple axel when he tried it for real. Other skaters had problems, too. So, when the event was over, Hamilton took to the public address system to ask the audience to please stay, because it was time for retakes. NBC and Stars on Ice were allowing the performers who had made mistakes a chance to clean up their acts for the cameras and, in the process, make the TV show picture perfect. They were giving out figure-skating mulligans. And they needed the audience to stay because it would look strange if NBC, when splicing the clean jumps into the original programs, suddenly found itself with a background of empty seats.

So Browning came back out and began skating. He moved into position for the triple axel, went up, and fell. The crowd groaned.

Take two. He got around on the jump, but landed with two feet.

Take three. Two-footed again.

Take four. Finally, success. Browning landed the jump. The restless audience erupted.

Browning breathed a sigh of relief. He finally could go back to the dressing room. After one try in the show and four retakes, NBC had its successful triple axel.

Browning was embarrassed about falling, but saw nothing wrong with the deception. "We're entertainers," he said.

Yet this was a production of NBC Sports, not the entertainment division.

The movielike takes were not over. Next came Witt, needing two new tries to land a double axel in her "Schindler's List" piece. Then, Hamilton himself, cleaning up a triple salchow and the footwork thereafter in two retakes. Then came two sets of pairs who had had bobbles during their programs.

During the January broadcast, NBC did not add a disclaimer to tell viewers about the mulligans. That was wrong, said NBC producer David Michaels, who handles most of the figure skating for the network.

"It was very, very disappointing," he said. "It will not happen that way again."

The network did inform viewers about Bezic's conflict of interest when commentator Hannah Storm announced that Bezic also was the director of Stars on Ice.

Then Bezic the NBC analyst went about the awkward task of critiquing her own work.

"What's exciting about Stars on Ice is we will see great athletes express themselves as entertainers and artists," she said near the beginning of the show. "This ice surface is their blank canvas. And with music, choreography, and dramatic lighting, they will create magic."

It came as no surprise that Bezic the skating analyst thought the show, put together by Bezic the director, was wonderful.

That night, at the packed ARCO Arena in Sacramento, most of the skaters had a difficult night jumping. In "All Alone," Browning went up for the triple axel—and popped it into a single. There was no retake. This one stayed with him all night.

It wasn't entirely his fault. The spotlights were supposed to point the way for his jump by flooding his takeoff point with light, like a giant flashlight in the dark. Instead, the light change came a split second before Browning jumped.

"To single something, it hurts more than falling," Browning said. "I think any skater would rather fall."

On the bus, Browning was not a barrel of laughs. "When I don't have a good skate, it really bugs me because I have to sit on the bus and go to another goddamn hotel and then sit on a bus and get on a plane and then sit on a bus and then wait for the next skate to see if I can get it back. So skating well on tour is really important to me."

Backstage at the San Jose Arena on Sunday, Wylie and Witt sat together at lunch. The topic of married men who have affairs with younger women came up. Wylie thought it was disgusting.

"You don't want to hear what I have to say," Witt replied. "I have been one of the women who has done that."

Wylie's eyes grew wide.

"It wasn't my fault and it wasn't the man's fault. Their wives were so cold," Witt explained.

"I don't want to hear this," Wylie said, sticking his index fingers in his ears. "I don't want to hear this."

Wylie finished eating, got up, and left the table. Witt shrugged. Wylie is a born-again Christian. Witt is not.

Witt doesn't always live such a daring life. She spends a lot of time alone. That's not unusual for some of the top women in skating; Debi Thomas is divorced from the man with whom she eloped after the 1988 Olympics, while Sumners has never been married.

Witt and Richard Dean Anderson, the actor who played MacGyver, were companions for a time in 1992. But Witt was dating no one in the winter of 1995. She didn't have the time.

"We're living in a modern world where you have to be sure of someone," Witt said. "Men today have problems with women. When men meet you for the first time, they are totally amazed, but they cannot handle it for a long time. Strong men most of the time have women which I call little mouses. But with strong women, we're so independent that we can live on our own and make decisions on our own. They love that at the beginning, then they get confused.

"When they see the weak side, the feminine side, then they don't understand you anymore. You sit there and cry and they say, 'How come you cry? I always thought you were so strong.' They just don't get it. And I think that's their problem."

For several seconds, a skater stands on the ice alone, in silence, waiting for the music to carry her on her way.

"The moment before the music starts during big competitions, I don't think you could feel any more insecure. You think you're going to forget your program or even forget how to skate."

That's the best female skater in the world talking.

Kristi Yamaguchi was one of only two women professionals who could win the Olympic-division world title in 1995. Ito, her 1992 Olympic rival, was the other. When Ito lands the triple axel, she is superb, but Yamaguchi's steadiness still can beat her.

As the Stars on Ice headliner, Yamaguchi skates a duet of sorts with Witt in one number, dabbles a bit in pairs skating, and trades double axels with Hamilton.

She also performs the most intriguing number on the Stars on Ice program. It's called "Doop Doop," an upbeat, techno-pop piece of music that Yamaguchi skates to dressed as a psychedelic bellhop. She wears a black body suit covered by a pink corset-vest with tails, yellow epaulets, and black-and-white-striped sleeves.

Yamaguchi heard the music in Japan the previous summer. Needing something for a short program in the upcoming professional competitions, Yamaguchi found the music at a store in Edmonton, where she trains. She took it to Bezic and they put it in the show.

Yamaguchi makes all kinds of quirky moves in the program, including strumming her face with her fingers, looking at her watch, and pressing both sides of her head with her hands as if it's caught in a vise.

But the true satisfaction of seeing Yamaguchi skate comes in watching her jump. She rarely misses. Three years after her Olympic triumph, she has never been a better skater.

As the show ended in San Jose, a man sitting in the tenth row jumped to his feet and began waving frantically at Yamaguchi.

"Kristi! Kristi!"

But she was on the other side of the ice and she couldn't hear him above the crowd or see him as she squinted into the bright spotlights that shone down upon her.

Yamaguchi knew Rudy Galindo was in the audience. She had left him two tickets at Will Call. Although they rarely talk anymore, she has fond memories of their time together. She spent parts of many days with him at his trailer-park home when they were skating together. They were kids growing up; they were a pair on the ice.

"He's actually done well, considering how far he's had to come," she said.

For Galindo, the show capped a difficult few weeks in a difficult few years in a difficult life. Richard Inglesi, his former coach, had died of AIDS complications the day Galindo was leaving to qualify at the sectionals in Portland, Oregon. He won the sectionals—called Pacific Coast—over a weak field, then came home for Inglesi's memorial service.

Galindo left the service quickly, unable to greet so many friends and parents. "Do I have bad karma or something?" he asked himself. "Am I killing these people?"

A few days later, he went to the show. For a couple hours, there was happiness in his life again.

"It was great," he said. "Kristi did so well. I tried waving at her, but I don't think she saw me. I guess it was the spotlights."

FEBRUARY

Nationals

14

TARA-MANIA

The ice in the deserted Providence Civic Center was perfect at 6 A.M. on Sunday, February 5. It was blue rather than white, without a scratch, untouched. Within a week, hundreds of skaters would perform thousands of jumps on this 85-by-200-foot rink at the 1995 U.S. figure skating championships, known, simply, as Nationals. But, at this moment on a bitterly cold, pitch-black winter morning, it was pristine, flawless, and waiting.

Of the three hundred skaters who were at Nationals, Jenni Tew was the first to touch the ice. At precisely six, she burst through the open door in the hockey boards and led a group of five girls onto the ice for the junior ladies Group A practice session. Dressed in a snappy yellow-and-black polka-dot outfit, with black gloves, Jenni had awakened at 4 A.M. after just five hours of sleep. She gave herself plenty of time to fix her dark brown hair into a perfect ponytail and do her makeup just right, even if no judges would be there to see her at such an early hour. Her audience for the next forty-five minutes would be her father, a few other parents, a couple of yawning custodians, and a local organizing-committee member. The security guards hadn't even arrived. But this was her first Nationals, and no matter how early it was, Jenni Tew told herself, nothing would be left to chance.

Tew had learned from the master. "Think like a man," was the philosophy of Carol Heiss Jenkins, "but look like a lady." This morning, Heiss was following her own advice. Her golden hair was pulled back tightly with a black ribbon. She was wearing a white turtleneck under a black sweater under a fur car coat. In the unofficial fashion shows that went on at Nationals, Carol Heiss always was the winner.

This practice session was designated a free-skating, or long-program, practice. Each day at Nationals, there were two practices for

every competitor: a short-program practice and a long-program practice. The skaters had several minutes to warm up, jump, and spin;
then the music for one competitor came on, followed by the next person's music, and so on, until all had had a chance to run through their
programs. Everyone kept on skating when another competitor's music
was going; the only deference to the person who was doing their program was that he or she had the right-of-way on the ice for those few
minutes.

After the five girls skated and warmed up, a sleepy-eyed public-
address announcer began the day's duties. Jenni's name was announced, reverberating off nearly twelve thousand empty seats. Her
music, a classical Boston Pops collection, began. Joel Tew sat seven
rows up in his winter jacket, his hands clasped in front of him, watching intently. He was thrilled that he could finally see his daughter on
the ice at Nationals, but he also knew how precarious her position
was. He told himself simply to be happy that she had made it there.
But of course he now wanted more for her. He figured this practice
could set the tone for the week. A spill or two and she could be doubt-
ing everything. But with a perfect run-through, she might begin believing that the third-place girl from the Midwestern sectionals really
could skate with the Tara Lipinskis of America.

Jenni Tew began with a double lutz, then moved across the ice for
her most difficult combination, triple toe loop–double toe loop. She
landed it. Her father beamed. The rest of the program, seven doubles
and another triple toe, went just as well.

"Clean!" Joel Tew exclaimed in the stands when the music ended
and his daughter stopped, posed for a split second, and skated over to
Heiss and choreographer Glyn Watts, who were dutifully sitting on
folding chairs beside the ice.

"Well done," Joel Tew said. "And at six in the morning. She's off to
a good start."

But Jenni was not done. As the other girls went through their programs, Heiss directed Jenni to practice her triple loop. So, in the middle of the ice, right in front of what would be judges' row during the
competition, Jenni Tew tried the triple loop. Again. And again. Five
times in all, with a fall each time.

The triple loop was not in Jenni's program at Nationals, either the
short program or the long, but Heiss was planning to have her try it
all week in practice. Heiss wanted the judges—and her competitors—
to see the jump, to see that Jenni could land it, to let them know that
even though they would see only the triple toe loop in competition,
this girl had a triple loop, too. It was psychological warfare, sublimi-
nal at worst, ingenious at best, the oldest trick in the coaching book.

With the judges watching and judging practice sessions, it made sense. With more than a dozen skaters and just ten to twenty seconds to make a decision after a program, the eyes can deceive. When the judges went to punch in Jenni Tew's scores Tuesday and Thursday, Heiss hoped that the triple loop would stay in their minds. It could be worth a placement here or there: from sixth to fifth, or fourth to third, something like that.

Now, of course, Jenni just had to land it.

By 6:45 A.M., the ice had become a tabletop of scratches. The Zamboni was waiting to make it new again. It was time for Jenni Tew to leave. Heiss smiled. What a nice way to start the week. But she had set her sights low for Jenni. Realistically low. Heiss knew Jenni would probably not be a factor in this competition. Other girls were doing far more difficult triples than the triple toe loop. Sydne Vogel, a fifteen-year-old from Anchorage, Alaska, even had a triple lutz, one step down from the triple axel. Jenni couldn't compete with that.

"If only she had one more triple!" Heiss said.

Quickly, she caught herself.

"But, it doesn't have to come that fast. She has time, plenty of time."

Heiss had acquired patience—a rare trait in figure skating—from watching the rise and fall of Lisa Ervin and from her own career, when waiting in the wings behind Tenley Albright in the 1950s allowed her to blossom as a teenage skater.

Others hadn't learned about patience yet; most especially a skater, a coach, and a family out of Newark, Delaware.

The second practice session for the junior ladies started at 6:55 A.M. The time was duly noted. At that moment, Tara-mania officially began at the national championships.

Whatever bleary eyes were present were cast on twelve-year-old Tara Lipinski as she shot onto the ice for her practice. At four feet five, a midget among children on the ice, Tara was joined by a team of three coaches, a miraculous number to have assembled before 7 A.M. on a Sunday. Her coach, Jeff DiGregorio, was present, of course, with a black baseball cap pulled low over his eyes. So was Ron Ludington—like Heiss, a venerable national fixture (in pairs skating) and mentor of all Delaware skaters and coaches. And finally, Megan Faulkner, Lipinski's coach from her Texas days.

Team Tara was firmly in place.

At the other end of the judges' row—the place where coaches sit for practice sessions—a lonely skater practiced by herself. Her coach was not there because of a scheduling conflict with another practice for another skater on another rink. Gangly and bowlegged, with braces and an awkward smile, that was the girl from Alaska, Sydne Vogel.

Tara was a sixty-nine-pound spinning top on the ice, never getting very far off the ground on her jumps, but rarely missing them either. She came back to the Team Tara coaching staff for a tip or a compliment after practically every jump, good or bad. It looked as if DiGregorio had her on a yo-yo string:

Jump. Skate over to the boards. Talk. Skate back out.

Jump. Skate over to the boards. Talk. Skate back out.

Meanwhile, Sydne Vogel had no one to talk with, so she simply skated.

She nailed the triple toe loop.

Then, triple flip.

Triple salchow.

Triple loop.

Triple lutz.

It was a clinic. She was landing the jumps of a senior woman skater—and doing them better than many seniors ever would. She wasn't as polished as, say, Nancy Kerrigan or Kristi Yamaguchi, not even close. She was abrupt at times, not entirely smooth, and in need of great doses of maturity. But she was only fifteen, not in her early to mid twenties, like Kerrigan and Yamaguchi. There was time, plenty of it.

At the junior level, this kind of jumping was something to behold. The coaches sitting rinkside couldn't help but watch. They sized her up. It was those bowed legs. Midori Ito's legs are bowed, and she is the greatest female jumper in skating history. This was a very good sign for Sydne Vogel.

By 7:25 A.M., just a half hour into the session, with fifteen minutes to go, Vogel did what few skaters will ever have the confidence to do:

Having accomplished everything, she left.

Heiss and Watts, coaching their other junior lady, Emily Freedman, in the second practice session, looked at each other with wide eyes.

"That," Heiss said, "was impressive."

At that hour, no daily newspaper reporters were there to see it. Already, some of them had written articles praising Lipinski. Most of them had never even heard of Sydne Vogel, which made sense, because reporters who rarely paid attention to figure skating never paid attention to the junior ladies. Until Tara.

The next day in the *Providence Journal-Bulletin*, Tara Lipinski was labeled "the clear favorite" to win the junior ladies title. The article listed five other names to watch, including Jenni Tew.

Sydne Vogel was not mentioned.

The previous summer, Tara Lipinski launched herself into the national figure-skating spotlight when she won a gold medal at the 1994 U.S. Olympic Festival in St. Louis. She defeated a group of junior skaters to become the youngest Festival gold medalist ever. Dozens of sportswriters were there covering the Festival, and happened upon her. She was cute, tiny, talkative, and she had a catchy story. What more could reporters want?

In October, the *New York Times* ran a long feature on Lipinski and what her family had done for her figure skating. Tara and her mother had moved to Delaware so she could train at one of the country's finest skating centers, while her father stayed behind in the family home in Houston. This wasn't unusual in skating, but no one outside the sport had heard much about split-up families until the story appeared in the *Times.* That day, the networks began calling the rink. DiGregorio and the Lipinskis looked over all the phone messages and settled upon ABC, because of its longtime coverage of their sport. Soon, Tara was on *Good Morning America,* and *Prime Time Live* was gearing up for a major piece.

It built from there.

By November, Tara was skating an exhibition at "Ice Wars" on Long Island at the invitation of promoter Mike Burg, who continued to lobby the Lipinskis to become her agent. He wasn't alone. International Management Group called the Lipinskis. ProServ, the company representing Nancy Kerrigan, also checked in.

Various East Coast newspapers, needing to write about an up-and-coming figure skater, beat a path to Delaware. Camera crews, agents, reporters: the precocious Tara had developed quite an impressive following.

An only child, Tara moved with her mother into a tiny apartment in Elkton, Maryland, just across the Delaware line, in 1993. They came for skating, nothing else. Her father stayed in Texas, working as vice president of refining for the Coastal Corporation, an energy company. Jack and Pat Lipinski, both forty-three, had decided to live apart after twenty years of marriage. They would see each other when they could.

This kind of living arrangement placed a dramatic financial burden on the family. The Lipinskis said they spent $58,000 in 1994 for Tara's skating, including living expenses in Delaware, travel, coaches' fees, ice time, skates, and costumes. To pay the bills, they refinanced the mortgage on their Texas home, a common decision for a figure-skating family.

By contrast, in Alaska, Vogel's family was paying about $25,000 a year for Sydne's skating. Vogel's father, Dennis, is a contractor who builds fire-sprinkler systems for commercial buildings. Her mother, Joy, keeps the books for her husband's company. Sydne, her parents, and her seventeen-year-old brother continue to live in the same four-bedroom home her family has lived in for her entire life. No one was moving anywhere for figure skating, the Vogels said.

"That's her support system," said Traci Coleman, Sydne's coach. "You get only one childhood. You can live life without an Olympic gold medal. You cannot live life without a firm family foundation."

But the Vogels were finding out that even with a stable home life, a young female athlete could run into trouble. Sydne was not eating properly, avoiding beef and pork, whole milk, oily foods, and desserts. She ate many other things, including chicken and fish, but she was deficient in some fats and proteins.

As she grew an inch over the past year to five feet four and a half, her weight dropped precipitously from 124 pounds to 104. In the nine months prior to Nationals, Sydne had left Coleman to train with a Russian coach working in Alaska. Vogel said the coach kept telling her she was "too fat." So, trying to please him, she cut down on what she was eating.

She did not become anorexic, Joy Vogel said.

"She got a little carried away," she said. "But we never felt she was spiraling down to something that could not be corrected. She's got to gain some weight, and she knows it."

Just two days before she flew to Nationals, Vogel asked Coleman, her longtime mentor, if she would coach her again, beginning in Providence. Coleman agreed, but she also was committed to another skater, which was why Vogel was alone for that first practice in Providence.

Another sign of upheaval in Sydne's life came that semester in school, when the Vogels took her out of the local high school and enrolled her in correspondence courses. She had been in public schools all her life, but because she was missing classes for skating competitions, her parents said it was impossible for her to keep up.

Sydne still took her tests at the school and went over for lunch a couple times a week to see her former classmates.

"She's a self-starter, so it's a good situation for her," Joy Vogel said.

"I do miss my friends," Sydne Vogel said.

•   •   •

The Lipinski family's sacrifice was being rewarded—outwardly, at least—by Tara's skating. It kept getting better and better. She went to the junior world championships in Budapest over Thanksgiving. She finished fourth, not a remarkable performance for an American, but a good one. When asked, inevitably, about her goals, she mentioned the 1998 Olympics. Or the 2002 Olympics. Or maybe 2006. She had three triple jumps in her repertoire and was working on the fourth and fifth, the flip and the lutz. Enchanted with his little sprite, DiGregorio began dreaming about quadruples: four-revolution jumps. The triple axel became a topic of conversation. The girl, obviously, was a jumping machine. DiGregorio thought she was going to be the greatest little jumper the world had ever seen.

But it wasn't just that she jumped, it was how she did it. Tara was so little, and her body was so compact, so perfect, that anyone watching had to smile. She launched herself into one tight spinning leap after another with a most determined look on her face. A mistake only set her jaw tighter. This twelve-year-old had perfected a palatable, pint-size, in-your-face style of skating. Tara was determined and confident; if she had to try a jump fifty times in one afternoon to get it right, she would do it. She thrived on the repetition of skating; she never got bored because there always was a new jump to try. DiGregorio saw to that.

The Lipinskis, meanwhile, professed amazement at their daughter's skating career. They told reporters they had tried to expose their daughter to many pursuits, including roller skating, horseback riding, piano, and modeling, but she wanted only figure skating. What could they do? They had to give in.

But the effort to keep their daughter well-rounded ended at the front door of the schoolhouse, as it did for other top skaters. Because of the demands of figure skating, they took her out of school and initiated private tutoring sessions for two hours each morning. Sometimes, those sessions would be canceled if travel or skating demanded all her time, which meant she would get extra tutoring another day. Her interaction with children her age would come almost entirely at the ice rink. In fact, the rink would become her life. She was there all day, practicing four or five hours a day, plus an hour of ballet and an hour of weight training on some days. She kept this schedule six days a week. If she could, she said, she would stay at the rink all night.

The Lipinskis also were shocked by the media's increasing interest in their little girl.

"It's already begun, so you really can't stop it," Pat Lipinski was saying at the rink in Delaware a few days before they headed to Providence. "With the media, I don't want to get anybody mad. I really don't. I figure if I'm good with them and I talk to them, they'll be good to Tara. You just hope they'll be soft and gentle with her when they see her in a down way."

They had to rearrange their lives for *Prime Time Live*'s cameras right before Nationals, and they did. Tara's tutoring was scuttled for the day so she could practice early for the network TV cameras. Pat was filmed watching practice and was interviewed for two hours. By late afternoon, Tara was still waiting around for her turn on-camera.

"You stop your running around," Pat said sternly as Tara bided time around the rink.

"I'm not running," Tara answered.

"You look a mess," her mother replied. "How do you think you'll look on TV?"

Pat, who wears the shaggy blond hair and long cloth skirts of a grown-up flower child, apologized to an outsider.

"This is not a normal day. Honestly, it's never like this."

Pat Lipinski wasn't sure how to react to what was happening in their lives. She reveled in it. She was embarrassed by it. As a parent, how could you turn down *Prime Time Live*? But television certainly turned your life upside down. Pat Lipinski was stuck in the middle of something that was growing larger than life—her twelve-year-old daughter's legend. Tara-mania was getting a grip on them all.

"If you keep telling yourself it's not a for-sure thing, you'll be okay, you'll survive it," she said. "Some people would get carried away and believe this is it, this is great. I'm more scared of it now than I was before. . . . She could be in an accident, and then skating would probably be the last thing I would think of. And imagine all these people in the media would be there to see it all, washed down the drain."

Because Tara was so young she presumably still had a bit of growing to do. People who know skating—coaches, professional skaters, ex-Olympians—thought she looked too perfect now. "It won't last" was the blunt comment of one veteran coach. She was not gangly like many growing children. She looked well-proportioned. Too much so. They would have liked her to look more awkward at twelve. When the inches or pounds arrived, where were they going to go? Tara was going to grow up or grow out, and either way, it probably would not be beneficial, at least in the short term, for her jumping.

But DiGregorio would hear none of that. He acknowledged that she would grow, but said Pat had taken Tara to the doctor to make sure it was okay for her body to continue to do the triples—as well as those quadruple jumps. They thought she would reach five feet one at most, and they believed she had the muscular structure to withstand the pressure.

"So," DiGregorio said, "I'm not going to hold back."

DiGregorio couldn't believe his good fortune. He had won the figure-skating lottery at the age of thirty. Unknown nationally even a year ago, he had been propelled into the stratosphere by the media's fascination with Tara, and he sure was happy to be there. He was going to take this kid and shoot for the moon.

"She hasn't come close to her potential," he proclaimed. "It's not like she's going to peak with triples. She'll have quadruple salchow and maybe quad loop. Those triples are so easy for her that I can see her doing quads. I watch the men, and I compare her to the men and what they're doing, and that's why she's always got a couple extra jumps more than the ladies."

Most men, in their lives, will never do a quad salchow or quad loop. The quad toe is as far as the best male jumpers usually get. Surya Bonaly has tried quads. Brian Boitano could do a quad toe in practice, but never completely landed one in competition.

But Tara was stopping at nothing.

"She's prepared. She's trained. She's worked so hard," DiGregorio said. "Last year, she had one triple in her program. Now she has six [repeating some of them]. People who don't see her every day are just amazed when they do see her. That's the response from the public and even from the judges when they see her. It's overwhelming. 'Oh my God, this little twelve-year-old!' The judges, they love her. They are just amazed at her consistency and her poise, and there's a lot of push for her [among the judges]. But she won't accept that push. She wants to prove to everybody that she can go out and do it."

As Nationals approached, the possibility of Tara actually losing in Providence was almost too much to discuss.

"I'll just feel horrible if she doesn't skate well or even if she doesn't win, because she's expected to win," DiGregorio said.

They all would feel horrible. Never had a junior skater been under so much pressure. Skating finally had a Jennifer Capriati—a prodigy with press clippings.

The record book lists all the girls who have been U.S. junior champion. It starts with the present and works backward:

1994: Jennifer Karl; 1993: Michelle Cho; 1992: Caroline Song; 1991: Lisa Ervin; 1990: Alice Sue Claeys.

1989: Kyoko Ina; 1988: Dena Galech; 1987: Jeri Campbell; 1986: Cindy Bortz; 1985: Jill Trenary; 1984: Allison Oki; 1983: Kathryn Adams; 1982: Lorilee Pritchard; 1981: Jill Frost; 1980: Vikki de Vries.

1979: Elaine Zayak; 1978: Jill Sawyer; 1977: Sandy Lenz; 1976:

Carrie Rugh; 1975: Lisa-Marie Allen; 1974: Barbara Smith; 1973: Laurie Brandel; 1972: Wendy Burge; 1971: Melissa Militano; 1970: Juli McKinstry.

1969: Louise Vacca; 1968: Barbara Ray; 1967: Julie Lynn Holmes; 1966: Janet Lynn; 1965: Sharon Bates; 1964: Carol S. Noir; 1963: Tina Noyes; 1962: Christine Haigler; 1961: Lorraine Hanlon; 1960: Karen Howland.

1959: Laurence Owen; 1958: Barbara Ann Roles; 1957: Carol Joyce Wanek; 1956: Joan Schenke; 1955: Nancy Heiss; 1954: Catherine Machado; 1953: Patricia Firth; 1952: Carol Heiss; 1951: Frances Dorsey; 1950: Tenley Albright.

And on and on, back to 1918.

Carol Heiss, sitting beside the rink at Nationals, was trying to answer a trivia question without the benefit of the list. With the junior ladies title seen as a stepping-stone to, well, somewhere, she was asked for the name of the last U.S. junior ladies champion who won the Olympic gold medal.

Heiss thought long and hard.

After several seconds, someone pointed at Heiss: "You were."

"You're kidding."

Peggy Fleming never won a junior title. Nor did Dorothy Hamill or Kristi Yamaguchi. Neither, for that matter, did Olympic medalists Linda Fratianne, Rosalynn Sumners, Debi Thomas, and Nancy Kerrigan.

Some superb skaters were on the list, including Albright, Heiss, Barbara Ann Roles, Janet Lynn, Elaine Zayak, and Jill Trenary. Others had fine careers, making an Olympic or world team. But the junior ladies winners are, by and large, a withering collection of the unknown, the discarded, the forgotten.

The USFSA has given this some thought. Kristin Matta, a spokeswoman for the Association, believes it's mostly the fault of Mother Nature. A girl is usually in juniors in her early teens, when puberty and growth spurts are lurking. The extra height and weight in certain crucial places can wreak havoc on a little girl's jumps. If she and her parents don't have the patience or the money to ride out the change to see if she can readjust to her new body, she's history.

And if it's not hips and breasts, it's boys. They enter the picture at about the same time.

There are other reasons: burnout; finding a life at school outside skating; an inability to cope with the increasing pressure of the senior division; and the fact that the Olympics come around once every four years, so even good skaters get left at home, ensuring their anonymity. All these things can play a part in a girl's decision to quit skating.

· · ·

The USFSA preached caution in the care and handling of junior ladies, but it did nothing to stop the spread of Tara-mania. Did the organization set the record straight and say that the Olympic Festival was not that big a deal, that Tara hadn't really won anything important yet, that there was a phenomenal young skater in the junior ladies, but it *wasn't* Tara? Did it stop trying to push its newest little star as it battled the professional ranks for TV ratings and sponsor support?

It did not. In fact, Claire Ferguson, the USFSA president, was quoted in a *Providence Sunday Journal* column tossing Tara's name in with some impressive company.

"Dorothy Hamill was an unknown twenty years ago. Michelle Kwan is here and Todd Eldredge. And there's a twelve-year-old named Tara Lipinski who is going to be something else."

In Tuesday's short program, the junior ladies were required to perform a jump combination, a single or double axel (they all end up trying doubles) and another double jump, plus various spins and footwork. By the luck of the draw, Tara went first on Tuesday afternoon. First was bad because judges tend to mark the first skater lower to allow for better performances later.

DiGregorio did what any coach would do; he turned a negative into a positive.

"She loves going first," he proclaimed.

In her little black velvet dress and tiny black gloves, Tara looked divine. She skated as well as advertised. Triple loop–double loop, no problem. Double axel, easy. Double flip, too easy. The judges doled out marks ranging from 4.6 to 5.2, with a total of four marks above 5.0. In juniors, those were good scores.

Ominously, however, seven of the nine judges gave her a lower artistic mark than a technical mark. Collectively, they said that you couldn't deny she had the jumps, but you also didn't have to love the look.

Before an audience of just 1,595 in the cavernous arena, the parade of girls kept coming. Amy D'Entremont, the polished seventeen-year-old who looks like Trenary and even wears some of her hand-me-downs, fell on her combination jump, but skated well the rest of the program. Two judges gave her high marks for artistry—5.2 and 5.3— and actually placed her ahead of Tara overall. So much for those deductions in the judges' guidelines; a stumbling D'Entremont was judged better than a perfect Lipinski by two of the nine people deciding their fates. This was bad news for Tara.

Soon, Sydne Vogel was on the ice, and in seconds it became clear that she was a much greater presence than Tara, and a better jumper, too. She breezed through her elements—triple flip–double toe, double axel, and double flip—and received ten marks above 5.0.

Vogel easily took the overall lead, nudging Lipinski into second.

The girls kept skating, fifteen in all.

The fourteenth was Jenni Tew.

Sparkling in hot pink, Jenni was one of only four juniors to be skating at the national championships for the first time. Her parents and her sister, Courtney, were sitting fifteen rows from the ice, near the corner where she tried her triple toe–double toe forty-five seconds into the program. She had never successfully completed the triple-double combination in the short program in a competition in her life.

That was why, as Jenni skated toward them, moving into her take-off, Deanie Tew put her hands in front of her face and buried her head in Courtney's shoulder. For a woman who used to stand in the rest room and flush the toilet so she couldn't hear the music when her daughter skated, it was quite an achievement to stay seated in the arena. Actually watching was another matter.

As Jenni threw herself into the air, Deanie peeked, then shrieked and threw a triumphant fist into the air. Jenni had landed both jumps and was on her way to a perfect program.

After a curtsy, she dashed off the ice and flew into Carol Heiss's arms. Heiss and Watts kissed and hugged her and she kissed and hugged them. It was the happiest moment of Jenni's skating life; maybe her whole life, period. She had come to Nationals and she had been flawless in her first two and a half minutes.

Watts likened a skater's first Nationals to the initial brushstrokes on a blank canvas.

"In seven years," he said, "the painting is done."

Jenni Tew already had a pretty picture in the making.

"Now, the judges' marks for Jenni Tew, for required elements," the PA announcer intoned: "4.6, 4.5, 4.4, 4.4, 4.5, 4.6, 4.3, 4.6, 4.6. And for presentation: 4.6, 4.5, 4.6, 4.5, 4.6, 4.8, 4.7, 4.9, 4.6."

The audience—what there was of it—rustled uncomfortably. Audrey Weisiger, Michael Weiss's coach, was sitting with some of her coaching friends. "That's wrong," she said. "She deserved better."

When all the short programs were over, Vogel was first, Lipinski second, D'Entremont fourth, and Tew eighth. Vogel won six judges, Lipinski won two, and D'Entremont won the other. Two girls who were ahead of Tew—D'Entremont and Serena Phillips, in fifth—had made mistakes.

Jenni's problem was not her performance. To have been judged better, she needed another triple jump, and she needed to have traveled back in time to have skated at Nationals a year earlier. Then the judges would have remembered her, felt comfortable with her skating, and probably placed her fifth or sixth—for the exact same program that earned her eighth place now.

They might even have tolerated a mistake and still put her fifth or sixth. That's called "holding up" a skater. D'Entremont, who had been sixth in juniors at the 1994 Nationals, got the benefit of the doubt this time. Grace Moore, a veteran judge from Convent Station, New Jersey, placed her second overall behind Vogel. Moore curiously put Lipinski seventh and Tew tenth.

Tew, who was a spectator at the 1994 Nationals, was "held down" by nearly every judge. "Held down" is not a common skating term, but it should be. One judge placed her fourth, another fifth. But the majority ended up with eighth. This kind of judging happens in every competition, including the Olympic Games, where Oksana Baiul received the benefit of the doubt in 1994 because she had won the world championships in 1993. Being "held up" means you're somebody in figure skating. To the judges, Jenni Tew still was a nobody.

As the spectators filed out, Joel and Deanie Tew stood in the aisle and waited for their daughter to pop up from backstage. They were ecstatic with her performance and trying with all their might to ignore the placement.

Jenni, however, didn't come up for quite a while.

She was sitting in the pressroom, by the entrance, far from most of the reporters. Heiss was standing in front of her. Jenni was in tears. She wasn't sad. She was angry.

"Listen, this is your first Nationals," Heiss said. "You cannot change your goals. Your job is to skate your very best—"

"And I did," Jenni said, disconsolate. "And I got eighth."

"Let's call Nancy Kerrigan!" Heiss said. "Nancy skates the performance of her life in the Olympics and gets the silver medal. And the judges say, 'But, honey, you have not been good before, you were fifth [at the 1993 worlds] in Prague.' And Nancy says, 'Yes, but I skated the performance of my life. It's worth the gold.'"

Heiss stared at Jenni and smiled, but Jenni still was glum.

"I could understand if everyone ahead of me had skated a perfectly clean program and had been to Nationals before," she said, "but to put someone ahead who fell, I don't understand."

"Jenni," Heiss implored in her sandpaper New York accent, "you are not going to understand it. Can you understand Tara Lipinski getting a seventh from one judge when Amy D'Entremont got a second from that same judge?"

Jenni sat in a plastic chair, silent and perplexed. Few reporters were paying any attention to them. Heiss was glad of that.

"Remember when we sat at breakfast with your parents at Midwesterns last year when you were last in novice and the big debate was, Do you go novice or do you go junior? And we said, 'Hey, what the heck, we'll go junior. You may not get out of Eastern Great Lakes. And you may not go to Mids. And, my God, if you go to Mids, your chances of making Nationals are one out of one hundred?' Remember? We discussed it. Now, if I had told you that day, 'We're going to juniors, and Jenni, you will sit eighth after the short program at Nationals,' what would you have said? You would have said, 'You're out of your cotton-pickin' mind, Carol.'"

"It would have been easier to take if I would have made a mistake," Jenni replied quietly.

"You've got to listen to the words I say," Heiss said. "I don't just say them to say them. I said to you, when you come to Nationals, enjoy it. Just take everything you've got and enjoy it. And, sometime, when you don't skate clean and you're on the podium, then I'll talk to you. We've all been through it, Jen."

"Are you telling me if I make Nationals again next year, since I've been here this year, if I skated this way, then I would get held up?"

"Probably, probably, because they like the consistent skaters," Heiss continued. "You've done very well in practices, but they also know you don't have any other triple beside the triple toe. They also know these other girls have a triple salchow and a triple toe. You have no other triple. We've said all along, 'If you had another triple . . .' That's what we know we have to do."

Jenni was slowly perking up.

"This is the way it goes," Heiss continued. "But that makes it fascinating, too. Besides, Jenni, you've just learned a very good lesson about life. There are lots of things in life that you're going to work hard for, deserve to get, and life doesn't give them to you. And this is probably one of the easiest things that you'll have to give up that you won't get. By the time you're finished skating, you'll be so well-prepared to deal with life that, for the rest of your life, everything's going to be a piece of cake."

Heiss gave Jenni a smile, a quick nod, and a hug. Jenni gathered up her skate bag and trudged up the stairs to find her mother and father. Heiss shook her head and grinned. All in all, it had been a charming afternoon with Jenni Tew. Despite having to administer that impromptu, welcome-to-the-big-bad-world-of-figure-skating pep talk, Heiss was thrilled by what had transpired. Jenni had been perfect, the judges had done a number on her, and she had responded the way any fourteen-year-old with a competitive soul would have: she got mad.

Heiss and Watts said it immediately after Jenni finished skating: Jenni Tew belongs here, she belongs at Nationals.

After the talk in the pressroom, Carol Heiss was even more certain of that.

The next day, the *Providence Journal* ran a front-page color picture of Tara Lipinski, with the headline, A NEW STAR SPARKLES. A front-page column ran underneath it, with another color photo of Lipinski and DiGregorio. In the column, Tara proclaimed her goal was to win the Olympics, "whichever one, just any Olympics." DiGregorio boasted that Tara would be the first woman in history with several quadruple jumps. Taramania took up about one-half of the front page on a slow news day.

Back on page D13, Sydne Vogel's name appeared in a headline over a tiny, ten-paragraph article. The only people quoted in the article were Lipinski and DiGregorio. There were no comments from the leader. Vogel was mentioned once, in the eighth paragraph. There also was no picture of her.

A coach who works at the Delaware rink wandered into the hotel health club, singing mockingly, "Tara, Tara, Tara."

"I wonder," the coach said, "what Sydne Vogel thinks of all this, the poor kid."

Nearly three thousand people had gathered for the junior ladies final—the long program—Thursday afternoon at twelve-twenty in the Civic Center. The short program had counted for one-third of the final score; the long would be the other two-thirds. Any one of the top three skaters would win the gold medal by winning the long program. But no one gave perky Brittney McConn of Atlanta, who was third, much of a chance. Many people didn't even know who exactly *was* third. This was going to be a battle between Sydne Vogel and Tara Lipinski. The others were setting themselves up for next year.

There would be a long wait, nearly two hours, before the top two girls skated. Before them would come all the girls who were simply trying to add a few more brushstrokes to the canvas, Jenni Tew included.

Jenni was the sixth of fifteen skaters, wearing her exquisite dress that was the color of the ice, a shining, shimmering, silvery blue. She was the mirror image of her early-Sunday-morning self, landing absolutely every jump she tried. The hardest jump she did was the triple toe loop, and she landed two of them. She would have to live and die with the triple toe, although if the judges had been watching practice carefully, they would have seen a few successful triple loops the previous few days.

When she finished after three and a half minutes, her father gave her a one-man standing ovation. The scores were better than Tuesday's and included three 5.0s and one 5.1. It was the first time Jenni had received more than one score of 5.0 or better.

"I'm so proud of her, I could just scream," Deanie Tew said. "I wouldn't have thought we could come to Nationals the first time and skate two clean programs."

It wasn't until breakfast the morning of the long program that Jenni finally put the judging in the short program out of her mind.

"I decided that I didn't care what they did," she said. "I just wanted to go out there and skate my best and let them do whatever they want to do."

Less than three months earlier, Jenni Tew had narrowly made it out of the Eastern Great Lakes regional in Lakewood, Ohio. Now she was talking like a wily veteran.

An hour after Tew was finished, Vogel was on the ice in red and gold, skating to "Les Misérables." Right out of the box, she nailed the triple lutz. She didn't wobble. Her landing was solid. She followed with the triple salchow and triple flip, the triple toe and triple loop.

But near the end, running out of gas, Vogel tried her double axel—and fell. She skidded across the ice in an ignominious slide. Did Lipinski now have an opening?

The program ended with one last jump. It was supposed to be a triple toe. But she popped that into a single. That was the mistake Tara needed, DiGregorio said to himself. He thought his kid could now win if she skated well.

Not so fast, the judges said. They spoke up for Vogel in a big way: 5.2s, 5.3s, and 5.4s for technical merit; a 5.0, two 5.1s, five 5.2s, and a 5.3 for artistry. A triple lutz carried a lot of weight in a junior ladies competition. Those marks would be tough to beat.

There were two more skaters, then Tara. She would be last, skating to "Samson and Delilah." DiGregorio was calling the final skating spot an "advantage" because he could scout the competition. First in the short, last in the long; either way, Tara loved it, according to her coach. DiGregorio could come up with a positive spin on almost anything.

Nervous and slow as she began, Tara swooped low on her triple toe loop, but somehow hung on. That, it turned out, was just the jump start she needed. She breezed through three combinations: double axel–triple salchow; triple loop–double loop; triple salchow–double toe. On her first-ever try at a triple flip, she was shaky, but she held on. Standing beside the boards, DiGregorio leaped into the air.

Finally, she zipped through a triple loop–double toe loop–double loop sequence.

DiGregorio and Lipinski thought they were the winners when she stepped off the ice and got lost in his arms. They were so happy. The first marks were outstanding, two 5.5s at the top of the spectrum and, overall, scores equal to Vogel's.

The artistic marks would break the tie.

They were not as good: 5.0s and 5.1s, with one 5.2 and one 5.3.

Given the chance to anoint Lipinski, something no one would have complained about, the judges did the exact opposite and handed Vogel a resounding victory.

The girl from Alaska won six judges' first-place marks; Lipinski, two; and McConn, one. Overall, combining the short and long, Vogel won with ease, followed by Lipinski, McConn, and D'Entremont. A contented Jenni Tew remained eighth.

Backstage, tears welled in Tara's eyes. Someone had told her she had won. DiGregorio had to tell her that was wrong.

"She's fighting mad," Delaware coach Ron Ludington said a half hour later. "She'd love to do it all over again, I'm sure. But they made it pretty unanimous. You can't argue with that too much."

Lipinski walked into an empty section of the stands and started crying. Her parents and some relatives were with her. A coach or two turned their heads and looked. They couldn't help it; this was a little skater too famous to ignore. Her mother later said that Tara was crying because one of the relatives who had come to watch her was leaving.

Tara and DiGregorio then went to the interview room.

"I thought we definitely had a chance of winning after the way [Vogel] skated," he said. "I would have put Tara first. She was the best in my eyes."

"I'll beat her next year," Tara vowed.

DiGregorio: "She's definitely moving to seniors. Definitely."

DiGregorio, again: "This keeps her hungry. There'll be a national title in her future."

What about the triple axel, Jeff?

"Sure, we're going to work on it when we get home. I think the quad salchow might be easier, though."

Tara?

"I would rather do the quad sal, because it is a little easier, but maybe both. I hope I get one of them."

And what of the media hoopla? Tara?

"I like the cameras. When I go home, I train hard, and next year I'll be back here and have the TV cameras here again."

Out in the hallway, silence enveloped Coleman and Vogel. Coleman was asked if all the attention for Tara bothered her or Sydne.

"We don't dwell on things like that," she replied. "We're here for something else. If Sydne does what she can do, and what she wants to do for herself, we don't worry about other people. I know what this kid can do."

Coleman, thirty-five, had been teaching Vogel for eight years. In the early eighties, when she finished at the University of Kansas, her parents gave her as a graduation present a round-trip airline ticket anywhere she wanted to go. She picked Alaska. When she got there, she liked it so much, she cashed in the return ticket and never left.

Alaskans, even the transplanted variety, are suspicious of many things in the Lower 48; chief among them, the media. So it was with a bemused look that Coleman stood and watched the horde of reporters following Tara. She said she never would have allowed that to happen to Sydne.

"Somebody in Tara's camp must think it's important," she said. "Otherwise, they would have put a stop to it."

Vogel herself had little to say. She explained that she played the piano and loved the Boston Pops. She also was going to move up to the senior division, where she hoped to be a factor in 1996. None of that was particularly enticing, so the media pack dashed back to Tara, where many of the pronouncements found their way into one publication or another.

Friday morning, *USA Today* had a picture of Tara Lipinski on the front page of the sports section. The Providence paper came out with a huge color photo of Tara and a small story about Sydne—but no photo.

A Providence columnist, however, questioned the media's devotion to Tara.

"We are told, confidently, that this twelve-year-old is doing what she wants to do," wrote Jim Donaldson. "How, I wonder, does a twelve-year-old know exactly what she wants to do? Especially a twelve-year-old who has spent most of her life in skating?"

Team Tara had an answer. The day before, Ludington had taken on the issue:

"I think you've got to understand something. Tara sets her own agenda, she loves to train, and she loves to skate. We're not looking at a burnout situation here. She just loves it. And she pushes herself. Nobody has to push Tara."

Tara, not Sydne, did *Good Morning America* on a remote from Providence. Tara then went off on her own for the remainder of the day. At 5 P.M., her parents still had not seen her.

Jack Lipinski asked USFSA officials to allow him to hold a news conference to dispute Donaldson's column. The USFSA's public relations staff let that idea die.

It was a tough day for the Lipinskis. The air had gone out of their sails. Their little girl had lost, decisively. The judges had spoken. All of a sudden, the world was swirling too fast for Pat Lipinski:

"I sometimes think if I could just close my eyes and go to sleep and wake up and then they would tell me how she did, that would be nice."

This was a tough loss to take. DiGregorio immediately fired Tara's longtime choreographer and asked Brian Wright to work with her. Wright said he would like to, but heard nothing further and, a month later, assumed the deal was off. Another choreographer eventually was hired to work with Lipinski.

Around the Civic Center, talk immediately turned to Tara's intention to join the ranks of the seniors for the 1996 Nationals.

"She doesn't have the skating ability yet to win *juniors*," said Denver judge Bonnie McLauthlin, who was not on the panel for the junior ladies, but watched every minute of the competition anyway. "She isn't a junior champion yet. Some judges had her third or fourth. What's she going to do in seniors?"

Pat Lipinski had a notion that the judges knew something they were about to learn:

"We're not going to win for a long time."

Prime Time Live's piece aired a few weeks later. Nearly eleven minutes long, it glorified the sacrifices of the Lipinski family. In a shot of Tara receiving her silver medal, there was a split-second glimpse of Sydne Vogel. No one bothered to mention her name.

Sports Illustrated ran a three-page story on the events in Providence, focusing mostly on the men's and women's competition. Included in the coverage was one photo of a junior lady.

It was, of course, the runner-up.

15

NATIONALS

Brian Wright arrived in Providence just in time to get fired.

Landing late on Sunday night due to a snowstorm, Wright went to the men's practice Monday morning and found Kathy Casey. Casey coached both Scott Davis, the two-time defending men's champion, and Damon Allen, a second-tier men's competitor. Wright, the choreographer for both men as well as Michael Weiss, was expecting to sit with Casey at practice sessions and also stand beside her when Davis and Allen skated in the men's competition Wednesday and Saturday.

"Do you want me to sit with you for Damon?" he asked Casey rather routinely when he first saw her in the Civic Center.

"No," she said. "We're going to do it ourselves."

Surprised, Wright stood still for a moment, then slowly wandered into the stands. As bad news went, this was the worst he had heard in, oh, about two weeks. His doctor in Indianapolis had told him that he could no longer officially be called HIV-positive. Based on blood tests and a falling T-cell count, Wright clinically had AIDS. Not full-blown AIDS. Not yet. Just the clinical variety.

Wright found a seat in the arena next to Audrey Weisiger. He quietly told her what had just happened. She was surprised. So was he, although he should have known he was in trouble. Casey had called a month earlier to ask him to come to Colorado Springs to work with Davis and Allen before Nationals, but he couldn't do it because he felt sick. Yet he never called her back to tell her. "He's great, very talented, and a gifted friend," Casey said, "but he didn't let me know what was happening. He's just not dependable."

Wright watched Allen and the other skaters in his practice group, then Davis and the others in his. When that group was done, Weisiger nudged him. "Come on," she said. Weiss's group was up next. Wright would have a seat beside the ice, at Weisiger's shoulder, to help Michael.

A couple hundred people were watching practice that day. These weren't fans, they were skating insiders: coaches, judges, parents, other skaters. Practices early in the week at Nationals—the grandest annual gossip session and skating competition on the Olympic-division calendar—established a pattern for the weekend results. They were not to be missed. Dick Button, preparing for his television broadcasts later in the week, pulled up a chair next to the ice, where the coaches sit for practice and the judges sit during competition, and began talking to Weisiger.

"Which one is Michael?" Button asked.

She dutifully pointed out Weiss. But Button already knew who Weiss was, and she knew he knew. He had commentated on the Goodwill Games the previous summer, where Weiss, one of three American men in the skating competition, had finished sixth. He had watched him at Nationals last year, too. Weisiger thought Button's question was rather surprising, but she also knew that if Dick Button asked her to identify Michael a thousand times, she would do it.

Evelyn Kramer, a coach from Lake Arrowhead, California, knew exactly who Weiss was. Kramer and Button shared the same skating lineage; both had been taught by one of the grand masters of the sport, Gus Lussi. Kramer had come along after Button left. Kramer had carved out a niche as a spin specialist—"the Spin Doctor"—and loved traditional skating. She was raving about Weiss in a cluster of coaches fifteen rows up.

"He's the last of the old-time skaters," she said. "When he skates, he really skates. The kids don't skate anymore. They only jump."

Peter Oppegard, the 1988 Olympic pairs bronze medalist and another Lake Arrowhead coach, was sitting close enough to hear Kramer.

"What do you mean, last of the old-time skaters?" he asked her. "He's eighteen."

"I know, I know," she said. "I mean, he skates like they used to skate."

Oppegard, one of Weisiger's good friends, liked Weiss's skating as well.

"Mike jumps a little bit like Christopher Bowman, and he's a better in-between skater than Bowman," he said. "He has a better upper body now than he used to. You can see he is working on upper-body presentation. Most skaters don't have all the ingredients. He does."

Down on the ice, Weiss lifted off and landed a soft triple lutz. "Oh! That was effortless," Oppegard said. "That was pretty."

But when it was his turn to do his short program and his music came on, Michael Weiss did not skate well. He popped the triple lutz into a double and touched down with his hand on the triple axel. Kramer and Oppegard were disappointed. They had been hoping for more.

A year earlier, Kramer had stopped Weiss and Weisiger to say something they had not expected to hear.

"Hey, Michael, good luck," she said. "You could be our first Jewish national singles champion."

Weiss shook his head. "Uh, I'm Methodist."

He and Weisiger chuckled with Kramer. She could be forgiven for her mistake. As a girl, she had not been allowed to join the blue-blood Skating Club of New York because she was Jewish. Exclusionary clubs had long since opened their doors to anyone who could skate well or pay for lessons, but the memories of those dark days of discrimination would stay with Kramer forever.

Todd Eldredge, a 1992 Olympian and former two-time national champion coming back from injuries, was the top skater in Weiss's practice group. He was the one Button was most closely watching. Down the row, rinkside, a man with a video camera was taping all the programs so ABC staffers could map out the performances for their cameras and also prepare the announcers for what they would see. When they go on the air, every commentator, whether it's Dick Button, Peggy Fleming, Sandra Bezic, or Scott Hamilton, is handed a list of the jumps a skater will do. These cheat-sheets—which occasionally fall into the hands of newspaper reporters, too—allow them to call jumps easily and also to report when a skater has changed what he or she had planned to do.

Having to be at practice, Button admitted, wasn't much fun. If only it were a professional event; one, say, that he promoted.

"That's where the action is," he said, standing beside the ice. "It's not here. This is sweet, but the action is elsewhere."

USFSA officials knew Button was taking shots at their event in private, but could do little to stop him. So they fumed. Their most prestigious event was being brought to the American public by a man who once won seven USFSA national senior championships but now seemed to be too involved in the professional world for their own good.

"I think Dick takes the titles that he won in that sweet world quite seriously," USFSA president Claire Ferguson replied, when told of Button's comment.

When the practice was over, Wright and Weisiger trudged through the snow back to Weisiger's room at the brand-new Westin Hotel, the headquarters for the skaters and coaches. Neither of them was happy. Weisiger was disheartened by the way Michael had skated. "Crappy" was the exact word she used. Propped up against the pillows on one bed, Weisiger joked, cynically, that it was all the choreographer's fault.

Wright was leaning on the pillows on the other bed in Room 902 (they called it 90210, in honor of the TV show).

"Go ahead," he said. "Fire me. I've been fired by bigger than you—today."

They decided to go to a coffeehouse on the other side of downtown Providence to get away from the hotel, which was filled with skating people talking about skating, a depressing thought for both of them at that moment. Before they left, Wright went into Weisiger's bathroom, shut the door behind him, pulled out a hypodermic needle, pulled down his pants, and injected a thousand units of the blood-thinning drug heparin into his upper thigh. If he didn't do this regularly, the blood clots that formed because of the HIV virus eventually would travel to his heart and kill him.

At eight-fifty that night, Weisiger and Wright were back in the arena, watching Michael skate once again. Also in the practice group, called Group A, was Rudy Galindo.

"What is Rudy wearing on his legs?" Casey exclaimed, sitting in the stands to watch the practice that didn't include either of her two skaters. Galindo, supposedly toned down by his coaches, had on yellow and gray tights with a black T-shirt. It was such a contrast with Weiss and Eldredge, who both wore black pants and white T-shirts. Weiss made three cosmetic concessions for Nationals: he visited a tanning booth two times in Virginia to get some color in his face (makeup was out of the question); he had his dark hair trimmed short on the sides and fashionably floppy on top in a salon, not by his usual barber—himself; and he left his hoop earring back in the hotel room, where it remained all week.

Once again, Wright and Weisiger didn't like much of what they saw in practice. Wright said Weiss looked as if he were moving "through thick water."

Weisiger admitted she was getting overly anxious. This was the time to get nervous: Nationals. A year of work synthesized into two performances. She asked Oppegard what he thought, and he bluntly told her that she was too nervous. Weisiger's mind was working overtime. After years of climbing, Weiss had reached the highest plateau. Now, he had to produce. It was easy being a rising phenom, the first kid on the block with a triple axel. The difficult part was proving your worth on an annual basis with the big boys.

None of the skaters did exceptionally well in practice that night, but Weiss did have a grand moment. Early in the session, with no fanfare, he attempted and landed a picture-perfect quadruple toe loop.

Jeff DiGregorio and several other coaching friends of Weisiger's cheered wildly. Weiss blew them a kiss. When he tried the quad in his long program run-through, however, he fell.

Wednesday night, Weiss was the eighth of fifteen skaters in the men's short program. He had practiced his routine at least three hundred times, all for this moment at Nationals. From last April, when he got the program from Weisiger and Wright, until that afternoon, when he last ran through it, his life on the ice had been consumed by his short and long programs. Although the long program weighed twice as heavily as the short in the scoring system, it was the short that was the most crucial. Required elements had to be completed. A mistake in the short could not be forgotten by the judges. It was supposed to count heavily against the skater. That was why Weiss's life for the past ten months had been consumed by the moves and jumps that constituted those two minutes and forty seconds.

So, needless to say, it came as quite a shock to him that, thirty seconds into his performance, he was sprawled on the ice, scrambling to get up on his hands and his knees in front of eight thousand people in the Civic Center. Ten months of work, hundreds of hours of practice, all of it wiped out by an ugly fall on the first jump he tried.

To make matters worse, the embarrassing error came on the combination jump, his planned triple axel–double toe loop. A fall on the combination in the short program usually was figure-skating death. Brian Boitano experienced it in Norway the year before. It's something from which you cannot recover. At that moment, Weiss knew any chance he had for a medal was gone. Thirty seconds and—poof— a whole year went up in smoke.

"Oh no, oh no," Wright muttered to himself as he stood by the boards with Weisiger. She didn't say anything. She kept her jaw up, nodded purposefully, and admonished every muscle in her face not to give away the sudden and overwhelming dismay that was welling up inside.

Wright's brain was firing fast: "Not just a bad fall. A disaster fall! You never get back on track after something like that."

Wright was absolutely correct. Weiss picked himself up and carried on, but he could muster no great desire to do anything but go through the motions. It was as if he were suddenly hollow, as if he had left most of himself there on the ice.

Then, another fall. Coming out of a spin, Weiss hit his knees—during some relatively simple footwork. Unbelievable, Wright said to himself. This was becoming a nightmare.

"Come on," Weiss told himself as he got up again. "At least make this respectable."

Weiss gathered himself to successfully complete the triple lutz and the double axel, shrugged as his music ended, and gladly accepted a soft hug from Weisiger when he stepped off the ice and through the swinging door in the boards.

"Can we start the tape over again?" he asked sadly.

The marks popped onto the scoreboard: a 4.6 all the way to two 5.1s technically, and 5.2s to 5.5s for artistry. The second set of marks was very good. If it was possible, Weiss, Weisiger, and Wright felt even worse than they had a minute earlier. When they saw the artistic marks, they knew that Michael really had blown it. With those high second marks for a seriously flawed program, the judges told Weiss they would have been willing to place him in the top four or five and give him a chance for a medal Saturday afternoon—if only he had not fallen. Twice!

Weiss left Kiss and Cry, clomped down the hallway in his skates, and entered the men's locker room. No one else was there. He had a water bottle in his hand. He threw it against the wall.

"Goddammit!" he yelled.

He picked up another water bottle and tossed it. He took off his skates and slammed them to the ground.

"You fool!" Weiss screamed. "You blew it! You're so stupid. How do you do something like that?"

He stood there for a second, thinking. That was his problem. He thought too much. He was thinking way too much about the triple axel before he jumped. You can't think about it. You just had to do it. From now on, he would try not to think.

Weiss trudged across the room, picked up the water bottles, and put them back where they belonged. He grabbed his skates and put them into his bag. He sat down. He couldn't help himself; he started thinking.

An hour later, Weiss calmly walked into the pressroom to talk to a few reporters from Washington, D.C., and Virginia who needed to write a couple paragraphs about him for the local readers. He explained that he had fallen because he was slightly off center in the air and slipped off the edge of his skate blade on the landing. It was a technical thing, he said. He had felt great coming into the program.

Suddenly, his head turned. He spotted a familiar face by a table with press releases stacked on it.

"Dad, what are you doing in here?"

Greg Weiss had sneaked into the pressroom and was munching on an apple. Michael went over to him. The five-foot-six bodybuilder wrapped his son in his arms and squeezed him hard around the chest.

"I love you," he whispered into Michael's ear. Still speaking quietly, he added the only admonition he would offer.

"You're too good to do that."

"I know," Michael said softly. "I know."

Near midnight, Brian Wright was standing outside the arena doors in the bitter cold, nervously smoking a Camel Light. He was perplexed about Michael.

"Making a mistake is okay, but to look that bad . . . There's very little salvation about it."

Disappointed as he was for Weiss, Wright was strangely pleased about the entire evening. When the short program had ended, Scott Davis was in first place, five judges to four over Todd Eldredge, who was undefeated all season. Third was Shepherd Clark, and Damon Allen was fourth. Weiss had ended up eighth, one place ahead of Rudy Galindo, who fell on his triple flip but landed his triple-axel combination. Galindo already was completely out of the running. Again.

Wright's skaters, whether he was standing by the boards for them or not, were first, fourth, and eighth. "Scott was great, and that made me really happy," Wright said. "Damon was great. I sat back and watched. That's not a bad way to earn a living, huh?"

Weisiger had left the arena quickly to go to a previously scheduled coaches' meeting at the Westin. She was mystified by Weiss's two falls and hurt by a chance encounter with Oppegard backstage after Weiss had skated. She asked him what he thought was going wrong.

"You're too close to him," Oppegard replied bluntly. "It's putting too much pressure on him."

Unable to say anything, with tears welling in her eyes, Weisiger walked away.

Friday at noon, before only 6,300 people, the women's short program began. It was an odd time to hold the glamour event of the competition, but the paid staff of the USFSA said the volunteers in the organization still called the shots. They ended up with a half-filled arena, but the TV cameras were rolling. That was what really mattered.

The short program was to be the beginning of the coronation of fourteen-year-old Michelle Kwan as the United States' top 1998

Olympic hopeful. There had been so much talk about Kwan. She had not won any competition since Sun Valley, but she had skated well throughout the fall in three different events and had been ahead of fellow teenager Nicole Bobek all three times they had met—at Sun Valley, Skate America, and a pro-am in Philadelphia in late November. They both had gone into seclusion for nearly two months to get ready for Nationals, practicing on their own with their coaches—and wondering, every now and then, what the other was working on.

Team Kwan came to Providence with a bit of an attitude, which was rare for people like Frank Carroll and Shep Goldberg, gentleman coach and gentleman agent. When pressed on the issue of little girls ruling the sport, Carroll asked, quite self-assured, whether reporters had watched any of Kwan's practices that week. It was a challenge: watch her, and you'll see how beautiful an artist she has become.

Goldberg took a good-natured jab at Newsweek's Mark Starr for writing these words: "Certainly, there will be no one performing in Providence who combines the technical skill and artistry of a former gold medalist like [Kristi] Yamaguchi."

Goldberg questioned Starr: What about Michelle?

Starr stood by his story. It was a good thing he did.

Kwan was not first after the short program. Nor was she second. She bobbled the triple-lutz/double-toe combination just enough to slip to third place after one-third of the competition. First Tara Lipinski, now Michelle Kwan. The little kids were going down fast.

The second-oldest woman in the competition was the leader, Tonia Kwiatkowski, the blue-collar skater who was going to turn twenty-four in two days. A college graduate (Ohio's Baldwin-Wallace), Kwiatkowski was known, as Paul Wylie had been, as a superb practice skater who choked when it counted. "She wins all the practice sessions," the skating community said derisively. She had made one world championship team, in 1993, and promptly missed the cut in qualifying, failing to make the main draw. She had been fifth at the '94 Olympic trials. There was nothing particularly remarkable about her career.

Kwiatkowski, one of Carol Heiss's stable of skaters, had been having fine practices all week, but this time, she carried them into the competition. She skated first, that awful starting position, but she proved that if you skate perfectly, and if almost no one else does, you can hold on to the lead.

The other serious contender was Bobek, the five-foot-four, 118-pound blonde whose only mistake was stepping out of her landing on her double axel. She found herself in second place, with two judges placing her first.

Bobek, not Kwiatkowski, was the skater Carroll feared the most. Carroll had taught her for one year, in 1989, and he knew she was capable of superb skating if she ever got herself into shape.

Carroll saw her at the Goodwill Games the previous summer. "I thought, 'Oh-oh, she can be a problem for me because she's changed, she's more disciplined, she's on time, she's sociable.' "

At Nationals, Carroll saw Bobek at practice and said, "I'm really in trouble."

Bobek had dropped about ten pounds.

She was the most fascinating Olympic-division skater in America. Without even training properly, she had become one of the best skaters in the country. And now she was starting to work hard, which was a shock to the coaches who were members of the Bobek Alumni Association.

"She might be one of the most talented kids I've ever touched," said Casey, who had coached her for four years before she bolted last summer. "But, boy, you've got to have a work ethic and guidance from home. If she learns a work ethic, she would be hard to beat."

Casey said those words in the fall of 1994. At that time, Richard Callaghan, who was her new coach in Detroit, was thinking the same thing.

"I require four programs each day in practice," he said, "and she probably didn't do that in the whole previous month before she came here. If she would skate four programs in one week, she probably thought she was doing great. It took a while for her to realize it wasn't enough."

In the last few months before Nationals at the Detroit Skating Club, Bobek began to get the idea. She shared the ice with straight-laced Todd Eldredge, skating's most noted workaholic. The old tricks— stopping her program mid-music because she fell or goofing off when a coach like Casey turned her head to help another skater—didn't work anymore. Eldredge didn't do that. Soon, Bobek stopped doing it, too. The rowdy teenager was beginning to grow up.

Bobek had finally found a home. And it showed. She was off to a good start at Nationals.

For the moment, though, Frank Carroll had not one problem, but two: Nicole and Tonia. Another Tonia! There always seemed to be one lurking in U.S. women's figure skating, although this one had a different spelling and never had caused a controversy in her life, as far as anyone knew. While Kwan and Bobek had spent the fall skating the marquee events on national television, Kwiatkowski the journeywoman was forced to qualify from the hinterlands, going to Eastern Great Lakes and Midwesterns, where the only cameras were the home variety held by mothers and fathers.

But, in the short program, reputation didn't mean as much as in the long. You've got to land the jumps and complete the other required elements. And the judges must mark what they see.

Heiss was nervous for Kwiatkowski heading into the short program, hoping she could hold it together. Heiss kept telling her, "Another day at the office. Another day at Winterhurst." With those words ringing in her ears, Kwiatkowski landed a triple-lutz/double-toe combination, a triple toe, and a double axel. She waited through a couple hours of skaters and found herself in first place. Whether she could stay there after the long program was another matter entirely.

Saturday was the first day in a week in which the ice melted outside the Civic Center. It was forty degrees, with a breeze that carried a hint of spring. Inside, where the ice was still frosty, winter was in command.

Michael Weiss's disappointment, carried over from three days earlier, was in not being in the final warm-up group for the long program. The field of fifteen men was separated into threes: the worst five after the short program skated first through fifth, in an order determined by a random draw; the skaters who were sixth through tenth after the short were in the middle group; and the top five were scattered, randomly, in the final group. Because of his fall on the triple axel, Weiss was in the middle group and skated eighth, just as he had on Wednesday. Skaters in the middle warm-up group were labeled as also-rans even before they skated; rarely if ever did a skater from that group pull up to win a medal.

Weiss had had a long time to think about what he was going to do in the long. His new goal was to leap into the top five, and the way he was going to do that was by becoming the first U.S. man to land a quadruple jump in competition.

Because Weiss was out of the running for a medal, and nobody in the media was paying attention to him, almost no one knew what was about to happen. Weiss himself didn't even realize that an American had never landed a quad in competition—until someone told him *after* he tried it.

Meanwhile, spectators never knew an attempt was made at U.S. skating history. No one announced it. Reporters didn't know, even after they saw the jump. They just assumed it was a triple. Things happened so fast when a figure skater was in the air that the difference between three and four revolutions was extremely hard to discern. The journalists were in good company. At least one of the nine judges thought Weiss had tried a triple.

•   •   •

Before Weiss tried the quadruple toe loop, before he began his program, he scared Weisiger to death. One time in practice earlier in the week, he had become disoriented during a spin and skated the wrong direction for several seconds before realizing his mistake. This can happen during spins, especially in arenas that are foreign to younger skaters, without easy points of reference. Weisiger had made a point of reminding Weiss that if he came out of the spin and was looking at her, he was facing the wrong direction and should make sure to turn around—subtly—to get his back toward her before continuing toward his next jump, the triple lutz. To make it easier for him, Weisiger said she would keep his water bottle on the ledge of the boards as another landmark.

Weiss knew Weisiger was worried about his sense of direction. As he stepped onto the ice to get ready to skate, he pointed to the other end of the ice and said, "So I start down there, right?"

Weisiger was horrified. "No! You start right here!"

Weiss, seconds from beginning, smiled broadly. "Just kidding."

He posed, his back toward Weisiger and Wright, waiting for his music to begin.

"I'm going to get you for that," Weisiger said in a voice just loud enough for him to hear in the hushed arena.

With that, Weiss was off. Boom! He landed the triple axel. He glided down the ice toward Weisiger and Wright to try the quad toe.

Up, up, up.

History in the making?

No. Spinning for what seemed like forever, he came down a fraction of a second too soon and stumbled onto the ice. The status quo remained; a successful quad was still yet to be done by an American in competition.

Weiss got up and moved into his troublesome spin. By the boards, Weisiger was distracted. A security woman was telling her that nothing could be placed on the boards. She would have to move the water bottle.

Weisiger balked. The bottle had to stay, at least for another few seconds.

"It could fall on the ice," the woman warned.

"That is my student out there," Weisiger replied. "I'll take the risk."

Weiss moved effortlessly through the spin, ended with his back to all the commotion, and continued on without a problem into his triple lutz.

Weiss landed that jump with a flourish, throwing his right arm out toward the crowd with the flair of a Shakespearean actor. (It wasn't his idea. That was a move courtesy of Weisiger and Wright.) As Weiss flung his arm, he looked into the crowd. Staring him in the face was none other than Viktor Petrenko, the 1992 Olympic gold medalist, who had come over for the day from his new home in Simsbury, Connecticut, and was sitting in the front row with Oksana Baiul.

"Viktor!" Weiss said.

Petrenko opened his eyes wide and smiled at Weiss.

Weiss laughed. What more could happen in the first half of a long program?

The rest was uneventful. After four and a half minutes, Weiss had landed four clean triples and stepped out of a fifth, a second triple lutz. When he finished, he skated toward the boards, where several women had come down through the stands and stood holding flowers they had bought at a booth on the concourse. One was an old girlfriend. Another was a current girlfriend. A third was his sister, Genna.

Weiss reached for Genna.

"I went with the safe one," he said.

The judges rewarded him with the highest marks of the afternoon to that point: mostly 5.3s and 5.4s for technical merit, a couple marks as high as 5.5 for presentation.

Bonnie McLauthlin, the judge from Denver, gave him 5.4, 5.5. She liked his flair—for an eighteen-year-old. But he didn't do as many triple jumps as the skaters who would come later. Another judge agreed with McLauthlin, handing out 5.4, 5.5. But no one went any higher.

Weiss was the leader in the clubhouse. But unlike in golf, where the wind might blow or the rain could come, there was almost no chance a skater from the middle of the pack could hold on to such a lead. Too many good skaters—better skaters at this point in their careers—were coming after him.

Aren Nielsen, yet another Heiss disciple, zipped past Weiss with a six-triple-jump performance. A couple others passed him as well. But all of them were nothing more than the warm-up act for the final two skaters: Eldredge and Davis, who would skate in that order. Barring a huge mistake, they would fill the two spots on the world championship team headed to Birmingham, England, in March.

Performing to the music of *Gettysburg,* wearing a little blue and a little gray, Eldredge was as rock solid as he had been all year, when he won Skate America, a pro-am title in Philadelphia, and an event in Japan known as NHK Trophy. Three competitions; that was a busy autumn for a top U.S. skater. Eldredge, twenty-three, was going through a second "career" as a skater. He had won two national titles before he turned twenty, but then succumbed to a bad back and had three difficult years before coming back in 1994. He was a solid athlete who shot in the eighties on the golf course and had industrial-strength training habits, but had trouble emoting on the ice. But he could jump.

Eldredge put both palms down to keep from falling on a triple lutz, but landed *two* triple axels and was otherwise perfect.

The judges gave him their highest marks to that point, but left room if Davis was superb.

McLauthlin, watching from her seat at center ice as judge No. 5, was happy to see Eldredge skate so well. It made her life so much easier. She had judged the senior men two years earlier at the Phoenix Nationals, where Eldredge had come in as a two-time national champion and 1992 Olympian. Eldredge's track record led McLauthlin, and all the judges, to believe he would be one of the top two skaters at that competition. But it didn't turn out that way.

"I had all my numbers in my mind for the last five skaters, how I'd mark them if they skated well," McLauthlin said. "After Todd missed the first jump, I thought, 'Well, now he's third.' And then he missed the second jump, and then I thought, 'Well, now he's fourth.' And then he missed the third jump and I thought, 'Well, now he's fifth.' After that, I had no place to put him, all my places were gone. So, the way my numbers worked, I had to give him either sixth or tenth, because I had seventh, eighth, and ninth together with no room between them. So I gave him sixth. You don't expect them to go that haywire."

This time, Eldredge was true to form and McLauthlin punched in 5.9, 5.8. But she left plenty of room if Davis skated better. If she had wanted to, McLauthlin could have put eight skaters ahead of a skater to whom she gave 5.9, 5.8. Needless to say, there was room for Davis to win on McLauthlin's, and everyone else's, scorecard.

Davis began strongly, with three powerful triples, including the triple axel. Halfway through the program, skating to music from *Dick Tracy* and *The Untouchables,* he attempted his second triple axel. But he stumbled and turned out of it. It was over, just like that. Eldredge had done two triple axels; Davis had managed only one. That was why he lost the national title for the first time in three years.

It was unanimous, nine judges for Eldredge, none for Davis. Nielsen was third. McLauthlin was generous in giving Davis 5.7, 5.8. She thought of dropping him into third place on her scorecard below Nielsen, but decided against it. Davis was a better spinner than Nielsen, she said, and that's what decided it in her mind. It was a split-second call, like most decisions in figure skating. A figurative flip of the coin in a judge's mind.

Among the also-rans, the results of the men who made it out of January's Eastern sectionals were turned nearly upside down at Nationals. Shepherd Clark, who had skated well in the short program and was in third place, failed miserably in the long program again and dropped to fifth overall. Weiss ended up sixth. Michael Chack, who landed only three triples in the long program after a messy short program, was tenth, and Jason Sylvia, who had been so good in Fitchburg, couldn't land the jumps on the national stage and finished eleventh.

Rudy Galindo, meanwhile, landed only two clean triples and fell twice to finish eighth. He was supposed to be a new Rudy. The hair *was* shorter. The makeup *was* lighter. But the outfit! He wore a one-piece black body suit with a maroon sequin top. He looked, and skated, like the old Rudy Galindo.

The women skated that evening. Forty-five minutes before the final skaters were to take the ice, they wandered by an open-air restaurant in the Westin on their way across the covered walkway to the arena. Sitting at a table beside the aisle, eating salads and sandwiches, were three agents taking a break from chasing clients—Jeanne Martin, Mike Burg, and Steve Woodward.

As each woman passed, the threesome cheerfully called to her and her entourage to sit down with them and have a beer, an invitation they knew would be turned down. (To Kwan, the offer was a Coke.)

Kwiatkowski stopped and talked for a couple seconds before moving along. Kwan was downright chatty for a moment before she kept going. But Bobek, the one who in the past really might have pulled up a chair and joined them, smirked, waved, and never broke stride.

"Bobek's going to win," Burg said, and the others didn't disagree.

Because Nancy Kerrigan turned pro and no U.S. woman won a medal at the 1994 world championships, the United States could send just two women to the 1995 worlds. Four skaters—Kwiatkowski, Bobek, Kwan, and Kyoko Ina, who was fourth in the short program—had a realistic chance at going. All four had wound their way from Sun Valley in October to Providence in February. The fifth skater in Sun Valley, Lisa Ervin, was sitting in a town house on Cape Cod, just a ninety-minute drive away, watching on television. At times she wanted to turn away from the TV set. She had beaten every single one of those skaters only two years ago in Phoenix. "I should be going on the ice right about now," she said to herself.

However, having watched the build-up for Kwan, Ervin found herself feeling sorry for her.

"I remember what it was like to be that age," the seventeen-year-old said of the fourteen-year-old. "Everything's peachy keen and the only thing you're worried about is how many double axels am I going to do today? I remember that. I really feel for her. She's going to wake up at fifteen or sixteen and she's going to say to herself, 'Oh my god, I'm number one or number two in the nation, and once you hit number one, there's no place to go but down.'"

Shep Goldberg was walking through the Civic Center concourse earlier in the day, pleasantly predicting the night's conclusion for his client, Michelle Kwan.

"She'll win," he said, just like a good agent should.

She did not win.

Kwiatkowski also did not win. She fell on a triple flip and two-footed a triple lutz, knocking herself out of contention. Ina, too, didn't win, finishing fourth.

The winner was the girl who had left only the very best coaches in her wake, the woman who had finally put her act together in Detroit: Nicole Bobek.

The skating order was the same as the men's. The two best came last; Bobek skated next to last, Kwan skated last. It was a position Kwan did not like, because of the long wait after warming up with the final group, and the pressure that created.

Kwan's fears, however, were minimal compared with the concern many experts had for Bobek. If she followed her own history, she would be such a disaster on the ice that Kwan could sleepwalk through her long program and win. Everyone in skating knew what Bobek probably would do. They knew she rarely practiced her long program straight through, so she of course never got through it at Nationals without several stumbles or falls. This had happened every year. She would land a few triple jumps, then get tired, then fall apart.

Would 1995 be any different?

Looking much older and more graceful than seventeen in a sparkling blue dress, Bobek attacked the ice. She didn't care if "Dr. Zhivago," her long-program number, started out slowly. She certainly wasn't going to.

"Attack," she told herself.

She skated so quickly at the start, she was in danger of getting ahead of her music. But she slowed down, the music caught up, and she let it lead her on. The capacity crowd gasped at her trademark spiral, lingering for fifteen seconds, one leg gliding on the ice, the other shooting toward the sky.

Bobek did make two mistakes. First, she put a hand down on the triple toe loop.

"Forget it," she told herself. "At least you didn't fall on your face or on your butt."

Later, she popped a triple salchow into a double. But, again, she did not fall. The practice had paid off. She had not been perfect, but she had not been her usual old self. The marks from the judges were very good, mostly 5.7s, 5.8s, and 5.9s. But those didn't matter right then. All that counted was how the last skater did.

The final performer in the entire national championships was Kwan. Everyone else was finished. Looking tiny and vulnerable on the ice all alone, she was doing just fine until the very end of her four-minute routine. She had her second triple lutz coming up and needed to pick up speed out of her footwork to get the power to get high enough to land the difficult jump. Carroll, standing beside the boards, saw that her speed wasn't there as she glided toward him. He knew what was about to happen.

She went up.

She came down—on her hip.

Kwan scampered to her feet and finished the program, but the damage was done.

Goldberg was sullen as he stood above the press section in a corner of the arena.

"One jump," he said. "The last jump. She was already cutting down the net, and . . ."

Kwan's scores had just been announced—5.6s through 5.9s—but Goldberg wasn't writing them down and no scoreboard in the arena was keeping track of the results.

"Was it close?" Goldberg asked.

No, he was told, it wasn't. It was eight to one, Bobek. Two judges even placed Kwan third behind both Bobek and Kwiatkowski. Even without her fall, Kwan probably wouldn't have defeated Bobek. Bobek looked too poised. Kwan looked too much like a kid sister.

This was a shocking disappointment for the Kwans—and for Goldberg. He had looked at the period from 1995 until the 1998 Winter Olympics as a time for his client to shine. He was expecting a four-year run for Kwan. He already had begun to worry about how a little girl like her could stay on top of such a volatile sport for so long.

Now, he no longer had to be concerned about any of that. Shep Goldberg was representing the two-time U.S. national silver medalist. How to keep a teenage girl on top of the sport was someone else's problem.

Richard Callaghan ended up as the most successful coach in Providence, training both the men's and women's champion, the first time that had happened at the same Nationals since 1950, when Gus Lussi coached Dick Button and Yvonne Sherman to national titles.

Eldredge the workaholic had helped turn Bobek into a fine skater. Their time together on the ice had meant everything to Bobek. He stood in the back of the interview room smiling as she told of her new work ethic in front of the cameras and reporters.

Bobek's life was changing right before her eyes. She was the national champion, the ladies champion. The lineage was stunning: Peggy Fleming . . . Dorothy Hamill . . . Nancy Kerrigan . . . and Nicole Bobek.

Bobek was about to become a busy and rich young lady, if she wanted it. Wanted it? She and her mother and her mother's friend had been chasing it her whole life, from her native Chicago to California, from Colorado to Cape Cod to Detroit. This was the moment they had been waiting for.

Late into the evening, Carroll sat in the lobby of the Westin with a couple of reporters and friends. He had thought Kwan was ready to take charge of U.S. skating, but he now knew he had been wrong.

In a news conference a couple hours earlier, glum and colorless, Carroll had proclaimed that Kwan would "live to skate another day." But that day now seemed farther away than he had thought. What a sad moment this was for Carroll, who was so hoping that Kwan would bring him not just stability in his coaching life, which she had done, but the joy that came in coaching the national champion. Christopher Bowman had been such a headache that his victories were muted in Carroll's memory. And it had been a long time since Linda Fratianne had nearly won the gold at the 1980 Olympics.

Everything was so strange to him now. He shook his head.

"I was just thinking," he said to Philip Hersh of the *Chicago Tribune,* "we've gone from Tonya Harding to Nicole Bobek. Oh my God!"

Earlier, at the press conferences, Heiss twice sat with a skater who had finished third and just missed making the world team. First it was Nielsen, then Kwiatkowski.

After a week of looking beautiful, Heiss finally was tired. She was having trouble smiling. There were no more events to handicap, no more judges to outguess.

When Carol Heiss stopped looking perfect, it was time for everyone to go home.

MARCH

To

GREAT BRITAIN

ANATOMY

OF A

RUMOR

The tiny room just off Kiss and Cry at the National Exhibition Centre in Birmingham, England, could not hold another person. There was space to seat fifteen people, but fifty had come for this special news conference. Working reporters and curious skating officials were jammed in the doorway. Boom microphones appeared from above. This was Monday, March 6, qualifying day for the women at the world championships. The event did not officially begin until the next day.

Already in the pressroom, there was the "Bobek Wall," as cynical reporters and press officials called it, with dozens of articles from London's tabloids and broadsheets about the latest blond American figure skater possessing an attorney and a court record.

BRASS KNUCKLE DUST-UP read a headline from the British paper *Today*. The story read, partially: "The tranquil world of figure skating suddenly finds itself the battlefield for a cold war poisoned with scandal and intrigue.

"Just when you thought it was safe to take to the ice after the Tonya Harding–Nancy Kerrigan crowbar drama, the sequins could fly again at next week's world championships in Birmingham.

"For America's latest hell-raiser, Nicole Bobek, is about to glide into the spotlight screaming smear and innuendo from the rooftops. The U.S. champion is no angel. A chain-smoking convicted burglar from Chicago nicknamed Brass Knuckles because she wears a ring on every finger, her seventeen years so far have been conducted on very thin ice."

The stately *Times* wrote that "had Bonnie and Clyde decided to enter the pairs competition at the world championships, they could hardly have caused more of a stir than the girl they call Brass Knuckles."

The *Daily Mail*: "A rum old business this ice skating. First we had Tonya Hardface and her heavies. Appearing soon in Birmingham is cigarette-smoking, blond U.S. champion Nicole Bobek, aka Brass Knuckles."

Into this maelstrom stepped Nicole Bobek. On November 2, Bobek had been arrested at the Bloomfield Township, Michigan, home of another skater in Bobek's club. According to Bobek's lawyer, Michael Friedman, Bobek had been given the security code to the house's alarm system. Friedman said Bobek entered the house and found no one home.

When the father of her skating friend arrived home, he found Bobek in the house. Published reports said Bobek had money in her hands, but her lawyer said nothing was stolen. The police were called and Bobek was charged with home invasion, a felony burglary charge. Bobek entered a conditional guilty plea and petitioned to have the case handled under a youthful-offender program. The program promised her confidentiality in exchange for the plea, and she was placed on two years' probation.

The program's guarantee of confidentiality didn't take into account that she was a figure skater.

Word of the arrest traveled quickly from rink to rink around the United States. Kathy Casey heard about it in December from Damon Allen, who had heard about it from other skaters. Soon, everyone was talking: judges, agents, U.S. Figure Skating Association officials, and reporters. Word reached the first journalist in late January, one week before Nationals.

This rumor mill sounded normal for figure skating, where gossip spread like a fast-growing vine, but Friedman told *USA Today* that he was suspicious. He said police told him a private investigator looked into the case. Friedman thought the camp of a rival skater hired the investigator to get copies of court documents and leak them to reporters.

"It is another example of jealousy and envy at work in skating," he said. "With Nancy Kerrigan, it was smash her knee. With Nicole Bobek, it was sully her reputation."

Richard Callaghan had been hoping the story would not get out, but he knew better. Reporters, dozens of them at times, followed the sport in the post-Tonya era. These weren't the old days where one skating club could gossip about another club with no threat of any of the sordid details hitting the papers. If skating people talked, some reporter now was there to listen. Figure skating was just too popular. The TV ratings from the weekend of Nationals showed that more people watched Bobek and Michelle Kwan skate on Saturday than watched Charles Barkley and Grant Hill play in the NBA All-Star Game on Sunday.

Yet Callaghan rather would have been in the old days—at least as long as he coached the explosive Nicole Bobek.

Callaghan did his best to sidetrack reporters. He told one journalist who called him that the incident at the house was a "misunderstanding."

Then, a group of reporters cornered him at Nationals.

"It's nothing," Callaghan told them. "Trust me. I wouldn't lie to you. I'm a good guy."

The reporters asked if Bobek had been arrested or charged with anything.

"No," Callaghan said.

When the *Detroit Free Press* broke the story February 17, six days after Bobek's victory at Nationals, it didn't run in the sports section. It was on the front page, upper right-hand corner, under this headline: BURGLARY CHARGE SHADOWS U.S. SKATING CHAMP.

The reporter who wrote the story, Michelle Kaufman, appeared at the Detroit Skating Club that afternoon. Bobek, her mother, and friend Joyce Barron had already come and gone.

"I was at the wrong place at the wrong time and that's it," Bobek said about the incident. "It was just a big mistake. No broken hearts, no tears about it. Stuff happens."

Callaghan—on skates, coaching Todd Eldredge that afternoon—wasn't taking the story quite as well as Bobek. When he spotted Kaufman, he left the ice, stomped into an office, found a club board member, and told him to remove Kaufman from the rink. The Detroit journalist who had paid the most attention to the club and its skaters the past five years was about to be escorted from the premises.

"You have destroyed this girl's life," Callaghan loudly told Kaufman on the sidewalk. "Your newspaper has destroyed this girl's life. She will never get over the word *burglary* in a headline on page one, and when she commits suicide next week, I hope those guys at your newspaper are happy."

"Was there anything false in the article?" Kaufman asked.

"No, it's not the story, it's the headline and the fact it was on the front page," he answered, according to Kaufman. "These two kids are not ready to go to worlds because of you, because of your newspaper. The *Detroit Free Press* is not destroying one skater, it's destroying two. You're destroying Todd, too."

The well-traveled Callaghan—he had been in upstate New York, Philadelphia, California, and Colorado—was known around skating as a control freak with a fast temper, as Kaufman was learning quickly. According to ten of his former skaters and associates, he closely monitored the personal lives of his students. One of his former male skaters said that when he was out on a date, he came out of a restaurant to find Callaghan waiting for him in the parking lot, telling him to go home. Another male skater said Callaghan waited outside a party and, when the coach spotted him, called him over and told him he was out too late. Both skaters were over eighteen at the time.

A female skater said Callaghan showed up unexpectedly at her front door one evening to check on her and her boyfriend.

"He got really possessive with people's outside lives," said Roman Fraden, a former Callaghan disciple who moved to follow his coach from San Diego to Detroit, then quit the sport. "Anytime anyone planned anything—a party, whatever—and he found out, it was a whole weeklong saga at the rink."

More than two weeks later, Callaghan had calmed down considerably as Bobek read a press release to reporters in the cramped interview room in England:

"The last two weeks have been very difficult for me. I have grown a lot as a result. All of you are aware of the things that have been brought up in the media. I'd like to say that there is nothing new. Mr. Callaghan and I have been able to put this behind me and focus my efforts on training for the world championships."

The rules of the press conference were that no questions were to be asked about the arrest, and every reporter went along. The USFSA's Kristin Matta had scheduled the news conference in a small interview room—not the main press-conference room—to make those reporters pressed together just uncomfortable enough not to want to sit around forever and bombard Bobek with questions. It was a brilliant move. They were in and out of there in fifteen minutes.

Bobek handled the media with the masterful touch of a savvy politician. She was neither snippy, like Tonya Harding, nor overwhelmed, like Nancy Kerrigan. She was charming, witty, and eminently likable. She understood better than both Tonya and Nancy—and her coach—that the rules governing her life had changed. She loved the trappings of the national title: the TV appearances, the agents leaving messages. She also understood that people would be keeping an eye on her now. She had become the new cover girl of one of the most popular sports in America.

In the press conference, she acted as if nothing had happened. (And, in fact, her case had been dismissed when its confidentiality had been breached.) She talked only about figure skating and gave credit to Callaghan for whipping her into shape.

"Mr. Callaghan has basically guided me the right way, and I put one hundred percent into whatever he says," she professed.

Callaghan, seated beside her at a little table facing reporters, rolled his eyes in jest.

"Don't I?" Bobek asked playfully. "I saw that look."

"Yes," Callaghan said dutifully.

"So he's doing his job," she said, "and I'm doing mine."

Asked if she read the tabloids, Bobek gave the perfect answer to set the local newshounds on their heels.

"I haven't had time," she said.

Callaghan wasn't sheltering Bobek from the tabloids; he said she could read them if she wanted. He seemed almost amused by them. He even took blame for having come up with the Brass Knuckles nickname the Brits so loved. He had used it once, he guessed, describing Bobek's old and discarded habit of wearing a ring on every finger and both thumbs.

"She can jump higher now," he said with a laugh.

The situation wasn't entirely humorous. Bobek and Co. still shuddered at the menacing headlines back across the Atlantic in the States. The *National Enquirer* had tagged its story with the cover headline AMERICA'S NEW SKATING CHAMP IS A BURGLAR and ran a photo of Joyce Barron with this line underneath: "Her Mom's Lesbian Lover."

People magazine was tamer, but still printed charges by outsiders of Jana Bobek's mistreatment of her daughter. None of the sports writers on the story could substantiate those charges. Still, they knew the Bobeks had lived a most unusual life. In all their moves, Jana Bobek and Joyce Barron molded their lives around Nicole's. They attended her practices and scheduled their jobs around her skating. They took her out of school and got her a tutor. Nicole said in the spring of 1995 that she was in the tenth grade, then, she said she was in the eleventh grade. It was unusual for a kid not to know. Jana, who left Czechoslovakia not long after the Soviet repression in 1968, made money running an ice cream concession in Chicago and, later, a tanning salon in Colorado Springs. But when her daughter was ready to move again, the jobs were easily jettisoned.

All the coaching changes were made because of Jana and Joyce, according to the coaches they left. Casey, Frank Carroll, and Evy Scotvold each said Jana and Joyce were looking for someone to give his or her undivided attention to Nicole. "That's really hard to do because if you do that, you lose your whole grassroots program because you've put all your time into Nicole and then they're gone and there you sit with nothing," Casey said.

The USFSA was delighted none of that was dredged up in the news conference and credited Bobek's statement as the preemptive strike. The U.S. delegation considered the news conference a complete success—after Tonya, they were getting pretty good at crisis management—and jauntily embarked on a five-minute walk around a lake from the NEC to the Metropole Hotel, the world championship head-quarters in the pastoral outskirts of industrial Birmingham.

Left behind were a dozen British journalists who, news conference be damned, were going to write what they pleased. Alan Fraser of the *Daily Mail,* however, sought out Kaufman to make sure he got his facts straight. She spent fifteen minutes trying to give him the sanitized American view of the Bobek drama. She left him thinking at least one member of the local press would get it right.

The next day, Fraser wrote this:

"The media information booklet for the World Figure Skating Championships lists the hobbies of Nicole Bobek as decorating old blue jeans, dancing, and roller-blading. The girl next door, one might imagine."

He went on to write disparagingly of Bobek and her mother, joking that she was the girl next door "if you happen to live in downtown Saigon."

The day Bobek faced the tabloids, Michelle Kwan went sight-seeing in London, a place she had never been.

"We woke up and we decided to go to London," she blithely announced at her own news conference the next day, attended by fewer than a dozen journalists in the main interview room that could accommodate several hundred.

Kwan and her father hopped on the train and, Kwan said, "saw Buckingham Palace and the Big Ben."

The Big Ben.

Once, Mary Lou Retton was asked about all the school she missed for gymnastics.

"While other kids were reading about the Great Wall," she said, "I was walking on it."

Kwan's teenage innocence had somehow remained intact, a delightful contrast with the wily Bobek. But as cute as she was, there was a serious, two-pronged strategy—partially cosmetic, partially technical—initiated by the Kwan camp that was worthy of the most veteran of competitors.

Having been rebuffed at Nationals in their efforts to portray Kwan as an artistic stylist, her father, her agent, and her coach had changed their tune. They began to downplay Kwan's chances. She was so young, they said. Too young. At fourteen, she was not even as old as the American junior champion, fifteen-year-old Sydne Vogel. Having learned their lesson with their great expectations in Providence, they earnestly began backpedaling to lower expectations in Birmingham.

At the same time they painted Kwan as a child with miles to go before she won, they were toughening her short program with an eye toward winning the world title right then and there.

Carroll went back to Lake Arrowhead after Providence and made two critical changes in Kwan's short program. First, he flip-flopped the order of her two biggest moves. At Nationals, she performed the double axel near the beginning and, ninety seconds into the program, the combination triple lutz–double toe loop, which she bobbled.

Carroll told Michelle and Danny Kwan that this had to be changed. The tough combination jump was going to come right out of the box, thirty seconds into the program, when Michelle was her freshest. The double axel, which was easier for her, would now move to the ninety-second mark. This would give her the best opportunity to succeed at both and skate a clean short, which Carroll knew was absolutely necessary at the world championships.

Change No. 2: Carroll gave Kwan a different triple jump as the second triple in the short program. He replaced the triple toe loop, which was her jump at Nationals, with the triple flip. Instead of doing the easiest triple, she would now do the third hardest. This jump would come last.

Carroll had packed Kwan's short program with the two most difficult triples any women would do at worlds—the lutz and the flip. In the process, he had given Kwan the most difficult short program in the women's competition, equaled only by France's Surya Bonaly's, and he didn't mind saying so.

"Flip and lutz are the most difficult jumps being done by the girls," Carroll said. "I wanted to go for doing the most difficult short program we could to try to get the highest first marks we could at worlds."

The first mark meant the technical mark. If Kwan was still too young to receive top-notch artistic marks, Carroll would go for broke with athleticism.

Within the U.S. delegation, the feeling was that with Carroll's guidance and all the attention being focused on Bobek's unstable life, Kwan would slide past Bobek at the worlds and win a medal. Or, if they both won a medal, Kwan's would rank higher. The Americans generally believed the results of Nationals were an aberration. It was just a hunch, but they thought Kwan's long reign as America's female star would begin this week—one month later than originally scheduled.

The world championships are nothing like the U.S. Nationals. Both are weeklong events, but there are no juniors or novices at the worlds; just seniors. The United States—a powerful influence in so many international sporting events—was just another country at this competition. The U.S. team was small; because the Americans had been shut out of the medals at the world championships in 1994—and 1993, for that matter—only two women, two men, two pairs, and one dance team qualified. To qualify three in any discipline, a country had to win a medal (finish in the top three) the previous year, or, in pairs, finish in the top five. If you didn't have someone in the top ten, you received just one entry the next year. Because of its slump, the United States was just the sixth-largest delegation in Birmingham. Russia was the biggest, with sixteen skaters.

An international competition meant, of course, that the decisions would be made by a panel of judges from all over the skating world: North America, Europe, and Asia. Europe didn't necessarily dominate skating, but it dominated skating judging. For the women's competition, the nine judges were from Italy, Japan, Austria, Great Britain, China, Russia, Canada, the Czech Republic, and Slovenia. Each country could send three judges; a draw determined who judged what. American judges would be on the panels for the men and the pairs, with the third substituting in ice dancing.

Prior to the competition, Carroll said that Kwan looked at figure skating "as being judged on a day-to-day basis. Whoever gets out there and skates well wins."

But Carroll had been around too long. He knew better.

In the women's short program, Kwan responded to the changes in her program by skating perfectly. She didn't make even the slightest of mistakes. Kwan skated right after France's Bonaly, the five-time European champion who had never won an Olympic or world competition. The contrast was stunning. Bonaly was as sloppy as Kwan was sharp, skating unevenly, with many sudden, lurching motions, which unfortunately have become her artistic trademark. She botched four of the eight required elements: she put her hand down in the middle of her triple-lutz/double-toe-loop combination to keep from falling; she traveled well off center on two different spins; and she performed an amateurish spiral. On her spiral, both knees were bent. Compared to Kwan's meticulous effort, or Bobek's stunning spiral later on, Bonaly looked like an uncertain rookie.

Bonaly, the seventh skater out of thirty-one competitors, got inexplicably high marks, mostly 5.6s for technical merit and 5.7s for presentation. The judges obviously were looking at that résumé: world silver medalist and two-time Olympic hopeful. Had a newcomer skated so poorly, she would have been near the bottom.

Kwan, on the other hand, flowed from one element to the next with an ease she had gained over the past year. She was everything Bonaly was not. And yet five of the nine judges gave Kwan *lower* marks than Bonaly. The judges from Italy, Japan, China, the Czech Republic, and Slovenia thought Bonaly was better than Kwan, not only artistically, but also technically.

When Kwan's scores flashed onto the scoreboard, the pro-American crowd (U.S. spectators were outnumbered only by the British in the arena) booed lustily.

Paul George, a respected U.S. Olympic Committee board member who has been involved with figure skating his entire life, had watched the two programs and casually kept an eye on the scores.

"Wasn't Michelle great?" he said to a fellow American.

"Yes, but she's behind."

When George worked out the math, he was incredulous.

"It's a travesty," he said, throwing up his hands and walking away. Even figure-skating veterans could get worked up about bad judging.

Outside Kiss and Cry, in an area of the hallway where French coaches and television commentators gathered, the reaction was very different.

Didier Gailhaguet, the French team director and the first coach in Bonaly's career, thought that the decision was right on the mark.

"It was faster skating," he said of Bonaly's performance. "Not junior skating."

To him, Kwan looked like a child.

"She skates extremely well, but she still skates like a junior skater. Well, you know, small jumps, slow skating, beautiful style, beautiful technique, excellent, very good hope for the future, but not there yet."

At a press conference after Kwan skated, Carroll sat beside his skater holding four stuffed animals that had been thrown onto the ice for her. Only in figure skating could a fifty-six-year-old man wrap his arms around stuffed animals and still be taken seriously.

Ever the diplomat, he said he saw only Bonaly's final spin as he got Kwan ready backstage.

"Skaters that are recognized and admired and have great track records are trusted by the judges more because they know, time after time, they've had success," he said in a soft, didactic tone. "They've gone out and proven it. This weighs against someone who is unproven. I think they tend to swing with a person who's a real champion.

"In any subjective sport, you're going to run into that. We don't have the stopwatch, we don't have the timer. We have different opinions from different people. So trying to form an opinion is very subjective, and as long as it's a subjective sport, you're going to run into that."

The translation: we got screwed.

"I skated like it's a sport, went for everything I've got, and just gave it my best shot," Kwan said in a meek voice. "It turned out great. I had nothing to lose. You might be the best in your heart, but not in other people's sight."

Carroll admitted that if what he was hearing about Bonaly's program was true, the judging was strange.

"It is interesting that Surya did have difficulty," he said. But, he added quickly, toeing the new party line, "We don't think Michelle's going to win anyway."

On his way out, Carroll mischievously caught the eye of a few American reporters. "I did see that final spin," he said of Bonaly's performance.

He took his arm and index finger and made a huge circle in the air, like an imaginary cowboy swinging a lasso. With a coy smile, he stepped out of the room.

The Americans' muted furor over Kwan's marks was tempered by what happened later in the short program, when Bobek, the twenty-ninth skater, also performed cleanly—and moved into first place. Ironically, her program was not as hard as Kwan's; her second triple jump was the toe loop, the easiest of the triples. But because she was the American champ, and because she looked so much older than Kwan, she was in the lead—and Kwan was fifth.

Wedged between the two U.S. skaters were Russia's Olga Markova, who completed the second-toughest program to Kwan's; China's Chen Lu, an elegant, steady skater; and Bonaly. The judges had sent Bonaly mixed signals. They gave her a gift and propped her up above Kwan, but they pushed her out of the top three, which meant she could not win the gold on her own. A year earlier, at the world championships in Chiba, Japan, she had initially refused to stand on the podium and accept her silver medal, then took it, cried, and took it off. Bonaly, one of the rare black skaters at the world level, had wanted to turn professional, like Oksana Baiul, and would have made a seven-figure income had she done it. But the French skating federation wouldn't allow it. The federation needed her for television ratings and, it hoped, that long-sought world title. If Bonaly didn't stay in the Olympic division, officials said they would not let her reinstate and come back in April. If the federation followed through on its threat, Bonaly would have been prevented from going to the 1998 Olympics. So she backed down.

Feeling very much alone and apart from the French team, Bonaly was hoping these world championships finally would bring her the respect she and her adoptive mother and sometime coach Suzanne felt she deserved. After the short program, she was bitterly disappointed when she realized that she did not control her fate, that she could win the title only if she won the long program, and Bobek finished third.

Bobek, meanwhile, was dancing on top of the world. Hers was one of the more remarkable turnarounds in recent figure-skating history. She didn't make the cut in the qualifying round at the world championships a year ago, and now she was leading after the short program and in the best position to win the women's world title, the most coveted prize in her sport during this non-Olympic year.

Six of the nine judges had her first. The Chinese judge gave her 5.9, 5.9, allowing her to pass Chen, whom the judge had given 5.8, 5.8. The Americans got a chuckle out of that; if you're the Chinese judge, why not, with two clean and equal programs, place your skater first?

With three of her ex-coaches—Kathy Casey, Frank Carroll, and Carlo Fassi—in attendance, Bobek showed exactly how good she could be. Not a one was surprised.

"When she's on, she's on," said Fassi. "Nicole has a sparkle that's incredible. She's a natural, she's exciting. It's nothing studied. Some have it, some don't. She has it."

The sound of dueling triple axels is a muffled, scrunchy thud, followed by another thud, equally muffled and scrunchy-sounding. It's a noise that's rarely heard. During a program, music drowns out the sound made when a 150-pound man turns three and a half times in the air and lands on the narrow outside edge of the blade of a figure skate. The six-minute warm-up period during a competition is one of the few times jumps can be heard as well as seen.

They came out for six minutes to stretch, skate around and jump. In the order they would skate, there was Russia's Alexei Urmanov, Todd Eldredge of the United States, Philippe Candeloro of France, American Scott Davis, Elvis Stojko of Canada, and Steven Cousins of Great Britain. They were the six best Olympic-division male skaters in the world. They looped around each other, searching for wide-open spaces to land their big jumps. Eldredge. Stojko. Candeloro. Blasting off, touching down. Davis spun swiftly and beautifully. Urmanov came down softly from a triple flip. Cousins's skate caught the ice just right on the end of a triple lutz.

Spread out before the audience, they were onstage, showing off their jumps, demanding attention. It ended too quickly. All that energy, released in six minutes, then bottled and saved for the real thing, the long program. They grabbed their skate guards and disappeared backstage. They said later that they didn't pay any attention to what the others were doing.

No one believed them.

Urmanov, the reigning Olympic gold medalist who is mocked in the West for his elaborate outfits, wore billowing sleeves to portray the swan from *Swan Lake*. Eldredge, in first place after the short program, was that Civil War soldier again—as he had been in Providence and throughout the fall—for his *Gettysburg* program. Candeloro was the godfather, as he always was, only an older one, with white powder in his long hair, turning it a fake kind of gray. Davis was Dick Tracy from the sound track of that movie, and *The Untouchables*. Cousins, the only man with almost no chance of winning the gold medal, was dressed as Sergeant Pepper, performing to a Beatles medley.

Stojko, in second place, had no identity but his own.

"Someone forgot to tell Elvis it was Halloween," exclaimed Terry Jones, an Edmonton journalist.

It turned out Stojko did have a role to play—he was Christopher Columbus, skating to music from *1492*. So everyone had a costume.

The outfits could not diminish the athletic battle that was about to unfold. There had been no other competition like this one all year. It came down to Todd Eldredge, the undefeated U.S. champion, having beaten everyone but one man over four competitions in the fall and winter. And that one man was Elvis Stojko, the reigning world champion, whom he had not yet faced.

Stojko, known simply as Elvis in the skating world, isn't frilly or beautiful or classical. His arms are short and his body is stocky. He wears black leather. He studies martial arts and relies on acupuncture twice a day. He talks to a kung fu teacher and relies on Zen techniques.

He had been injured severely in January when, trying to stop after landing a double axel in a practice rink at the Canadian nationals, he slid and jammed his right toe into the boards. When his toe pick stuck into the wood, his right knee caved in and his ankle rolled to the side, ripping a tendon and straining ligaments and muscles from his foot into his lower back.

The right leg is Stojko's landing leg. It was so badly injured that a month went by before he could do a double jump without pain shooting through it. But, doctors assured him, it was okay to try. The only way to reinjure himself would be to do the exact same thing he had done to injure himself in the first place. A skater the likes of Stojko was likely to wedge his toe into the boards only once in his life.

Eldredge, a fisherman's son from Chatham, Massachusetts, was every bit Stojko's competitive match. In a sport of ice-cream-shop number-takers, Eldredge believed nothing was given to you. One year, he had gone to Skate Canada, a big annual event, not to compete, but simply to scout the competition. This was very rare, almost unheard of, in skating. Usually, skaters were so caught up in their own lives and practices and problems that they never took time to watch others. But Eldredge saw skating as a sport, not an art, something to compete at, not marvel over. As long as they picked a winner, he wanted to be that guy. He wanted it so badly he came back from three full seasons of disappointment—1992, 1993, and 1994—to keep skating. He, like Stojko, had returned from injuries and illness, but his comeback took more than two years, not less than two months. Every day during the tough years after a tenth-place finish at the 1992 Olympics, through 1993 and 1994, Eldredge looked deep into his soul and asked himself if he should quit. And every day, he heard the answer: "No."

So he stayed.

In the first forty seconds of his long program, Eldredge planned to open with his triple-axel/triple-toe-loop combination. This was the crux of his battle plan to beat Stojko, who skated after him. A triple axel–double toe was not good enough.

Eldredge skated to the far corner and lifted off the ice, but was slightly off-balance coming out of the axel. The landing was shaky. The next jump was to come immediately afterward. But Eldredge, floundering slightly, could not get enough lift for the triple, so he doubled the toe loop.

This presented him with a problem. He needed the triple-triple combination. His mind clicked through his program on fast-forward even as his body stayed in the present. Where could he improvise and throw in the triple-triple?

His answer came quickly enough: the second triple axel. That came in front of the judges nearly three minutes later. He would add the triple toe to the triple axel there.

When the time came, Eldredge pushed off harder than usual, knowing he needed an extra effort to tack on the triple toe. But he lifted too high, overrotated, and came crashing down to the ice, landing on his hands and his right knee.

So now he was in big trouble. He was missing the triple-axel/triple-toe combination *and* the second triple-axel jump by itself. Stojko, presumably, would have both. With only a minute to go in his program, Eldredge had more choices to make. He gave up on the triple-axel/triple-toe combination. There was no time for it. But he thought he knew a spot where he could squeeze in that second triple axel by itself. As his mind worked, his face belied nothing but calm. He would not give away his fears.

With just fifteen seconds to go, four minutes and nineteen seconds into an exhausting routine, Eldredge scrapped his planned jump.

"The hell with it," he said. "Go for it. You're not that tired yet. You've come this far, you've worked so hard. Don't let it go on just one jump. Stick it in, go for it. Nail it. This is your only shot."

He tried the triple axel.

Eldredge spun in the air three and a half times and landed perfectly. The crowd cheered wildly. The spectators realized what Eldredge had done. That was stunning in itself. The fans actually recognized a figure-skating jump.

This was one of the rarest of moments in figure skating, when a skater changed a program on the fly. Christopher Bowman did it, but that was Bowman. Oksana Baiul did it at the 1994 Olympics when she threw in a double-double combination at the very end of her program. But this was the triple axel.

Eldredge knew this was his only chance to win the gold medal. He was willing to risk not winning a medal at all to try for the gold.

But there was a doubt about what Eldredge had done. Was it legal? The rules said a skater can do a triple jump only twice, once by itself, once in combination. The word used in the judges' regulations is *repeat*. What was the definition of *repeat*? To try it? Or to land it? The judges weren't sure.

Janet Allen, the U.S. judge on the panel, gave Eldredge 5.8, 5.9 and, ultimately, first place. She said Eldredge deserved the benefit of the doubt. The referee never questioned her.

Claire Ferguson, the USFSA president and a judge herself, was so thrilled with Eldredge's move that she didn't care what the rules said.

"I haven't read the rule book and I'm not going to. I thought what he did was fabulous," she said.

With Eldredge in first place, Stojko came out to skate. He is a jumper. And that is what he did. He outjumped Eldredge, eight triples to seven. And he won. Victory was assured when he landed his second triple axel, one of which was the combination that Eldredge never accomplished.

But Stojko, like Eldredge, was not letting conventional skating thinking get in his way. He tried the quadruple toe loop early in his program, but fell. And, with fifteen seconds remaining, he tossed in a triple-triple combination. This was not what you would call protecting a lead.

Stojko's grin was gritty as he stepped through the boards. His ankle had throbbed throughout the four and a half minutes.

The judges gave Stojko his second straight world title, six to three. Allen was joined by the judges from Italy and Norway in voting for

Eldredge, who earned the silver. Candeloro won the bronze. Davis, the other American, made mistakes on three jumps and dropped like a rock from third in the short program to seventh place overall.

In the seventy-two years that there has been competition in pairs skating at the world championships, Americans have won only twice: Karol and Peter Kennedy in 1950 and Tai Babilonia and Randy Gardner in 1979. It's a problem of national personality traits; individualistic Americans would rather skate by themselves than rely on anyone else. It's also a problem of instability; American pairs and American marriages have something in common. They have a tendency to break up. U.S. pairs skaters just do not stay together like the Russians (and former Soviets), who have won every world title but four since 1965.

Calla Urbanski and Rocky Marval won the U.S. title in 1992 and 1993. They split up three different times and are now together as professionals. "I've had six different partners," Urbanski said.

Two-time Russian Olympic gold medalists Ekaterina Gordeeva and Sergei Grinkov, on the other hand, were paired up when she was eleven and he was fourteen. They now are married, which has become a tradition of sorts in pairs skating.

The Russians also never had to worry about who would pay the bills, Gordeeva said.

"We always had four hours of ice a day," she said. "I don't know what parent could pay for that. It was only because the government was paying for it."

Jenni Meno and Todd Sand won Nationals this year, defeating Kyoko Ina and Jason Dungjen, who finished second and qualified for the world championships as well.

Meno and Sand were married on July 22, 1995. They met and began dating at the 1992 Olympics, where they were skating with different partners. They became the nation's best pair because Meno was a strong singles skater—and because they have an emotional relationship.

"Often during my instructional periods with Todd and Jenni," said John Nicks, the most respected pairs coach in the country, "I feel like an intruder."

At the worlds, Meno and Sand went into the long program in fifth place and did nothing particularly grand to warrant a leap into the medals. They looked as if they would stay in fifth. But because certain judges flip-flopped the Americans with the fourth-place Russians and a German pair who had been second in the short, the United States won the bronze, the Russians stayed fourth, and the Germans dropped to fifth. Ina and Dungjen were eighth.

That kind of serendipitous leap occurs every now and then in the sport. Fassi coached an Italian named Gilberto Viadana at the world junior championships in 1992. Viadana skated and then watched himself bounce from eighth to twelfth and back to ninth on the computer as the judges ranked all the others in the men's event.

With one skater to go, Viadana was ninth. When that skater was done, and all the marks were in, Fassi's boy had moved up to fifth.

"This is a wonderful sport," Viadana said. "I gain four places while sitting on a bench."

The winners in the pairs at worlds were Radka Kovarikova and Rene Novotny of the Czech Republic—not Russia—who train at Lake Arrowhead and are coached by three-time Olympic pairs gold medalist Irina Rodnina, a former Soviet. Evgenia Shishkova and Vadim Naumov of Russia won the silver.

The competition resembled *The Dating Game.* Each of the medal-winning pairs was engaged to be married, a prerequisite, it seemed, for good pairs skating. Seven of the previous nine Olympic gold medalists in pairs were either married to each other or about to be, including Rodnina, who was the Olympic champion from 1972 to 1980.

Meno and Sand kept up the image by dressing like bride-and-groom wedding-cake ornaments for their short program, he in a black tuxedo, she in a white dress.

For two minutes in the ladies long program, Bobek was headed for the world title. She had landed the most difficult triple-triple combination jump a woman had ever tried, the triple lutz–triple toe; she was successful on two other triples; she was skating beautifully and she looked unbeatable.

Unfortunately for Bobek, the program was four minutes long. Just as she had so often in her career, she ran out of gas at the end.

In the last half of her performance, fading fast, Bobek fell on both of the triple jumps she attempted. Just when Bobek looked as if she were unstoppable, she faltered. Her body began to cave in as she took off on a triple loop. She fell. The crowd groaned. She slipped again a minute later, on the triple salchow. One fall could have been ignored. But two? She had lost the gold medal. Bobek, looking at least twenty-five with a blond French braid and her shimmering blue, backless dress, dissolved into tears on the ice. She shook her head as she reached Callaghan at the boards. It had been hers to win, and she had blown it.

Bobek's performance, immediately preceding that of Chen Lu,

opened the door for Chen to finally win something other than a bronze medal. After finishing third at the 1992 and 1993 worlds and 1994 Olympics, she did it, winning the gold medal with a steady, if unspectacular, performance. For the second consecutive year, and fifth out of the last seven, a skater of Asian descent had won the women's world title.

Bobek didn't win the silver medal, either. That went, just barely, to Bonaly, who landed six triples but once again lacked the artistry of her peers.

Prior to the last skater, the computer ranked the competitors to that point. Chen was first, Bobek second, and Bonaly third. But then came Kwan, and, like a bowling ball crashing into pins carefully arranged, she changed everything.

Kwan was skating for more than honor. The way the judging had gone in the wake of Bobek's mistakes, if Kwan won the long program, she would win the gold medal. Of course, Carroll and Danny Kwan and Goldberg already knew she wouldn't win the long program. They got the message loud and clear from the short program: *She's cute. Come back and see us next year.*

No matter what Kwan did, they knew she could please a couple of the judges, but not a majority of them.

Kwan started solidly, as she always did, but this time she just kept building. Near the end, after having already landed five triples, she came to her second triple lutz, the jump she fell on in Providence.

She had the right speed cutting across the ice. Carroll knew it would be good. She nailed it. And, as an added flourish, she tacked on a double toe loop, right then and there. Her smile was a mile wide.

By the time her last triple was attempted and landed, tears were welling in her eyes. She looked as if she weren't going to stop skating. The way she was going, they would turn out the lights and everyone would go home—and Michelle Kwan would still be jumping. But she did stop, and when she did, the capacity crowd of seven thousand couldn't help themselves. They had no choice but to stand and applaud wildly. It was the only standing ovation of the night.

Kwan's effort had required every last ounce of her energy. The little girl had nothing left to give. Alone in the middle of the ice, Kwan put her hands to her face and sobbed. A year of pressure, a season of expectations, four minutes of performing; her tiny shoulders could not bear the weight of all these things.

"It was just so overwhelming," she said later, "all the American flags waving and everyone standing."

Carroll felt tears welling in his own eyes as he watched her skate toward him. He somehow willed himself to stop and gave her a small kiss on the top of her head.

"I didn't want both of us crying," he said.

Six of the nine judges ranked Kwan above Bobek, but because she was so far behind after the short program, she could not quite catch her American rival. Unwittingly, Kwan knocked Bobek from silver to bronze, and she finished fourth. She was the only skater to perform both of her programs perfectly. And she didn't win a medal.

Not only did she have the toughest short program, Kwan also had the most difficult long program. She was the only skater to land seven clean triple jumps in the long. Bonaly was next with six, Chen had five, and Bobek, four. The only thing Kwan couldn't do in front of the judges was grow up and become sixteen, which is what they were waiting for. They wanted Kwan taller, older, and a bit faster on her feet before they gave her the gold medal. Otherwise, Kwan was perfect. No one in recent memory ever had performed so much so well and not won some kind of a medal at a worlds or Olympics. After a season in which she had had a slip or mistake at every competition, Kwan had corrected everything on the grandest stage of the year.

She actually received the first-place votes of two of the nine judges, from Great Britain and the Czech Republic. Chen received three first-place votes, Bonaly three, and Bobek one, from the Austrian judge.

When all the marks were put together, Chen had won the long program, with Bonaly second, Kwan third, and Bobek fourth.

But Kwan was also extremely close to winning the whole thing. Had she received three more first-place votes in the long program, giving her five overall, she would have moved from fourth in the final standings to first. That's how quirky skating judging is. That would have been enough to jump over Chen, Bonaly, and Bobek for the gold.

Bobek was close to winning, too. She didn't have the performances Kwan did, but she had the look. *That* look. Sophisticated, athletic, tantalizing. Richard Callaghan was overjoyed that the judges had embraced the idea of giving her the gold medal, if she only could have held herself together on the ice.

"Third in the world is excellent, and third in the world with two mistakes shows that minus those mistakes, she has a great future," he said.

Even with her spills on the ice, Bobek had reason to rejoice. She had turned herself around in less than five months. She had not been able to land a triple jump at Skate America. Now she was four for six in the long program and a world medalist.

"I've always known I wanted to skate and I wanted to win the gold medal," she said. "But I wasn't really sure how to get everything packaged together. I knew what I wanted, but I was scattered in little pieces. And it wasn't until I came here and Mr. Callaghan said, 'We're going to tie you all back up together in one piece,' that he glued my broken pieces together and gave me the whole package."

Bobek's bronze was the first medal for a U.S. woman at the worlds since Kristi Yamaguchi and Nancy Kerrigan won the gold and silver, respectively, in 1992 in Oakland, California. It meant the United States could send three, not two, women skaters to next year's worlds in Edmonton, Alberta. And the three-four finish for the U.S. skaters signaled three seasons of jockeying for position leading to the 1998 Winter Olympics in Nagano, Japan.

Bobek-Kwan; Kwan-Bobek. There was reason to believe that both would be there in 1998: Bobek because of the discipline and control Callaghan demanded, assuming she stayed with him; Kwan because of her impeccable technical ability and the strong family she had surrounding her.

For the moment, though, the world was ruled by Chen, an eighteen-year-old who lives in Beijing and often trains in Los Angeles. Her stack of bronze medals signified that Chen is nothing if not consistent. And it was that dependability that won the first world figure-skating gold medal by a Chinese athlete. She didn't try a triple-lutz/triple-toe combination as Bobek did, and she doesn't have the overall might of Bonaly, but she combined strong jumping ability with a graceful style that was just enough of a balance to swing the judges in her favor.

Because she grew up in China, Chen never saw much figure skating on television and never had a role model until she watched Yamaguchi skate a couple years ago. As role models went, Chen picked a perfect one. If she could emulate Yamaguchi's work ethic, it was possible to envision her winning for a very long time.

For Bonaly, twenty-one, the competition ended just as the last two worlds had. She was a disappointing second and, for the third straight year, would have won had just one judge changed his or her mind.

Last year, she yanked off her medal and pouted. This year, she smiled.

"I used to feel disappointed, but this time is different," she said. "I am happy. I'm sure it could be better, but I am very happy. There's always next year."

Perhaps. But with a group of teenagers upon her—and one already above her—Bonaly's career already might have seen its best days.

That night, Kwan went to the traditional competitors' party with her parents. The three of them then wandered into the Metropole lobby and joined Goldberg and a cluster of American reporters. Kwan sat on the edge of a chair and listened, mostly.

Michelle said her father was giving her a gift for her performance at worlds: a trip to Cleveland for Jenni Meno and Todd Sand's July wedding.

"And," Michelle added, mischievously peering at her father, "a boat."

"We'll see," Danny Kwan said.

The Kwans were ecstatic—over fourth place, no less. It was doubtful they would ever again be happy with an out-of-the-medals placement at worlds, figure-skating expectations being what they are, especially for her. But it was gratifying to know that for this one time, they were.

17

"FACE THE MUSIC"

The ice arena was not an arena at all, but a musty old exhibition hall with girders running from the floor to the ceiling, blocking the view of a fair number of hearty Scottish souls. If this place had been located in a cornfield in Indiana, not beside the foreboding North Sea in Aberdeen, Scotland, someone would have called it an old barn and surely would have scheduled a high school basketball game.

But there was ice on the floor, and when the lights went down, the spotlights came on and made headlines on the shiny surface. "Gold in Sarajevo," proclaimed one. A row of 6.0s—nine of them—appeared.

At the end of the earth, there was an ice show. Torvill and Dean were touring Great Britain one final time—and it was going to be a very long good-bye. There were 115 shows in all, stretching from March until August. There were nine shows in Aberdeen in March 1995. Each one drew 4,200 people.

Jayne Torvill and Christopher Dean originally were scheduled to be elsewhere. They had planned to be in Birmingham, playing the NEC. But organizers asked them to stay away from Birmingham in March because the world championships were scheduled there, and if Torvill and Dean came, people wanting to go to only one figure skating event would buy tickets to see them and not show up for the worlds.

Torvill and Dean obliged and ended up in Scotland.

The costumes still fit. The purple ones, the ones that flowed across the ice to the gold medal eleven years ago in Sarajevo. Torvill and Dean have fourteen copies of those costumes hanging in various dressing rooms and closets. They don't wear the ones they wore at the 1984 Olympics; those clothes are hanging in a museum in their hometown of Nottingham. But they wear the same sizes still, which the thirty-seven-year-old Torvill and thirty-six-year-old Dean acknowledge is quite an achievement.

They open their show—the "Face the Music" World Tour—in those costumes, skating to "Bolero" in a dramatic beam of white light. Same steps, same program. "The people come for that," Dean said. They close the show with "Face the Music," their 1994 Olympic free-dance program that brought them controversy, a bronze medal, and a whole new life. They might as well be rock stars doing the songs they've made famous. They don't jump; they're not allowed to. They are ice dancers, the artists of figure skating, teetering over the athletic edge, often falling onto the side of pure show. But these are artists who have competed, who have won and lost, who have been done in by a silly system, who have become legends during their time.

The Olympic loss was on everyone's mind. Every day. Every show. How could anyone look at Torvill and Dean and not think of Norway? All they went through—to win the *bronze?* It was bizarre, and everyone knew it. Judges and officials had told them to change their free-dance program a few weeks before the 1994 Winter Olympics. So they had scurried around, and because they didn't have much time, they threw in moves they had done before. They've been together for nearly two decades, so there are very few moves they haven't done. But then they were criticized for stealing from themselves—"poaching," Torvill said—and finished third.

"You know when you get a feeling when you're slightly not welcome?" Dean asked. "When you've known somebody and then you go away and you come back and it's all different, they're very much, like, standoffish? It was like that."

"We were totally confused about what was required," Torvill said. "We were so aware to not go in as show business people, which we could have done quite easily, or to not go in as so artistic that it would be way above everyone. We wanted to be part of the competition.

"If they wanted dance holds and dance steps, then we could try and do that. That's what we did. Then suddenly it needed more highlights, so we just put in lots of highlights, a lot of which we had used before because we really didn't have time to invent new ones. But we knew the ones that worked from experience and shows, so we did that, and obviously that wasn't right, so then you wonder, would anything be right anyway?"

Torvill and Dean never toed the line before 1994. With Dean as the creative genius and Torvill as the steadying sidekick, they always pushed the envelope, came up with their own stuff, and dragged ice dancing in the direction they felt it should go. Now the judges were grabbing it back from them. So Torvill and Dean went along. The judges wanted the ice to convert to a dance floor. Torvill and Dean became Fred Astaire and Ginger Rogers, joyously gliding around to Irving Berlin's "Face the Music and Dance." But the judges wanted to be picky. They had a chance to confer upon Torvill and Dean one more Olympic title. They skated superbly. It would have been easy. But the judges saw a move they didn't like, gave them marks hovering around 5.7 and 5.8, and gave the gold medal to a lightning quick, young Russian couple named Oksana Gritschuk and Evgeny Platov performing rock and roll. It was the first time Torvill and Dean had been beaten in a major competition in fourteen years.

Ice dancing is so peculiar. The best moves are almost always illegal, but the great thing is, no one actually is certain of that. At the end of their free dance, Dean spectacularly lifted Torvill from behind his back and helped her somersault over his head onto the ice in front of him. It was a move spectators could not forget. But it was illegal, according to the referee overseeing the event, because Torvill flipped over Dean's head. Lifts above the shoulders were not allowed. Torvill and Dean said her momentum carried her over his head, but most of the judges penalized them for it.

HANG THOSE JUDGES suggested the *Sun,* a London tabloid.

"We think maybe in hindsight we should have not listened to any of what they were telling us," Torvill said, "come up with an idea for a routine like we normally do, find a piece of music we want to use, and then just gone in and done it. But if we had done that and not taken any advice about steps and dance holds, I think maybe still they would have gone the way they did. That's the only thing that leaves us feeling really confused and a little bit bitter about the whole thing because we would have tried to do any style if it would have been accepted."

"It was a big thing for us to make that decision [to come back]. It motivated us for a year. I think we experienced nerves we hadn't had in a while. Whenever we think about anything bad now, we always say, 'Well, remember that night at the Olympics. It can't be as bad as that.' "

As Christopher Dean talked about it a year later, there was irony in his voice, not bitterness. The night of the loss, they were in shock. Natalia Linichuk, the 1980 Olympic ice-dancing gold medalist who coached Gritschuk and Platov, approached Torvill in the dressing room and congratulated her. "I thought that was very interesting because when we won European's, she didn't say anything. So now we're third and her skaters are first and she said, 'Congratulations,' " Torvill said.

After it was over, Torvill and Dean were concerned. They loved to tour—America, Australia, England, it didn't matter. Dean thought up new things and they thoroughly enjoyed performing them for their fans. But what would their loss do to their reputations? It had been a gamble to come back. They knew it, and Brian Boitano and Katarina Witt and the others knew it, too. The International Skating Union opened the door to let them back in to increase interest in the Olympic Games. The ISU got everything it wanted, and more. Torvill and Dean wondered if they hadn't been duped.

"We didn't know what we were going to head into," Dean said, "whether we were going into a big depression after all of that. You feel like you're only as good as your last performance. We skated well. Then, it became, 'Well, is that it? Are we going to be able to put a show together? Are people going to want to come and see it? Do we still have any popularity? Maybe we're yesterday's news.' "

Relief settled upon them as they started to put their last tour together. Said Dean, "It seemed like we gained so much popularity out of not winning. There was a lot of support, whether in sympathy or whatever. When we went to start the tour, it was incredibly successful."

The bronze medal might have been the best thing to ever happen to them, they have come to realize. Before they came back, people always asked them what they were doing, if they had retired. They said they were touring. People nodded and gave them a blank stare. But then they did a grand job at the Olympics—and they didn't win. Millions of their fans were united in their outrage. In a way, it was perfect. People cared about them again.

"Mum called the minute we saw the advertisement on TV," said fifteen-year-old Stacey Milne of Peterhead, Scotland, who was sitting in the front row at the Aberdeen Exhibition and Conference Center. "Whenever ice skating is on, me and Mum sit glued to the TV. It wasn't fair what happened to them. We couldn't believe they lost."

Milne and her family joined the more than four thousand other Scots in the old barn to say good-bye to Torvill and Dean, who have said this *really* is good-bye. They will pop in on other people's tours, but this is their last. "Every night at seven-thirty or eight, for five or six days of the week, you've got to go out there smiling," Dean said. "It's like going out each night for that one competition a year."

It's a thrill and it's a headache putting on a show. A few months earlier, they were chipping white paint off the ice two hours before a show in Chicago. The idea was to have white ice. But the paint had been put on too late and not enough ice had formed on top of it. All the chipping made the ice a mess. The skaters danced around ruts all night.

In Aberdeen, there was a different problem. The ice was not flat. The far end of the ice was fourteen inches higher than the other end. "It's a real struggle up one way," Dean said, "and you come blazing down the other."

But that was a minor problem they would live with.

The show is Dean's mind come to life, and his chance to take some gentle jabs at the judges from the 1994 Olympics. In a number entitled "Strictly Skating," portraying a ballroom-style competition, the announcer said, "Any couples trying classy, crowd-pleasing steps unfortunately will have marks deducted from their final score."

Torvill and Dean got a chuckle out of that one.

The number ended with everyone stripping down to their underwear.

Torvill and Dean gave ice dancing legitimacy. On that alone, they should have been awarded their second gold medal. Without them, it's just so silly.

At the 1991 Nationals in Minneapolis, Michael Janofsky of the *New York Times* was rushing to send his story on a tight deadline. He quickly wrote that the team of Elizabeth Punsalan and Jerod Swallow competed "dressed as racing flags."

Later, he was informed he had made a mistake. Punsalan and Swallow weren't racing flags. They were racing *cars*. He had to call his office with the correction. On the other end of the phone was a grizzled veteran, a man more used to dealing with major-league box scores than with the sequins and glitter of figure skating.

Janofsky swallowed hard as he sat in the pressroom.

"See where it says 'dressed as racing flags'?" he asked within earshot of a dozen chuckling reporters. "We need to change it to . . . 'dressed as Indy 500 race cars.' "

The next year, at the 1992 Olympic trials, Punsalan and Swallow came up with another idea. They decided to portray all the Winter Olympic sports in their program. They were going along fine until he dropped her as they were imitating the luge. Only in figure skating would you find this: a crash in the luge taking out an ice-dancing team.

Three years later, Ron Kravette was in the dance competition at the 1995 Nationals with his partner, Wellesley graduate Amy Webster. A month earlier, Kravette, sitting in an Italian restaurant just off Harvard Square, had predicted that Renee Roca and Gorsha Sur, the American and ex-Soviet who had become all the rage in the United States the last few years, would win the competition. He thought the husband-and-wife team of Punsalan and Swallow, who had written letters trying to block Sur's citizenship so he couldn't go to the 1994 Olympics (they were successful; they went, Sur didn't), would be second. He guessed that he and Webster, veterans who performed to "Phantom of the Opera," would be third.

And he was right. It was difficult to believe it was all not prearranged.

At the world championships in Birmingham, Gritschuk and Platov won again, followed by Finland's Susanna Rahkamo and Petri Kokko and France's Sophie Moniotte and Pascal Lavanchy. The French couple was notable. They lost the European championships a month earlier to the Finns at least partially because Moniotte's dress had been too long and kept flying into her face, distracting the judges. Now that was a reason to lose a sports title.

"I can see how people think of this as a nonsport," said U.S. ice dancer Susie Wynne, a 1988 Olympian and a Torvill and Dean tour member.

At the 1993 world championships, she and her partner, Russ Witherby, noticed one of their judges looking down for the entire two and a half minutes of their original dance program. After not watching, the judge actually moved them up a notch, from fifteenth to fourteenth.

Making a leap up the standings in ice dancing is almost impossible. In fourth place at the 1995 worlds were the most appealing skaters in the competition, Canada's Shae-Lynn Bourne and Victor Kraatz, who had the audacity to actually try new things. Their problem was that they just have not been around long enough, only since 1993.

They had been tied for fourth after the compulsory dances and then, with the speed of a glacier, had gone into fourth all alone after the original dance, the second phase of the—ahem—competition.

"They've gone from a tie for fourth to fourth all by themselves," mused Terry Jones, the reporter from Edmonton. "It normally takes five years to make that kind of a move in ice dancing."

Roca and Sur moved from eleventh to tenth after the free dance, the last event. This was a titanic leap. It meant they captured a second ice-dancing spot for the United States at the 1996 worlds. Other than clicking their skate blades in their first compulsory dance, they looked just as good to the naked eye as any of the top five teams. In a matter of time—oh, five to ten years—they might reach the top five. Did this frustrate them?

"No," Sur said.

"Lie, lie, lie," Roca shot back.

"I don't know," Sur said through his thick Russian accent. "We're sick people."

As close as they are, as sensually as they skate, Torvill and Dean say they have never been romantically involved.

"No, in a word," Dean said. "We've stayed together most probably because we don't have romantic involvement. No matter what happens on the ice, you go your separate ways at nighttime and it's over, and you come back the next day and carry on from where you left."

Dean was married to Isabelle Duchesnay, the French ice dancer, for two years, then, after a messy breakup that led to divorce, began dating Jill Trenary, whom he married in the fall of 1994. Dean proposed to Trenary, the 1990 world champion, moments after skating at the Olympics in Norway. At their Minneapolis wedding, Torvill sat in a pew as her husband, Phil Christensen, a sound engineer, served as Dean's best man.

Torvill and Dean might as well be family. They have been together so long, twenty years now, that they finish each other's sentences. Their cast and crew and business associates know there is no point complaining to one about the other. They won't listen.

Theirs is an unspoken agreement: whatever they have felt for each other over the years, they have portrayed on the ice, and left it there. "Jayne is very good at putting up with him," Trenary said. "He's obviously very intense on the ice and very high-strung. He needs to have someone like Jayne, who's very mellow."

Now facing retirement, Torvill and Dean say they are ready to begin to slowly fade away.

"We know we can't skate forever," she said.

"There's a time clock running out for us, isn't there?" Dean added.

Won't they miss each other?

"If we said, at the end of this week, we are not going to see each other for the rest of our lives, we would have been upset," Dean said. "But we always see each other."

"For dinner, anyway," Torvill added. "Jill's a good cook."

APRIL

Epilogue

After the world championships, the official 1994–95 figure-skating season was over. But the annual world tour was yet to start. Mike Burg had more exhibitions and made-for-TV competitions to put on. And Oksana Baiul had a decision to make.

As Baiul's deadline for reinstatement into the Olympic division moved closer, it became apparent that at the stroke of midnight, Cinderella was going to remain Cinderella. She liked the lifestyle she had. She did not want to dive back into the competitive world of triple lutzes.

And so it came as no surprise when she announced that she was not reinstating April 1, that she would remain professional. Unless the International Skating Union decided to turn to a completely open competition for 1998, or make some other concession to the pros, she would be lost to the Olympic division forever.

Midori Ito, however, decided to return. This came as quite a shock; those close to the twenty-five-year-old skater said they had not heard her mention the idea. But it immediately made sense. The 1998 Winter Olympic Games are in Nagano, Japan; Ito, with that amazing triple axel, immediately became the favorite to win the gold medal in her homeland. But the pressure would be unbearable. It had been too much for her in Albertville in 1992. It would be worse in 1998.

The ISU did everything it could to try to get Baiul back and keep the Olympic-division skaters happy. Trying to catch up with the professional promoters, the federation initiated a grand prix of five existing competitions with prize money of $1.25 million, and a grand prix final worth $700,000, scheduled for February 23–25, 1996, in Paris.

There also would be prize money at the world championships, and countless other opportunities for skaters to make money in mixed Olympic-division/ineligible-professional events.

"Had she returned," said Baiul's agent, Michael Carlisle of William Morris, "she probably would be making about what she's going to make this way. This is not driven by money. It's driven by lifestyle. Do you want to train from September to March and have it depend on one moment? Oksana's had that life. She's seventeen, she wants to have fun, and it's more fun the other way."

Nicole Bobek was definitely going to stay in the Olympic division. She was hot. Steve Disson became her manager, but other jobs still needed to be filled.

Steve Woodward watched, amused, as agents and public relations people lined up to sign Bobek.

"It would be like being caretaker to a vial of nitroglycerin," he said. "The decision is whether you want to stay in figure skating or go into pyrotechnics."

All of a sudden, Woodward found himself playing with fire.

At Disson's urging, Woodward and Jeanne Martin drove to Detroit to meet Bobek, her mother, and Joyce Barron for dinner at a pasta place outside the city.

Woodward and Martin didn't win the right to do public relations for Nicole Bobek. A New York PR man named Ira Silverman got the job. Later on, she signed with William Morris as her agent. Bobek had a coach, an agent, a manager, and a PR man.

One of Bobek's first ventures was a campaign in which she visited schools to talk to children. Bobek hadn't been to school herself in three years, but she went to Potomac Elementary School in the exclusive suburb north of Washington to talk about many things, including the importance of staying in school.

After the hour-long session in the school gym, Disson whisked Bobek into the teachers' lounge, where a crew from the tabloid TV show *American Journal* was waiting to talk to her. When the reporter asked about the publicity over Bobek's arrest, Disson stepped in and abruptly ended the interview.

He and Silverman had not followed the two rules agents were supposed to know while representing figure skaters in the 1990s.

Rule No. 1: When *American Journal* (or *Inside Edition* or *Hard Copy*) called, say no.

Rule No. 2: When *American Journal* called and the figure skater they wanted to talk to had been arrested within the last five months, definitely say no.

Before the competition began at Nationals, Bobek said, "You can't make money as an entertainer if you don't have a title."

Now she had the title. And she wanted to make the money. Bobek's schedule was filling up quickly. One of the most interesting decisions she and her numerous advisers made was to schedule her in the skating production of the Nutcracker, December 1–30, 1995. Todd Eldredge also would skate in the show, and their coach, Richard Callaghan, would be there to oversee practice sessions at the twenty-two tour stops.

Their decision to do the tour stunned rival coaches, skaters, agents—and even the U.S. Figure Skating Association. The 1996 Nationals were January 14–21, 1996. In the past, skaters always stayed close to home for intense training in the month or so leading up to Nationals. They never *went on tour*.

"It's the dumbest thing in the world," Scott Hamilton said. "I told Todd he was crazy for doing the Nutcracker tour. They're acting like pros. Instead of building a résumé, they must feel like they already have one. If you're more worried about the by-product than the product itself, you're toast."

At the end of April, Michael Weiss flew to Indianapolis and spent a week learning his 1996 short and long programs from Brian Wright. The results of the world championships had been particularly pleasing to Weiss. Eldredge's silver medal meant there would be three places on the world championship team next March in Edmonton. He was hoping to fill that third slot.

By the middle of May, Wright was in the hospital, bleeding internally. He stayed nearly a week, then went home. He had weighed 170 pounds in November. He was down to 148 by Memorial Day.

Audrey Weisiger was frantic during Wright's hospital stay. When they spoke on the phone, he talked about his funeral.

"You get to choreograph this one," he told her.

Three junior ladies were going through skating growing pangs.

For her thirteenth birthday, Tara Lipinski got an agent. After an eight-month courtship, the Lipinskis finally signed with Mike Burg in June.

There were guarantees of a certain number of appearances that would bring in as much as $100,000 over the next few years. All of a sudden, the Lipinskis' $58,000 a year in expenses didn't seem so bad.

Throughout the spring and summer, Jeff DiGregorio was being warned by skating judges and friends not to let Lipinski take the skating test to become a senior but to stay back in juniors another year.

"What they don't understand is that Tara wants to do it," he said. "She wants the next challenge."

DiGregorio said their only goal for their first year in seniors would be to qualify out of regionals and sectionals for Nationals in 1996.

Her agent, however, had a different view.

"That third spot is wide open," Burg said. He was dreaming about a place on the world team.

DiGregorio had watched the videotape of Tara's performance from Nationals again and again, and each time, he thought she won. "It might be a blessing in disguise, because it will make her work harder," he said. "Her ultimate goal is to be the Olympic champion, and she's not going to stop until she does it."

By the summer, Lipinski had grown two inches to four feet seven and still weighed sixty-nine pounds. She was skating well, but those quadruple jumps promised in February weren't coming exactly as planned.

"She's trying the quad salchow," DiGregorio said, "but she's not doing all the quads."

And the triple axel?

"Her double axel is one of the weaker of her jumps, so we're not working on that yet," DiGregorio said. "I'd rather she be more proficient on the stuff she does."

DiGregorio still thought Lipinski was headed for greatness.

"I firmly believe she will be the best," DiGregorio said, "but maybe I can't see past her."

Burg also was interested in signing Sydne Vogel, but the Vogels and Traci Coleman decided to take things slowly. They agreed to have Sydne skate in a show or two, nothing more.

Others had their eye on Vogel. Carlo Fassi, for one. The skating grapevine in America got word to Coleman that Fassi was interested in taking on Sydne. Coleman wasn't worried. The Vogels said Sydne wasn't going anywhere.

Throughout the spring, Sydne worked on her triple axel. She wasn't landing it, but she was getting close. She went to a competition in Italy and finished a disappointing fourth. In the summer, she competed with a bad hip in the Olympic Festival, which she had injured attempting to land the triple axel and other triple jumps.

Reporters raced to interview Vogel at the Festival. She finished sixth of eight skaters. The winner, national novice champion Erin Sutton, was virtually ignored. Her name was barely mentioned in the newspapers. Most reporters were too busy writing about Vogel.

Sydne's performance at the Festival frustrated her parents. Coleman thought she might get fired. After a couple weeks of uncertainty, the Vogels gave Coleman a vote of confidence, but said that they were taking Sydne to train with Kathy Casey in Colorado Springs for "a couple weeks to get her up to par."

All of a sudden, Sydne was leaving home—if only for a few weeks—for figure skating.

When Jenni Tew got home from Nationals, she returned to the ice at Winterhurst outside Cleveland with one goal. To do better in next year's junior competition, she needed more triple jumps. She spent a good month trying to get that second triple jump, the triple loop, the one she was trying at Nationals. It never happened.

So, one day in late March, she tried another jump, one that is considered harder than the loop—the triple flip. Soon, she was landing it. She began to try another one, the triple lutz. At first, it was hard for her to trust herself, to loft herself into the air after that long glide down the ice into the corner. But then, she got the hang of it, and she began landing the toughest jump most women ever do. Jenni is a good toe jumper—and the toe loop, flip, and lutz are toe jumps. The loop, salchow, and axel are not.

Down in Florida, Joel Tew was hearing about the flip and lutz over the telephone. Finally, Deanie Tew told him, "You really need to come and see this."

Joel flew to Cleveland on a Thursday night in late April and went to the rink the next day. And, like clockwork, Jenni treated her father to a couple clean triple flips, followed by three perfect triple lutzes.

Carol Heiss beamed as she watched.

"Hey, this is a good deal," she teased Joel Tew. "Only six weeks for the triple flip and triple lutz. What a bargain."

"Yeah, but it took two years for the double axel," he said with a laugh.

Joel Tew had always told himself never to think of the money, the hundreds of thousands of dollars they were shelling out to live apart and pay for lessons and ice time and everything else.

"Carol," he said, "let's put it this way. We're about even."

Stars on Ice wound its way around the country, finally finishing on the East Coast, in Amherst, Massachusetts, April 1. Kurt Browning had totally given up on his triple axel by then. Hamilton was skating better than ever. Everyone was tired and wanted to go home.

Several weeks earlier, Rosalynn Sumners and Bob Kain became engaged after five years of dating. By the summer of 1995, Sumners and Katarina Witt were filming a movie in Berlin. It was a "Cinderella"-style fairy tale in which they skated and also acted in full period costumes.

Witt had become a very kind, understanding friend to Sumners. In the dressing room on tour, as Sumners put on her makeup, she told an outsider how difficult it had been to lose to Witt in 1984. As Sumners spoke, Witt stood beside her, brushing her teeth.

"Is it okay if I stand here?" Witt asked Sumners.

"Sure, sure," Sumners said. "You know all this stuff anyway."

Sumners had learned to deal with it by talking about it.

"Right now, we're filming the part where they want to marry me off to the prince before he chooses Katarina," Sumners said from Berlin.

So she got the prince?

"No," Sumners said with a laugh, "Katarina does."

Tina Noyes graduated from Boston College with her business administration degree on May 22, 1995. She and a friend went to Aruba for a week, then she began her job search.

"I'm considering a mass mailing," she said.

On a brilliant Saturday in June, Lisa Ervin graduated with high honors from Dennis Yarmouth High School on Cape Cod. She had quit skating with Evy and Mary Scotvold earlier in the spring. She liked the Scotvolds very much, but she just wasn't happy in a big-time rink.

Ervin said when she stopped skating seriously, she began eating properly. Her weight was on the high side, 125 pounds or so, but for once in her life she said she didn't care. She was feeling much better about herself again.

"Sometimes, things just don't work out the way you hope they would," she said. "But I know somewhere in life, I'll be successful."

Ervin was accepted by both Boston University and Hamilton College in Clinton, New York. She chose Hamilton and began classes in the fall.

After taking a break from figure skating "to see what it's like to not be a skater," Ervin was ready to try it again. She went to a nondescript rink in upstate New York for a summer training session that extended into the new school year.

"I just want to skate with some no-name coaches in a relaxed setting," she said. "I want to skate where no one has any expectations for me. I want to skate where no one knows my name."

Michelle Kwan spent most of her spring and early summer skating in a different arena in a different city almost every night on the world tour. She skated in sixty-five of the seventy-six shows; Bobek performed in sixty-nine of them. Kwan brought her homework with her and did it in her hotel room. Bobek said she was calling her tutor long-distance.

Most days at practice, Kwan worked on her triple axel with Brian Boitano and Elvis Stojko.

"Michelle closes her eyes and looks down and relaxes her shoulders right before she goes onto the ice," Boitano said admiringly. "I do the same thing."

Bobek was drawing raves for her skating on tour, but there was something about Kwan's work ethic that attracted Boitano. She might not be flashy, but no one worked harder. Boitano liked that.

When the tour went to Oklahoma City in May, Boitano suggested the skaters donate their paychecks from that show to help build a day-care center to replace the one destroyed in the April bombing. Everyone went along. They raised $125,000.

Boitano was skating consistently well on tour, not bad for someone who was going to turn thirty-two in the fall. In Philadelphia, however, he fell on a simple move, the one-legged spiral. A spiral! It was the ultimate embarrassment.

"Bi-taska," Baiul said warmly to him backstage, in broken English, "you no robot."

That was Boitano's reputation: the machine that rarely made mistakes. But, as the expanding figure-skating world continued to take shape, Boitano and his professional peers still were banned from future Olympic or world competition. An "open" figure-skating world, like that in tennis or golf, seemed far away. Too many promoters and federations were worried about turning profits and controlling their turf to figure out a way for Kristi Yamaguchi to compete against Kwan and Bobek in truly meaningful events such as the U.S. and world championships.

The troubles continued for 1976 Olympic gold medalist Dorothy Hamill. She and her second husband, Ken Forsythe, announced in August that they had "mutually agreed to separate after eight years of marriage." The couple has one child, Alexandra, who turned seven in September. Hamill's marriage to Dean Paul Martin ended in divorce in 1984. Three years later, Martin, the son of entertainer Dean Martin, was killed in a plane crash.

Tonya Harding showed up once every week or so to skate at the Clackamas Town Center rink, the shopping mall ice now known as the Dorothy Hamill Skating Center, in the outskirts of Portland. Hamill, of all people, had purchased Harding's rink.

"I am looking forward to possibly doing some skating shows," Harding said. "Even though I haven't done too many things in the last year doesn't mean that I'm dead and that I've ended my career. I think that you will see a comeback and it will be within the next year."

After she was kicked out of the USFSA not long after the 1994 Olympics, rumors of professional skating deals were circulated by an agent, but no one officially and publicly invited her to skate anywhere.

Still, Harding had an eventful year and a half after the Olympics. She performed more than 400 hours of community service as part of her felony plea of hindering the prosecution in the attack on Nancy Kerrigan. Most of her work involved preparing and serving meals to the elderly.

She paid a $100,000 fine to the state of Oregon, $10,000 to the district attorney to repay court costs, and $50,000 to the Special Olympics as part of her deal with the state. Where her money came from, no one was certain. She did play the part of a restaurant owner in *Breakaway,* which was playing in Europe.

Both she and ex-husband Jeff Gillooly went through changes; he changed his name, she changed her body. He became Jeff Stone; she had breast-enhancement surgery.

In the spring and summer of 1995, Harding devoted time to a new career.

"My singing is coming along really well," she said.

The audience that heard her first concert wasn't so sure. On Labor Day weekend, Harding performed three songs with her new group, the Golden Blades, at a riverfront concert in Portland. Spectators reacted to her performance by booing and throwing soda bottles and cans at her. In hindsight, figure-skating judges were much more forgiving.

Said Harding: "I'm just trying to go on with my life and be happy and not associate myself with abnormal people."

Nancy Kerrigan announced her engagement to agent Jerry Solomon in March—in a backstage television interview at a skating show. They were married September 9 in Boston.

In April, for the first time in more than a year, Kerrigan smiled on the ice in a competition. She landed two triple lutzes in West Palm Beach; it was her best performance since the Olympics.

She and Brian Boitano were partners in that event.

"What if we lose by one-tenth of a point?" she asked in front of several skaters and coaches.

Kerrigan and Boitano won by one-tenth of a point.

Kerrigan said that because of the attack on her knee, she still flinched when someone came up beside her quickly. "It must be someplace on the right side that I see something black or somebody's passed something near my head," she said. "I might just jump. It's just a reaction. It doesn't happen often, though."

She was asked if she thought Harding was involved in the attack.

"Everybody has their thoughts on it," Kerrigan said. "It's just . . ."

She stopped.

"It's over."

AIDS continued to cast a dark shadow over figure skating. In the spring, former U.S. junior champion William Lawe died. Then, in late June, more than three hundred people showed up at the Fairfax Ice Arena for a skating exhibition benefiting Brian Wright. Michael Weiss was there, breaking in his new long program, the one for the 1996 Nationals. Mozart had been dumped. Santana was in. Weiss was happy and skating well.

Wright had driven from Indianapolis to Virginia for the exhibition. He had been in and out of the hospital throughout the spring and summer. Money was tight. The medical bills were soaring. Even though he looked tan and rested, when people hugged him, they noticed how easily they could feel his ribs.

It was Weisiger's idea to put on the show as a benefit to help her best friend with medical expenses. That afternoon, they raised more than $3,000 and gave it all to him.

Wright took the microphone.

He looked at Weisiger.

"To you, Audrey, 'thank you' doesn't work," he said. "So I'll just have to promise you the first dance in heaven."

Janet Lynn lost seventeen pounds through the winter and spring, with twenty-three still to go. When Stars on Ice went to the Palace at Auburn Hills, Scott Hamilton invited her to come. She brought her baby son to the practice and her other four boys to the show.

Lynn's brief forays into skating, however, did not necessarily convince her to return to the sport in some way.

"I have a list of things I'd like to do someday," she said. "If I can be of service, perhaps be an inspiration to have skating go in a good way, then maybe. I'd never do it to be recognized. That would make me uncomfortable. But I still do love skating. It is a wonderful memory."

NOVEMBER 1995–
MAY 1996

Afterword

The figure skaters gathered slowly in the mahogany-paneled lobby of the majestic Mirror Lake Inn in Lake Placid, New York, flashing no smiles, barely saying a word. The collection of gregarious entertainers had been reduced to silent, wide-eyed stares. The crackling wood in the fireplace made the room's only noise.

They had met in hotel lobbies in fancy street clothes hundreds of times in the past, but never for an event as devastating as this. On a cold night in late November 1995, they were to travel through snow-swept Adirondack mountain roads to a nearby funeral home for a private wake for Sergei Grinkov, their colleague and friend who died of a massive heart attack during a skating practice the day before.

Scott Hamilton, who always has been the leader of the Stars on Ice tour, came down from his room first. He had not yet heard the news of the day, that an autopsy performed on Grinkov revealed that his left anterior artery, which feeds the heart muscle, was virtually closed. The autopsy also found that the twenty-eight-year-old Grinkov's heart was enlarged from high blood pressure and that the two-time Olympic gold medalist had suffered an earlier heart attack within twenty-four hours of his death.

"I talked to him that morning," Hamilton said when told the news. "I couldn't tell that anything was wrong. He was talking about Dasha [Daria, the three-year-old daughter of Grinkov and his wife and skating partner, Ekaterina Gordeeva] coming to be with them, and he was great and very excited. If anything was wrong with him, I never knew."

Grinkov collapsed while he and Gordeeva were practicing for the opening performance of the 1995–96 Stars on Ice tour. Gordeeva and Grinkov were running through a program on the USA rink, one of four ice surfaces in Lake Placid's Olympic Center, when he was stricken. Several skaters said that after lifting Gordeeva, Grinkov set her back down and then stopped skating.

"Are you okay?" Gordeeva asked her husband.

"I just feel a little dizzy," he told her.

She helped him sit on the ice. He then started to lay back and lost consciousness. Rescue workers arrived within three or four minutes but they couldn't revive him. By then, word of Grinkov's collapse had reached the other skaters working in an adjacent rink. They all frantically raced to the USA rink and were standing or kneeling beside Grinkov when he was carried off by paramedics and taken to Adirondack Medical Center, where he was pronounced dead at 12:28 P.M. Monday, November 20, 1995, three days before Thanksgiving.

"They're devastated, obviously," Hamilton said about the Stars on Ice cast. "They can't make sense out of any of it, and neither can I. He was the biggest, strongest, most capable of all of us, and he's gone."

Paul Wylie, like Hamilton, said he never saw any indication that Grinkov was having heart pain or shortness of breath.

"The guy was on the bike every day," Wylie said. "One of my last vivid memories of him was last Saturday, working out in the hotel gym with him. We were both on the bikes and he was lifting weights too. He looked over at me and said in his Russian accent, 'Good boy, good boy.' He was always like that."

Wylie said the skaters all are responsible for their own medical checkups, adding he knew only that Grinkov was seeing a doctor for a back that had been giving him problems for months.

"It's not like a team sport," he said. "We're all independent contractors. If I miss a show, I don't get paid. We all know it's our responsibility. I think Sergei did look out for his health."

The day after Grinkov died, Wylie wandered into the USA rink, a place most of the others were avoiding.

"I had to walk out there, even though my mind was flashing back to what happened there on Monday, to seeing him lying on the ice with the paramedics around him, putting my hand on Katia's back, touching his skate, praying that he would be okay," Wylie said. "I didn't want to go, but I told myself, 'No, you are going to get on this ice.' It was a haunting thing, especially skating over the patch of ice where he lay and that feeling of helplessness that came rushing back to me, but I had to face it head on."

Gordeeva and Grinkov, who was five foot eleven and weighed 180 pounds, won the 1988 and 1994 Olympic gold medals in pairs skating, as well as four world championships. They had settled into a lucrative professional career that allowed them to perform their graceful and romantic programs before more than half a million spectators a year. In addition, they regularly appeared in televised professional events.

"What they had is what everyone wants," Kristi Yamaguchi said. "My first year on tour, I watched them almost every night. I'd go out and stand in a corner and just watch them. They just floated across the ice."

"Rosalynn Sumners and I stood on the ice during a number last year as they skated, and we always said to each other, 'Isn't that amazing?' " Wylie said. "The way she looked at him, this power between them, so beautiful and pure, yet so effortless in appearance. They reminded me of Romeo and Juliet."

On the 1994–95 tour, Hamilton led into a romantic duet by the pair by standing alone on the ice after being snubbed by various female skaters. He told the audience: "Then something catches your eye, something so pure, so genuine, so incredible, that you realize that, yes, you can in fact have it all."

At the private wake, Gordeeva told several of her fellow skaters, "Maybe it was too perfect."

Living and traveling in a new land, often without their daughter and with so many American stars, was not always easy, Gordeeva and Grinkov said during a wistful interview ten months before his death.

"Sometimes I think people like us and think we're so good," said Gordeeva, who spoke for the both of them. "But when people like Paul Wylie and Katarina Witt skate, the fans give them their hearts. I can't think we're the best here. I still feel like we're guests [with the American fans].

"I know for sure we will never get a standing ovation. We had one once, at Madison Square Garden, but the fans do that mostly for other skaters. A standing ovation would be the best for me. A standing ovation is the only thing we wish for. But maybe I need to change my mind, because it's hard [for Russians] to take America's heart. Americans like, 'Wow,' but we are more like, 'Awwww . . .' "

As Gordeeva talked, Grinkov, who spoke little English, nodded his head and smiled.

Two days after Grinkov's death, the day before Thanksgiving, Wylie dashed out of the inn to get his picture taken for a Russian visa. He was preparing to go to Moscow for Grinkov's funeral.

Asking for directions to get to the photographer, Wylie was told by the other skaters to "make a turn at the road that goes up to Sergei and Katia's."

The condominium where Grinkov and Gordeeva had been living was just up the street.

"You always said their names together, and that's the way we'll always think of them," Wylie said. "The two of them, together."

"You don't think of one without the other," Hamilton said.

While Hamilton and Wylie prepared to fly to Russia, Gordeeva, her parents, and 1992 Olympic gold medalist Viktor Petrenko drove from the condo to her permanent U.S. home in Simsbury, Connecticut. There, they picked up Daria and left for Moscow. Gordeeva and her daughter observed a traditional Russian Orthodox forty-day mourning period before returning to the United States.

In late February 1996, Gordeeva and the Stars on Ice cast skated a memorial for Grinkov in Hartford, Connecticut. As a national television audience watched on CBS, Gordeeva performed on her own in public for the first time, with a spotlight shining where Grinkov would have been.

Even a day or two after Grinkov's death, the other skaters knew Gordeeva would return to the ice.

"She'll come back to us," Hamilton said. "That's what she is, a skater. She understands we are her family and she'll come back to us when it's time."

"It's hard for us as Americans to understand, because we're not from that culture, but skating is of the utmost importance to her family and to her," Wylie said. "I really do hope she comes back. She's just a precious, precious person."

In January 1996, the U.S. figure skating world turned its attention to San Jose, California. On a quiet corner across the street from San Jose Arena, five columns featuring abstract mosaics rose twenty feet into the air from the grounds of a public art project. They were erected to honor four world or Olympic champions from the vast suburban sprawl south of San Francisco—Peggy Fleming, Brian Boitano, Kristi Yamaguchi, and Debi Thomas—plus one other skater, Rudy Galindo.

Boston and Philadelphia and, yes, even Portland, home of Tonya Harding, have their skating heritage, but no area of the country has been more productive for U.S. skating in the past thirty years than the one that hosted the 1996 national championships. Fleming, the 1968 Olympic gold medalist, grew up in San Jose, although she trained for her Olympic triumph in Colorado Springs. She lives in the hills in nearby Los Gatos and is a community activist who helped convince city officials to build the arena where the 1996 Nationals were held.

"To use a movie comparison, without Peggy fighting for that arena, it would be like Bedford Falls if George Bailey didn't live," former San Jose mayor Tom McEnery told the *San Jose Mercury News*.

Boitano, the 1988 Olympic gold medalist, grew up in Sunnyvale and lives in San Francisco. He still trains in rinks throughout the area. Thomas, a world champion and the 1988 Olympic bronze medalist, is from San Jose, and Yamaguchi, the 1992 Olympic gold medalist, is from Fremont. Galindo, the only one of the five still competing in skating's Olympic division, also is from San Jose.

Among them, they held fourteen national senior championships, including two won by Yamaguchi and Galindo when they skated pairs together in 1989 and 1990.

It was undeniable that the first four would be chosen for the art project. But Rudy? Heading into the 1996 national championships in San Jose, he was known as Yamaguchi's pairs partner who, when he went off on his own, had been a failure.

After a disappointing eighth-place finish at the 1995 Nationals in Providence, Galindo quit for eight months. He taught children how to skate so he could pay his bills. He lived with his mother in a trailer park and didn't have the money to buy a car, so he rode a bicycle to and from the rink.

At twenty-six, with nowhere in particular to turn, he decided to come back to skating because the Nationals would be held in his hometown. His sister Laura would be his coach. But no one expected much of him. He was so far removed from his sport that his picture and biography weren't even in the U.S. Figure Skating Association's press guide.

Then came the men's short program. The two favorites, Todd Eldredge and Scott Davis, who had won three and two men's national championships, respectively, skated well. Eldredge was his usual perfect, workmanlike self, landing a triple axel followed by a double toe loop for his required combination. Davis, who had been battling vertigo in the weeks leading up to Nationals, looked to be ready to challenge Eldredge with an energized techno-pop program until he put a hand down on a wobbly double axel. He, too, completed the triple axel–double toe.

Next came Galindo, who had had several days of magnificent practices leading into the competition. One of the most artistic, balletic skaters of his day, Galindo began with his combination. He easily landed his triple axel. He then took off for his second jump—another triple, the triple toe loop. It was the most difficult combination of the night, and he had nailed it.

He skated the rest of the program flawlessly, and cautiously at times, with some slow footwork. But when he stopped, he hopped into the air, then covered his face with his hands.

As Galindo stood in the middle of the ice, blinking back tears, the crowd in his hometown roared its approval. At that moment, some men might have thought of triple axels successfully landed or hundreds of hours of practice before dawn in a cold, lonely rink.

But Galindo's mind turned to death: "I thought of all my friends and family who have passed away."

Galindo, who has lost two coaches and a brother to AIDS, turned in the performance of the evening in the men's short program.

Within a minute, the audience that had stood and cheered Galindo was hissing and booing. Galindo's marks were as low as 5.4, and merely reached 5.8—and there were just two of those. Only three judges placed Galindo ahead of Davis in the technical mark, even though Galindo completed a harder combination and Davis had a flawed jump. So Galindo ended the night ranked third behind Eldredge and Davis.

Galindo, who has been so critical of the judging in the past, wouldn't let that ruin his evening. "I'm really happy with the marks. Todd and Scott are Olympians and world-ranked. I'm happy with this."

Whether he was first or third, Galindo knew he had the same opportunity to win the national title Saturday afternoon, January 20. A skater in first, second, or third place after the short program can win the title simply by winning the long program.

Two days later, the talk leading into the men's long program concerned only Rudy. Could he hang on for a medal and a trip to the world championships in Edmonton? He needed to be in the top three to do that. Already, however, pressure was building. After talking about being gay for this book months earlier, he was now not commenting on his sexuality. Galindo was unaccustomed to the spotlight. The world was beginning to spin too fast. This was not going to be easy for him.

Dick Button was standing in the ABC booth, grasping for words that usually came so easily. In San Jose Arena, the crowd of 10,869 was on its feet and roaring. Some spectators stood in the aisles crying. Rudy Galindo still had half a minute of skating to go, but it didn't matter. The crowd knew. Dick Button knew. And when the judges' scores popped up—and two perfect 6.0s lit up the scoreboard—Galindo knew too. He had become the most improbable national champion in U.S. figure skating history.

"Thank you, Dad," Galindo screamed to the rafters. "Thank you, George, Jim, Rick!"

All of them—his father, his brother George, and coaches Jim Hulick and Rick Inglesi—were dead. All but his father died of complications related to AIDS.

An hour after his victory, Galindo, the second-oldest man ever to win a national singles title, said, "I'm still in shock."

Galindo thought this day never would come. If he ever dreamed of it, he would push the idea out of his mind. How could he win the men's national figure skating championship? How would the conservative world of figure skating ever allow an openly gay Mexican-American to take even third place, much less the national title? he had asked aloud. How could someone who never had been higher than fifth in seven previous national men's competitions rise up to beat the top skaters in the country?

In his hometown, he found the answer. If he skated better than everyone else, and if the defending champion faltered, he would not be given the title—he would earn it himself.

Galindo landed eight triple jumps, and each was lofty, lilting, and perfect. His balletic skating won the first-place marks of seven of the nine judges; two surprisingly voted for Eldredge, the defending champion who skated an uncharacteristically shaky program with only five clean triples. Eldredge, who had chosen to spend the month of December touring with Nutcracker on Ice rather than training at home, finished second; upstart Dan Hollander came in third.

Two-time national champion Scott Davis was dreadful, making five mistakes in the final three minutes of his program to drop to fourth.

Michael Weiss, the nineteen-year-old from Fairfax, Virginia, finished right behind Davis. Weiss, four years younger than any of the other men in the top five, stumbled twice in his short program, but was dropped only to fifth place. The judges clearly were waiting to place him higher, if only he hadn't faltered.

In the long program, Weiss did not fall on any of his eight triples, but had slight trouble with the landings on two of them, and stayed in fifth. His steady rise in the senior men's division continued; he was eighth in 1994; sixth in 1995; and now fifth. But Weiss had been hoping for more. He had finished a strong second at Skate America in Detroit in October 1995 and had been thinking of a trip to the worlds in 1996. Now, he would have to wait another year, at least.

"Even when he makes mistakes, he still has an aura about him," said his coach, Audrey Weisiger. "I would prefer, however, that the aura would nail it."

Missing from the Weiss team in San Jose was choreographer Brian Wright, who, while battling complications due to AIDS, decided not to come to Nationals.

"I don't want to have to say good-bye to everybody," Wright said.

*　*　*

Galindo—who has said he never fits the image the judges want with a hoop earring, goatee, and extremely dramatic moves—gasped in delight at the sight of his perfect 6.0s for his artistry (although one of the 6.0s came from a judge who put him behind Eldredge overall). It was the first time a male skater had received a perfect score at Nationals since Wylie received six 6.0s in the short and long programs at the 1990 Nationals.

Galindo's life changed in the four and a half minutes he was on the ice. He soon was signed for the seventy-five-city Campbell's Soups Tour of World Figure Skating Champions, making an estimated $5,000 a night—or $375,000 for four months' work. There would be a book, there would be appearances, there would be made-for-TV competitions! The gay community embraced him. He soon would get rid of the bicycle and buy himself a car.

As spectators streamed out of the arena that day, they walked by the five columns commemorating the careers of the area skaters. All of a sudden, Galindo's presence among the others made sense. Each column was to include a quote from the skater about some aspect of their career—and in Galindo's quote, there was controversy. During his interview, Galindo said, "It's hard enough being a Mexican-American skater when the judges are looking for an all-American boy."

When Galindo realized months before Nationals that that quote would be used, he hired an attorney and eventually got a chance to submit a new quote, one that did not refer to ethnic issues: "I never imagined when I started skating that I'd win the junior world title and the U.S. pairs championship twice with Kristi Yamaguchi.

"I didn't want to create controversy," he said. "I didn't want that to be the way people remembered me."

But controversy followed Galindo no matter how majestically he skated or how cautiously he spoke.

"I've never heard any comments inside the judges' room about [his ethnic background or his sexuality]," USFSA president Morry Stillwell said as he wiped tears from his eyes moments after Galindo's victory.

Then, Stillwell added, "There are a lot more weird people in this sport than Rudy, and you all know that."

In the women's competition, what the fourteen-year-old Michelle Kwan couldn't do in 1995, a more mature fifteen-year-old Michelle Kwan accomplished in 1996. Kwan completed seven triple jumps to become the youngest national women's champion since Fleming in 1964, while defending national champion Nicole Bobek dramatically withdrew right before she was to skate the long program when her tender right ankle swelled after warming up. When Bobek petitioned to make the world championship team anyway, the USFSA turned her down and took two other skaters instead: Tonia Kwiatkowski, the old lady of the club at twenty-four, who finished second at Nationals with a brilliant program featuring six triples, and thirteen-year-old phenom Tara Lipinski, who was third.

But the Nationals belonged to Kwan. A year earlier, she had worn a little-girl dress with only a touch of lipstick and a ponytail that spun in the air. However, for the 1995–96 season, things changed.

"I think Michelle's beautiful," coach Frank Carroll said. "She has a beautiful face. But the hair hanging down doesn't do anything to enhance that. So I told [her family], 'Wait a minute. She's not going to the school yard here. She's appearing before eighteen thousand people and millions on television. This would not be extraordinary if she were in ballet. You want to look the part.' I tried to explain that there's nothing extraordinary about wearing makeup. It's part of the schtick. She's not performing a school exam. She's performing before thousands."

In the summer and fall of 1995, Kwan started to adapt to her new look. Her ponytail was gone, replaced by a stylish bun that required her hair to be braided and sewn into place, which took half an hour. The teenager who wore no makeup the year before began to cake it on. And Carroll picked music and programs for the 1995–96 season that demanded maturity on the ice; she would be playing a Spanish flamenco dancer in the short program, a seductress in the long.

But for all the cosmetic changes Carroll insisted upon, Kwan's greatest strength was her smooth, fluid jumping style—and a graceful presence across the ice.

The results were remarkable. The judges actually began thinking of Kwan as a mature skater, almost as a different person from the child they'd seen a year ago. She became the world's best skater all season, winning major international competitions as well as the coveted national title, her first ever. She made at least $750,000 in earnings and show fees.

While Kwan became the perfect skating package, Bobek, the flashy defending national champion, was a study in confusion. She moved to her ninth coach in fifteen years of skating just before Nationals—splitting with Richard Callaghan and returning to one of her previous coaches, Barbara Roles Williams. She angered the USFSA by spending a month of valuable training time touring with Nutcracker on Ice in December (for a reported $90,000) rather than buckling down and getting ready for Nationals. To compound the problem, Bobek injured her right ankle on the tour, and when she went to the USFSA to plead for mercy—and a bye into the world championships—officials said no. Had the injury occurred in training, or if she had taken time off to rest, the USFSA would have been more sympathetic.

When she withdrew before the long program due to her throbbing ankle, the USFSA's international committee met for more than an hour and, once again, turned down her request to go to worlds. The committee decided this was the time to make a statement about exactly who controlled Olympic-style figure skating. The USFSA looked at the flood of agents, promoters, and managers entering the sport and felt powerless. It couldn't stop the pseudo-competitions, shows, and tours that were diluting its product.

But the night of the women's long program at Nationals, the organization suddenly was in control. It sent a message to Bobek—and her manager, agent, and public relations man. And that message was simple: we're in charge here.

Bobek went home and looked for another new coach. Kwan, Kwiatkowski, and Lipinski went off to the worlds in Edmonton.

The junior ladies of 1995 found out that success at times could be fleeting. Sydne Vogel, skating as a senior at Nationals for the first time, looked as if she were headed to the world championships until she made two mistakes at the end of her long program and dropped to fourth behind Lipinski.

Jenni Tew went for her big jump—the triple lutz—at the Midwesterns in December. She fell on it and failed to qualify for Nationals. It was a crushing blow for a girl who had hoped to reach the medal stand in San Jose in the junior division in 1996, but she remained with the sport and stayed a junior heading into 1997.

Shelby Lyons, a fourteen-year-old pairs and singles skater who trains with Vogel in Colorado Springs, won the junior ladies title, and also qualified for the world team with senior pairs partner Brian Wells.

As for Lipinski, her star continued to rise even as coach Jeff DiGregorio quit after a blowup with Tara's mother at the world junior championships in Australia a month before Nationals. Mother and daughter picked up and left Delaware, moving to Detroit so Tara could train with Callaghan, her new coach.

In March, the figure skating world gathered in Edmonton Coliseum for what experts assumed would be the coronation of Canadian native son Elvis Stojko as the three-time men's world champion. Instead, with a thud heard across the land, Elvis fell on his triple axel in the short program and dropped right out of medal contention. Taking his place at the top of the medal stand was Eldredge, who was joined by Kwan to give the United States its first men's and women's world titles in the same year since 1986, when Brian Boitano and Debi Thomas both won.

Eldredge, second in the short program, held off Ilia Kulik, the baby-faced, eighteen-year-old from Moscow, who had been in the lead after the short program. Galindo once again did not fall in either program—although he wasn't as sharp as he had been at Nationals—and won the bronze medal, giving the United States its best men's finish at a world championships or Olympic Games in fifteen years.

Eldredge, Kulik, and Galindo each landed eight triple jumps in the long program before eighteen thousand spectators, but the difference between Eldredge and Kulik was one triple-triple combination. Eldredge landed two in the first ninety seconds of his long program; Kulik managed just one triple-triple in his entire four-minute, thirty-second program.

Eldredge beat Kulik, 6–3, on the judges' scorecards. He won fifty thousand dollars, the first time prize money had been given out at the event. Kulik earned thirty thousand; Galindo, who actually finished fourth in the long program but third overall, earned twenty thousand.

Kulik, a former world junior champion, was the last man to skate and could have knocked Eldredge out of first place—just as Stojko did the previous year at the worlds. But Kulik, a tremendous jumper, lacked the polish of Eldredge, the 1995 world silver medalist, and Galindo's grace.

After stumbling at Nationals due in part to his participation in the Nutcracker tour, Eldredge buckled down, rejecting offers to tour for a month so he could stay in the rink and practice.

"I have to thank Rudy for beating me at Nationals," Eldredge said with a smile.

That night was significant for figure skating in other ways. The sport won a major battle in the sports TV wars. The men's long program, shown live on ABC, received a 10.1 rating (a rating point equals 956,000 households). Going head-to-head with the skating was the highly publicized NCAA men's basketball tournament on CBS. The basketball earned just an 8.8.

When the men finished, the women began. Kwan easily won the short program, with defending world champion Chen Lu of China second, followed by Russian teenager Irina Slutskaia.

While Kwan won the hearts of the nine judges, fellow Americans Kwiatkowski and Lipinski did not fare nearly as well. Kwiatkowski, the college graduate among children, performed a flawless short program including the triple lutz, the most difficult jump landed in the competition. But the judges did a number on her, giving her scores of 5.1 to 5.6, with one 4.9. She ended up ninth, lower than two women who fell.

Lipinski fell twice and dropped to twenty-third out of thirty skaters, barely making the cut to the top twenty-four for the long program. After hanging on to a shaky triple lutz landing, Lipinski unexpectedly fell on her double loop, a very easy jump for her. She also tumbled to the ice on her triple flip. After that fall, she glanced plaintively at Richard Callaghan beside the boards, then kept on skating.

The next night, with a daring triple jump in the final second of her four-minute long program, Kwan won the women's world title, becoming the third-youngest world champion in the sport's history. Only Sonja Henie, who won the first of her ten world titles at fourteen in 1927, and Oksana Baiul, who was fifteen in 1993, were younger than Kwan.

Kwan upset Chen, the nineteen-year-old defending world champion from China, who performed a flawless classical program filled with six triple jumps. Kwan, who came three skaters later, was holed up backstage with Carroll in the flower girls' room as Chen performed, but still heard her scores, which included two perfect 6.0s.

Knowing she had to pull off the skating equivalent of knocking out the defending champion in boxing, Kwan needed to land all seven triple jumps she planned. But she pulled back on one of them early in her program, doing just a double toe loop as the second jump of a triple-triple combination. So, at the very end, as her music, "Dance of the Veils" waned, she improvised, turning a double axel into a triple toe loop. The nine judges responded in the kindest way possible, giving her two perfect 6.0s as well, and a 6–3 victory over Chen.

Slutskaia won the bronze medal despite a sliding fall on a triple lutz. Japan's Midori Ito, the 1992 Olympic silver medalist who returned from the professional ranks to make a run at the 1998 Winter Games in Nagano, Japan, finished seventh after falling on her triple axel in the short program. Right behind Ito was Kwiatkowski, who moved up to eighth with a solid, six-triple jump effort. Lipinski came back to finish fifteenth after landing seven triple jumps.

But Kwan was the American of the moment. Three years earlier, she was a gangly twelve-year-old who finished sixth in the United States. In Edmonton, she ruled her world. Her career was carefully managed, with practice time weighing heavier than all her tantilizing money-making opportunities. She had become the nerviest U.S. women's skater since Yamaguchi, with an unprecedented five international victories in 1995–96 alone.

Said her agent, Shep Goldberg, "She had a career in one season."

In mid-April, a letter arrived at the *Washington Post*. It came on USFSA letterhead and was addressed to the sports editor, George Solomon, with a copy mailed to me.

"It is our opinion that Ms. Christine Brennan no longer is reporting figure skating on an impartial basis and has interjected her personal opinions into her coverage of the sport whether it be for additional sales of her book or her notion that she is the protector of the sport of figure skating," wrote USFSA president Morry Stillwell and executive director Jerry Lace.

"Whatever the reason, this is to inform you that Christine Brennan will no longer be afforded the media services normally offered to members of the media at USFSA events. We would more than welcome any of the *Washington Post*'s reporters with the exception of Christine Brennan and they will be afforded the normal media services."

Never before had the national governing body for a U.S. Olympic sport tried to ban a reporter from covering its events, according to the records and memories of various experts. It was a bold move, and a curious one, considering Stillwell and Lace had had numerous opportunities to complain in person about the book after receiving a prepublication copy from me in December—and never did. Their action led to an immediate letter of protest from the *Washington Post*, and a threatened boycott of USFSA events by the Associated Press Sports Editors, an organization of sports editors representing more than three hundred newspapers.

Ultimately, and not surprisingly, the USFSA's effort failed. In late May, the organization backed down, and my credentials were restored.

But in its ill-fated attempt to get rid of a reporter it didn't like, the USFSA showed that it was having trouble adjusting to the glare of the post-Tonya national spotlight.

"The boneheads who run the U.S. Figure Skating Association proved this week that despite the sport's huge TV ratings and popularity, the folks who run it are amateurs," wrote Michelle Kaufman in the *Detroit Free Press*, under a headline reading, "SKATING'S HONCHOS DO A PERFECT DOUBLE-KLUTZ."

"THIN SKINS AND THIN ICE," a headline reported in the *Blade* in Toledo, Ohio.

"It's the stupidest thing they could ever do," said Philip Hersh of the *Chicago Tribune*.

"Would someone please call out the Zamboni to clean up this mess?" asked the *Pittsburgh Post-Gazette*.

As negotiations between Solomon and Stillwell and Lace carried on for six weeks, it became clear that the USFSA wasn't exactly certain what it was angry about. At first, it was "no longer . . . reporting . . . on an impartial basis," but not specifically the book, the USFSA said. Then, officials mentioned an article I wrote for the *Post* on Tara Lipinski, a piece filled with on-the-record information from Tara's mother about the difficult life of a skating family.

Next, it was an interview on "Primetime Live," in which Rudy Galindo's controversial third-place finish in the short program at Nationals was discussed.

"Is it fair or right? No . . . Welcome to figure skating," I said in that interview.

A few weeks later, USFSA sources were floating two rumors, both inaccurate. The first was that I had held a news conference at Nationals to promote my book, and the second was that I had tried to twist the arm of a USFSA sponsor, State Farm, to help sell my book. Had the banishment gone on for a few more weeks, the USFSA might have tried to link me to the clubbing of Nancy Kerrigan's knee.

In mid-May, after a month of negotiations, the USFSA's second letter arrived at the *Post*. Stillwell and Lace took a new approach.

". . . the [USFSA] media credential guidelines clearly state that freelance reporters, writers, or photographers are not eligible to receive media credentials for USFSA events. Individuals writing books or pursuing outside commercial ventures are considered free-lance reporters.

"Based on these guidelines, the USFSA will issue media credentials to Ms. Brennan when she is covering USFSA events for the *Washington Post*. If, in addition, she is actively promoting an outside commercial venture involving figure skating while she is covering the events, she will not be eligible to receive media credentials for such purposes."

The USFSA's pressroom at any given event is filled with free-lance reporters and photographers trying to earn a living in "outside commercial ventures." Were the USFSA to pursue the policy outlined in that letter, its pressroom would be empty.

Finally, in a letter dated May 29, the USFSA relented. But it got in its final jabs.

"Should Christine's activities go beyond covering activities for the *Post* and fall into the commercial interest, you can be assured we shall be in touch with you to let you know her credentials will be rescinded."

Throughout this bizarre situation, I tried to keep a sense of humor. My efforts were made much easier by the hundreds of journalists, readers, skaters, parents, coaches, judges, and agents who supported me.

Of all the phone calls, letters, faxes, and messages I received, my favorite came from Jody Meacham, who covers figure skating and the Olympics for the *San Jose Mercury News*. He called me after the USFSA had backed down. He left this message:

"I just saw on the wire that you have your credentials back from the USFSA," Meacham said. "If you need any notes on all the figure skating competitions that went on while you were suspended, give me a call. I'd be glad to share anything that I've got with you."

How many figure skating competitions were held in April and May? None.

Despite the USFSA's efforts, I had missed nothing.

In the suburbs north of Detroit, a woman began dragging herself out of bed before dawn to drive to the Detroit Skating Club to skate alone. As her husband and five boys slept back at home, she laced up her skates and walked onto the ice and began to remember why she had skated for so many years and what she had missed when she gave it all up for her family.

She, too, blamed this on me. Not that I minded at all. Having read in a certain book how beloved she is, how many people in her sport consider her the greatest skater ever, Janet Lynn made the only decision she could think to make.

She began skating again.

ABOUT THE AUTHOR

Christine Brennan has been a sportswriter for the *Washington Post* for eleven years, specializing in the Olympics and international sports. She is also a commentator for National Public Radio. She has appeared on ESPN, CNN, and a variety of network talk shows. Brennan received undergraduate and master's degrees from Northwestern University and lives in Washington, D.C.